PRIX ARS ELECTRONICA 96

Bildnachweis

S. 19, Margherita Spiluttini; S. 20, Pilo Pirchner; S. 27–32: ORF; S. 130, Kris Snibbe; S. 136, Otto Piene; S. 139, Mikio Kurokawa; S. 140, Digital Aesthetics; S. 164, 169: Disney/Property of Pixar; S.170, Jean-Baptiste Mondino; S. 171, 173, 175, 177, 191: BUF Compagnie; S. 174, Partizan Midi Minuit; S. 179, Toshiba/Ex Machina; S. 184, Tony Walsh; S. 187, TriStar; S. 191, Taarna Studios; S. 192, PDI/Terry Lorant; S. 200, Bernard Lafontaine; S. 210, Bobby Neel Adams; S. 211, Tobi Christiansen; S. 213, Gerald Place; S. 214, J.M. Pharisien; S. 215, Marco Borggreve

Die Portraitfotos auf den Seiten 6, 11, 21, 27, 37, 42, 43, 53, 58, 63, 68/69, 116/117, 158/159, 194/195 und 218 stammen von Erwin Wimmer, Fotostudio Stasny, Linz.

Die Bildrechte der Werkphotos liegen — wenn nicht anders angegeben — bei den Künstlern. Der Bildnachweis gibt die uns bekannten Rechteinhaber an. In einigen Fällen konnten die Rechteinhaber leider nicht oder nur ungenau ermittelt werden. Sollten dadurch Urheberrechte verletzt worden sein, wird der ORF-Landesstudio Oberösterreich nach Anmeldung berechtigter Ansprüche diese entgelten.

Der Prix Ars Electronica – Internationales Kompendium der Computerkünste – World Wide Web Sites, Interaktive Kunst, Computeranimation, Computermusik – **Edition 96** – **Herausgeber:** Dr. Hannes Leopoldseder, Dr. Christine Schöpf – **Redaktion:** Peter Klimitsch, ORF, Landesstudio Oberösterreich, Europaplatz 3, A-4010 Linz – **Übersetzungen:** Aileen Derieg – Cover-Design, **Layout:** Arthouse, Hansi Schorn – **Titelbild:** John Lasseter, Luxo jr.; Andy Kopra, Fire; Joan Staveley, Broken Heart; Myron Krueger, Videoplace; Karl Sims, Panspermia; Andrew Witkin/Michael Kass, RD Texture Buttons; ILM, Terminator 2; Ludger Brümmer, The Gates of H.; Robin Hanson, Idea Futures; John Lasseter, Toy Story; **Koordination/deutsches Lektorat:** Ingrid Fischer-Schreiber – **Englisches Lektorat:** Aileen Derieg – **Technischer Support:** Thomas Riha – **Satz, Offsetreproduktion, Montage:** Typeshop Linz – **Copyright** 1996 by Österreichischer Rundfunk (ORF), Landesstudio Oberösterreich.
Druck: A. Holzhausens Nfg., A-1070 Wien
Gedruckt auf säurefreiem, chlorfrei gebleichtem Papier – TCF
Das Werk ist urheberrechtlich geschützt. Die dadurch begründeten Rechte, insbesondere die der Übersetzung, des Nachdruckes, der Entnahme von Abbildungen, der Funksendung, der Wiedergabe auf photomechanischem oder ähnlichem Wege und der Speicherung in Datenverarbeitungsanlagen, bleiben, auch bei nur auszugsweiser Verwertung, vorbehalten.
Prix Ars Electronica – Internationaler Wettbewerb für Computerkünste – **Veranstalter:** Österreichischer Rundfunk (ORF), Landesstudio Oberösterreich – **Idee:** Dr. Hannes Leopoldseder – **Konzept:** Dkfm. Heinz Augner, Dr. Christine Schöpf, Wolfgang Winkler – **Kontaktadresse:** Prix Ars Electronica, ORF, Europaplatz 3, A-4010 Linz, Telefon: 0043/732/6900-267, Telefax: 0043/732/6900-270, Telex (02)1616, E-mail: prixars@aec.at

The Prix Ars Electronica – International Compendium of the Computer Arts – World Wide Web Sites, Interactive Arts, Computer Animation, Computer Music – Edition 96 – **Publisher:** Dr. Hannes Leopoldseder, Dr. Christine Schöpf – **Editors:** Peter Klimitsch, ORF, Landesstudio Oberösterreich, Europaplatz 3, A-4010 Linz – **Translations:** Aileen Derieg – Cover-Design, **Layout:** Arthouse, Hansi Schorn – **Frontispiece:** John Lasseter, Luxo jr.; Andy Kopra, Fire; Joan Staveley, Broken Heart; Myron Krueger, Videoplace; Karl Sims, Panspermia; Andrew Witkin/Michael Kass, RD Texture Buttons; ILM, Terminator 2; Ludger Brümmer, The Gates of H.; Robin Hanson, Idea Futures; John Lasseter, Toy Story; **Coordination/German Proof-reading:** Ingrid Fischer-Schreiber – **English Proof-Reading:** Aileen Derieg – **Technical Support:** Thomas Riha – **Offset reproduction, assembly:** Typeshop Linz – **Copyright** 1996 by Österreichischer Rundfunk (ORF), Landesstudio Oberösterreich. **Prix Ars Electronica** – International Competition for Computer Arts- **Organizer:** Österreichischer Rundfunk (ORF), Landesstudio Oberösterreich – **Idea:** Dr. Hannes Leopoldseder – **Conception:** Dkfm. Heinz Augner, Dr. Christine Schöpf, Wolfgang Winkler – **Liaison Office:** Prix Ars Electronica, ORF, Europaplatz 3, A-4010 Linz, Telefon: 0043/732/6900-267, Telefax: 0043/732/6900-270, Telex (02)1616, E-mail: prixars@aec.at

©1996 Österreichischer Rundfunk (ORF), Landesstudio Oberösterreich
ISBN 3-211-82863-X SpringerVerlag Wien New York

Hannes Leopoldseder
Christine Schöpf

PRIX ARS ELECTRONICA 96

SpringerWienNewYork

Computer Animation

Computer Music

Prix Ars Electronica - Jury

Prix Ars Electronica - Participants 96

MIRRORING MEDIA TRANSFORMATIONS

Mehr denn je ist der Prix Ars Electronica — heuer in seiner zehnten Auflage — in seinen Ergebnissen ein Spiegel des radikalen Wandels der digitalen Medien in den letzten Jahren.

More than ever, the Prix Ars Electronica – now in its 10th year – has become a mirror of the radical transformation of digital media in recent years.

Als der ORF/Landesstudio Oberösterreich den Prix Ars Electronica 1987 ins Leben rief, war das primäre Anliegen, ein offenes Forum für den Einsatz des Computers als Werkzeug in den verschiedenen Kunstbereichen zu schaffen. Dementsprechend wurden zu Beginn die Wettbewerbskategorien Graphik, Animation und Musik etabliert. 1990 kam Interaktive Kunst als vierte Wettbewerbssparte dazu und 1995 wurde die Graphikkategorie durch die für World Wide Web ersetzt. Stand das World Wide Web als Werkzeug noch im Vorjahr auf Grund seiner klaren Bauweise und seiner Benutzerfreundlichkeit gerade für Nutzungen im kulturellen Kontext im Vordergrund, wird nun aufgrund verschiedenster technischer Neuerungen das Netz an sich zum Hypermedium, das, wie viele der insgesamt 939 Einreichungen aus den vier Bereichen zeigen, Kommunikation auf der visuellen und akustischen Ebene vereint und in dem Interaktivität zur gemeinsamen Kulturtechnik wird.

When the Upper Austrian regional studio of the Austrian Broadcasting Company (ORF) initiated the Prix Ars Electronica in 1987, the primary aim was to create an open forum for the use of the computer as a tool in the various areas of art. In accordance with this aim, the competition categories of computer graphics, animation and music were established.
In 1990, interactive art was included as a fourth category, and in 1995, the category of computer graphics was replaced by a new category for the World Wide Web. Last year, the World Wide Web as a tool was a focal point, since its clear construction and user-friendliness made it particularly useful in a context of art and culture. In the meantime, however, various technical innovations have transformed the Net itself into a hypermedium, and as many of the total of 939 entries in all four categories demonstrate, it has united visual and acoustic levels of communication and enabled interactivity to become the technique that the different fields of cultural activity have in common.

PRIX ARS ELECTRONICA
NACH NATIONEN

1996 verzeichnet der Prix Ars Electronica eine neuerliche Rekordbeteiligung mit 826 Personen aus Kunst, Wissenschaft, Forschung und Unterhaltung und aus 38

PRIX ARS ELECTRONICA
ACCORDING TO COUNTRIES

In 1996, the Prix Ars Electronica has set a new record in the number of entries with a total of 826 participants from the fields of

art, science, research and entertainment,
from 38 countries around the world. As in
previous years, the USA is most strongly
represented, followed by Germany and
France. The dominance of the USA in the
Prix Ars Electronica demonstrates once again
the position of leadership that this country
has attained in the area of digital media.
However, if we compare numbers, it appears
that a consolidation is beginning to take
place in the Old World: 468 entrants are
from Europe.
This year's four Golden Nicas go to the USA,
Japan, Canada and into Cyberspace. The
eight awards of distinction go to France, the
USA, Canada, Austria and Italy.

THE WINNERS
OF THE PRIX ARS ELECTRONICA

12 money prizes amounting to a total of ATS
1.25 million have been awarded in the Prix
Ars Electronica 96. The sponsor this year is
Siemens Nixdorf; the competition is made
possible through the support of the VOEST-
ALPINE STAHL, the city of Linz, the province
of Upper Austria and the Gerhard Andlinger
Foundation.

COMPUTER ANIMATION
In the category of computer animation, the
Golden Nica (ATS 300,000) is awarded to
John Lasseter for "Toy Story", the first
completely computer-generated feature film.
The jury's decision emphasizes the importance of "Toy Story" not only in the history
of computer animation, but also in the history of film making as a whole. With this
award, the jury particularly honors not only
the technical excellence and multifaceted
details evident in the film, but also its dramatic structure. John Lasseter is the first
award winner to receive this award for the
third time (he was also the award winner in
1987 and in 1988).
The two awards of distinction, amounting to
ATS 100,000 each, for computer animation
are awarded this year for two productions
from the French BUF Compagnie based in

*Ländern in aller Welt. Spitzenreiter unter
den Nationen sind, wie auch in den vergangenen Jahren, die USA, gefolgt von
Deutschland und Frankreich. Die Domi-
nanz der USA im Prix Ars Electronica
zeigt einmal mehr deren Vormachtstel-
lung im Bereich digitaler Medien, wobei
sich, zählt man zusammen, offensichtlich
auch auf dem Alten Kontinent eine Kon-
solidierung anzubahnen scheint: 468 Ein-
reicher sind Europäer.
In die USA, nach Japan und Kanada und
in den Cyberspace gehen die vier Goldenen Nicas in diesem Jahr, die acht Auszeichnungen nach Frankreich, USA, Kanada, Österreich und Italien.*

DIE GEWINNER
DES PRIX ARS ELECTRONICA

*12 Geldpreise im Gesamtwert von öS
1,25 Mio werden im Prix Ars Electronica
96 vergeben. Preisstifter ist in diesem
Jahr Siemens Nixdorf. Die Durchführung
des Wettbewerbes ermöglichen die
VOEST-ALPINE STAHL, die Stadt Linz,
das Land Oberösterreich und die Gerhard
Andlinger Stiftung.*

COMPUTERANIMATION
*In der Kategorie Computeranimation er-
hält die Goldene Nica (öS 300.000) John
Lasseter für „Toy Story", den ersten zur
Gänze computergenerierten Spielfilm. Mit
dieser Entscheidung unterstreicht die
Jury den Stellenwert, den „Toy Story" sowohl in der Geschichte der Computeranimation als auch in der Filmgeschichte
einnimmt. Nicht nur die technisch-gestal-
terische Brillanz und die Vielschichtigkeit
der Details, sondern auch die Dramaturgie des Filmes werden von der Jury in
besonderer Weise honoriert. John Lasseter ist der erste Preisträger, der (nach
1987 und 1988) die begehrte Trophäe
bereits zum dritten Mal erhält.
Die beiden mit je öS 100.000 dotierten
Auszeichnungen für Computeranimation
gehen in diesem Jahr an zwei Produktio-*

nen der französischen BUF Compagnie mit Sitz in Paris. Dort entstanden die Spezialeffekte für den Spielfilm „Stadt der verlorenen Kinder", Regie Marc Caro und Jean-Pierre Jeunet, und für das Musikvideo der Rolling Stones „Like a Rolling Stone", Regie Michel Gondry. Beide Werke zeigen ein Höchstmaß an Perfektion in Bezug auf die Integration von computergenerierten Effekten in Spielhandlungen, demonstrieren kreative Anwendung der Technologie innerhalb des dramatischen Prozesses.

COMPUTERMUSIK

Aus 287 Werken, die 1996 in der Sparte Computermusik eingereicht wurden, sprach die Jury die Goldene Nica (öS 150.000) einstimmig dem Kanadier Robert Normandeau zu. Das ausgezeichnete Werk, die akusmatische Komposition „Le renard et la rose", ist ein Stück „Kino für das Ohr". Es nimmt bezug auf eine Hörspielbearbeitung des gleichnamigen Kapitels aus dem „Kleinen Prinzen" von Antoine de Saint-Exupéry.
Die beiden Auszeichnungen (je öS 50.000) erhalten der in Italien lebende Amerikaner James Dashow und der Franzose Régis Renouard Larivière. James Dashows Werk „Media Survival Kit", ein Radioprogramm, ist eine satirische Vision darüber, wie Computer und Netzwerke in unser Leben und Denken eindringen. Für sein Werk verwendet Dashow Sprech- und Singstimmen, ein Instrumentalensemble sowie computerbearbeitete und -generierte Klänge.
Ein Stück für Lautsprecherensemble ist „Futaie" („Hochwald") von Régis Renouard Larivière. Das Werk stellt die herkömmlichen Vorstellungen vom Ablauf musikalischer Zeit in Frage und besticht in der zeitlichen Dramaturgie, in der sorgfältigen Behandlung der Töne und des Raumes zwischen den Tönen.

INTERAKTIVE KUNST

Interaktivität als Kulturtechnik und das

Paris. They were responsible for the special effects for the feature film "City of Lost Children", directed by Marc Caro and Jean-Pierre Jeunet, and for the Rolling Stones music video "Like a Rolling Stone", directed by Michel Gondry. Both of these works are distinguished by perfection with regards to the integration of computer-generated effects in the action of the film, and both demonstrate the creative use of technology within the dramatic process.

COMPUTER MUSIC

Of the 287 works entered in 1996 in the category of computer music, the jury unanimously agreed to award the Golden Nica (ATS 150,000) to the Canadian Robert Normandeau. The award winning work, an acousmatic composition entitled "Le renard et la rose", is a piece of "cinema for the ear". It is based on a radio play adaptation of the chapter "The Fox and the Rose" from "The Little Prince" by Antoine de Saint-Exupéry.
The two awards of distinction (ATS 50,000 each) go to James Dashow, an American living in Italy, and to Régis Renouard Larivière of France. James Dashow's work "Media Survival Kit", a radio program, is a satirical vision of the way that computers and networks are invading our lives and our minds. Dashow uses speaking and singing voices and an instrumental ensemble for his work, as well as computer processed and computer generated sounds.
"Futaie" (High Forest) by Régis Renouard Larivière is a piece for a loudspeaker ensemble. This work challenges conventional notions about the course of musical time and is notable for its temporal dramatic structure and the thoughtful treatment of the notes and the spaces between the notes.

INTERACTIVE ART

Interactivity as a technique of culture and the Net as a hypermedium are the characteristic features of the installation "Global Interior Project" by Masaki Fujihata from the Keio University in Japan, the winner of the Golden Nica 96 (ATS 200,000). Actual room installations in separate locations are connected via networks, thus establishing virtual communities. This is a new form of art work addressing the issue of communication per se, which is also the theme of the two winners of the awards of distinction (ATS 50,000) in the categroy of interactive art: "Motion Phone" by the American Scott Sona Snibbe, and "Scavengers" by the Canadians Louis-Philippe Demers and Bill Vorn.

"Motion Phone" demonstrates interactivity as an open playground where visitors can communicate visually. Visitors to this installation may change the form and the motion of the pre-set graphic patterns.

In "Scavengers", interactivity is determined by the interactions of autonomous robot systems among themselves. Visitors enter a complex environment exemplifying the issue of the relationship of humans to machines, to artificial life.

WORLD WIDE WEB

Cyberspace is the home of the artist group "etoy", with servers in Vienna, Manchester, Zurich and other places; they are the winners of the Golden Nica (ATS 100,000) for the WWW category, awarded this year for the second time. "etoy" demonstrates digital anarchy, piracy, subversiveness, hacker culture and art. "etoy" uses conventional forms of art (music, graphics, sculptural design, animation, text), transfers these to the Net and transforms them into a self-sufficient "Gesamtkunstwerk" that could only exist in the Internet.

The two awards of distinction (ATS 50,000 each) go to the American Ed Stastny for "HyGrid" and to Manuel Schilcher of Linz for "VVV – Journey as an exile". "HyGrid" is an artists' colony on the Net: Stastny places images on the Net, and other artists may add their own images. The over-all image is continuously changed by means of a special algorithm.

"VVV – Journey as an exile" interprets everyday life in the Net in an individualist-

Netz als Hypermedium charakterisieren die Installation „Global Interior Project" des Japaners Masaki Fujihata von der Keio University, die die Goldene Nica 96 (öS 200.000) erhält. Reale Rauminstallationen an getrennten Orten sind über Netzwerke verbunden und etablieren so virtuelle Gemeinschaften — eine neue Form von Kunstwerk, das die Kommunikation an sich zum Thema hat.

„Motion Phone" des Amerikaners Scott Sona Snibbe und „Scavengers" der Kanadier Louis-Philippe Demers und Bill Vorn sind die beiden Auszeichnungen (je ÖS 50.000) in der Sparte Interaktive Kunst. „Motion Phone" demonstriert Interaktivität als offenes Spielfeld, in dem Besucher visuell kommunizieren. Die Besucher dieser Installation verändern vorgegebene Graphikmuster in ihrer Form und Bewegung.

Die Wechselbeziehung autonomer Robotersysteme untereinander bestimmen die Interaktivität von „Scavengers". Das komplexe Environment, das der Besucher betritt, thematisiert die Frage nach dem Verhältnis des Menschen zu Apparaten, zum künstlichen Leben.

WORLD WIDE WEB

Der Cyberspace ist die Heimat der Künstlergruppe „etoy" mit Servern in Wien, Manchester, Zürich etc., die die heuer zum zweiten Mal vergebene Goldene Nica (öS 100.000) in der Kategorie WWW erhalten.

„etoy" demonstriert digitale Anarchie, Piraterie, Subversivität, Hackertum und Kunst. „etoy" benutzt althergebrachte Kunstformen (Musik, Graphik, skulpturale Gestaltung, Animation, Text), transferiert sie ins Netz und kreiert daraus ein neues eigenständiges „Gesamtkunstwerk", das nur im Internet so entstehen kann.

Die beiden Auszeichnungen (je öS 50.000) erhalten der Amerikaner Ed Stastny für „HyGrid" und der Linzer Manuel Schilcher für „VVV-Journey as an exile".

„Hygrid" ist eine Künstlerkolonie im Netz: Stastny setzt Bilder in das Netz. Andere Künstler können dazu eigene Bilder setzen. Ein spezieller Algorithmus verändert kontinuierlich das Gesamtbild.
„VVV-Journey as an exile" interpretiert den Alltag im Netz auf individuell-künstlerische Weise. Das alltägliche Instrumentarium wie Suchroboter, Gebrauchsgraphiken, Texte werden in ungebräuchlicher Weise einander gegenübergestellt.

PRIX ARS ELECTRONICA PRÄSENTATION
Die traditionelle Verleihung der Goldenen Nica findet am 4. September 1996 im ORF-Landesstudio Oberösterreich statt. Die von Mercedes Echerer präsentierte Gala wird von 21.00 bis 22.00 Uhr live im Satellitenprogramm 3sat übertragen und ab 23.15 Uhr in ORF2.

PRIX ARS ELECTRONICA DOKUMENTATION
Wie jedes Jahr erscheint auch heuer wieder eine dreiteilige Dokumentation über den Prix Ars Electronica. Das Buch „Der Prix Ars Electronica 96", das im Springer Verlag erscheint, dokumentiert über den aktuellen Anlaß hinaus die Ergebnisse des Wettbewerbes 96. Zum Buch erscheinen ein Video mit ausgewählten Animationen und eine CD mit den preisgekrönten Musikstücken.

PRIX ARS ELECTRONICA SPONSOREN
Der Prix Ars Electronica in seiner Gesamtheit ist nur durch das finanzielle Engagement von Sponsoren und der öffentlichen Hand möglich.
1996 wird der Prix Ars Electronica von Siemens Nixdorf gestiftet. Die Durchführung des Wettbewerbes ermöglichen die VOEST-ALPINE STAHL, die Gerhard Andlinger Stiftung, die Stadt Linz und das Land Oberösterreich.
Für weitere Unterstützung dankt der Prix Ars Electronica der Lufthansa, der Casinos Austria AG, dem Ramada Hotel Linz, Mailfast, Silicon Graphics Österreich und dem EDV-Zentrum der Universität Linz.

artistic way. Common instruments such as search engines, commercial graphics, texts are counterpoised in an unusual and unexpected way.

PRIX ARS ELECTRONICA PRESENTATION
The traditional Golden Nica award presentation will take place on September 4, 1996 in the ORF Upper Austrian regional studio. The gala will be hosted by Mercedes Echerer and will be broadcast live from 21:00 to 22:00 on 3sat, the satellite program, and in ORF 2 beginning at 23:15.

PRIX ARS ELECTRONICA DOCUMENTATION
As in previous years, a three-part Prix Ars Electronica documentation will be published again this year. The book "The Prix Ars Electronica 96", published this year by Springer Publishing Company, positions the results of the 1996 competition in a broader context. In addition to the book, there is also a video with selected animations and a CD with award winning music works.

PRIX ARS ELECTRONICA SPONSORS
In its entirety, the Prix Ars Electronica is only made possible through the financial support of sponsors and public institutions. The 1996 Prix Ars Electronica is sponsored by Siemens Nixdorf. The competition was made possible through the support of the VOEST-ALPINE STAHL, the Gerhard Andlinger Foundation, the city of Linz and the province of Upper Austria.
The Prix Ars Electronica would also like to thank Lufthansa, Casinos Austria AG, the Ramada Hotel Linz, Mailfast, Silicon Graphics Austria and the EDP center of the University of Linz.

ARS ELECTRONICA, ALL ABOARD
bitte einsteigen

John Lasseter, 10 years ago the winner of the first Golden Nica, the Prix Ars Electronica for computer animation, will receive his third Golden Nica in September 1996 for his work on "Toy Story." If, following the landing of his San Francisco-Vienna night flight, he decides to take an early train to Linz, he may be in for a bit of a surprise at Vienna's Western Station.

Wenn John Lasseter, der vor zehn Jahren der erste Gewinner der Goldenen Nica für Computeranimation beim Prix Ars Electronica war, im September 1996 nach einem Nachtflug aus San Francisco in Wien landet und einen Frühzug nach Linz zur Verleihung seiner dritten Goldenen Nica, für „Toy Story", nimmt, ist er auf dem Wiener Westbahnhof vielleicht verwundert.

The station's loudspeaker will inform him that "Eurocity train EC 562, Ars Electronica from Vienna West with stops in Linz, Salzburg and Bregenz is now departing from Track 6. Ars Electronica, all aboard!" Since June 1, 1996, the EC train linking Vienna and Bregenz, the longest single route in Austria, has been named in honor of Ars Electronica, the festival of art, technology and society. The list of such names, spanning the full spectrum of Austrian culture and including Mozart, Kepler and the Vienna Philharmonic, now includes that of a contemporary media festival which, since its founding in 1979, has established a rich tradition unsurpassed by any festival of its kind. Austria's 1,000-year anniversary in 1996 marks a further milestone for Ars Electronica. With the opening of the Ars Electronica Center as a Museum of the Future, the development of this festival has reached another high point, and one that simultaneously points the way for its subsequent evolution in the years immediately ahead. The theme of this year's festival, though, directs our attention toward an even more distant future, measured in millennia rather than in centuries. The point of departure is Richard Dawkins' theory of the meme, which he defines as a cultural DNA analogous in a certain sense to that found in the gene of a living cell. Along with the rhetorical reference implicit in this

„Der Eurocity, EC 562, Ars Electronica" — so hört er die Zugankündigung — „von Wien-Westbahnhof über Linz und Salzburg nach Bregenz fährt von Gleis 6 ab. Ars Electronica, bitte einsteigen, bitte Türen schließen!" Seit 1. Juni 1996 ist einer jener EC-Züge, die in Österreich die längste Strecke zurücklegen, nämlich die von Wien nach Bregenz, nach Ars Electronica, dem Festival für Kunst, Technologie und Gesellschaft benannt. Ein Spektrum der österreichischen Kulturszene – die Züge werden nicht nur nach Mozart, Kepler oder den Wiener Philharmonikern benannt, sondern auch nach Ars Electronica, einem zeitgenössischen Medienfestival, das durch seine Gründung im Jahre 1979 das traditionsreichste Festival dieser Art ist.

Das Jahr 1996, Österreichs Millenniumsjahr, ist für Ars Electronica ein weiterer Meilenstein. Mit der Eröffnung des Ars Electronica Centers als Museum der Zukunft erfährt die Entwicklung dieses Festivals einen vorläufigen Höhepunkt, gleichzeitig wird damit der Weg in die nächste Zukunft der Jahrtausendwende anvisiert. Das Festivalthema 1996 zielt allerdings noch in eine weitere Zukunft, mehr auf eine Jahrtausendzahl denn auf ein Jahrhundert. Ausgehend von Richard Dawkins' Theorie der Meme, unter denen er in Anlehnung an die Gene in einem gewissen Sinn die kulturelle DNA versteht, will sich Ars Electronica 96 — mit dem Kunstwort „Memesis" als Motto — neben dem dialogischen Bezug auch bewußt

HANNES LEOPOLDSEDER

*auf die Genesis berufen und damit eines der
großen Themen des nächsten Jahrtausends
ansprechen: die Zukunft der Evolution des
Menschen, die mit dem digitalen Zeitalter in
eine neue Ära eintritt. Mit der Entfaltung der
virtuellen Systeme erhält die Verschränkung
von Mensch und Maschine eine neue Dimension. Klangen die Ausführungen von Marvin
Minsky bei Ars Electronica 1990, man werde in
50 Jahren einen Chip in die Cortex implantie-
ren können, noch utopisch, läßt das „Things
That Think"-Projekt von Nicolas Negroponte
vom MIT Media Lab diese damals noch utopi-
schen Gedanken nun bereits in eine reale Dis-
kussionsphase rücken.*

*Die Auseinandersetzung mit Themen, die aus
dem Spannungsfeld von Kunst, Technologie
und Gesellschaft heraus unser Leben bewegen, ist eines der Charakteristika des Festivals
Ars Electronica, das sich gerade auch durch
diese Zielsetzung seine besondere Position innerhalb der Szene der Medienfestivals weltweit über nahezu zwei Jahrzehnte sichern
konnte.*

*Ars Electronica 96 will aber nicht nur in seiner
thematischen Orientierung über das Jahr 2000
hinauszielen, sondern präsentiert sich gleichzeitig in einem neuen Umfeld, das dem Festival selbst seine Schubkraft und seine Vitalität
über die Jahrtausendwende hinaus sichern
soll. Wie jedes Produkt in bestimmten Zeitrhy-
thmen verändert werden muß, um die entsprechende Kundenattraktivität zu halten, hat
auch Ars Electronica von Beginn an versucht,
als Festival in bestimmten Zeitabschnitten
entscheidende Neuerungen und Erweiterungen
seines Wirkungsfeldes zu erreichen.*

*Nach den Pionierjahren der Gründung von Ars
Electronica 1979 durch das Brucknerhaus Linz
und durch den Österreichischen Rundfunk,
Landesstudio Oberösterreich, in denen das
Festival seine erste Positionierung erhält, erfährt das Festival 1986/87 durch die schärfere
Thematisierung, durch die philosophische und
künstlerische Ausrichtung durch Peter Weibel
sowie durch den nunmehr jährlichen Rythmus
und dank der Initiative des ORF zum Prix Ars
Electronica als Wettbewerb für Computerkünstler eine Ausweitung und eine weitere*

artificially coined term "memesis," Ars
Electronica 96 also explicitly evokes an
association with genesis and thereby raises
one of the most important issues of the
next millennium: the future of human
evolution which has entered a new era with
the arrival of the Digital Age. With the
emergence and spread of virtual systems,
the interlocking of man and machine had
assumed a new dimension. The prediction
of chip implants in the brain cortex within
the next 50 years, elaborated by Marvin
Minsky at Ars Electronica 1990, may still
sound utopian, but the "Things That Think"
project by Nicolas Negroponte of MIT Media
Lab has already shifted this concept from
the realm of utopian fantasy into a very real
discussion phase.

The lively debate of issues which lie before
us — issues which emerge from the tense
and mutually stimulating interaction of art,
technology and society, issues which move
our very lives — is one of the definitive
elements of the Ars Electronica Festival, and
it has been precisely this fundamental aim
which has enabled Ars Electronica to attain
its unique position within the international
media festival scene over the almost two
decades of its existence.

It is not only in term of its thematic orientation, however, that Ars Electronica 96 directs
its aim out beyond the year 2000; rather, it
strives to simultaneously present itself in a
new context whereby the festival itself is
assured of maintaining its thrust and vitality
into the next millennium. Like any product
which must be modified in a certain time
rhythm in order to remain attractive to consumers, Ars Electronica has made an effort
from the very outset to introduce decisive
innovations in the festival format and to
broaden its field of effectiveness.

Ars Electronica was founded in 1979 by the
Bruckner House in Linz and the Austrian
Broadcasting Company (ORF) studio in the
Province of Upper Austria. Following the
early pioneering years during which the
festival's initial positioning was established,
Ars Electronica underwent a process of

expansion and internationalization in
1986–87 due to a sharper thematic focus
and the philosophic and artistic realignment
carried out by Peter Weibel, as a result of its
being held on a yearly basis as well as the
initiative leading to the creation of the ORF's
Prix Ars Electronica as a competition for
computer artists.

Ten years later, the next step, which had already been initiated in 1992, is being successfully completed with the opening of the
Ars Electronica Center. Thus, Ars Electronica
is not simply the name of a festival or one
connected with an artistic competition — or,
for that matter, with the EC train covering
the Austrian Federal Railway's longest route
— but rather that of an established institution in Linz, the Ars Electronica Center, the
Museum of the Future.

With the completion of this step, Ars Electronica is no longer only an event which takes
place once a year in Linz, providing a temporary forum for intensive encounter. Rather,
Ars Electronica is now present on a daily
basis, existing in a fixed, real form as one of
the first digital media centers. It thereby
makes its facilities available not only to
virtual visitors in the WWW, but also to the
broad general public, as well as to specialists in the field whose projects at the leading
edge of digital media are revealing the
capabilities and applications of these new
technologies.

The Ars Electronica Center occupies a position at the interface of art, technology and
science. It sees its mission as that of a
"house of progress," a living organism not
only providing the public with a glimpse into
virtual reality, data visualization, networks
and the applications of digital media in
education, science and the arts, but one that
makes its foremost contribution in actively
promoting interactivity.

Above all, the Ars Electronica Center will
strive to be a place dedicated to the
formation of consciousness — of the Digital
Revolution, of the radical nature of the
breakthroughs and shifts brought about by
digital media and thus of the new stage of

Internationalisierung.

*Zehn Jahre später erfolgt 1996 der nächste
Schritt, der allerdings bereits 1992 eingeleitet
wurde: Die Eröffnung des Ars Electronica Centers. Damit ist Ars Electronica nicht nur mit
dem Namen eines Festivals oder mit einem
Wettbewerb verbunden – oder mit dem läng-
sten EC-Zug Österreichs von Wien nach Bregenz –, sondern auch mit einer ständigen Institution in Linz, dem Ars
Electronica Center, dem Museum der Zukunft.*

*Ars Electronica ist damit nicht mehr nur ein
Ereignis, das einmal im Jahr in Linz stattfindet
und zur Begegnung einlädt, sondern Ars Electronica ist täglich präsent. Das Ars Electronica
Center lädt nicht nur die virtuellen Besucher
im World Wide Web (WWW) ein, sondern existiert auch real als eines der ersten digitalen
Mediencenter, das ein breites Publikum
ebenso anspricht wie Fachexperten, die dort
die Gelegenheit erhalten, sich mit den digitalen Medien in beispielhaften Projekten auseinanderzusetzen und die Möglichkeiten und Anwendungen neuer Technologien kennenzuler-
nen.*

*Das Ars Electronica Center liegt an der
Schnittstelle von Kunst, Technik und Wirtschaft. Das Center, das sich bewußt als
„house in progress" versteht, will ein lebendi-
ger Organismus sein und dem Publikum nicht
nur Einblick in Virtual Reality, Datenvisualisie-
rung, Netze oder in den Einsatz digitaler Medien in Bildung, Wissenschaft und Kunst geben, sondern vor allem auch aktiv zur Interaktivität einladen.*

*Das Ars Electronica Center will vor allem eines
sein: ein Haus der Bewußtseinsbildung für
den digitalen Wandel, für die Radikalität des
digitalen Medienbruchs und damit für die
neue digitale Kulturstufe, die sich vor uns
auszubreiten beginnt.*

*Wir stehen in der Morgendämmerung dieser
neuen Zeit. Vieles ist noch nicht sichtbar und
erkennbar, vieles liegt noch verborgen, niemand weiß letztlich, wohin die digitale Revolution in einem neuen Jahrhundert führen
wird.*

*Vor zehn Jahren, zu Ars Electronica 86, habe
ich in einem Aufsatz zehn Indizien für das*

Werden der Computerkultur darzustellen versucht. „Würden wir das Computerzeitalter auf 100 Jahre ansetzen," schrieb ich damals, „könnten wir uns vielleicht jetzt im Jahre 10 befinden. Die jetzigen Kindergartenkinder, die mit
Videoclips und Homecomputer aufwachsen, werden von Anfang an den Computer als vorhandenes Instrument, als vorhandenes Werkzeug betrachten." In der Zwischenzeit sind seit 1986 zehn Jahre vergangen; wenn wir von einem Jahrhundert ausgehen, wären wir im Jahre 20. Eines hat sich in diesem letzten Jahrzehnt allerdings verändert: die neue Goldgräberzeit hat — zumindest in den USA, wenn man die Zahl der sprunghaft ansteigenden Unternehmensgründungen betrachtet — längst begonnen. Noch etwas ist in diesen zehn Jahren passiert: der Inhalt der Datenbanken der Welt übersteigt heute die Kapazität des menschlichen Gedächtnisses. Wir haben den Punkt der kritischen Masse erreicht. In einem sind sich alle Prognosen einig: Die neue digitale Zeit verändert das Leben eines jeden einzelnen. „Wir werden die Welt", sagt Peter F. Drucker, „nach einer Generation nicht wiedererkennen."
Das Ars Electronica Center, vor allem das Festival Ars Electronica, geht von der Kunst aus: Kunst erweist und versteht sich mehr denn je als Sensor für neue Entwicklungen, die schließlich das ganze Leben umfassen. In diesem Sinne versteht sich das Ars Electronica Center als „Evangelist": als Evangelist für die digitale Zeit der Virtuellen Realität, des Cyberspace und der Evolution der Kommunikation, in der erstmals die Qualität des Geistes verstärkt wird, im Gegensatz zu den bisherigen Tools, die Verstärker unseres Körpers waren. Ars Electronica, Prix Ars Electronica und Ars Electronica Center bilden ein Triangel, um Linz damit verstärkt positionieren zu können.
Wie jedes neue Medium bestimmte Orte hervorgebracht hat — der Buchdruck die Bibliotheken, das Telefon die Telefonzelle, der Film das Kino oder wie das Fernsehen jedes Wohnzimmer verändert hat —, wird die digitale Medienkultur ebenfalls neue Plätze, neue Orte, neue Einrichtungen schaffen: das Ars Electro-

digital culture which has already begun to unfold before us.
We stand at the dawning of a new age. Much remains unseen and unrecognized, much still lies hidden. Ultimately, no one knows where the Digital Revolution will lead in the coming century.
In an essay written 10 years ago on the occasion of Ars Electronica 86, I attempted to elaborate 10 indicators of the emergence of computer culture. "If we visualize the Computer Age as a timeline of 100 years," I then wrote, "we are now, perhaps, in Year 10. Today's kindergarten kids, growing up with video clips and home computers, will, from the very start, regard the computer as an available instrument and a useful tool." In the meantime, 10 more years have elapsed since 1986; on our timeline, we are now in Year 20. One thing has certainly changed during this decade: the gold rush has long since gotten underway, at least in the USA, when one considers the extraordinary number of newly founded firms that has achieved spectacular growth. And something else has taken place during these 10 years: the content of the world's data banks today exceeds that of human memory. We have reached the point of critical mass. All prognoses agree in one respect: this new digital age means change in the life of each and every individual. "In another generation," Peter F. Drucker says, "we will no longer recognize the world."
Art constitutes the point of departure for the Ars Electronica Center and, above all, for the Ars Electronica Festival. More than ever, artists consider themselves, and have proven to be, sensors of new developments that ultimately encompass life in its entirety. In this sense, the Ars Electronica Center sees its role as that of an "evangelist" of the digital age of virtual reality, of cyberspace and of the evolution of communication serving for the first time to augment the quality of the human spirit and in stark contrast to the tools strengthening our bodies we have had up to now.
The Ars Electronica Festival, the Ars

Electronica Center and the Prix Ars Electronica constitute a triangle enabling Linz to assume a key position in this process. Just as every new medium has brought forth certain physical locations — printing produced the library; the telephone, the telephone booth; film, the cinema; or television, making its presence felt in every living room — digital media culture will likewise lead to the creation of new places, new sites, new installations, and the Ars Electronica Center seeks to become the prototype of such a location of the new stage of digital culture. Linz will thus continue to support the leading role played by Ars Electronica, and through the Ars Electronica Center establish itself as prototype of a vibrant nucleus of digital culture.

The Ars Electronica activities undertaken by Linz thus encompass a time frame of almost two decades: from 1979, when the personal computer was in its infancy, to 1996, a time in which Internet is in the process of unifying within it all previously existing media and thus contributing to the full-blown breakthrough of the new digital era — whether within the network structure which has emerged to date or something closer to Craig McCaw's vision of "Teledesic" and the 840 satellites orbiting 435 miles above the earth which, it is claimed, will make Internet accessible to every point on the planet in broadband audio quality by the year 2002. In conjunction with the opening of the Ars Electronica Center, the activities of Ars Electronica will also be reorganized. Whereas up to now, Ars Electronica has been organized by the Bruckner House, a cultural facility of the City of Linz, and by the ORF, in the future, management of all Ars Electronica activities will be consolidated in the hands of the center's board of directors within the City of Linz. The ORF's Upper Austrian studio will remain a co-sponsor of the Ars Electronica Festival; the prime focus of its involvement within the festival's framework will be the judging and awarding of the Prix Ars Electronica. The project idea proposing an Ars Electronica Center can likewise be traced

nica Center will ein Prototyp eines solchen Ortes der neuen digitalen Kulturstufe sein. Linz will damit die Vorreiterrolle der Ars Electronica weiter ausbauen und sich durch das Ars Electronica Center als Prototyp eines neuen Kraftortes digitaler Kultur festigen.

Die Ars Electronica Aktivitäten von Linz umfassen daher fast zwei Jahrzehnte, von 1979 — einer Zeit, in der gerade der Personal Computer im Aufbruch war — bis 1996 — einer Zeit, in der das Internet dabei ist, alle bisherigen Medien in sich zu vereinen und damit der neuen digitalen Ära voll zum Durchbruch zu verhelfen: sei es in der bisherigen Vernetzungstruktur oder in der Vision von Craig McCaw mit „Teledesic" und den 840 Satelliten, die ab 2002 in einer Höhe von 435 Meilen die Erde umkreisen und Internet in Breitbandqualität an jedem Punkt der Erde zugänglich machen sollen.

Mit der Errichtung des Ars Electronica Centers werden auch die Aktivitäten der Ars Electronica neu organisiert: Wurde bisher Ars Electronica von Brucknerhaus Linz, einer städtischen Kultureinrichtung, und dem ORF organisiert, werden künftig innerhalb der Stadt Linz die Aktivitäten der Ars Electronica in der Ars Electronica Center Betriebsgesellschaft zusammengeführt. Mitveranstalter des Festivals Ars Electronica ist, so wie bisher, der Österreichische Rundfunk, Landesstudio Oberösterreich, der als besonderen Schwerpunkt innerhalb des Festivals den Prix Ars Electronica betreut. Das Ars Electronica Center geht ebenfalls als Projektidee auf den ORF zurück, der damit bewußt seine Rolle als Impulsgeber im Bereich der digitalen Medienaktivitäten vorantreiben will.

Die Geschichte des Ars Electronica Centers reicht nahezu fünf Jahre zurück, also in eine Zeit, in der WWW, Netscape oder Yahoo noch nicht erfunden waren.

Das Ars Electronica Center basiert auf einer von mir 1992 vorgelegten Projektidee, für deren Realisierung sich die Stadt Linz im Zuge der Nutzungsdiskussion des bereits planmäßig bestehenden Gebäudes „Donautor" der Architekten W. H. Michl und K. Leitner nach einem Hearing und einer Präsentation von

insgesamt fünf Projektideen im März l992 entschieden hat. Daraufhin wurde ART+COM, Berlin, unter Prof.Edouard Bannwart mit einer
Machbarkeitsstudie beauftragt. Die Projektlei-
tung lag bei Mag. Sigbert Janko, Stadt Linz,
und Dr. Hannes Leopoldseder, ORF. Aufgrund
der Machbarkeitsstudie entschied die Stadt
Linz im März l993, das Ars Electronica Center
mit einem Kostenaufwand von 180 Millionen
zu errichten, wobei sich das Land Oberösterreich mit 30% und der Bund mit 10% in Form
eines ERP-Kredites beteiligten. Mit dem Bau
des AEC wurde die Bau-und Errichtungsgesell-
schaft der Stadt Linz mit ihrem Geschäftsführer Dipl.-Ing. Fritz Angerhofer beauftragt. Für
die Innengestaltung ist Architekt Rainer Verbizh verantwortlich. Für den Betrieb des Ars
Electronica Centers wurde 1995 die Ars Electronica Center Betriebsgesellschaft ins Leben
gerufen. Zum Geschäftsführer wurde mit Juli
1995 der Medienkünstler Gerfried Stocker be-
stellt. Gerfried Stocker ist sowohl für den Betrieb des Ars Electronica Center verantwortlich, als auch, gemeinsam mit Dr. Christine
Schöpf vom ORF, für das Festival Ars Electronica.
Ein digitales Mediencenter wie das Ars Electronica Center bedarf in besonderer Weise
auch der Kooperation und der Partnerschaft
der Industrie, insbesondere im Elektronik-und
Technologiebereich.
Die wichtigsten Partner des AEC sind: Creditanstalt, Digital Equipment, Ericsson Austria,
Hewlett Packard, Kapsch AG, Brau AG, Microsoft, Oracle, Quelle Versand, Siemens Nixdorf,
S plus S, Silicon Graphics. Ebenfalls ein besonderer Partner des Ars Electronica Centers
ist der ORF.
Mit dem Triangel Ars Electronica, Prix Ars Electronica und Ars Electronica Center will sich
Linz nicht nur regional, sondern weltweit im
Cyberspace positionieren. Das Ars Electronica
Triangel von Linz zielt schließlich darauf ab,
den digitalen Wandel unserer Kultur hin zu einer kognitiven Gesellschaft, deren entscheidende Ressource das Wissen ist, im Einklang
mit den wirtschaftlichen und sozialen Gege-
benheiten zu bewältigen.
Für Linz ist Ars Electronica Vorreiter und Zu-

back to the ORF, which has thereby taken
another step forward in advancing its role
as a driving force in the field of digital
media.
The history of the Ars Electronica Center
goes back almost five years, and thus to a
time in which the WWW, Netscape or Yahoo
had not yet been invented.
The Ars Electronica Center is based upon a
project proposal which I submitted in 1992.
Following a hearing and a presentation of a
total of five project ideas in the course of
the proposed use discussions in March 1992
regarding the Donautor Building already
completed as planned by the architects
W. H. Michl and K. Leitner, the City of Linz
decided in favor of the realization of this
idea. ART+COM Berlin, under the direction of
Prof. Edouard Bannwart, was then
commissioned to perform a feasibility study.
The project managers were Mag. Siegbert
Janko representing the City of Linz and Dr.
Hannes Leopoldseder from the ORF. As a
result of the feasibility study, the City of Linz
decided in March 1993 to go ahead with
construction of the Ars Electronica Center at
a cost of 180 Million Schillings, of which
30% was to be provided by the Province of
Upper Austria and 10% by the Austrian
Federal Government in the form of ERP
credits. The Ars Electronica Center project
was then assigned to the Building and
Construction Corporation of the City of Linz
headed by Dipl. Ing. Fritz Angerhofer.
Architect Rainer Verbizh was given
responsibility for the interior design. For the
management of the center, the Ars
Electronica Center Board of Directors was
created in 1995, and media artist Gerfried
Stocker was appointed its managing director
in July of that year. Gerfried Stocker is
responsible for the day-to-day operation of
the Ars Electronica Center as well as,
together with Dr. Christine Schöpf of the
ORF, for the Ars Electronica Festival.
A digital media center like the Ars
Electronica Center has an especially urgent
need for the cooperation and partnership of
private firms, particularly those in the

electronics and technology sectors. The Ars Electronica Center's most important sponsors are Creditanstalt, Digital Equipment, Ericsson Austria, Hewlett Packard, Kapsch AG, Brau AG, Microsoft, Oracle, Quelle Versand, Siemens Nixdorf, S plus S, Silicon Graphics. Last but not least, I would like to mention our very special partner, the ORF.

With the triangle Ars Electronica Festival, Prix Ars Electronica and Ars Electronica Center, Linz has established itself in a leading position in cyberspace, both regionally and worldwide. The ultimate aim of this Ars Electronica triangle in Linz is to enable us to work together, bringing economic and social efforts into harmony in dealing effectively with the digital transformation of our culture as we move further along the way to a cognitive society in which knowledge is the most decisive resource.

For Linz, Ars Electronica has functioned both as leader and signal in the process of change which for this city, as for so many other cities and regions, has run parallel to the development of an iron and steel metropolis into a modern industrial center, where steel is today regarded quite properly as a high-tech product. Ars Electronica personifies the future-orientation of this city on the threshold of a new cultural epoch in the next millennium. For Austria, Ars Electronica constitutes an ambassador, providing this country with a presence abroad which expands the traditional image of Austrian culture. Thus, for example, the Prix Ars Electronica as an award recognizing excellence in digital media, presented by a land such as Austria with its long and rich European cultural tradition, has enjoyed an extraordinarily positive reception, particularly in the USA.

Seit 1979 hat Ars Electronica in der Welt der „Electronic Community" viele Freunde gewonnen. Ars Electronica hat für viele den „Spirit of Linz" geschaffen, um mit dem ersten Preisträger der Goldenen Nica in der Computergrafik, Brian Reffin Smith, zu sprechen. Es ist ein Treffpunkt von Persönlichkeiten aus unterschiedlichen Bereichen geworden: aus der Wissenschaft, der Kunst, Philosophie, aber auch Wirtschaft.

Mit der Goldenen Nica des Prix Ars Electronica sind seit 1987 insgesamt weit über eine Million Dollar an Preisgeldern an digitale Künstler gegangen, ein Betrag, der kaum anderswo in dieser Kontinuität direkt den Neuen Medien und ihren Gestaltern gewidmet wurde. An dieser Stelle ist all jenen Unternehmen zu danken, die in diesen Jahren durch die Förderung des Prix Ars Electronica dazu beigetragen haben: Siemens AG, Kapsch AG, Austria Tabak AG, Gerhard Andlinger Foundation, VOEST-ALPINE Stahl AG, Siemens.

Für den Österreichischen Rundfunk bedeutet das Ars Electronica Center einen Markstein im Engagement und in den Initiativen zu den Ars Electronica Aktivitäten seit 1979. Mit diesem Engagement will der ORF bewußt seine offensive Haltung im Zusammenhang mit den digitalen Medien, den Herausforderungen, die daraus für alle bisherigen Medien erwachsen, zum Ausdruck bringen.

Gleichzeitig ist für den ORF sein Einsatz für das Ars Electronica Center eine Einladung an das Publikum der Zukunft, eine Einladung zum Kennenlernen der neuen Medienwelt, die sich vor uns auszubreiten beginnt. Darüber hinaus wird der ORF, zusätzlich zum Festival Ars Electronica, mit dem Ars Electronica Center als Partner weitere gemeinsame Projekte realisieren, sei es auf dem Gebiet künstlerischer Medienprojekte, sei es in der Entwicklungsarbeit bei der Nutzung der ATM-Strecke zwischen dem Ars Electronica Center und dem Rundfunkstudio, sei es in der Zusammenarbeit bei der Produktion von Radio- und Fernsehprogrammen.

Die Geschichte der medialen Kommunikation bewegt sich in säkularen Zeiträumen — von den Höhlenmalereien über Gutenberg zu Tele-

Over the past 10 years, as a result of its continuity, its high artistic judging criteria and its wide-ranging media impact, including book publications, exhibitions and TV documentaries, the Prix Ars Electronica has become a sensor of artistic developments in the field of digital media. This is attributable as well to the variety of new categories, corresponding to media developments such as the World Wide Web in 1995, which have been continually added. Since 1979, Ars Electronica has made many new friends in the world of the "electronic community." For many, Ars Electronica has created a new "Spirit of Linz," to recall the words of Brian Reffin Smith, the first winner of the Golden Nica in computer graphics. It is a meeting place of the most prominent figures from the most diverse fields of science, art, philosophy as well as business. Along with the Golden Nica of the Prix Ars Electronica, digital artists have also been awarded a total of well over 1 Million Dollars in prize money since 1987 — thus, an award of virtually unparalleled continuity that has been expressly dedicated to the advancement of new media and their creators. At this point, an expression of gratitude is due to the corporate sponsors whose support of the Prix Ars Electronica this year has contributed to this goal: Siemens AG, Kapsch AG, Austria Tabak AG, Gerhard Andlinger Foundation, VOEST-ALPINE Stahl AG and Siemens. For the Austrian Broadcasting Company, the Ars Electronica Center represents a milestone in the long-term commitment and great initiative it has displayed in Ars Electronica activities since 1979. Through this engagement, the ORF wishes to express its positive attitude and active approach to digital media in confronting the challenges which they now pose.

At the same time, the ORF's tremendous efforts on behalf of the Ars Electronica Center should be understood as an invitation extended to the public of the future, an invitation to get to know the new world of media that has begun to unfold before us. Furthermore, in addition to its involvement with the Ars Electronica Festival, the ORF will continue to pursue cooperative ventures in partnership with the Ars Electronica Center, including projects in the area of artistic media, developmental work regarding the utilization of ATM conduits linking up the Ars Electronica Center and the ORF studio, as well as collaborating in the production of radio and television programs. The history of communication using media has tended to display a series of secular epochs — from cave painting to Gutenberg to the telegraph, telephone, radio, television and finally to the universal medium of the computer, which appears like a werewolf threatening to devour all the others. Thus, everything starts anew. New forms of storage and transmission, new design, new formats, a new society. These all require new places for their elaboration. The Digital Age with its universal medium, with its on-line existence, creates new sites, new places, new homes. If this new Digital Age requires vibrant new centers, beyond the capitals of the electronics industry, which embody the social reflection of the Digital Revolution, centers functioning as both nexus in the real world and simultaneously as interface and point of contact in cyberspace, then Linz, in the form of its Ars Electronica Center, has boldly announced its readiness to act as prototype and test field, extending an invitation to all those who, with optimism and critical reflection, are prepared to encounter the new era of digital culture.

graf, Telefon, Radio, Fernsehen und schließlich zum Universalmedium Computer, der die bisherigen Medien wie ein Werwolf aufzufressen scheint. Damit beginnt alles neu. Neue Speicherung, neue Übermittlung, neues Design, neue Formate, eine neue Gesellschaft. Dies alles braucht zur Manifestation neue Orte. Die digitale Ära mit ihrem universalen Medium, mit ihrem Online-Sein, schafft neue Orte, neue Plätze, neue Häuser. Wenn das neue Zeitalter des Digitalen über die Standorte der Elektronik-Industrie hinaus neue Kraftzentren der gesellschaftlichen Reflexion dieses digitalen Wandels benötigt, die ein Knoten in der realen Welt sind, gleichzeitig aber auch ein Knoten und Ansprechpartner im Cyberspace, dann will Linz mit seinem Ars Electronica Center Prototyp, Testfeld und Einladung an alle sein, die mit Optimismus und kritischer Reflexion der neuen Ära der digitalen Kultur begegnen.

Ars Electronica Center Team: Erich Berger / Hardware Engineering, Sandra Brandstetter / Administration, Maria Falkinger / Press & Information, Oliver Frommel / Network and Coding, Doris Haider / Assistant Manager, Horst Hörtner / Technical Director, Elisabeth Kapeller / Administration, Jürgen Kern / Cave-Engineering, Wolfgang Modera / Consultants, Chris Mutter / Web-Master, Dietmar Offenhuber / Computeranimation, Michael Pointner / 3D Graphics, Christa Schneebauer / Web Editor, Peter Schöber / Marketing, Sponsoring, Matthew Smith / Media Design, Romana Staufer / Marketing Assistant, Gerfried Stocker / Managing Director, Tom Teibler / House Supervisor, Tom Weber / Networkadministrator, Birgit Brandner / Festival PR, Patricia Futterer / Festival Assistance, Patricia Maier / Festival Assistance, Karin Rumpfhuber / Festival Assistance, Jutta Schmiederer, Festival Producer

There are numerous reasons – of which its name is only one – for assuming that a unique project such as the Ars Electronica Center could never have come about without its "godparents".

Es gibt viele Gründe anzunehmen, daß ein einmaliges Vorhaben wie das Ars Electronica Center nicht nur seiner Namensgebung wegen ohne seine „Paten" nicht hätte zustande kommen können.

GERFRIED STOCKER

The most important reason for its coming into being, however, is the knowledge which has grown out of the internationally-acclaimed Ars Electronica Festival and the Prix Ars Electronica: the knowledge that a future-oriented approach is essential for understanding and dealing with the present. A knowledge which, at the leading-edge of cultural development, is an indispensable element of competence in engaging those areas targeted from the start – the arts, technology and society – as an integrated field of endeavour. One fundamental consideration in the setting of an agenda is therefore its positioning in that environment in which the Ars Electronica Center, derived as it is from the activities of the Festival and the Prix, is rooted. Thus the raison d'être of the Ars Electronica Center is established in part by a functioning model: that is, artistic commitment as the guiding principle for navigation through a world in the throes of a media-led transformation; as the driving force for society's confrontation with the new contextual realities of our age; and as a resource for the impending tasks of design and acculturation of the new media-based environment.

Against this programmatic backdrop, the Ars Electronica Center cannot be regarded simply as a centre of cultural competence, but – where culture is understood as technological evolution - as itself an art-project of this cul-

Der wesentlichste Grund seines Entstehens ist jedoch das aus dem international akklamierten Ars Electronica Festival und dem Prix Ars Electronica gewachsene Wissen um die Notwendigkeit eines zukunftsorientierten Umgangs mit der Gegenwart. Ein Wissen, das Voraussetzung ist, sich im Vorfeld der kulturellen Entwicklung den zu Anbeginn programmierten Zielbereichen, Kunst, Technologie und Gesellschaft als einem gemeinsamen Aufgabenbereich kompetent zu stellen.

Eine Grundüberlegung zur Programmatik betrifft daher die Positionierung in jenem Umfeld, in dem das Ars Electronica Center durch seine Ableitung aus den Aktivitäten des Festivals und des Prix wurzelt. So wird dem Ars Electronica Center auch seine Bestimmung durch ein funktionierendes Modell vorgegeben: nämlich künstlerisches Engagement als Leitbild für die Navigation durch die in einer Mediamorphose begriffenen Welt; als Motor für die gesellschaftliche Konfrontation mit den neuen Rahmenbedingungen unserer Zeit; als Ressource für die anstehende Gestaltung und Akkulturation der neuen medialen Lebensräume.

Angesichts dieses programmatischen Hintergrundes ist das Ars Electronica Center nicht nur als ein kultureller Kompetenzträger zu verstehen, sondern – infolge des Verständnisses von Kultur als Techno-Evolution – selbst als ein Projekt der Kunst dieser Kultur. Konsequenterweise verhält sich dieses Projekt wie ein "work in progress" – im Hinblick auf seine Integrationsfähigkeit ebenso wie auf seine Kompatibilität mit den Interessen einer breiten Öffentlichkeit; andererseits verlangt ein Projekt, das sich so sehr im Sturm der Veränderungen und Neuerungen exponiert, eine starke Identität, die es über Technikmoden und kurzlebige Hypes hinausstellt.

Das Ars Electronica Center darf sich daher nicht nur als Anbieter und Galerie begreifen, sondern als Partner, als Infrastuktur und Impulsgeber. Das heißt, es muß selbst an seiner eigenen Notwendigkeit, der Schaffung eines fruchtbaren Umfeldes mitwirken. Denn, was unterscheidet das Ars Electronica Center als „Museum der Zukunft" von einem Werbecamp der Computer- und IT-Industrie? Im wesentlichen wohl, daß die Inhalte dieses „Museums" nicht von Produktherstellern oder Softwareentwicklern designt werden, sondern aus einer künstlerisch motivierten Herangehensweise resultieren.

Das Ars Electronica Center legt es darauf an, eine Art Magnetfeld zu entwickeln, das nicht nur verstärkt internationale Kapazitäten, sondern auch neugierige, experimentierfreudige Kreative (welcher Ausbildung auch immer) nach Linz zieht. Gedacht ist, auf diesem Wege einen Pool von kompetenten, interessierten, innovativen Menschen ins Leben zu rufen, die sich der Gravitationskraft des Centers nicht nur physikalisch, sondern auch in ihrem Denken „ausliefern" werden; insofern, als sie — von dem modus operandi, aus großer Distanz die Dinge in ihren Köpfen zu disponieren, in die unmittelbare Nähe zur Technologie gebracht — zwangsläufig ihre Herangehensweise an die Dinge werden ändern müssen. Ein solches Naheverhältnis evoziert automatisch eine ganz andere Art von Ideen, als sie bisher mehrheitlich die Gestalt von ästhetischen Ferndiagnosen erhielt.

Schon in den Monaten vor dem offiziellen Betriebsbeginn herrschte im Ars Electronica Center keine sterile institutionelle, konzeptionell gesteuerte Arbeitsatmosphäre, es präsentierte sich vielmehr als offene Werkstatt, in der kreative Intelligenz ihr Vermögen an den Geräten und dadurch deren Leistungsvermögen er-

ture. As a logical consequence, this project has the nature of a "work-in-progress", both in regard to its capacity for integration and in terms of its compatibility with the interests of a broad public. On the other hand, a project so exposed to the elements of change and innovation requires a strong identity that sets it above considerations of transient techno-chic and the short-lived hype.

The Ars Electronica Center cannot, therefore, content itself with simply being a collection or a gallery, but sees itself as a partner, as infrastructure and initiator. This means that it must itself participate in the establishment of its own necessity, in the creation of a fertile environment.

What is it then that distinguishes the Ars Electronica Center, as a "museum of the future", from a publicity barrage of the computer and IT industry? Essentially it is the fact that the content of this "museum" was not designed by manufacturers of products, or software developers, but is the result of an artistically-motivated approach.

The Ars Electronica Center seeks to develop a kind of magnetic field, attracting not only international capacities in greater number and scope, but also inquisitive, experimentally-oriented, creative people (whatever the nature of their training might be) to Linz. The idea is in this way to create a pool of competent, interested, innovative individuals who will "surrender" to the gravitational pull of the Center, not only in physical terms but also in their thinking. That is to say that they will be obliged to abandon the modus operandi characterised by internal deliberations at a distance and, brought now into direct proximity with the technology, to alter their approach to the objects of their deliberation. A close physical relationship of this kind automatically evokes an entirely different category of ideas than that which hitherto, in the majority of cases, had rather the nature of aesthetic remote-control.

Even in the months prior to the official inauguration, the working atmosphere at the Ars Electronica Center was not one of sterile institutional process control – it was more like an open workshop, in which creative intelligences tested their capabilities on the equipment, and in doing so probed the extent of the latter's performance capability. In a concentrated engagement with the machine itself, of a kind peculiar to this new generation of hacker-artists and scarcely conceivable for outsiders, in the identification with – practically a fusion with – the computer (and the network behind it), the digital revolution that now has our society in its thrall took on a graphic and concrete form.

Much of what will never leave the home directories of these "freaks", what they are unlikely even to put in the official web server of the Center, is notable above all for the process of its creation and the matter-of-factness (not to be confused with laid-back indifference) of approach to the process which characterises this, the third generation of computer users. An undeniable sign of the emergence of a new culture, identified as "memesis" in this year's Festival. Thus the Festival, this year dominated by the inauguration of the Center, is itself also focused on the opening up of such zones of activity, on a new phase in the evolution of interaction with media technology, and of media art, which is needed to confront the technological revolution with that very force which it has unleashed. This is the great opportunity for the Ars Electronica Center, which must ally itself with its users, must engage with them and grow with them. The same applies to the collaboration with artistic, innovative individuals: they must be attracted and encouraged to accept and make use of the Ars Electronica Center as their laboratory and their platform.

However, it has to be more than just a question of using electronic media as a tool. On the one hand the encounter between technologists and artists will give birth to projects which are founded on knowledge of the technological processes, on the appropriate selection of means, and on the idea of multimedia networking and its reflexion. On the other, artistic expertise will be opened up for

probte. In einem dieser neuen Hacker-/Künstlergeneration eigenen, für Außenstehende kaum nachvollziehbaren konsequenten Einsatz am Gerät selbst, der Identifizierung, geradezu Verschmelzung mit dem Computer (und dem dahinterliegenden Netzwerk) wurde die digitale Revolution, die unsere Gesellschaft heute erfaßt, konkret.

Vieles davon, was die „Home-Directories" dieser „Freaks" niemals verlassen wird, was sie wohl auch nicht in den offiziellen Web-Server des Centers stellen werden, ist vor allem im Zusammenhang mit seinem Entstehungsprozeß und dem von Selbstverständlichkeit (nicht zu verwechseln mit unreflektierter Gelassenheit) geprägten, erst für die dritte Generation der Computeruser bezeichnenden Umgang so bemerkenswert. Unleugbares Zeichen des im diesjährigen Festival als „Memesis" bezeichneten Entstehens einer neuen Kultur.

So spielt das Festival, das zugleich ganz im Zeichen der Eröffnung des Centers steht, auch auf die Eröffnung solcher Aktionsfelder an, auf eine neue Phase der Arbeit mit Medientechnologie und der Medienkunst, der es bedarf, um der technologischen Revolution auch mit jener Kraft zu begegnen, die durch sie wirksam geworden ist.

Hier liegt die Chance für das Ars Electronica Center, das sich mit seinen Usern verbünden, auf sie einlassen und mit ihnen wachsen muß. Dies gilt auch für die Zusammenarbeit mit den künstlerischen, innovativen Kräften: Sie müssen gewonnen werden, das Ars Electronica Center als Labor, als ihre Plattform anzunehmen und zu nutzen.

Wobei hier über den bloßen Einsatz elektronischer Medien als Werkzeug hinauszugehen, hinauszudenken ist. Zum einen sollen der Begegnung von Technikern mit Künstlern Projekte entspringen, die, in Kenntnis der technologischen Prozesse, auf der adäquaten Wahl der Mittel ebenso wie der Idee der intermedialen Vernetzung und deren Reflexion basieren. Zum anderen soll künstlerisches Knowhow für Techniker und Theoretiker erschlossen werden — ein Ansatz, der angesichts der zunehmenden Bedeutung von „kreativen Problemlösungsstrategien" durchaus nicht ver-

*messen ist. Nur in der Öffnung zu verschiede-
nen Interessenskreisen, in der Koexistenz von
Vermittlungs- und Forschungsstätte, von Labor und Infopool kann eine den Anforderungen entsprechende Schnittstelle entstehen —
eine Vernetzung, Verstrickung, in alle Lebens-
bereiche, die wiederum ein kulturelles Para-
digma der neuen Informationsgesellschaft ist.
Man wird lange suchen müssen, um eine historische Analogie zu jenem Phänomen zu finden, das derzeit unter teilweise sehr
gegensätzlichen Vorzeichen abläuft:
Künstler/innen, die bisher auch im Medien-
kunstbereich isoliert und unbeachtet gearbeitet haben, sehen sich unverhofft dem außer-
ordentlich großen Interesse einer Öffentlichkeit gegenüber, die sich Schlüsselbegriffe und
ideologische Stereotypen der digitalen Revolution aneignet. Diese neue Aufmerksamkeit
gilt jedoch weniger der eigentlichen künstlerischen Arbeit als vielmehr den Künstlern selbst
als im weitesten Sinne gestalterisch kreatives
und daher dienstbares (Arbeits-)Potential der
neuen Medientechnologien. Die beklemmende
Erkenntnis, daß die Technologie ohne „content" nicht zu verkaufen sein könnte, öffnet
viele Kanäle und schürt zugleich die äußerst
fragwürdige Hoffnung, daß sich in Technolo-
gie-Angelegenheiten verdienende Kunst bald
selbst ihr Brot verdiene und folglich den aus-
gezehrten öffentlichen Kulturtöpfen etwas Ent-
lastung zukommen könne.
Dem Künstler geht es in den latenten Grenzen
seines Selbstverständnisses wie seines gesellschaftlichen Rollenbildes an den Kragen. Hatten seinesgleichen in den klassischen Gattungen noch Theater, Galerien und Konzerthäuser
als approbierte Formen ihrer abgrenzbaren Öffentlichkeit — Distributionspraktiken, die
selbst in den Einweg-Massenmedien Rundfunk
und TV noch einigermaßen konserviert werden konnten -, so stellt sich eine virtuelle Öffentlichkeit, wie sie das Internet exemplarisch
ausformt, vielen als unwertes oder bedrohli-
ches Nichts dar. Als ein schwarzes Loch, in
dem alles verschwindet, weil es sich so
schwer auszeichnen und hervorheben läßt in
dem allgemeinen „Kommunikationsmüll" (als
ob eine Galerie in Hongkong oder ein guter*

technologists and theoreticians – an approach which, in view of the increasing sig-
nificance of "strategies for creative problem-
solving" is in no way presumptuous. Only in
the mutual accessibility of different interests, in the cohabitation of research and
dissemination, the twin functions of laboratory and information pool, can an interface
be set up which meets the requirements
made of it – a networking, an interweaving
in all areas of life, which is itself a paradigm
of the new information-based society.
One would need to look for a long time to
find a historical analogy for that phenomenon which is currently taking place, based in
part on highly contrasted premises: artists
who hitherto, even in the field of media art,
have worked alone and unnoticed, are now
unexpectedly confronted with an extraordinary level of interest from a public which is
mastering the key terms and ideological ste-
reotypes of the digital revolution. However,
this new awareness relates in fact less to
the artistic activity than to the artists themselves as being, in the broadest sense, the
designers, the creators, the human resource
potential for the new media technologies.
The uneasy feeling that without "content"
the technology might not be marketable
opens up many channels, and at the same
time fuels the extremely dubious hope that
art which makes itself useful in the service
of technological matters will soon be able to
earn its own crust, thus to some extent re-
lieving the overburdened public cultural
purse.
In terms of the latent limitations of his self-
conception and of his social role, the artist
is in a bad way. Whereas his colleagues in
the classic fields still have theatres, galleries
and concert-halls as approved formal contexts for their definable public persona –
distribution systems which even in the one-
way mass media of radio and television are
still to some extent preserved –, a virtual
public on the other hand, such as is represented for example by the Internet, is seen
by many as an unworthy or indeed threatening void. A black hole into which ever-

ything disappears because it is so difficult to identify and to evaluate among the general „communication garbage". (As though a gallery was easier to track down in Hongkong, or a good article among all the newsprint in an airport kiosk ...). Because everybody can take what he wants, and because – and this at least is an aspect which must be taken very seriously – it is not possible to make a living from it. Notwithstanding all of which, an artist can no longer afford to stand aloof from these developments; home pages and E-mail are now self-evident components of an artist's biography.

The implementation of artistic ideas is nowadays frequently only possible with considerable technological resources, so that the traditional venues of art can only seldom provide the right framework. The "disappearance" of art and of artists – heralded and long since anticipated and rehearsed in the interdisciplinary cross-dressing of the genres – is now, aside from the exciting theoretical redefinition of self-conception and role model, becoming a real possibility.

The altered framework conditions demand from us new concepts. This applies equally to production, transmission and reception. In the face of the enormous challenge with which contemporary art is confronted, of establishing itself in "electronic-digital space" and maintaining a balance between the fascination of our high-tech environment and a necessary critical reflexion, interdisciplinary, networked activity has today, rightly, become a key concept, and not only of artistic endeavour. To be genuinely contemporary, the artist must conceive of himself as a node in a technologically-determined social environment – and in doing so assume a highly political responsibility.

An institution such as the Ars Electronica Center, by virtue of its specific infrastructure in terms of hardware and of personnel, of its twin functions as a place of production and of presentation, and also by virtue of its positioning "between the fronts", assumes in this connection the nature and function of a model for its time.

Die Umsetzung künstlerischer Ideen ist oft nur mehr mit beträchtlichem technologischem Aufwand zu bewerkstelligen, so daß die herkömmlichen Orte der Kunst nur mehr selten den richtigen Rahmen abgeben. Das „Verschwinden" der Kunst und ihrer Künstler — angekündigt und lange schon in der interdisziplinären Verschränkung der Genres vorgedacht und geprobt — wird abseits der spannenden theoretischen Neudefinition von Selbstverständnis und Rollenbild zu einer realen Möglichkeit.

Die geänderten Rahmenbedingungen fordern uns neue Konzeptionen ab. Dies gilt gleichermaßen für Produktion, Vermittlung und Rezeption. Angesichts der großen Herausforderung, mit der sich die zeitgenössische Kunst konfrontiert sieht, sich einzurichten im „elektronisch- digitalen Raum", sich zu behaupten zwischen den Faszinationen unseres High-Tech-Environments und einer notwendigen kritischen Reflexion und Distanz, ist interdisziplinäres, vernetztes Arbeiten heute zu recht ein Schlüsselbegriff — nicht nur des Kunstbetriebs — geworden. Um tatsächlich zeitgenössisch zu sein, muß sich der Künstler als Knoten in einem technologisch determinierten gesellschaftlichem Umfeld begreifen — und damit eine auch höchst politische Verantwortung übernehmen.

Eine Institution wie das Ars Electronica Center, mit seiner spezifischen gerätetechnischen und personellen Infrastruktur, mit seiner Doppelfunktion als Produktions- und Präsentationsort, aber auch mit seiner Positionierung „zwischen den Fronten" hat in diesem Zusammenhang zeitgemäßen Modellcharakter.

Betrachtung und Reflexion des Spannungsfeldes von Kunst, Technologie und Gesellschaft erfolgte oft nur in den internen Zirkeln des Festival-Publikums, doch die Virulenz dieser Themen übersteigt ein bloß medientheoretisches Interesse bei weitem und ist eine Herausforderung, der sich Festival und Center gleichermaßen stellen müssen.

Denn nicht nur die von Künstlern besiedelten Nischen geraten aus den Fugen, ihr Schicksal teilt auch die Welt der klassischen Berufsbilder im Verlust eines langbewährten Regelwerks der gesellschaftlichen Ordnung und Hierarchie. Auf Arbeit als sinnstiftenden Lebensunterhalt hin orientiert, mental wie auch ökonomisch, sehen wir dem Näherkommen einst moderner Visionen einer durch Technologie von ihrer Arbeit befreiten Menschheit mit großer Skepsis entgegen, blieben doch in der ersten Annäherung alle schillernden Utopien und Verheißungen auf der Strecke. Gegenwärtig folgt die Durchsetzung der Informationstechnologien noch ziemlich einfallslos den Leitlinien des klassischen Kapitalismus zu Ungunsten sozialstaatlicher Ideen. Derartige „banale" Aspekte werden im Fieber der gutgemeinten Euphorie noch viel zu selten angesprochen und leisten einer zunehmenden Verunsicherung und auch Abwehrhaltung Vorschub. Hier ist eine laufende offene und öffentliche Diskussion und Konfrontation gefordert.

Für diesen Diskurs ist Linz dank seines frühen Engagements in der Auseinandersetzung mit der Krise einer Gesellschaft an der Wende des Industriezeitalters zum Informationszeitalter nur ein Vorteil.

Consideration of and reflexion on the interaction of art, technology and society has often only occurred within the circles of the Festival's visitors – and yet the urgency of these topics far exceeds a merely theoretical media-oriented interest, and represents a challenge which both Festival and Center will have to confront.

Because it is not only the niches occupied by the artists that are coming adrift; their fate is shared by the world of classic "job descriptions" in the loss of a well-tried and tested set of rules of social order and hierarchy. Oriented as we are, mentally and economically, to the concept of work as the provider both of a livelihood and of the means to imbue it with meaning, we are intensely sceptical of the approach of once-futuristic visions of a humanity freed from labour by the benefits of technology – each of these shimmering Utopias and Promised Lands to date having, on closer inspection, proved illusory. At the present time the process of the acceptance and establishment of information technologies is still adhering rather unimaginatively to the guidelines of classical capitalism, to the detriment of ideas of social welfare. "Banal" aspects of this kind are still much too infrequently addressed in the fever of well-meaning euphoria, fostering an increasing insecurity and indeed an attitude of resistance. This makes an ongoing, frank and public debate essential.

With its early commitment to confronting the crisis of a society at the turning-point between the industrial age and the age of information, Linz can only be of benefit in such a debate.

One evening in June 1994, just a few days before the beginning of the Ars Electronica: The motto for the opening this year is "Everyone Play", reminiscent of "Everyone Waltz", with which balls are usually opened in Austria. The opening work is the first public presentation of the interactive system Cinematrix, developed by the computer guru Loren Carpenter.

Ein Abend im Juni 1994, wenige Tage vor Beginn der Ars Electronica. Eröffnet wird in diesem Jahr unter dem Motto „Alles Spiel" – in Anlehnung an das in Österreich bei Balleröffnungen übliche „Alles Walzer" – und mit der ersten Präsentation des von Computerguru Loren Carpenter entwickelten interaktiven Systems „Cinematrix" im öffentlichen Raum.

CHRISTINE SCHÖPF

Cinematrix allows the audience/participants to interact with images on a screen, play games, answer questions and make decisions about adventures in a virtual world individually and in real time. Cinematrix is pure interaction. For days, Loren has been busy measuring the location for the event, the baroque main square of Linz. On this particular evening, Loren, his wife Rachel and I are having dinner in a restaurant. We talk about all kinds of things: whether the weather will be good for the opening event, how the audience here in Linz will participate

(Cinematrix had only been presented before a large audience once before, at the Siggraph 91 in Las Vegas, but there the audience had been composed of 5,000 computer experts, whereas in Linz a mixed audience was expected.); we talk about cryptopgraphy in general and Phil Zimmerman and his PGP in particular, and about how work is progressing at Pixar – where Loren Carpenter is Senior Scientist – on the new film (n. B.: "Toy Story"), and, of course, about the Prix Ars Electronica, in which Loren has received an award of distinction this year for "Cinematrix" – the Golden Nica of the Prix Ars

Bei „Cinematrix" können die Zuschauer/Akteure individuell und in Echtzeit mit Bildern auf dem Bildschirm interagieren, Spiele spielen, Fragen beantworten und Entscheidungen über Abenteuer in einer virtuellen Welt treffen. Cinematrix ist Interaktion pur. Bereits seit Tagen ist Loren damit beschäftigt, den Ort des Geschehens, den barocken Linzer Hauptplatz, zu vermessen.

Loren, seine Frau Rachel und ich sind an diesem Abend zum Essen in einem Restaurant. Wir reden über alles Mögliche: ob das Wetter wohl für den Eröffnungsevent halten werde, wie das Publikum hier in Linz mitmachen werde (bisher wurde „Cinematrix" erst einmal bei der Siggraph 91 in Las Vegas mit großem Publikum gespielt, dort freilich waren es 5.000 Computerexperten, während man in Linz ein völlig gemischtes Publikum erwartet), wir reden über Kryptographie im allgemeinen und Phil Zimmerman und sein Verschlüsselungsprogramm PGP im Speziellen und darüber, wie man bei Pixar, wo Loren Carpenter Senior Scientist ist, mit dem Film (Anmerkung: „Toy Story") weiterkommt, und natürlich über den Prix Ars Electronica, bei dem Loren in diesem Jahr für „Cinematrix" eine Auszeichnung bekommen hat – die Goldene Nica erhalten beim Prix Ars Electronica 94 Christa Sommerer und Laurent Mignonneau für „A-Volve". „Nica – wo kommt dieser Name eigentlich her?", fragt Rachel. Ich erzähle die Geschichte.

Am 12. September 1977 wird in Linz, im Park-
gelände an der Donau, „Forum Metall" eröffnet – eine Schau von Metallgroßplastiken internationaler Bildhauer wie Uecker, Rinke, Luginbühl, Heerich, Rabinovich, Donald Judd
und anderer. „Forum Metall", getragen von
der Linzer Kunsthochschule, thematisiert das
Spannungsfeld Kunst–Technologie und formuliert erstmals ein neues Kulturverständnis der
Industriestadt Linz. Symbol und Werbeträger
für „Forum Metall" wird die hoch über dem
Hauptplatz installierte Skulptur der Künstlergruppe Haus-Rucker-Co – eine 8 Meter hohe
Nachbildung der im Louvre befindlichen griechischen Siegesgöttin Nike von Samothrake.

Wissend um die mit der Nike
verbundene Provokation rät
der Katalogtext: „Die mit
den Materialien unserer Zeit
und dem Nichtverdecken ihrer Technologie vollzogene
Geste der Vergangenheit
gegenüber ist Anlaß für einen komplexen Prozeß des
Nachdenkens und Relativie-
rens." In weiten Teilen der
Linzer Bevölkerung löst die
Haus-Rucker-Nike von An-
fang an heftige Proteste aus.
Die Stadtpolitiker leisten der im Katalog for-
mulierten Einladung nicht Folge. In einer
Nacht- und Nebelaktion wird die Plastik im
Auftrag der Stadt demontiert.
Knapp acht Jahre später: Die Stahlstadt Linz
ist Ars-Electronica-Stadt geworden. Den Im-
puls dafür setzte 1979 der Intendant des ORF-
Landesstudios Dr. Hannes Leopoldseder. Jetzt,
1985, geht es ihm um den nächsten Schritt:
zum Festival für Kunst, Technologie und Gesellschaft soll der Wettbewerb kommen –
branchenübergreifend (für Musik, Graphik und
Animation), offen für Kunst und Forschung, offen auch in Bezug auf die Veränderbarkeit der
Kategorien (1990 kommt interaktive Kunst
dazu, und 1995 wird die Kategorie Graphik
durch die Kategorie World Wide Web ersetzt)
und bewußt hoch dotiert: mit Preisgeldern
von ATS 1 Million, vergleichbar denen in Literatur, Musik oder bildender Kunst, um auch

Electronica 94 goes to Christa Sommerer
and Laurent Mignonneau for "A-Volve".
"Nica" , asks Rachel, "where does the name
actually come from?" I tell them the story.
On September 12, 1977, the Forum Metall
was opened in Linz – an exhibition of large-
scale metal sculptures by international
sculptors such as Uecker, Rinke, Luginbühl,
Heerich, Rabinovich, Don Judd an others in
the park grounds along the Danube. Forum
Metall, under the direction of the art college
of Linz, addressed the issue of the relationship between art and technology and
provided the industrial city of Linz with the
first statement of its new understanding of
culture. Forum Metall's symbol and promo-
tional figure was a sculpture by the artists'
group Haus-Rucker-Co, installed high above
Hauptplatz – an 8 meter high copy of the
Greek goddess of victory, Nike of Samo-
thrace, on display in the Louvre. Knowing
the provocation the Nike represents, the
catalogue text advised: "The gesture toward
the past, made here with the materials of
our time and the exposure of its technology,
compels us to engage in a complex process
of reflection and contextualization."
The Haus-Rucker Nike set off a steam of
strong protests throughout the population
of Linz. The politicians of the city decided to
ignore the catalogue's advice. By order of
the city, the sculpture was covertly removed.
Barley eight years later: The steel city of
Linz has become the city of the Ars Electronica. The initial impulse for this transformation was given in 1979 by Dr. Hannes Leopoldseder, Director of the ORF Regional
Studio. The next step was to enhance the
festival for art, technology and society with
a competition – interdisciplinary (for music,
graphics and animation), open for art and
research, and also open to the possibility of
changes in the categories (interactive art
was added in 1990, and the computer
graphics category was replaced in 1995 with
one for the World Wide Web). The
competition was purposely endowed with
prize money (ATS 1 million), comparable to
competitions for literature, music and fine

arts, in order to indicate recognition and respect for computer art. Siemens AG came in as a partner and generous sponsor. Three money prizes were to be awarded for each category: one main prize and two distinctions of equal value. The concept for the competition had been prepared, the competition regulations were ready to be printed, and we (Hannes Leopoldseder, the graphics designer Hansi Schorn and I) were discussing the trophy for the main prize – what it should be called, what it should look like. The name Nica (the last syllable of "Electronica") was mentioned, and suddenly everything fell into place: Nica is the prize from the Ars ElectroNICA, Nica is the goddess of victory for the electronic arts, and in conjunction with the Haus-Rucker Nike, the Nica of the Prix Ars Electronica retrieves what was lost (reflection and contextualization) eight years earlier to a spirit of narrow-mindedness. And so it was also obvious, what the Nica should look like: it should not be some kind of kinetic object, but rather a representation of the goddess of victory.

The figure was designed by the sculptor Prof. Alfred Seidel, cast in bronze and gilded, 39 cm high on a glass crystal pedestal – baroque and perfectly formed, just as she stands in the Louvre today and in earlier times, in 190 BC, as she stood at the ship's prow proclaiming victory.

In 1987, the first year of the Prix Ars Electronica, more than 700 works were sent to Linz form all over the world. In the final round of the jury for computer animation and graphics – with ten from a total of 116 works left for consideration in this round – jury member Alex Graham from the Institute for Contemporary Art in London posed the central question: What do we want to award the prize for? We want to give the Nica for excellence! The jury, made up of experts such as the artists Oswald Oberhuber and Richard Kriesche, the director Tony Verità and the art critic Alfred Nemecek, reached a unanimous decision: the first Nica, also the most valuable money prize (ATS 300,000), was awarded to "Luxo Jr." by John Lasseter, who has now

dadurch die Anerkennung und den Respekt der Computerkunst gegenüber zu signalisieren. Partner Siemens AG als großzügiger Sponsor steigt ein. Drei Geldpreise gib es pro Kategorie – einen Hauptpreis und zwei gleichrangige Auszeichnungen. Der Wettbewerb ist konzipiert, die Wettbewerbsbedingungen sind druckfertig, wir (Hannes Leopoldseder, Graphiker Hansi Schorn und ich) diskutieren die Trophäe für den Hauptpreis, wie sie heißen soll, wie sie aussehen soll. „Nica" (Endsilbe von „Electronica") taucht als Name auf, und plötzlich ergibt sich alles fast von selbst: Nica ist der Preis der Ars ElectroNICA, Nica ist die Siegesgöttin für die elektronischen Künste, und in Bezug zur Nike der Haus-Rucker bringt der Prix Ars Electronica mit der Nica das zurück (Nachdenken und Relativieren), was vor acht Jahren der Ungeist entfernt hat. Und so war auch ihr Aussehen klar: nicht irgendein kinetisches Objekt, sondern von Bildhauer Prof. Alfred Seidel in Bronze gegossen und vergoldet, 39 Zentimeter hoch, auf einem Sockel aus Kristallglas – die

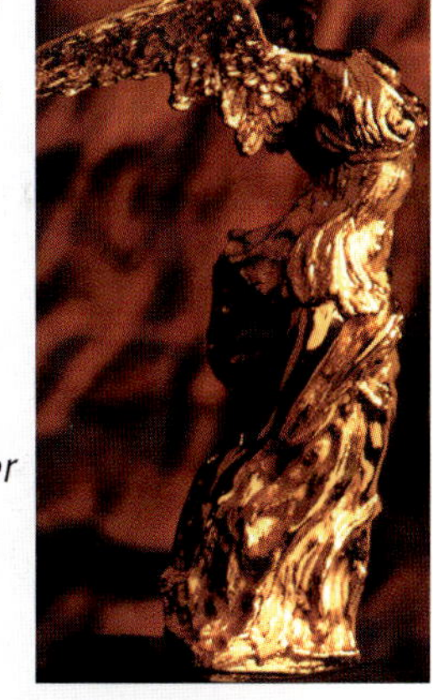

Nachbildung der griechischen Siegesgöttin, barock und formvollendet, wie sie heute im Louvre steht und wie sie einst, 190 v. Chr., im Schiffsbug stehend den Sieg verkündete.

1987, im ersten Jahr des Prix Ars Electronica, kommen über 700 Arbeiten aus aller Welt nach Linz. In der Endrunde der Jury für Computeranimation und Computergraphik – zehn aus insgesamt 116 Arbeiten sind in diese Runde gekommen – stellt Juror Alex Graham vom Institute for Contemporary Art in London die Gewissensfrage: Wofür wollen wir den Preis geben? We wanna give the Nica for excellence!

Die Entscheidung der Jury, in der u. a. Künstler wie Oswald Oberhuber und Richard Kriesche, der Regisseur Tony Verità und Kunstkritiker Alfred Nemecek vertreten sind, ist einstimmig: die erste und gleichzeitig am höchsten dotierte Nica (ATS 300.000) geht an

„Luxo jr." von John Lasseter, der knapp zehn Jahre später mit „Toy Story" den ersten zur Gänze computergenerierten Spielfilm in der Geschichte vorstellt und damit wieder einstimmig die Goldene Nica 96 gewinnt.
In der damaligen Jurybegründung liest man: „Die in ‚Luxo jr.' geschaffene Bildwelt ist derzeit mit keinem anderen Medium als dem der Computeranimation zu realisieren." Die von Alex Graham gestellte Frage wiederholt sich seither immer wieder. Denn jedes Jahr gerät der Prix Ars Electronica zur Diskussion über Kriterien, die an eine neue Kunstform anzulegen wären, in der es noch keine festgeschriebenen Beurteilungsgrundlagen gibt.
Computerspezifität ist eines der Hauptargumente im Lauf der Diskussionen auch in den Folgejahren, wenngleich die Interpretation immer wieder neu zu formulieren ist.
Zitate aus zehn Jahren Prix Ars Electronica illustrieren den Diskurs. Im Katalog zum ersten Prix Ars Electronica bringt Rolf Herken (Mental Images, Berlin), Preisträger und späterer Juror, die zentrale Fragestellung auf den Punkt: „Die Faszination, die von dem neuen Werkzeug zur Erzeugung von Bildern, Filmen und Klängen ausgeht, ist enorm. Die Möglichkeit, jedes imaginierte Bild, jeden imaginierten Vorgang anschaulich zu machen, rechtfertigt auch größte Anstrengungen, die unternommen werden müssen, um zu einer exakten Beschreibung davon zu gelangen. Die Visualisierung ermöglicht dem Betrachter, das so gewonnene Verständnis für sich zu reklamieren, und dem Urheber, neue Einsichten zu gewinnen. Im Gegensatz zu dem von dieser Faszination und dieser Zweckvorstellung geprägten, sich rapide entwickelnden Computerkunsthandwerk der Dienstleistungsbetriebe (...) wird Computerkunst eher an dem Versuch zu messen sein, diese Konvention in Frage zu stellen und für sich die Natur und die Grenzen

presented, just ten years later, the first entirely computer-animated feature film in the history of film making, "Toy Story", and thus has once again been awarded by unanimous decision the Golden Nica 96. The 1987 Jury Statement states: "It would not be possible to realize the image world created in 'Luxo Jr.' at this time in any medium other than computer animation." The question that Alex Graham originally posed has been repeated since then again and again. Every year, the Prix Ars Electronica generates discussions about the criteria that may be applicable for a new art form, for which there are as yet no predetermined guidelines for evaluation.
"Computer-specific" is one of the primary concerns continually expressed in the course of discussions throughout the years following the first award, although the interpretation of what this means has had to be redefined every time.
This discourse may be illustrated by quotations from ten years of the Prix Ars Electronica. In the first Prix Ars Electronica catalogue, Rolf Herken (Mental Images, Berlin) award winner and later jury member, focuses on the central issue:
"The fascination emanating from the new tools for creating images, films and sound is incredible. The possibility of visualizing any imagined picture, any imagined process justifies even the greatest exertions that must be made to achieve an exact representation. Visualization enables the viewer to claim the understanding thus achieved for himself and provides the author with new insights. Contrary to the rapidly developing computer artistry of service industries, which is marked by this fascination as a means to an end, computer art will be judged more

on the basis of its attempts to question this convention and to explore the nature and limitations of our capability of perception and imagination, as well as our creativity. In this sense, the computer could become the preferred instrument of an artistic avant-garde, to whom the separation of art and science makes no sense."

Brian Reffin Smith, also both a former award winner and jury member, wrote in 1988: „Is it not possible that a completely new aesthetic may be found? I mean an aesthetic that is different from everything that is made by hand, but which counters the impression of "oh no, not computer graphics again". What would one need to think about when producing this kind of image? Which dimensions would have to be taken into consideration when searching for new forms of representation and reproduction?

John Lansdown, professor at Middlesex Polytechnic, London, 1990:

"When I look at a particular work, too, I ask myself, 'Why has computer animation been used in this case? What has been gained by this choice?' This is a harder question to answer. This is because we are inventing the medium as we go along, and we don't yet know its limits. ... Computer Anitmation has its own mode of voice: perhaps one day too its own aesthetic. In some of the many excellent works submitted for the Prix Ars Electronica we can just begin to see this aesthetic emerging, but it is hard for us yet to articulate what exactly it might be."

Milan Knizak, artist and art professor form Prague, 1992:

"With all due respect to the possibilities computers have to offer us, they are still not yet perfect. The means they put at our disposal are still extremely limited. But perhaps the problem lies not so much in the imperfection of the machines, or the humans who use them, as in the relationship between the two parties themselves. Perhaps we should try to overcome the differences between these phenomena, i. e., try to remove human nature from humans and machine-like qualities from machines. Clearly we are talking

des Wahrnehmungs- und Vorstellungsvermö-gens, mithin der Kreativität zu erforschen. So gesehen könnte der Computer zum bevorzug-ten Instrument einer künstlerischen Avant-garde werden, für die die Trennung von Kunst und Wissenschaft keinen Sinn macht".

Brian Reffin Smith, ebenfalls Preisträger und Juror, schreibt 1988: „Kann nicht vielleicht eine völlig neue Ästhetik gefunden werden? (...) Ich meine eine Ästhetik, die von allem verschieden ist, was mit der Hand gemacht wird, aber die gegen das ,Schon-wieder-Computergraphik-Gefühl' ankämpft. Woran würde man bei der Produktion eines solchen Bildes denken? Welche Dimensionen müssen bei der Suche nach neuen Formen der Darstellung und Wiedergabe berücksichtigt werden?"

John Lansdown, Professor am Middlesex Polytechnic, London, 1990: „Wenn ich mir ein Werk ansehe, so frage ich mich auch: Warum wurde in diesem Fall Computeranimation eingesetzt? Was wurde durch diese Entscheidung gewonnen? Und diese Frage ist schwer zu beantworten. Wir erfinden ja das Medium, während wir damit arbeiten, und kennen seine Grenzen noch nicht (...) Die Computeranimation hat ihre eigene Sprache und vielleicht eines Tages auch ihre eigene Ästhetik. In einigen der vielen hervorragenden Werke, die für den Prix Ars Electronica eingereicht wurden, können wir gerade eine solche Ästhetik heraufdämmern sehen, aber wir erkennen noch nicht, wie sie wirklich aussehen wird."

Milan Knizak, Künstler und Kunstprofessor aus Prag, 1992: „Computer sind – bei allem Respekt ihnen gegenüber – noch nicht perfekt. Und deshalb bieten sie uns ein sehr begrenztes Angebot an Mitteln. Aber möglicherweise liegt das Problem nicht an der Unvollkommenheit der Maschinen oder in der Unvollkommenheit der sie bedienenden Menschen, sondern im Verhältnis dieser beiden zueinander. Vielleicht sollten wir die Unterschiede zwischen diesen Phänomenen beseitigen, d. h. das Menschliche vom Menschen und das Maschinelle von der Maschine entfernen. Offensichtlich soll hier der Zustand einer Partnerschaft bis hin zu einer Symbiose in irgendeiner dritten Instantwelt entstehen, wo

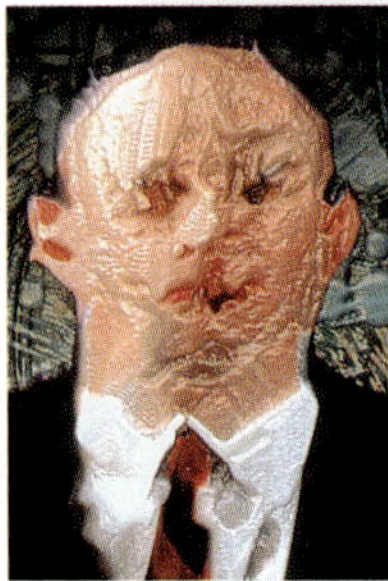  

about creating a partnership, if not a symbiosis, where both computer and man might then share equel chances. ... I am in favour of the relationship between machines and human beings becoming clearer and more transparent."

In 1993, Peter Weibel, artist and "spiritus rector" of the Ars Elctronica for many years, stated in reference to the award winning "Founders Series" by Michael Tolson: "Computer graphics and animation have finally reached the stage where they no longer aesthetically transfigure the works but can throw a spanner into them. ... The incessant crime of the entertainment industry actually consists solely of its forcing the infantility of its under-complex forms on the world as a global standard of culture. A subversive aesthetic that deviates from this is becoming more and more necessary. Computer art was for a long time just a descendant of this apparently harmless, industrial standard aesthetic. Only now is it slowly beginning to uncover/ discover the dangerous, the subversive, the obscene, the critical, the dirty. It es recognizing that this is the only way it can redeem its artistic promise. ... Criticality, complexity, and art are laying the new foundation for computer culture."

And Michael Tolson himself, artist and software developer, wrote in 1994: "As to artists/scientists: they just might represent an avant-garde tugging the medium towards not only the Dionysian, but towards a Dionysian return. ... The computer scientists and artists discover what other artists have know – intuitively – all along. The deepest dreams of reason become Dionysian rages. If we consider computer art as an evolutionary medium embedded in a cultural/economic medium, the selection pressures exerted by the mass media market are enormous and growing (with the advent of interactive media). These pressures are terribly conservative and banal. In this context I fear that the real dinosaurs will not be found in 'Jurrassic Park', but rather will be certain artist/ scientists."

And Sally Rosenthal in 1995: "Fewer than 1 years ago, production of photorealistic, synthetic images by computer on a mass scale was not possible. Now, we witness thousands of synthetic images each day ... Computer Graphics has hit the culture. We (modern westerners) now perceive these images differently. We understand that synthetic and photographic images represent merely their creator's point of view. A photograph is no longer 'The Truth'. We have seen a videotape of Rodney King's beating deconstructed for the jury, so dissected that the perpetrators are acquitted – how postmodern. Images are rhetorical. They can support any point of view. ... Technology remains an uncivilized, wild frontier. But it is not a destination. ... Technical virtuosity again provides the opportunity to acknowledge the value of the artist, the power of the hacker."

Ten years of Prix Ars Electronica: The issues involved are not only the discourse on artistic and technological criteria in computer arts, but also the discourse on the political and economic strategies of the media industry that has grown explosively in recent years. This is also the continuation of a discourse, although under different conditions, that is already as old as media art itself. In the early 70's, for instance, the exhibition "Art and Technology" in the Los Angeles County Museum sparked heated reactions on the part of the art critics. The participating artists were accused of having blind faith in machines, leading to totalitarian ideologies and moral blindness. The American artist and art critic Douglas Davis stated in response: "A number of intellectual machine-iconoclasts tell us we must restrain ourselves. Of course, this position cannot be maintained for long. Art can no more reject technology and science that it can reject the world. Even if the future does not turn out to be better, at least it has not yet been determined and therefore may still be formed. It will only disappoint us, if we leave knowledge and technology to the utilitarians."

tionäres Medium begreifen, das in ein kulturell-ökonomisches Umfeld eingebettet ist, dann wird der Auswahldruck durch den Markt der Massenmedien enorm stark, und er wird durch das Auftreten der interaktiven Medien noch wachsen. Dieser Druck ist schrecklich konservativ und banal, und in diesem Zusammenhang fürchte ich, daß die echten Dinosaurier nicht in ‚Jurassic Park' zu finden sind, sondern unter gewissen Künstler-Wissenschafter-Persönlichkeiten."

Und Sally N. Rosenthal 1995: „Vor weniger als zehn Jahren war die Massenproduktion von photorealistischen, synthetischen Bildern nicht möglich. Heute sehen wir jeden Tag tausende synthetische Bilder (...) Computergraphik ist Bestandteil der Kultur geworden. Wir (Zeitgenossen der westlichen Welt) nehmen diese Bilder jetzt anders wahr. Wir verstehen, daß synthetische und photographische Bilder lediglich die Anschauung ihres Erzeugers darstellen. Eine Photographie ist nicht mehr ‚die Wahrheit'. Wir haben gesehen, daß eine Videoaufnahme der Verprügelung von Rodney King für die Geschworenen so zerlegt wurde, daß die Täter freigelassen wurden (...) wie postmodern. Bilder sind rhetorisch. Sie können jeden Standpunkt unterstützen. Die Technologie bleibt ein unzivilisiertes Grenzland. Sie ist jedoch nicht das Ziel der Reise (...). Technische Virtuosität bietet wieder die Gelegenheit, den Wert der Künstler, die Macht der Hacker anzuerkennen."

Zehn Jahre Prix Ars Electronica: Das ist also nicht nur der Diskurs über künstlerische und technologische Kriterien in der Computerkunst, sondern auch der Diskurs über politische und ökonomische Strategien der in den letzten Jahren explodierenden Medienindustrie. Er führt damit unter veränderten Vorzeichen einen Diskurs weiter, der so alt ist wie die Medienkunst selbst. So löste bereits Anfang der 70er Jahre die Ausstellung „Art and Technology" im Los Angeles County Museum heftigste Reaktionen in Kreisen der Kunstkritik aus. Man wirft den beteiligten Künstlern Maschinengläubigkeit und damit totalitäre Ideologie und moralische Blindheit vor. Der amerikanische Künstler und Kunstkritiker Douglas

Davis nimmt dazu Stellung: „Eine Vielzahl intellektueller Maschinenstürmer erklärt uns, wir müßten uns zurückhalten. Natürlich kann diese Position nicht von langer Dauer sein. Kunst vermag sowohl die Technologie wie die Wissenschaft so wenig zurückzuweisen, wie sie die Welt zurückweisen kann (...) Die Zukunft ist, wenn sie schon nicht besser sein sollte, zumindest noch nicht festgelegt und daher gestaltbar. Sie wird uns nur enttäuschen, wenn wir Wissen und Technologie den Utilitaristen überlassen."

Wurde zu dieser Zeit, auch aus dem Bewußtsein des Kalten Krieges, jegliche Annäherung von Kunst und Technologie per se für unvereinbar gehalten, stellt sich in unseren Tagen die Frage nach der Position der Computerkunst neu. Entscheidend dafür ist die sich allmählich anbahnende Annäherung zwischen Kunst und Wissenschaft im Zusammenhang mit dem Computer als gemeinsamem Medium zur Visualisierung abstrakter Daten.

Damit gilt es auch, die Person des Computerkünstlers neu zu definieren: An die Stelle des Künstler-Ingenieurs der 70er tritt die neue Generation der Künstler-Wissenschafter. Michael Tolson, Michael Joaquin Grey, Yoichiro Kawaguchi, Christa Sommerer/Laurent Mignonneau oder Michael Kass/Andrew Witkin – allesamt Preisträger im Prix Ars Electronica in der ersten Hälfte der 90er Jahre – stehen dafür. Biochemische Prozesse, Evolutionsmodelle, mathematische und physikalische Modelle liegen ihren Arbeiten zugrunde. Ein herausragender Vertreter ist der Amerikaner Karl Sims, Gewinner der Goldenen Nica für Computeranimation 1991 und 1992. Seine Computeranimationen basieren auf mathematischen Formeln und Modellen von Wachstumsprozessen. Seine Arbeiten verbinden mehrere Konzepte: Chaos, Komplexität, Evolution. Karl Sims verwendet eigene Software, um Strukturen und Bewegung prozedurell zu generieren. „Für mich ist es wichtig, den Computer nicht als ein bloßes Medium der bildenden Kunst zu verstehen, sondern als ein künstlerisches Werkzeug, dessen Grenzen erweiterungsfähig sind." Seine Bilder sind, so besehen, nicht zu trennen von den Werkzeugen, mit Hilfe derer sie produ-

If art and technology were held at that time, against the background of the Cold War, to be mutually and absolutely exclusive, the question of the position of computer art must be reconsidered today. The decisive issue here is the gradually increasing proximity between art and science in conjunction with the computer as a common medium for visualizing abstract data.

This means that it has also become necessary to redefine the characteristics of the computer artist: a new generation of artist/ scientists has replaced the artist/ engineers of the 70's. This new generation is represented by people like Michael Tolson, Michael Joaquin Grey, Yoichiro Kawaguchi, Christa Sommerer/Laurent Mignonneau and Michael Kass/Andrew Witkin – all of them Prix Ars Electronica award winners in the first half of the 90's. Their works are based on biochemical processes, models of evolution, mathematical and physical models. One outstanding representative of this group is the American Karl Sims, winner of the Golden Nica for Computer animation in 1991 and in 1992. Karl Sims' computer animations are based on mathematical formulas and models of growth processes. His works combine various concepts: chaos, complexity, evolution. Karl Sims uses his own software to procedurally generate structures and motion. "For me, it is important not to understand the computer merely as a medium of the fine arts, but rather as an artistic tool with limitations that may be extended." In this sense, the images he creates may not be separated from the tools used to produce them. Although this perspective is not entirely new in an age of the art work and its potential for reproduction, it now takes on a radically new aspect as the program itself, or even just the interface, becomes the actual art work. This means that the program not only provides a framework for that which is possible, at the same time it also allows for the generation of a world that is no longer a reflection of the external world, but rather originates entirely in the programmer's imagination. One of the first popular examples of this was "Terminator 2"; although Gerhard Johann Lischka, philosopher of culture and also a member of Animation Jury in 1992, which awarded ILM Studios an honorary Nica for "Terminator 2", conceded that the film demonstrates artistry with respect to the special effects, he nevertheless maintained that it is not to be understood as art (perhaps in the traditional sense). He went on to say: „And yet these effects toss us back and forth, because they point to a new aesthetic that no longer operates mimetically or materially, but rather springs from pure imagination. Kandinsky posited a distinction between the "great reality" and the "great abstraction" that he established, and if art has consequently been divided between these two positions, computer animation now dissolves this polarity and becomes transformed in all its possible manifestations into a pan-animism of the here and now. The fixation of a photographic or film image now gives way to the magnetism of the pixels, which may be here and there at the speed of light.

It may be a mere coincidence that "Terminator 2" conquered movie box offices in the same year that the computer – the computer image – lost its innocence: the year of the Gulf War, the first "today electronic war" (Paul Virilio). The first laser-directed bomb that hit its target on January 17, 1991, practically became a video-clip in people's minds, which edited out the horrors of war and turned the fighters into movie stars. Jean Baudrillard referred to this war as the epitome of simulation, as it was conducted on two fronts simultaneousley: the battlefield in the Arabian desert and the minds of people around the world as it was visually "processed" through a world-wide media network. This was the war of real-time images, the first live world war film involving people all around the world via their television screens. The Gulf War removed the myth of the artificial from the ivory towers of academic discussion and placed it firmly in the midst of the world of hyperreality, the world of war.

ziert wurden.

Dieser Gesichtspunkt ist im Zeitalter des Kunstwerkes und seiner Reproduzierbarkeit nicht an sich neu, verschärft sich nun allerdings radikal, indem das Programm selbst bzw. das Interface zum eigentlichen Kunstwerk wird. Damit steckt gleichzeitig das Programm den Rahmen des Machbaren ab und ermöglicht die Generierung einer Welt, die nicht das Abbild der Außenwelt darstellt, sondern der Imagination des Programmierers entspringt.

Eines der ersten populären Beispiele dafür ist „Terminator 2", und wenngleich der Kulturphilosoph Gerhard Johann Lischka – Mitglied der Jury für Computeranimation 92, die den ILM-Studios für „Terminator 2" eine Ehrennica zuspricht – dem Film respektive den Special Effects wohl Artistik zugesteht, aber nicht das, was man unter Kunst (vielleicht im traditionellen Sinne) versteht, meint er dann: „Und doch sind wir hin- und hergerissen von diesen Effekten, denn sie weisen auf eine neue Ästhetik, die nicht mehr mimetisch oder material operiert, sondern aus der reinen Vorstellungskraft stammt. Unterschied Kandinsky noch das „große Reale" vom „großen Abstrakten", das er etabliert hat, und ist die Kunst in der Folge in diese beiden Lager gespalten, so löst die Computeranimation diese Polarität auf und verwandelt sich in alle möglichen Gestaltungen, in einen Pan-Animismus des Hier und Jetzt. Das Fixieren eines photographischen oder filmischen Bildes weicht einem Magnetismus der Pixel, die lichtgeschwind hier und dort sind."

Es mag ein Zufall sein, daß „Terminator 2" genau in jenem Jahr seinen Siegeszug in die Kinos antrat, in dem der Computer/das Computerbild die Unschuld verlor – im Jahr des Golfkrieges, des ersten „total elektronischen Krieges" (Paul Virilio). Die erste lasergesteuerte Bombe, die am 17. Jänner 1991 ihr Ziel trifft, gerät in den Köpfen der Menschen geradezu zum Videoclip, der die Grauen des Krieges ausspart und die Krieger zu Moviestars umfunktioniert. Ein Paradebeispiel für Simulation nennt Jean Baudrillard diesen Krieg, der zwei Schauplätze hat: das Schlachtfeld in der

*arabischen Wüste und, visuell „aufbereitet"
durch ein weltumspannendes Mediennetz,
die Köpfe der Menschen.
Der Krieg der Echtzeit-Bilder, der erste Live-
Welt-Kriegsfilm, der die Menschen in aller
Welt via Bildschirm involviert. Der Krieg am
Golf hat den Mythos des Künstlichen aus
der akademischen Diskussion geholt in die
Welt des Hyperrealen, in die Welt des Krieges. Orientierte sich der Prix Ars Electronica
in seiner Anfangskonzeption mit den Kategorien Animation, Graphik und Musik noch
mehr an den traditionellen Künsten, nimmt
er mittlerweile vorrangig zur technokulturel-
len Diskussion Stellung. Dies signalisiert u.
a. auch das Einbeziehen der Interaktiven
Kunst als vierte Wettbewerbskategorie und
die Einführung der Sparte World Wide Web
anstelle der Graphikkategorie im Verlauf der
Jahre. Virtual Reality, Cybertechnologie, Neu-
rocomputer, Nanotechnologie, Things That
Think stellen den kreativ Tätigen vor grund-
sätzlich neue Herausforderungen. Nicht mehr
die Kommunikationsmedien sind das Objekt
künstlerisch-wissenschaftlicher Begierde,
sondern die Kommunikation an sich. Das
aufgezeigte Entwicklungsfeld, das zudem einer immer rapider werdenden Beschleuni-
gung unterworfen ist, stellt eine Herausforderung an uns alle dar. In besonderem Ausmaß aber trifft sie die Computerkünstler als
die von den Innovationen direkter Betroffe-
nen und als diejenigen einer Stellungnahme
der ersten Stunde. Der Prix Ars Electronica
wird für sie auch in den nächsten Jahren
nicht nur Präsentations-, sondern auch Dis-
kussionsforum sein.*

Although the initial concept of the Prix Ars
Electronica with the categories of animation,
graphics and music war oriented more to
traditional arts, it has meanwhile adopted a
stance primarily revolving around techno-
cultural discussions. Signs of this shift over
the course of time include the introduction
of interactive arts as a competition category
and the replacement of the computer
graphics category with a new one for World
Wide Web. Vitual reality, cyber-technology,
neuro-computers, nano-technology, Things
That Think have posed fundamentally new
challenges to creative minds at work. It is
no longer the communication media which
are the object of artistic-scientific desire, but
rather communication per se. The fields of
development indicated here, which are
additionally subject to increasing accelera-
tion, pose a challenge to all of us. However,
this challenge especially applies to computer artists as those who are immediately
affected by innovations and as those whose
task is to formulate a position in the initial
phase. In the years to come, the Prix Ars
Electronica will continue to be not only a
forum for presentation, but also a locus of
discussions.

Some things never change. Last year's jury complained about the heavy traffic on the Net, which turned loading the frequently large homepages that were entered into an exercise in patience.

Es gibt Dinge, die sich nie ändern. Letztes Jahr klagte die Jury, daß das Netz überlastet sei und das Runterladen der häufig sehr großen Homepages zum Geduldspiel wurde.

KARIN SPAINK

This year was no different, except that we had more homepages to review: two hundred and twelve, against last year's eighty-something. So in order to be able to visit all of them, we had to work in the afternoon and mainly at night, when traffic was lower; usually we went on until 4 or 5 am. And because we were offered a plentitude of fine beverages during dinner, these were strange evenings and nights indeed. Coffee, alcohol, computers and nicotine: quite an addictive mixture.

After previewing about a third of these homepages before the jurors met, I could already draw several conclusions. Some were minor (for example, that black homepages are currently de rigueur), others more pertinent: for instance that quite a lot of homepages use state of the art Net technology (VRML and Shockwave) and include sound, often RealAudio.

Another was that too many homepages need an endless amount of clicking before you finally get to see an index or anything of that nature: the first page unnervingly takes ages to load, so you wait and wait; and then it turns out that all it contains is a picture that serves as a frontispiece. When you've clicked that one, you get the credits and another slow-loading clickable picture; then, on the third page, you're finally where you wanted to be in the first place. We suspected that this circuitous way of going about things was characteristic of pages that

In diesem Jahr war es nicht anders, außer daß wir noch mehr Einreichungen hatten: zweihundert und zwölf gegen die irgendetwas über achtzig im letzten Jahr. Um wirklich alle diese Homepages durchschauen zu können, arbeiteten wir am Nachmittag und hauptsächlich in der Nacht, zu einer Zeit, als weniger los war, und dann meistens bis 4 oder 5 Uhr in der Früh. Da wir jeden Abend eine Fülle an guten Getränken angeboten bekamen, wurden diese Abende und Nächte doch sehr seltsam. Kaffee, Alkohol, Computer und Nikotin; eine durchaus süchtigmachende Mischung.

Nachdem ich ungefähr ein Drittel der eingereichten Homepages bereits vor der Jurysitzung durchgesehen hatte, konnte ich für mich bereits einige Schlüsse ziehen. Nebensächlichere zum einen (z. B., daß schwarze Homepages zur Zeit „de rigueur" sind), andere waren schon sachdienlicher: zum Beispiel daß viele Homepages jetzt den aktuellsten Stand der Netztechnologie (VRML und Shockwave) und Sound, oft RealAudio, verwenden. Weiters stellte ich fest, daß man bei allzu vielen Homepages endlos weiterklicken muß, bis man schließlich zu irgendeiner Art von Inhaltsangabe kommt: Schon das Laden der ersten Seite dauert unheimlich lang, und man wartet und wartet; und was dann schließlich am Bildschirm erscheint, ist bloß eine Graphik, die ein Titelbild darstellen soll. Wenn man das Titelbild anklickt, kommt dann der Vorspann mit noch einem furchtbar langsam zu ladenden Bild, erst auf der dritten Seite sieht man endlich das, was man von Anfang an gesucht hat. Wir hatten den Verdacht, daß diese umständliche Vorgangsweise auf Auftragswerke zurückzuführen ist, da Homepage-Auftragnehmer ihre Preise oft nach der Anzahl der einzelnen Seiten richten. Zynisch gesehen heißt das, das Brot des einen ist des anderen vergeudete Zeit (außerdem werden dadurch die Telekom-Profite gefördert). Solche Seiten würde ich als „kommerziellen Kreislauf" bezeichnen. Angesichts der ganz anderen Natur des Netzes waren wir auch überrascht, daß doch sehr viele Homepages eine einigermaßen lineare Struktur aufweisen; da anklicken, dann da anklicken, und dann da – alles nach der vorgeschriebenen Ordnung, wobei der Autor dich an der Maus nimmt und dich leitet. Während meiner ersten Sichtung der Einreichungen, zu Hause, habe ich außerdem festgestellt – das ist meine persönliche Meinung – daß sehr viel Kunst im Netz verschwendet wird, und es wird vielleicht sogar noch mehr Netz für die Kunst verschwendet.

Ich gewann allerdings den Eindruck, es handle sich hier nicht bloß um meine persönliche Einschätzung. Unter den Webseiten gibt es scheinbar hauptsächlich zwei Gattungen. Zunächst gibt es Hobbyseiten. Das ist keineswegs geringschätzig gemeint: Es geht in diesem Fall um Homepages, die speziellen Interessen gewidmet sind: solche Homepages spiegeln die echten Sympathien, Freizeitbeschäftigungen, Hobbies, Schwerpunkte oder Berufe der Autoren in ihrem wirklichen Leben wider. Wenn sich jemand besonders für Käfer interessiert und sich ein umfassendes Wissen über diese Spezies angeeignet hat, wird er sobald er einmal im Netz ist, wahrscheinlich eine Homepage zusammenstellen, die sich dem Thema Käfer widmet. Für andere Käfer-Fans mag diese Seite dann von größter Wichtigkeit sein, doch der Interessentenkreis wird eher klein bleiben. Es geht nur darum, ob man Käfer liebt oder zumindest Interesse dafür hat. Solche Homepages gibt es wie Sand am Meer. Der Interessentenkreis mag einmal größer, einmal kleiner sein, er bleibt jedoch immer begrenzt. In diesem Sinne ist Kunst wie ein Käfer.

Zu viele Künstler oder Galerien oder Museen, die am Prix Ars Electonica Wettbewerb teilnahmen, haben lediglich ihre Portfolios auf die Homepage gestellt, oder sie haben die Werke, die normalerweise an der Wand hängen, ins Web geladen. Es war nicht die Aufgabe der Jury, die Schönheiten oder den Wert der Käfer zu beurteilen; das können wir gar nicht.

Die Aufgabe der Jury war Webseiten zu beurteilen.

Kein Medium ist neutral. Da jedes Medium eigene Möglichkeiten bietet und eine eigene Bedeutung birgt, verändert das jeweilige Medium den Inhalt – so daß Form und Inhalt oft untrennbar werden. Dieses Prinzip ist den Künstlern eher vertraut als anderen Menschen: Bei jedem Werk, das sie schaffen, müssen sie sich für ein

were done jobs. After all, paid homepage makers often price their work by the number of individual pages. Thus, cynically, one person's bread is another person's wasted time (and it sponsors Telecom's revenues, too). I'd label these pages as "commercial circuitry". And quite surprisingly, considering the nature of the Net, we discovered that quite a lot of homepages have a more or less linear structure: click here, then click here, and then here; all in a prescribed order where the maker takes you by the mouse and leads you. Also, – but that's a very personal observation – during my previews of the entries at home, I found that there's a lot of art wasted on the Net, and perhaps even more Net wasted on the arts.

But, on second thought, that was not a personal issue after all. There seem to be two major genres in pages on the Web. On the one hand, you have hobby pages. That's not to be taken in a derisive sense, it simply means a special interest homepage, a homepage that is a direct reflection of somebody's real-life sympathies, pastimes, hobbies, urges or profession. A person who is devoted to beetles and has extensive knowledge of the species, is, once they are on the Net, bound to end up making a homepage about beetles. While such a page might be of prime importance to other beetle-fans, the amount of people that it will appeal to is rather restricted. You just have to love beetles, or at least be curious about them. There's literally an immeasurable amount of such homepages. The groups they draw may vary in size, but are basically limited. Art, in this respect, is like a beetle. There are too many artists or galleries or museums who entered the competition for the Prix Ars Electronica, when all they did was to upload their portfolio to their homepage or take whatever is on their walls and paste it to the Web. The jury was not asked to judge the beauty or value of beetles; we are not even capable of that. The jury was asked to judge Web pages.

No medium is neutral. Since each medium

has its own possibilities and carries its own meaning, each medium modifies content – to the extent that often form and content are inseparable. Artists are more familiar with this principle than many other people: they have to make a choice for a medium for every piece they make. Will it be oil, marble or words; crayons, wood or bronze; celluloid, cloth or computers? Simply transporting an existing art object into another medium will not do, no matter what its original quality was. Like any medium, technology is not neutral. To ignore that principle leads, alas, to beetles; or to put it in a slightly more dignified way: it leads to nothing more than an art catalogue. But the catalogue is not art. We decided to dismiss those pages. In our first few hours, we agreed that we would only nominate homepages that did something that could only be done on the Net. (And of course this principle was not rigidly adhered to. What else would you expect, with five stubborn people who sometimes argued feverishly, defending their own pet pages? Sometimes we bowed to one another, just to maintain a sense of balance.) Then there's the second genre of homepages. These are true Net pages: they use technology and narrative structures that are only available and only meaningful on the Net. Linearity is common to many media, and it usually can't be avoided. You just can't go back to a previous version of a painting, or take a different route through a book and branch off at an interesting point. On Web pages, linearity may be abandoned. You can always retrace your steps, you can go though homepages in a variety of ways, none of them "better" than the other, none of them more meaningful than the other. Nor have homepages a locus, other than the Net itself – whose locus is global, or almost global. Some pages make use of the fact that they're situated on the Net, in a context of other pages and programs, for instance by linking to other people's pages or to other Net-resources. Others, unfortunately, don't ever – which is often outright silly. Why not make use of the luxurious wealth surround-

Medium entscheiden. Können sie ihre Ideen besser mit Öl, Marmor oder Worten verwirklichen? Oder mit Wachskreiden, mit Holz oder mit Bronze; mit Zelluloid, mit Textil oder mit Computern? Unabhängig von der ursprünglichen Qualität, genügt es nicht, ein bestehendes Kunstobjekt einfach in ein anderes Medium hinüberzustellen. Wie jedes andere Medium ist die Technologie auch nicht neutral. Die Folge davon, wenn man dieses Prinzip ignoriert, sind – leider – „Käfer". Oder etwas vornehmer formuliert: Die Folge davon ist nicht mehr als ein Kunstkatalog. Doch ein Katalog ist nicht Kunst. Wir beschlossen, solche Seiten aus dem Wettbewerb zu nehmen. In den ersten Stunden der Jurysitzung wurden wir uns einig, daß nur solche Seiten nominieren würden, die etwas zeigen, was nur im Netz passieren kann. (Natürlich haben wir uns nicht immer streng an diese Regel gehalten. Es ist auch nicht anders zu erwarten, wenn fünf Sturköpfe leidenschaftlich streiten und die je eigenen Lieblingsseiten verteidigen. Manchmal gaben wir abwechselnd nach, um das Gleichgewicht zu halten).

Dann gibt es die zweite Gattung der Homepages. Diese sind die echten Netzseiten: Sie verwenden jene Technologien und narrativen Strukturen, die ausschließlich im Netz verfügbar und sinnvoll sind. Das Lineare haben viele Medien gemeinsam; nur selten kann man überhaupt darauf verzichten. Es ist einfach nicht möglich, eine frühere Version eines Gemäldes hervorzuholen oder einen anderen Weg durch ein Buch zu nehmen, um bei einer interessanten Stelle abzuzweigen. Bei Webseiten braucht man das Lineare nicht. Man kann seine Schritte immer zurückverfolgen, kann die Seiten auf verschiedene Weise durchblättern, und keine Möglichkeit ist „besser" als eine andere, keine ist sinnvoller als eine andere.

Außerdem sind Homepages nirgendwo „beheimatet", außer im Netz selber – und das Netz ist eine globale bzw. fast globale „Heimat". Bei manchen Seiten wird die Tatsache mitberücksichtigt, daß sie im Netz in einem Zusammenhang mit anderen Seiten und Programmen positioniert sind. Links werden auf die Seiten von anderen oder auf Internet-Ressourcen angelegt. Leider gibt es auch Seiten, wo das nie getan wird – und oft ist das einfach blöd. Wenn man schon von einem solchen Reichtum umgeben ist, warum sollte man nichts davon nehmen? Es ist wie eine Art geistiger Anorexie, wenn man auf die Fülle des mit einem einfachen Klick erreichbaren Angebots verzichtet und freiwillig verhungert. Doch wir wissen ja schon: Manchmal steckt eine

Absicht dahinter, wenn eine Homepage so abgeschirmt ist, vor allem wenn es sich um Institutionen oder kommerzielle Einrichtungen handelt. In diesem Fall fürchtet man, die angelockten Besucher an andere Seiten zu verlieren, sobald ein Link auf eine andere Seite angelegt wird, und deshalb wird versucht, die Besucher hinter verschlossenen Türen in einem eingegrenzten Bereich zu halten. Aber Homepages unterscheiden sich von Geschäften oder Cafés oder konkurrierenden Filmen und haben diesen inhärenten monopolistischen Zugang nicht. Sie ernähren sich gerade von der Konnektivität, vom Eingebettetsein, von der Erweiterung; Seiten, die eine Anzahl hilfreicher, interessanter, lustiger, sinnvoller und zusammenhangsbezogener Links bieten, werden tendenziell öfter besucht.

Der Nachteil bei den echten Netzseiten ist, daß sie manchmal mit neuen Technologien überfrachtet werden, auch wenn die Autoren noch nicht ganz wissen, was sie damit alles anstellen können. Es ist schon erstaunlich, wieviele VRML verwenden. (VRML ist eine Sprache, die eine Vorlage für die Verwendung von 3D-Objekten bietet; sowie HTML eine Vorlage für die integrierte Darstellung von Worten, Bildern und eventuell Sounds bietet, kann man mit VRML geladene 3D-Objekte mit einer Maus drehen, verschieben, schwenken und mit Zoombewegungen verkleinern und vergrößern.) Leider ist das aber oft ein klarer Fall von Technologie um der Technologie willen, und wenn das anfängliche Staunen über das 3D-Bild nachgelassen hat, bleibt nicht mehr viel übrig. Trotzdem gibt es sehr viele Seiten, die in VRML ganz vernarrt sind, als ob sie stolz verkünden wollten: „Toll! Schau mich an! Ich habe VRML! Ist das nicht großartig, bin ich nicht clever?"

Doch die sinnlose Verwendung einer Technologie ergibt nur Unsinn. Es ist nicht nur langweilig, es ist auch oft sehr oberflächlich, eine Art Maske. Wie der Juryassistent Thomas Riha bemerkte: „Es ist leicht, einen Mangel an Ideen hinter technischem Overkill zu verbergen. Dann kann zumindest keiner sagen, man habe nicht viel gearbeitet."

Nachdem wir Kunst um der Kunst willen und Technologie um der Technologie willen abgelehnt hatten und versuchten, die Stellen zu finden, wo diese beiden Welten sich treffen, verblieben uns noch einige Feinheiten zu diskutieren. Wenn man versucht, jene Seiten zu identifizieren, die sich als Teil des Netzes begreifen und dies intelligent ausnützen, so bieten sich viele Überlegungen an. Welche Seiten versuchen, eine neue Grammatik für Webseiten zu entwickeln, z. B. indem sie

ing you? It seems a bit anorectic to forego all that abundancy that's only a click away and to voluntarily starve oneself. Ah yes, we know: having an insulated homepage is often policy, especially for institutions and commercial sites; they're afraid they'll lose their visitors to the next page once they offer you a link to follow, so they try to keep you inside, behind closed walls. But homepages are not shops or cafes or competing films, and do not have this inherent monopolistic approach. They thrive on connectedness, on being embedded, on getting expansions, and one tends to go back to the pages that offer a number of helpful, interesting, funny, meaningful and related links.

On the down side, these true Net pages sometimes gorge themselves on new technologies, regardless of whether they know what to do with it yet. The number of pages on which VRML is used, is astonishing. Just as HTML provides a template in which to present words, pictures and perhaps sounds in an intergrated fashion, VRML is a language that provides a template for 3D objects that may be turned, slid, panned, zoomed in and out from, by using one's mouse. But often, it's a clear case of tech for tech's sake, and after the first suprise of the 3D image has worn off, there's nothing much left. And yet there's so many pages doting on it, pounding their chest as it were; "Gee! Look at me! I've got VRML! Ain't that great? I'm smart huh?" But a technology without a use is nonsense. In fact, it's not only boring, it's also often superficial and a bit of a mask. As Thomas Riha put it: "It's easy to hide lack of ideas behind a technical overkill. So no one can say that you didn't at least work hard."

Having thus ruled out both art for art's sake and tech for tech's sake, trying to find the places where both those worlds met, we were left with a multitude of fine points to debate. When you try to single out the pages that make smart use of the fact that they're part of the Net, there's so much you can dwell upon. Which pages try to evolve a new grammar for Webpages, for instance by using links in a novel way? Ah, but there were a good many to chose from. We selected Lisa Hutton for that reason, and "McSpotlight". Which pages had that special smell of self-reflectiveness, and somehow showed that they were aware of what else was going on on the Net and used that as a treasure, as a joke, or as something to dwell upon? "etoy" scored very high in this respect, and the "SuperCollider" had that same sense of irony. There was even an art-page doing precisely that: "Journey as an Exile" spins you off down into AltaVista's guts and lets you search the Web for some pre-programmed sentences. Which pages were non-linear? "etoy" for sure. We lost our way there each time we tried to retrieve a page we wanted to show to another juror, and while searching for it, we kept finding new interesting places there. It's truly a maze, "etoy". And as for new ways of telling stories, my ... there's a whole archive of stories, some huge and political (such as Ron Newman's never-ending and very reliable documentary about Scientology's war against Internet), some small and tentative, like "Hegirascope", which attempts to create Web fiction.

And speaking of fiction and reliability: one thing which we hotly debated was how sure we were that what we saw was what it purported to be. Was "etoy", our prospective winner, perhaps a hype, as one of the jurors suspected? Was "Hegirascope" letting you evolve the story, or was it pre-programmed? How were we to know? All we had was the Web, and the Net. But that was precisely what we were judging: the Webpages, and not their relation to any outside world. So if something might turn out to be a spoof in the real world, that was – to reformulate a worn-out adage – "too bad for reality". So that turned out to be our major touchstone: what is happening on the Net itself, and is it done in character? If so: kudos to you! If not: get a life. An e-life, that is.

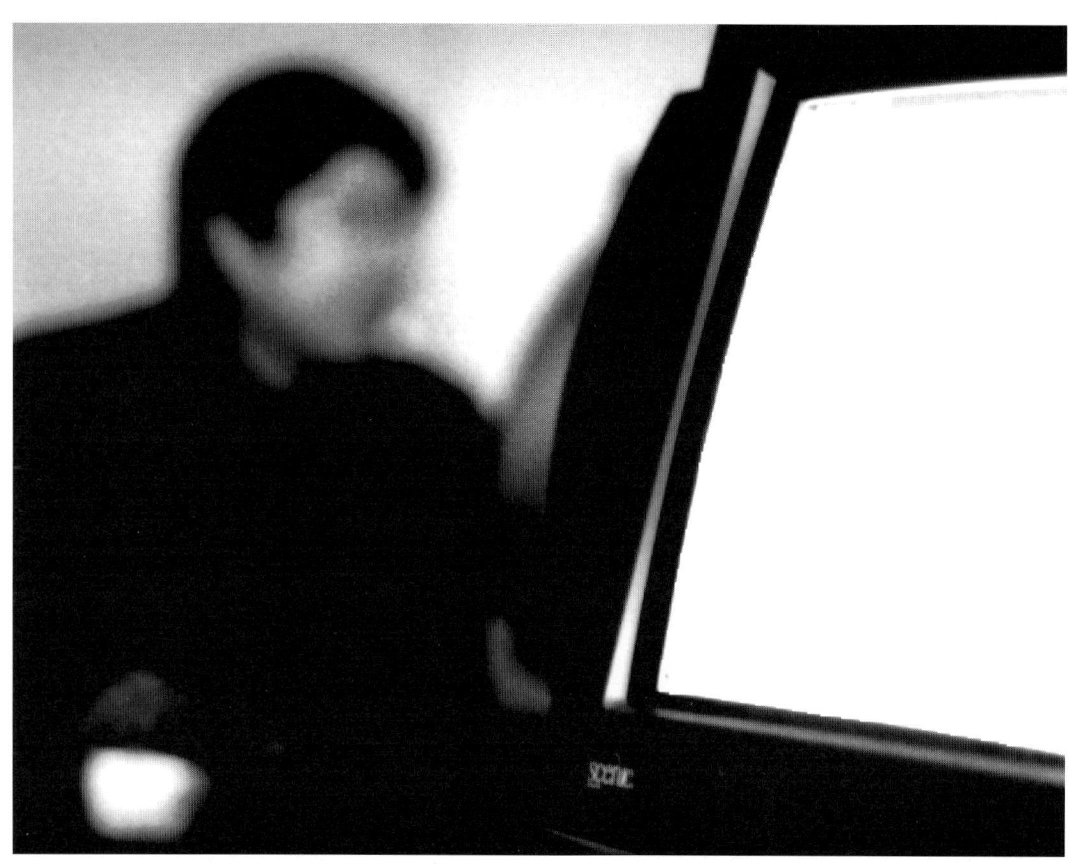

A NEW UNDERSTANDING OF IDENTITY

In 1995, the Computer Graphics category of the Prix Ars Electronica was replaced by a new category for the World Wide Web. This decision and the timing of the decision were not based on the all-pervasive hype surrounding the Internet since 1994.

Im Jahr 1995 ersetzte der Prix Ars Electronica die Kategorie Computergraphik durch die Kategorie World Wide Web. Diese Entscheidung gründete sich zu diesem Zeitpunkt nicht im Hype, den das Internet seit 1994 in den Massenmedien erlebte.

JOICHI ITO

It rather reflected the way in which the WWW that had been created by Tim Berners-Lee was increasingly becoming a basis for artistic-cultural activity manifesting itself in the world-wide networks. The criteria that were developed in the Prix Ars Electronica 1995, such as Webness, Community Forming, Virtual Id/Entity, etc., were the result of a discourse oriented to philosophical and communications-theoretical issues.

With the advent of new programs, the addition of 3D graphics and sound, the Internet as a whole has evolved into a new medium for artistic design.

Joichi Ito, webmaster and network specialist, has been a mastermind of the WWW category of the Prix Ars Electronica since 1995. (Ed.)

Regina Patsch: What has changed over the course of this past year with regards to the criteria defined last year?

Joichi Ito: From the point of view of the people involved, I don't think that they are thinking about it as philosophically, but more personally. So we have very different views: we have a movie maker, we have a political writer, we have technical persons. Of course, this means we are going to get quite a mixture of different types of things that appeal more to these people and the appeal is more subjective. We may have more discussions about what is good and what is

Anlaß dafür war vielmehr die Art und Weise, wie sich das von Tim Berners-Lee kreierte WWW zunehmend als die künstlerisch-kulturelle Keimzelle im weltweiten Netz manifestierte. Die im Prix Ars Electronica 1995 erarbeiteten Kriterien wie Webness, Community Forming, Virtual Id/Entity etc. waren das Ergebnis eines vor allem philosophisch und kommunkationstheoretisch orientierten Diskurses. Neue Programme, das Hinzukommen von 3D-Graphik und Sound haben das Internet insgesamt zum neuen Medium künstlerischer Gestaltung werden lassen.

Joichi Ito, Webmaster und Netzwerkspezialist, ist seit 1995 Mastermind der Kategorie WWW im Prix Ars Electronica. (Hrsg.)

Regina Patsch: Was hat sich im Laufe des letzten Jahres hinsichtlich der Kriterien, die im Vorjahr von der Jury definiert wurden, verändert?

Joichi Ito: Was die Beteiligten betrifft, so glaube ich, daß sie jetzt weniger philosophisch, sondern eher von der persönlichen Warte darüber nachdenken. Wir haben in der Jury jetzt sehr verschiedene Perspektiven: ein Filmemacher ist dabei, eine politisch involvierte Schriftstellerin, und Techniker. Das heißt natürlich, daß wir eine Mischung der verschiedensten Aspekte haben, die diese Menschen mehr ansprechen, und die Weise, wie diese Menschen angesprochen werden, ist viel subjektiver. Vielleicht diskutieren wir eher darüber, was gut und was schlecht ist.

Vom technischen Standpunkt her war das Internet im letzten Jahr noch sehr neu; seitdem haben sich sich die Aktivitäten im Web alle zwei Monate verdoppelt, und das Netz selbst wächst jeden Monat um fast zehn Prozent. Heuer haben wir 200 Einreichungen gegenüber

den 80 Einreichungen im letzten Jahr. Außerdem haben wir jetzt Audio und Video und Java-Applets und alles mögliche an neuer Technologie. Das heißt, daß es jetzt viel intensiver ist und es ist viel Arbeit, alles wirklich anzusehen.

Auf der anderen Seite ist der Kern der Sache — nämlich die Kriterien — nur linear gewachsen. Wir dürfen uns nicht auf die oberflächlichen Technologien konzentrieren, sondern tiefer schauen, um den Inhalt genauer zu betrachten. Ich glaube, es ist in diesem Jahr viel schwieriger, aber wir versuchen, etwas zu finden, das wirklich Neuland betritt.

RP: Was ist im Vergleich zum letzten Jahr jetzt wirklich neu an den Webseiten? Welche tatsächlichen Veränderungen gibt es?

Ito: Zunächst haben wir natürlich HTML, das sich ganz schön weiterentwickelt hat — jetzt gibt es Frames, und damit kann man den Client von der anderen Seite steuern; dazu gibt es nun Audio und auch Java, das viel interaktiver ist, und Dinge wie Shockwave, womit der Client eher wie eine CD-ROM aussieht, und andere derartige Dinge. Die Schwierigkeit besteht aber darin, daß alles so blendend aussieht und dem Künstler mehr Macht gibt, während man jedoch die eigentliche Ästhetik oft in den einfachen Dingen findet. Im letzten Jahr hatten wir viele textbasierte Anwendungen, obwohl Graphik schon möglich gewesen wäre. Heuer gibt es weit mehr Technologie – alles sieht sehr schön aus –, aber in Wirklichkeit haben nur wenige Entwicklungen die Komplexität verändert. Andererseits habe ich den Eindruck, als gäbe es jetzt viel mehr Künstler, die all diese Technologien verwenden. Die meisten Leute, die wir letztes Jahr auswählten, hatten nur zufällig Kunst geschaffen. Jetzt ist es viel wichtiger geworden, daß ein Künstler seine Arbeit wirklich durchdacht hat und Kunst nicht nur ein Zufallsprodukt ist. Ich habe den Eindruck, daß sich jetzt sehr viel mehr Menschen ernsthaft mit künstlerischen Fragen im Netz auseinandersetzen.

RP: Was meinen Sie mit künstlerischen Fragen – bezieht sich das auf den Inhalt oder auf die Form, in der die Kunst präsentiert wird? Das ist ja ein Unterschied.

Ito: Ich glaube, es ist beides. Nehmen wir eine beliebige Kunstgemeinschaft: In den USA z. B. gibt es viele Leute, die letztes Jahr Experimentalfilme machten, die aber jetzt ins Netz eingestiegen sind. Und viele Leute, die letztes Jahr experimentelle CD-ROMs produzierten, sind jetzt ebenfalls im Netz – weil das Netz nichts kostet und weil der Vertrieb fast nichts kostet und weil man Rückmeldungen bekommt. Das heißt, viele Künst-

bad. From the technical point of view, last year the Internet had just come out; since then the activity on the Web has been doubling every two months and the Net itself is growing by almost ten percent each month. This year we have 200 entries, whereas last year we only had 80. Now we also have audio and video and Java applets and all kinds of new technologies. That means it is much more intensive and it is a lot of work to look at all the different things.

But on the other hand, the core part, which is the criteria, has only grown lineally. I think that what we have to focus on is not the superficial technologies, but rather to delve into what the content is. This year, I think, is much more difficult, but we have been trying to come up with something that really breaks ground.

RP: What is actually new about WWW sites now, as compared to a year ago? What are some of the actual changes?

Ito: Well, the fact is that you have HTML, which has grown quite a bit — so now you may have frames and you can control the client from the other side; then you have audio, you have Java, which is more interactive, and things like Shockwave, which now makes the client look more like a CD-Rom, and things like that. So the difficulty is that it's very dazzling and gives the artist much more power, but often it is in the simple stuff where real aesthetic happens. So last year we had many text-based applications, even though they were capable of doing graphics, but this year, the technology has increased quite a bit — it looks very nice, but there are only a few developments which have changed the complexity. But on the other hand, I think this year there are many more artists using all that. Last year, most of the people we chose had inadvertently turned it into art. But this year, it is more important that the artist has thought it out and the art is not just accidental. I think this year there are more people really working on contemporary art issues on the Net.

RP: What do you mean by art issues —

does that refer to the content, or does it refer to the form in which the arts are presented? That makes a difference.

Ito: I think it's both. But if you look more at just a general art community as in the US in particular, a lot of the people who were doing experimental film last year have now shifted to the Net. And a lot of the people who were doing experimental CD-Rom are on the Net, because the Net is free, and the distribution cost is almost nothing and you get feedback. So most of the artists who were in CD-Rom and film because of expression and not to make money, come to the Net, because on the Net you may not make money, but you get your pieces distributed. So the people who are still commercial are staying in the traditional media forms, but most experimental artists are coming on the Net. So that's very exciting to see and I think a lot of talent is coming out — well, we will see; it is still not clear whether anyone has a great grasp of the really deep meaning of using the Net, because they are coming in from other fields. But on the other hand, I think that this period before the medium fully matures is actually where all the exciting things are happening.

RP: What does "art" or "artistic" mean in terms of the WWW? A year ago, there was a discussion going on about how something is not necessarily art, just because an artist uses it.

Ito: Going back to the discussions we had last year: it's a new medium and so we have to look at what is unique about the Web. This takes us back to the criteria: so you can do distributed, you can do communities, it is interlinked, it is self-organizing, it can grow by itself, and so an artist has to look at the Web as something that is active and it is a completely different medium. Some people might not even call that art, more like an aesthetic or philosophy or even religion. You know, one discussion I have going with my art students is about identity — and I am going to go off on a tangent here — but most art is static. So when you make a

ler, die früher wegen der größeren Ausdrucksmöglich-keiten — und nicht wegen des Geldes — mit Film und mit CD-ROM arbeiteten, steigen jetzt ins Netz ein: Im Netz verdienen sie zwar vielleicht auch kein Geld, aber ihre Arbeit kommt unter die Leute. Leute mit kommerzi-ellen Interessen bleiben bei den traditionellen Medien-formen, aber die meisten experimentellen Künstler übersiedeln ins Netz. Es ist wirklich spannend, wenn man das beobachtet, und ich glaube, es werden noch mehr Talente auftauchen — doch das bleibt noch abzu-warten, denn es ist immer noch nicht klar, ob die tie-fere Bedeutung der Arbeit im Netz wirklich schon be-griffen wird, weil alle aus anderen Bereichen kommen. Andererseits glaube ich, daß gerade diese Phase, bevor also das Medium voll ausgereift ist, die spannendsten Ergebnisse bringt.

RP: Was bedeutet „Kunst" oder „künstlerisch" im Zu-sammenhang mit dem WWW? Vor einem Jahr wurde diskutiert, daß etwas noch lange nicht Kunst ist, nur weil ein Künstler es verwendet.

Ito: Um die Diskussionen im letzten Jahr wieder aufzu-greifen: Das WWW ist ein neues Medium und deswegen müssen wir uns mit dem beschäftigen, was dem Web eigen ist. Damit sind wir wieder bei den Kriterien: Es ist ein distribuiertes System, es ist gemeinschaftstiftend, es ist auf gegenseitiger Verbindungen aufgebaut, es ist selbstorganisierend, es wächst aus sich heraus, und das alles bedeutet, daß ein Künstler das Web als etwas betrachten muß, das aktiv ist; es ist ein ganz anderes Medium. Manche Leute würden das nicht einmal als Kunst bezeichnen, sonderen eher eine Ästhetik oder eine Philosophie oder sogar eine Religion. Es gibt ein Thema, das ich immer wieder mit meinen Kunststuden-ten diskutiere: die Frage der Identität — das ist jetzt ei-gentlich ein ganz anderes Thema: Ich behaupte, Kunst ist in erster Linie statisch. Wenn man ein Werk geschaf-fen hat, dann gehört es einem, es gehört zum eigenen Ich, und alle müssen es aus der Perspektive des Künst-lers betrachten, auch wenn manche experimentelle Künstler dem Betrachter erlauben, das Werk aus ver-schiedenen Perspektiven anzusehen und verschieden zu interpretieren. Das Web ist da weitaus extremer: Wenn man etwas ins Netz stellt, dann nimmt es ein an-derer her und verändert und verändert und verändert und verändert es — und zum Schluß weiß man nicht mehr, daß es einmal einem selbst gehört hatte. Doch wenn man einen guten Fluß und eine gut Ästhetik hat, dann stellt man noch etwas und noch etwas ins Netz, und es muß im Fluß sein. Was dann geschieht, ist daß

piece, it is yours, your own ego, and everybody has to look at it from your point of
view, and some experimental artists will
allow the viewer to look at it from different
points of view and interpret it. But the Web
is even more extreme, because you put
something on the Net and somebody will
take it and change it and change it and
change it and change it — and in the end
you don't know that it was yours. But if you
have a good stream and you have a good
aesthetic, then you keep putting stuff on the
Net, and it has to be a stream. What happens is that each piece you put on the Net
gets changed. But just like a child that you
bear is changed by the environment, and
you cannot control the child, the child is still
yours. The child grows up to an adult, to be
better than you, and the Net is the environment. So you can think about the Net as
something — something like a community
— that you put some idea into and the idea
grows. Then it is not bad that it changes, it
is good, because that means it is growing.
And then you put another one in and you
see how it changes, and then you learn
more about the environment. You see how
your identity changes on the Net, and real
identity is your ability to create new work. It
is not the work that is already made. So it is
very important to look at that Net information not as a noun, but as a verb, and it is a
living thing, it is a relationship with the Net.
That is the effect when you are a part of the
Net — an artist on the Net is a performer
rather than somebody who puts something
on and tries to get it to stay the same. So I
think maybe it is like raising children, and
maybe it is like a natural science and artificial life, and maybe it is like performance.
But even though the tools look like CD-Rom
and film making and computer graphics, it is
a completely different aesthetic that you
have to approach the Net. Some of these
artists have a very good sense of aesthetics
and they also understand how to use the
tools, but they need to learn how to create
their own identity on the Net. And identity
on the Net is not just an image. I think that

is an important thing that we see some of
the people coming up with.
RP: Is the image, or the appearance of a
Web page, as important as the content?
Ito: I think that it is important, but it is also
very important to remember that the web
net is slow and the screen that we have has
a very low resolution in comparison to computer graphics. So if it is something that can
be done with CD-Rom, then it should be in
the interactive category. If it is something
that is just a graphic, it should be in the
computer graphics, animation category. The
Net — this category should focus on things
that really happen better on the Net than on
anything else. So what that brings us to is
yes, this aesthetic is important, but it is
more about layout, it is more about timing,
it is more about the way that things move
and so it is more in motion and active and
also more linked with what is happening on
the outside.

So you need a very keen, critical eye, because you can't just be dazzled. A lot of sites
we looked at made us think, this is very
beautiful but it would be better on the CD-
Rom, so we threw it out. How it looks is
important, but it is not just a surface.
RP: The number of homepages on the WWW
has also increased a lot since last year,
and you find very nice, shiny homepages
that probably do not have much content. On
the other hand, you also have subculture
homepages, which from an aesthetic or
formal point of view immediately look
strikingly different. How do you find the right
ones? Which path do you take here? What is
your point of orientation?
Ito: The good thing about the Net and the
Web is that everybody links to everybody
else. So if you find a good thread of good
pages, you find them clumped in little
communities of pages. So in the Internet,
even if people don't know each other, but
they appreciate each other, one artist will
link you to another artist who will link you
to another artist — so it is a kind of an
artist's word-of-mouth introduction, but it
happens very digitally. So in that sense,

*diese Kategorie sollte sich auf die Dinge konzentrieren,
die im Netz besser stattfinden können als irgendwo
sonst. Die Antwort auf Ihre Frage ist deswegen „ja":
Die Ästhetik ist wichtig, aber noch wichtiger ist das
Layout, das Timing; es geht darum, wie sich die Dinge
bewegen, damit mehr Bewegung und Aktivität miteinbezogen werden, und es geht auch darum, daß es mehr
Links zu dem gibt, was außerhalb stattfindet.
Das bedeutet, daß man sehr scharfe, kritische Augen
braucht, damit man nicht einfach verblendet wird. Wir
haben uns schon viele Seiten angesehen, bei denen wir
dachten, das Werk ist wirklich wunderschön, aber es
wäre auf CD-ROM besser aufgehoben, und dann haben
wir es gestrichen. Wie eine Seite aussieht, ist zwar
wichtig, aber es geht uns nicht bloß um die Oberfläche.
RP: Die Anzahl der Homepages ist im letzten Jahr stark
angestiegen, und man findet sehr schöne, glänzende
Homepages, die aber wahrscheinlich nicht viel Inhalt
aufweisen. Andererseits findet man auch Subkultur-
Homepages, die von der Ästhetik oder von einer forma-
len Perspektive her sofort auffallen. Wie findet man die
richtigen? Welche Wege schlagen Sie hier ein? Wie
orientieren Sie sich?
Ito: Das Gute am Netz und am Web ist, daß jeder Links
zu jedem anlegt. Das heißt, wenn man einen guten Fa-
den für gute Seiten findet, dann findet man kleine Gemeinschaften von Seiten gebündelt vor. Die Leute im
Internet mögen sich gegenseitig gar nicht kennen, aber
sie schätzen einander, und so legt ein Künstler einen
Link zum nächsten Künstler an, der wiederum einen
Link zum nächsten Künstler anlegt — es ist eine Art
Mundpropaganda der Künstler, aber eben eine digitale
Mundpropaganda. Nach diesem Prinzip kommen die
guten Seiten immer mehr an die Oberfläche, selbst
wenn sie nicht viel beworben wurden. Natürlich gibt es
auch viele kommerziellen Seiten im Netz. In den USA
werden bereits 5 Millionen Dollar für Homepages ausgegeben, und alle großen Nachrichtenagenturen zum
Beispiel gehen online.
Was auch noch im Netz passiert, ist, daß alles kräftig
durchgebeutelt wird, weil es eben so viele Webseiten
gibt. In den USA heuer sind mehr alte Seiten ver-
schwunden als neue dazugekommen. Es ist ungefähr
vergleichbar mit den Anfängen der CD-ROMs: Die wirklich schlechten Titel verschwanden, als der Markt immer
gesättigter wurde. So rücken jetzt auch im Netz die
guten Seiten immer mehr in den Vordergrund. Außerdem gibt es Suchmaschinen, mit denen man nach
Schlüsselwörtern suchen kann. Wenn man eine Seite*

*RP: In den traditionellen Kunstformen bleibt der Künst-
ler mit einem Werk verbunden. Was bedeutet es dann
für den Künstler als Person, wenn er sein Werk ins Netz
stellt und danach bloß zuschaut, um zu sehen, was als
nächstes passiert?*

*Ito: Im Netz bleibt man immer mit dem Werk verbun-
den. Wenn man etwas ins Netz stellt, sieht man auch,
wo es hingeht. Es entwischt dir nie. Wenn jemand das
Werk findet, können sie auch dich finden, und es ist
wie ein Kind, das nie vergißt, wer seine Eltern sind, so
sehr sich das Kind auch verändern mag. In diesem
Sinne ist es nicht wie mit der herkömmlichen Kunst, wo
man nicht weiß, wo ein Kunstwerk hinkommt, wenn es
einmal verkauft wird und die Galerie verläßt. Das ist ein
großer Unterschied: Solange man Werke in einem Fluß
schafft, wird alles, was hinausgeht, auch zurückkehren.
Man kann sich einen Philosophen wie McLuhan vorstellen, der eine große Idee hat und sie aussendet, sie jedem zur Verfügung stellt, und irgendwann beginnen
dann alle, McLuhan zu glauben. Auf einen Künstler
übertragen würde das heißen, er verschenkt alles, und
irgendjemand wird vielleicht „The medium is the message" auf viele verschiedene Weisen interpretieren,
aber dabei werden sie immer von McLuhan inspiriert.
Das ist die Erkenntnis, die man braucht. Wenn man im
Netz Erfolg haben will, muß man nicht nur Künstler,
sondern auch Evangelist sein, weil man im Netz nichts
schützen kann. Das geht gar nicht, es gibt keine Kontrolle. Man kann die Kontrolle nicht behalten — man
kann es zwar wollen, aber es ist sehr schwer, ein auf
Kontrolle orientierter Künstler zu sein; es ist viel leich-
ter, ein interaktiver Mensch zu sein. Ich glaube, es war
Thomas Jefferson, der es einmal sehr treffend formuliert
hat: Vor langer Zeit schrieb er etwas über Ideen und
verwendete dafür die Metapher des Feuers. Wenn jemand seine Kerze an deinem Feuer anzündet, verlierst
du dein Feuer nicht; aber das Feuer geht rund um die*

even without much advertising, the good
pages start to surface to the top. Of course,
there is a lot of commercial stuff out there,
too. You know, in the US people are
spending 5 million dollars on homepages
now, and all the big news agencies are
coming online.

The other thing that is happening on the
Net is that there is a shake-up, because
there are so many Web pages. This year in
America there were more pages going away
than coming up. In a way, it is similar to the
beginnings of CD-Rom: the really trashy
titles disappeared when it started to get
saturated. So on the Net now, the good stuff
is starting to surface. There are also search
engines, so you can search for key words.
So when people are making pages, they
have certain key words: say if you have
McLuhan and aesthetics, for instance, then
you can do search on the Net, and AltaVista
and Infoseek will find those pages for you.
So that is also really wonderful: there is
linear searching with the search engines,
and there is an introduction from other
pages. This means that it is very important
for artists to introduce those who inspired
them, and so you can find your way along
and that is a very good system. It is not
organized, but it is effective.

RP: In traditional art forms, the artist
remains connected with a work. So what
does it mean to an artist as an individual, if
he places a work in the Net and then simply
watches to see what happens next?

Ito: On the Net you are always connected.
So when you put something on, you see
where it is going. It never gets away from
you. When somebody finds it, they can find
you, and it is your child who always
remembers that you are the parent, even
though a child changes. So it is not like
normal art, where you don't know where it
goes after it is sold in the gallery. That is a
big difference, and as long as you are
creating a stream of work, all of the stuff
that goes out will come back and find you.
So if you think about a philosopher like
McLuhan, who comes up with a great

thought, and he sends it to everybody and everybody starts believing in McLuhan, but as an artist he is giving everything away and somebody may interpret „the medium is the message" in many different ways, but they are very inspired by McLuhan, and that is the kind of sense you need to have. You have to be an evangelist as well as an artist to be successful on the Net, because you cannot protect anything on the Net, there is no way, there is no control. So you can't be a controller — well, you can, but it is difficult to be a control-oriented artist; it is much easier to be an interactive person. Thomas Jefferson, I think, said it very well: he wrote a piece a long time ago about ideas. He used the metaphor of fire. You know, when somebody lights a taper from your fire, you don't loose your fire, and the fire goes around the earth. And it is a network of people that are setting each other on fire, but you don't loose your own fire that way. I think we have to get into that philosophy or the Net is a very scary thing.

RP: In our society, you usually receive money for what you have created: what happens to the creator in the Net? He doesn't get any money out of the Net by putting ideas in it. In comparison, if you write a book and you sell the book, then you sell something — it is material. Or you sell a painting or you sell a piece of music. What happens in the Net?

Ito: Well, the Net is an interesting thing, if you look at it from a view of performance rather than a product. Then it makes sense because now you can pay people with Digicash and other things. So if you are a musician, now with Streamworks you can perform on the Net and so, let's say, do a performance every month. And every month, since you don't have a middleman, you get the cash directly. So if a thousand people pay you a dollar each and listen to your song every month, that may be more money than you could get from a CD. And maybe I broadcast in CD quality, so they can copy it, but they want to hear every live performance I have. So if you are competent in creating content or performance, it becomes very

Erde. Und hier haben wir ein Netzwerk von Menschen, die alle ihre Kerzen am Feuer der anderen anzünden, ohne daß aber einer sein eigenes Feuer verlieren würde. Ich meine, wenn wir uns diese Netzphilosophie nicht aneignen, dann bleibt das Netz für uns etwas ganz Unheimliches.

RP: In unserer Gesellschaft wird man normalerweise für das bezahlt, was man schafft: Was passiert dann hier, wenn jemand etwas geschaffen hat? Er bekommt vom Netz kein Geld, wenn er etwas hineinstellt. Wenn man dagegen ein Buch schreibt und das Buch verkauft, dann verkauft man etwas Materielles — genauso ist es bei einem Gemälde oder einem Musikstück. Was passiert im Netz?

Ito: Das Netz ist besonders interessant, wenn man es unter dem Aspekt der Performance anstatt des Produktes betrachtet. Dann macht es Sinn, denn jetzt ist es möglich, mit DigiCash und ähnlichem zu bezahlen. Wenn man also Musiker ist, kann man z. B. mit Streamwork jeden Monat eine Performance im Netz anbieten. Nachdem es in diesem Fall keinen Vermittler gibt, bekommt man das Geld dafür direkt. Wenn dann Tausende Leute je einen Dollar bezahlen und das Lied jeden Monat hören wollen, bekommt man unter Umständen mehr Geld als für eine CD. Und vielleicht sendet dieser Musiker in CD-Qualität, dann können die anderen die Musik auch kopieren, aber trotzdem wollen sie die Musik jeden Monat auch live hören. Wenn man ein Talent dafür hat, Inhalt oder Performance zu gestalten, wird es sehr einfach, Möglichkeiten für Performance zu schaffen. Da das Netz immer verlinkt ist, bezahlt man für Live-Information, nicht für vorgefertigte Information. So gesehen, verliert Information im Netz sehr schnell am Wert. Börseninformationen von vor 15 Minuten gibt es gratis, obwohl die jeweils aktuellste Information teuer ist. Die gestrige Zeitung im Netz ist gratis, während man für die heutige Zeitung bezahlen muß; Information steht also sehr schnell gratis zur Verfügung. Wenn man in diesem Zusammenhang Performance anbieten kann — nehmen wir z. B. Performance-Musiker wie Grateful Dead: Leute verwenden das Netz, um ihre Aufnahmen auszutauschen, und beim einem Auftritt der Grateful Dead wurden mehr Konzertkarten verkauft als für irgendeine andere Band auf der ganzen Welt, weil sie das nötige Selbstvertrauen in ihre Performance-Fähigkeit haben. Solche Künstler können im Netz bezahlt werden. Oder nehmen wir das Beispiel einer Rundfunkstation wie den ORF: Sie werden für das bezahlt, was Sie noch produzieren werden, nicht für das, was sie bereits produziert haben. Leute wollen morgen Ihr Nachrichtenprogramm, nicht das gestrige Programm hören. Wenn man es so betrachtet, wird auch ein Künstler für das bezahlt, was er morgen schaffen wird, nicht für das, was er bereits geschaffen hat, und dadurch ist alles, was er bereits geschaffen hat, gratis verfügbar. So wie bei Zahnärzten, Ärzten und Anwälten — alles, was sie vorher getan haben, ist jetzt gratis, und sie werden dafür immer berühmter. Wenn man heute jungen Künstlern, die noch ganz am Anfang stehen, zuhört, sind sie viel mehr daran interessiert, berühmt oder bekannt zu werden — bzw. nicht einmal daran, bekannt zu werden, sondern daran, andere Leute mit ähnlichen Interessen zu finden — als daran, Geld zu verdienen. Für einen Künstler ist es am Anfang wichtiger, bekannt zu werden als Geld zu verdienen. Ich glaube, die meisten Künstler nehmen es schon in Kauf, daß sie zunächst am Hungertuch nagen, bis ihr Name bekannt wird. Und in dieser Hinsicht bietet das Netz den Künstlern einen sehr guten Einstieg. Hier gibt es keine solche Hürden wie Plattenfirmen und Filmproduzenten und CD-ROMs. Jeder kann einfach produzieren.

RP: *Noch einmal zu Thema Prix Ars Electronica: Sollte die Jury jetzt andere Kriterien definieren, um die Werke zu beurteilen, oder gelten noch die Kriterien vom Vorjahr?*

Ito: *Die meisten Preisträger des Vorjahrs hatten nicht die Absicht, Künstler zu sein. „Idea Futures" war ein ökonomisches Experiment. „Ringo" war ein Anwender/Modell-Experiment. Und weil die Jurymitglieder in erster Linie Philosophen waren, entdeckten wir Kunst in den Werken der anderen. In diesem Jahr wollen wir dezidiert Kunst auszeichnen. Um das zu tun, müssen wir Künstler finden, die über alle diese Möglichkeiten nachgedacht haben und auch mit dem Werkzeug umgehen können. Wir suchen Sound, wir suchen Aktivität, aber wir suchen auch vielmehr Konnektivität, weil es im Netz inzwischen sehr viel mehr an Inhalt gibt und einige der interessantesten Seiten Elemente von anderen Seiten aufnehmen und einbauen, damit mehr als bloß ein Link entsteht. Das heißt, wir verwenden die gleichen Kriterien, aber wir suchen etwas, das einerseits bewußt als Kunst geschaffen wurde, andererseits auch den Kriterien entspricht. Und wir haben gute Arbeiten gesehen.*

RP: *Wie würden Sie das Netz jetzt im Jahr 1996 beschreiben? Welche Perspektiven hat das WWW, und welche Tendenzen sehen Sie im Vergleich zum Vorjahr?*

Ito: *Ich glaube, ein großer Unterschied besteht darin, daß die Technologie seit letztem Jahr gewachsen ist,*

easy to perform. Since the Net is always linked, you are paying for live information and not for packaged information.

So on the Net, information depreciates very quickly. This means that stock information that is 15 minutes old is free, even though now it is expensive. Yesterday's newspaper on the Net is free, but today's costs money, and information becomes free very quickly. So if you can perform in there — take performance musicians like the Grateful Dead: people use the Net to exchange their tapes and when the Grateful Dead were performing, they sold more concert tickets than any other band in the world, because they had confidence in their performance ability. So artists like that can get paid on the Net. Or take a news agency like ORF: you are getting paid for what you are going to produce, not for what you have already produced. They want to listen to your news programm tomorrow, not yesterday's. So I think if you think about it in that sense, that you want to pay an artist for what he is going to make tomorrow, not what he has already made, then everything he has already made is free. Like dentists and doctors and lawyers — everything they have done is free and they are getting more and more famous. And if you listen to young artists these days, when they are starting out, they are more concerned about becoming famous or well-known — or not even well-known, but in finding other people whose interests are similar — than they are about making money, because it is more important for an artist to become familiar to his audience then it is for him to make money in the beginning. So I think most artists are willing to starve to become a familiar name. And on that side the Net is a very good entry for artists, because there is not that barrier of record companies and movie producers and CD-Roms. It is very easy for anyone to produce.

RP: Coming back to the Prix Ars Electronica: is it necessary now for the jury to determine new criteria for judging the works, or are last year's criteria still valid?

Ito: Last year most of the winners were not intentional artists. "Idea Futures" was an economics experiment. "Ringo" was a user-modelling experiment. And the jurors — since we were mostly philosophers — we found art in somebody else's piece. This year, we are seeking to distinguish art. This involves finding an artist who is has thought about this stuff and also used all the tools. We are looking for sound, we are looking for activity, we are also looking for a lot more connectivity, because there is a lot more content out there and some of the really interesting pieces take things from all these other sites but integrate it, so it is not just a link. So I think we are following the same criteria, but we are looking for something that is intentional and also fit the criteria quite well. And we have seen some good pieces.

RP: How would you describe the Net now in 1996? What are some of the perspectives of the WWW, and where do you see the trends in comparison to a year ago?

Well I think the big difference is that the technology has grown and the community has grown. So two things have happened. Now you have commercial people on the Net, you find scientologists on the Net, you have all kinds of people on the Net. So this very small happy community of Internet people has become a big open city. That means you have crime and you have lawsuits and all the things that happen in a big city. So in that sense it is not the small happy family it used to be. That is one thing. The other thing is that technology has gotten better. Now you have audio and video and this is a big difference because last year it was mostly photographers and writers doing electronic publishing, and that was the Internet. But now it is not just a World Wide Web. You have all kind of new technologies, so you have musicians coming online and television producers coming online and now with Digicash you have economists coming online. There is a whole new community out there. So the type of content and the type of aesthetic control you

genauso wie die Netz-Gemeinschaft. Zwei Dinge sind dabei geschehen. Jetzt findet man Leute aus dem kommerziellen Bereich im Netz, man findet Scientology-Anhänger im Netz, man findet alle möglichen Leute im Netz. Das bedeutet, daß aus einer kleinen, zufriedenen Gemeinschaft von Internet-Usern eine große, offene Stadt geworden ist. Folglich gibt es nun Verbrechen und Klagen und all diese Dinge, die eben in einer Großstadt passieren. So gesehen, gibt es diese kleine, glückliche Familie nicht mehr. Das ist das eine. Das andere ist, daß die Technologie besser geworden ist. Jetzt gibt es Audio und Video, und das ist ein großer Unterschied: Letztes Jahr waren es hauptsächlich Photographen und Schriftsteller, die sich mit „Electronic Publishing" beschäftigten — und das war das Internet. Jetzt ist es aber nicht mehr bloß ein World Wide Web. Da es alles Mögliche an neuen Technologien gibt, gehen Musiker online, Fernsehproduzenten gehen online, und nun, in Zeiten von DigiCash, gehen auch die Wirtschaftswissenschafter online. Da draußen ist eine ganz neue Gemeinschaft entstanden. Die Art der Inhalte und die Art der ästhetischen Kontrolle haben sich stark vermehrt. Eigentlich ist es das, was Multimedia sein soll. So gesehen, glaube ich, daß die Art von Menschen, die online sind, daß die Gemeinschaft als Ganzes sich stark geändert hat.

RP: Welche andere Entwicklungen können Sie sich in nächster Zeit vorstellen?

Ito: Ein Projekt, an dem wir gerade für die Internet 1996 World Expo arbeiten, ist die „Brain Opera", ein Werk von Tod Machover vom MIT. Da es noch nicht ganz fertig ist, konnte es jedoch bei dieser Jurysitzung nicht berücksichtigt werden. Es geht dabei um eine ganz neue Idee: Musik, Bilder, Ideen und Inhalte werden aus dem Netz entnommen und dank des Knowhow, über das das MIT im Bereich der künstlichen Intelligenz verfügt, mit neuen Musikinstrumenten und neu entwickelten „Hyperinstrumenten" kombiniert, die mit Sounds und Signalen aus dem Netz arbeiten. Dadurch können die Musiker elektronisch interagieren und Instrumente spielen, und eine Interaktion mit dem Netz gehört ebenfalls dazu. Durch künstliche Intelligenz wird gewährleistet, daß es noch Musik bleibt, gleichzeitig aber kann jeder zur Musik beitragen. Es ist besonders interessant, weil wir schon vorweg eine ganze Datenbank im Netz haben und während einer Live-Performance die Musik im Netz stattfindet. Menschen interagieren also mit den Musikern, die Musiker spielen tatsächlich in einem Theater oder Konzertsaal und inter-

agieren dabei mit dem Publikum. Dadurch werden die interaktiven, medialen Aspekte auf eine Ebene mit den interessantesten Aspekten des Netzes gestellt, und das Gesamtwerk verwendet einige sehr hochentwickelte KI-Computer. Ich freue mich schon darauf, das Werk hier beim Ars Electronica Festival zu sehen.

(Das Gespräch mit Joichi Ito führte ORF-Redakteurin Regina Patsch)

have has heavily increased. So it is really what multimedia needs to be. And in that sense I think that the type of people who are online and the whole community has changed quite a bit.

RP: What are some of the other developments that you can see happening in the near future?

Ito: One of things that we are working on for the Internet 1996 World Expo is the "Brain Opera", which is Todd Rendgren's work at MIT. It is not finished yet, so it couldn't be considered at this jury meeting. It is a whole new idea of taking music and images and ideas and content from the Net using the artificial intelligence know-how from MIT, plus new musical instruments and the hyperinstruments they have, which take the sounds and the signals from the Net, allow the musician to interact electronically and play instruments, and to have the Net also interact with it. Artificial intelligence is used to make sure that it still stays music, but allow everybody to add their influence to the music and it is very interesting, because we have the whole build-up of the database beforehand on the Net, and then during a live performance we have the music happening on the Net. We have people interacting with the musicians, we have the musicians actually playing in a theater or a concert hall, and then we have them interacting with the audience. So it is really leveraging the interactive, media side along with all the really interesting aspects of the Net and using some very sophisticated artificial intelligence computers. I am really looking forward to seeing it here at the Ars Electronica.

(Joichi Ito spoke with Regina Patsch from the Austrian Broadcasting Company)

Freie Wahl
FREE CHOICE OR CONTROL
oder Kontrolle

In interactive art, we can find two seemingly opposite tendencies in the approaches to interaction: on the one hand, a sharing (or even an abdication) of responsibility (or intentionality) on the part of the author; and on the other, a remarkable extension of the author's domain, an unprecedented attempt to control his/her audience and their response on every level.

In der interaktiven Kunst finden wir zwei scheinbar gegensätzliche Tendenzen, was den Zugang zu Interaktion betrifft: Auf der einen Seite sind Autoren bereit, Verantwortung (oder Intentionalität) mit dem Publikum zu teilen (oder gar zu überantworten); auf der anderen Seite wird die Bestimmungsmacht des Autors merkbar erweitert, und es entsteht ein noch nie dagewesener Versuch, das Publikum und die Reaktionen des Publikums auf jeder Ebene zu kontrollieren.

PERRY HOBERMAN

This distinction is complicated by the fact that these are not, in fact, mutually exclusive opposites, but qualities that can coexist in the same work. For instance, a stance of shared responsibility can be used to ensnare an audience within a arena where the unstated (but nonetheless primary) objective is absolute control. (One might say that this is the strategy em-ployed by mainstream media and advertising: an offer of "free choice" is presented, but simply as a way to get you to consider only certain highly delimited options.) In fact, these two tendencies (towards sharing and control) may well exist in any interactive work. The audience is integrated into a system of immediate feedback, which offers the possibility of "customizing" each person's experience via their actions; but this very customization works the other way round too, as each member of the audience is integrated into the work, and becomes what the work "needs".

Digital technologies are often spoken about as though they have somehow become autonomous systems, cut off from their producers, operating strictly on their own. This is clearly not the case with interactive artworks (and may actually be more generally false). Perhaps we might extend our idea of interaction and imagine it more along the lines of "deferred, technologically mediated interaction between a producer and audi-

Diese Unterscheidung wird dadurch verkompliziert, daß diese zwei Möglichkeiten sich keineswegs gegenseitig ausschließen, sondern Qualitäten darstellen, die in einem Werk gleichzeitig vorhanden sein können. Es ist zum Beispiel möglich, diese geteilte Verantwortung dazu zu verwenden, das Publikum in einem Gebiet „einzufangen", in dem das unausgesprochene (jedoch hauptsächliche) Ziel die absolute Kontrolle ist. (Man könnte behaupten, das sei die Strategie, die von den kommerziellen Medien und der Werbung verwendet wird: eine „freie Auswahl" wird angeboten, doch nur damit man bestimmte, stark eingeschränkte Wahlmöglichkeiten in Betracht ziehen kann.) Tatsächlich können diese zwei Tendenzen (Teilhabenlassen bzw. Kontrolle) ohne weiteres in jedem beliebigen interaktiven Werk nebeneinander existieren. Das Publikum wird in ein System sofortigen Feedbacks integriert, wodurch jeder seine Erfahrungen durch direktes Handeln „maßgeschneidert" bestimmen kann, doch gerade dadurch wird auch das Gegenteil erreicht: Während jeder Teilnehmer in das Werk integriert wird, wird er gleichzeitig zu dem, was das Werk „braucht".

Über digitale Technologien wird oft so gesprochen, als ob sie irgendwie autonome Systeme geworden wären, die losgelöst von ihren Herstellern gänzlich unabhängig funktionieren würden. Bei interaktiven Kunstwerken ist das offensichtlich nicht der Fall (und ist möglicherweise auch generell nicht der Fall). Vielleicht sollten wir unsere Vorstellung von Interaktion erweitern und sie eher als „verschobene, technologisch vermittelte Interaktion zwischen Produzent und Publikum" auffassen. Auf jeden Fall kann das Konzept der Interaktion scheinbar nicht als formale Eigenschaft verwendet werden, um ein

Medium wie Malerei oder Skulptur zu definieren. Interaktion ist möglicherweise nicht ein Medium an sich, sondern eher ein Signal dafür, daß es zu einer radikalen Neubewertung bestehender Medien kommt, wodurch wir vielleicht sogar unsere Vorstellung eines „Mediums" an sich neu definieren und dieses Konzept auf eine andere Bedeutung zurückführen müßten, d. h. „Medium" als Substanz, durch die etwas fließt, zu definieren. In diesem Sinne würde sich Interaktion auf ein Medium (ein technologisches Gerät) beziehen, das den Fluß zwischen Produzent und Benutzer öffnet.

Die Vorstellung einer interaktiven Kunst existiert schon seit einiger Zeit; noch nicht so lange existiert das entsprechende Werkzeug (im Form von relativ leistungsfähiger digitaler Ein-/Ausgabe-Technologie), mit dessen Hilfe diese Vorstellung weitgehend umgesetzt wird.

Doch die spezifischen Apparate der Interaktivität sind möglicherweise wichtiger als das Konzept der Interaktivität an sich. Wenn ein Künstler ein interaktives Kunstwerk konzipiert hat, kann er noch immer beschließen, ohne digitale Logik, ohne Elektronik, (vielleicht) sogar ohne Strom zu arbeiten.

Was bedeutet das für eine Jury, die die Aufgabe hat, den Bereich der interaktiven Kunst im Jahre 1996 zu evaluieren? Es war, als wären wir mitten in einen chaotischen Sturm hineinkatapultiert worden, in einen gewaltigen Wirbelwind aus gegensätzlichen Ideen, Zugängen, Motivationen, Begründungen, Materialien und Systemen. Wir sahen uns immer damit konfrontiert, wie schwierig es ist, ein Werk rational und formal zu betrachten (d. h. zu versuchen, ruhig und unparteilich eine Liste unbestrittener Kriterien anzuwenden).

Der Bereich, wie er in diesem Wettbewerb festgelegt wurde, ist fast schon überdimensional. Die Werke, die er umfaßt, gebrauchen (bzw. mißbrauchen) zusammengebastelte Systeme, die von der Industrie übernommen wurden; Projekte, die von (bzw. in Zusammenarbeit mit) Technikern entworfen wurden, die oft die erstaunlichsten Innovationen, was Interface oder Hardware betrifft, miteinbeziehen; Werke, die ein streng festgelegtes Format (CD-ROM) verwenden oder sich im allgemeinen an die heilige Input/Output-Dreifaltigkeit Maus/Tastatur/Bildschirm festhalten; Software-"Welten", die mit (beinahe) Massen-VR-Apparaten (bzw. am Bildschirm) betrachtet werden sollen; kurzlebige „Experimente", die bestehende oder modifizierte Systeme auf diversen Ebenen untersuchen sollen; Werke, die teilweise oder ausschließlich in Netzwerken existieren sollen; Werke, die „Interaktion" nicht als Mensch/Maschine-Interaktion,

ence". In any case, it doesn't seem that the concept of interaction can be cast into a formal property that can be used to define a medium such as painting or sculpture. More than a medium in itself, interaction may signal a radical revision of any existing media, perhaps even forcing us to redefine our idea of a "medium" itself, bringing that concept back to another sense; that is, the "medium" defined as a substance through which something flows. In this sense, interaction would refer to a medium (a technological apparatus) that opens up flows between producers and users.

The idea of an interactive art has been around for some time now; for somewhat less time, there have been adequate tools (in the form of reasonably powerful digital technologies for input and output) to implement it widely. But the specific apparatus of interactivity may be less important than the concept of interactivity itself; once the artist conceives of an interactive art, s/he might choose to work without digital logic, without electronics, even (perhaps) without electricity.

So where does all of that put a jury charged with evaluating the field of Interactive Art, circa 1996? It felt a bit like being airlifted into the middle of a chaotic storm, a turbulent hurricane of conflicting ideas, approaches, motivations, rationales, materials and systems. At every moment, the difficulty of taking a rational and formal approach to the work (that is, calmly and impartially trying to apply a set of uncontested criteria to each work in turn) was apparent.

The field as it has been defined in this competition is almost absurdly broad. It includes works that use (or misuse) jury-rigged systems appropriated from industry; projects created by (or in collaboration with) engineers, often involving startling innovations in interface or hardware; works that utilize an already rigidly defined format (the CD-ROM) or more generally, that utilize the holy I/O trinity of mouse, keyboard and screen; software "worlds" designed to be viewed with (nearly) "off the shelf" Virtual

Reality apparatus (or on a screen); ephemeral "experiments" designed to interrogate existing and modified systems on a variety of levels; works designed to exist partially or solely on networks; works that define "interaction" not as human/machine interaction, but as the behavior of autonomous machine systems; therapeutic works, designed both for the inclusion of the disabled and the recasting of the "abled"; this list could go on and on. Further, "Interactive Art" was here defined as encompassing certain works that were neither art nor interactive (at least in the usual senses of these words).

And all of this seemed entirely appropriate. Our conception of an interactive art should probably remain radically provisional, emerging as much as possible from the work itself rather than being imposed from outside. The circumstances that gave rise to the field in the first place are undergoing constant change and innovation, and this is not about to stop. Therefore, any judgment of interactive art is undeniably bound to a particular moment in time and history. I doubt that anyone can imagine that we are setting the ground for a final definition of an exclusive realm of any category called "interactive art".

The jury was made up of five individuals, all extremely well versed in our field, but each with our own frames of reference and preconceptions. A good portion of our discussions were categorical in nature. Could a CD-ROM be judged in the same context as an interactive sculpture? Was it useful to compare a networked installation to a newly-invented interface? These discussions led to a number of attempts to develop provisional categories, categories that we generally found only partially and temporarily useful. Of course, we looked for works with a high degree of interactivity. But exactly how to quantify this "interactivity" was always an open question.

Sylvia Müller, who was charged with the Herculean task of organizing the material for us, not only prepared detailed data sheets

sondern als das Verhalten autonomer Maschinensysteme definieren; therapeutische Werke, die Behinderte miteinbeziehen und für „Nicht-Behinderte" eine neue Rolle schreiben sollen; diese Liste könnte noch lange fortgesetzt werden. Außerdem wurde „Interaktive Kunst" in diesem Fall so definiert, daß auch Werke darunter fallen, die weder Kunst noch interaktiv sind (zumindest nicht im herkömmlichen Sinne dieser Begriffe). Und das war alles gut und recht so. Wahrscheinlich sollte unser Konzept von interaktiver Kunst radikal provisorisch bleiben und sich so weit wie möglich aus dem Werk selbst ergeben, anstatt von außen drübergestülpt zu werden. Die Bedingungen, aus denen sich dieser Bereich ursprünglich entwickelt hat, sind stets im Wandel begriffen und bringen Innovationen hervor, die so bald nicht werden erschöpft sein. Jede Beurteilung interaktiver Kunst ist deswegen untrennbar von einem bestimmten Moment der Zeit und der Geschichte bestimmt. Ich bezweifle, daß irgendjemand annehmen könnte, wir würden jetzt das Fundament für eine endgültige Definition eines abgegrenzten Bereichs einer Kategorie namens „Interaktive Kunst" legen.

Die Jury setzte sich aus fünf Persönlichkeiten zusammen, die alle profunde Kenntnisse unseres Bereichs, doch sehr unterschiedliche Bezugspunkte und vorgefaßte Meinungen mitbrachten. Unsere Diskussionen waren zum großen Teil kategorischer Natur. Kann man eine CD-ROM in demselben Kontext wie eine interaktive Skulptur beurteilen? Bringt es etwas, wenn wir vernetzte Installationen mit neu erfundenen Interfaces vergleichen? Diese Diskussionen mündeten in dem Versuch, provisorische Kategorien zu entwickeln, die sich jedoch nur zum Teil und nur vorübergehend als nützlich erwiesen. Natürlich suchten wir nach Werken mit einem hohen Interaktivitätsgrad. Aber die Frage, wie wir diese „Interaktivität" genau quantifizieren sollten, blieb immer offen.

Sylvia Müller, die die enorm mühevolle Aufgabe übernommen hatte, das Material für uns zu organisieren, hatte nicht nur ein detailliertes Datenblatt für jede einzelne Einreichung vorbereitet, sondern auch ein anspruchsvolles Dokument mit dem Titel „Kategorisierungsvorschläge" verfaßt. Damit wurde versucht, spezifische Unterscheidungen in Hinblick auf die tatsächlichen Einreichungen zu formulieren. Diese Unterscheidungen waren u. a.: Einzel- / Mehrfach- /Massenbeteiligung; freiwillige / unfreiwillige Interaktion; unmittelbare / mittelbare Interaktion; vernetzte / Standalone-Werke; Mensch/Mensch- bzw. Mensch/Environ ment-Interaktion; kommunikative / kollaborative / „reine" interaktive Werke.

Später entwarfen wir noch eine — etwas willkürliche — Liste von Kategorien in Bezug auf die Werke, die wir konkret betrachteten. Diese Kategorien waren: Telepräsenz, Virtual Reality, Robotics, Bildschirmwerke, Interaktivität, Audio, Internet und Hardware/Interface.

Schließlich stellten wir eine Liste von Werkqualitäten zusammen, eher um unsere Entscheidungen für uns zu erklären, als um weitere Kategorisierungen vorzunehmen. Diese Liste umfaßte u. a.: Zusammenarbeit, algorithmisches Denken, Interface-Innovationen, philosophischer Kommentar, Anpassungsfähigkeit oder Stabilität, Humor, kritischer Kommentar und „Scalability".

Diese Auflistungen sollten uns in erster Linie dabei unterstützen, das Ausmaß des Beurteilungsfelds nicht aus den Augen zu verlieren und bestimmte Werke nicht deswegen zu übersehen, weil sie den Definitionen, die uns momentan durch den Kopf geisterten, gerade nicht entsprachen.

Doch trotz aller höherer Organisationsprinzipien fanden wir uns durch die kalte, harte Wirklichkeit einfach blockiert. Es gab schlicht und einfach nicht genug Zeit, um jedes Werk mit der verdienten Aufmerksamkeit zu würdigen. Im Bereich der interaktiven Kunst ist die Zeit ein besonders heikler Aspekt. In den temporalen Künsten (wie z. B. Musik, Tanz oder Film) wird die Zeit als ungebrochener Fluß erlebt; in den nicht-temporalen Künsten (wie z. B. Malerei, Skulptur und Fotographie) wird die Zeit als angehalten oder erstarrt erlebt. Doch in der interaktiven Kunst setzt sich die Zeit sehr unregelmäßig fort; Zeit ist die Zeit der Teilnehmer, und diese Art Zeit ist für die Außenstehenden oft schwer begreiflich.

Unvermeidbar war, daß die Werke in erster Linie durch Videodokumentation repräsentiert wurden. Und auch wenn man noch so viel Verständnis dafür hat, daß ein Künstler sich kaum in der Lage sieht, sein Werk mit einem zehnminütigen Videoclip adäquat darzustellen, steht trotzdem fest, daß die Qualität der Dokumentation ein wichtiger Faktor bei unserer Reaktion auf das Werk war. Dabei waren hohe Produktionswerte weit weniger wichtig als Klarheit und Überblick bei der Präsentation. Es war z. B. nützlich, wenigstens eine Teilerklärung des Werkes (in der Form von Voiceover oder Titeln) zu haben oder sehen zu können, wie die Teilnehmer tatsächlich mit dem Werk umgehen, oder eine Vorstellung davon zu bekommen, wie sich das Werk anhört.

on every single entry, but came up with an ambitious document entitled "Categorization Suggestions" that attempted to draw up some specific distinctions based on the entries received. These distinctions included: individual vs. multiple vs. mass participation; voluntary vs. involuntary interaction; indirect vs. direct interaction; networked vs. stand-alone works; human-to-human vs. human-to-environment interaction; communicative vs. collaborative vs. "pure" interactive works.

Later, we came up with another, somewhat arbitrary list of categories, based on the works we were looking at. These categories were: Telepresence, Virtual Reality, Robotics, Screen Works, Interactive, Audio, Internet and Hardware/Interface.

Finally, we made up a provisional list of qualities, more to explain our decisions to ourselves than to perform any further categorization. This list included: collaborativeness, algorithmic thinking, interface innovations, philosophical commentary, adaptability or robustness, humor, critical commentary, and scalability.

In each case, we tried to use these inventories to remind ourselves of the breadth of the field we were judging, attempting to avoid overlooking certain works because they didn't fit into whatever definitions were foremost in our minds at any given moment. But in spite of any higher organizing principles, in certain cases, we found ourselves simply blocked by cold, hard reality. There was simply not enough time to give each work the attention it deserved. Time is an especially acute factor in the field of interactive art. In the temporal arts (such as music, dance or cinema) time is experienced as an unbroken flow; and in the non-temporal arts (for instance painting, sculpture and photography), time is experienced as paused or frozen. But in interactive art, time moves in fits and starts; the time is the time of the participant, and this kind of time is often difficult for an outside observer to grasp.

Unavoidably, works were represented primarily by video documentation. And while it is more than easy to sympathize with the plight of an artist who feels unable to adequately represent their work in a ten-minute video clip, the fact remains that the quality of the documentation was an important factor in our response to the work. High production values were not nearly as important as clarity and breadth of presentation. For instance, it was useful to have at least some explanation of the work (in the form of voiceover or titles); to actually see participants using the work; and some sense of what the work sounded like.

Entries that didn't include a videotape were unfortunately not considered. There simply wasn't time. A number of CD-ROMS were unfortunately submitted without videotapes. It is understandable that many artists were reluctant to include videotapes; since it is logistically possible in the case of CD-ROMs to submit the work itself, they may have regarded the inclusion of a videotape (justifiably) as both reductive and redundant. Allowing CD-ROMs some special status would be unfair to other works, where presentation of the actual work is an impossibility.

There were also many discussions of possible revisions in the competition classifications in the future. Should there be a separate CD-ROM category? (The general opinion was no.) Should the World Wide Web category be expanded into a more general Internet/network division? (Yes.) Other ideas: to distinguish between "screen-based" (including both CD-ROM and the Web) and "installation" works; or between single-user and multi-user; or even between "closed" and "open-ended" approaches.

In the end, we paid most attention to the various qualities and degrees of interactivity in the works selected for prizes and honorable mention. In certain cases, we chose to pass over well-realized, even admirable works in which interactivity was limited to pure navigation or multiple choice.

"Computer Music" per se is, at least for the moment, at something of a dead end. This is the result of a bizarre sort of inverse development over last few decades.

Derzeit scheint die „Computermusik" an sich in eine Art Sackgasse geraten zu sein. Das ist die Folge einer bizarren inversen Entwicklung während den letzten paar Jahrzehnte.

BOB OSTERTAG

Damals, in der „guten, alten Zeit", war die elektronische Technologie, die in der Musik verwendet wurde, ziemlich primitiv, doch das Spektrum der Musikversuche, die damit angestellt wurden, war erstaunlich groß, und es herrschte ein regelrechter Entdeckergeist.
Heutzutage verfügen unsere Computer über technische Fähigkeiten, die zu Zeiten eines Varese oder eines frühen Cage und Stockhausen undenkbar waren.
Während aber die technischen Fähigkeiten erweitert und verbessert wurden, wurde der Bereich, in dem musikalische Forschung stattfand, immer enger.
In ähnlicher Weise war der Zugang zur elektronischen Musikerzeugungstechnologie „damals" einigen wenigen Menschen, die in Forschungsinstitutionen arbeiteten, vorbehalten. Heute ist der Computer in der Musik allgegenwärtig. Es gibt fast keine Musikaufnahme mehr, die sich nicht auf irgendeine Art und Weise des Computers bedient, und dank der immer niedrigeren Kosten der Technologie ist ein echtes Computermusikstudio zu Hause für so ziemlich jeden interessierten Durchschnittsmenschen in der westlichen Welt erschwinglich.
Während sich aber der Computer in der Musik vom unsichtbaren zum geradezu unvermeidbaren Handwerkzeug entwickelt hat, ist das Spektrum jener Musik, die als Computermusik betrachtet wird, zunehmend rigid und festgefahren geworden.
Wie kommt es also zu dieser widersprüchlichen Entwicklung, die gesellschaftliche Grenzen scheinbar genauso schnell setzt, wie die Technologie neue Freiheit bietet?
Wie kommt es zur Entstehung einer „Computermusik" anstatt zu einer Offenheit sämtlichen durch Computer ermöglichten Musikarten gegenüber?
Zwei Gründe: Der eine hat mit künstlerischer Stagnation zu tun, der andere mit sozialem Eigeninteresse.

Back in the "old days," the electronic technology used in music was quite primitive, yet the range of music that was attempted was staggering, and a freewheeling spirit of adventure was prevalent.
Today, we have computers with technical capabilities inconceivable at the time of Varese and the early works of Cage and Stockhausen. Yet as the technical capabil-ities have expanded, the range of musical possibilities which are being explored has become increasingly restricted.
Similarly, in the "old days" access to the electronic music-making technology was limited to a handful of individuals working in a few research institutions. Today, computers are ubiquitous in music. There is almost no recorded music that does not involve the use of a computer somehow or other, and the ever decreasing cost of the technology means that a bona fide home computer music studio is within the means of any erstwhile member of the middle class of the western world.
Yet just as computers' presence in music has mushroomed from nearly invisible to downright unavoidable, the range of music considered to be Computer Music has become increasingly fixed and rigid. Why this contradictory evolution, which seems to impose social restrictions as fast as technology seems to offer new freedom? Why this emergence of Computer Music, instead of an openness to all the musics which computers make possible? Two reasons: one having to do with artistic stasis, and the other to do with social self-interest.

1. Artistic Stasis. For all the self-professed interest in using digital technology to create new musical forms, in fact the agenda of "computer music" quickly ossified around the concerns of the Western avant garde prevalent at the time of the introduction of computers into music (in fact, concers which pre-dated the appearance of the computer in music): algorithmic composition (which is really a digital extension of serial music), and extended timbral exploration.

When considering the 287 works submitted for the Ars Electronica prize this year, it is remarkable how little the focus of Computer Music has strayed from these early concerns over the intervening decades. This is even more apparent when one considers that, formally speaking, the large majority of pieces involving computer response to live instrumentalist are simply variations in algorithmic composition.

2. Social Self-Interest. The emergence of Computer Music as a thing we isolate off to consider on its own, to confer advanced academic degrees in, publish journals and organize conferences about, and award prizes to, is of course intimately linked to the careers, salaries, and prestige of the individuals and institutions which benefit. Here the logic of the inverse development of the broadening use of computers in music against the narrowing of the concerns of Computer Music at least has a clear and rational basis in the self-interest of those involved. In fact, it is a phenomenon seen time and time again in academia: the more an area of knowledge becomes diffused in the public, the louder become the claims of those within the tower to exclusive expertise in the field, and the narrower become the criteria become for determining who the "experts" actually are.

The cul-de-sac these trends have led "Computer Music" into is a considerably less enjoyable place to tarry due to a technological barrier that is becoming increasingly obvious: despite the vastly increased power of the technology involved, the timbral sophistication of the most cutting edge

1. Künstlerische Stagnation. *Trotz all des prophezeiten Interesses an der Verwendung digitaler Technologien zur Gestaltung neuer musikalischer Formen, hat sich in Wirklichkeit die „Computermusik" sehr schnell rund um die Interessen der zur Zeit der Einführung des Computers in die Musik vorherrschenden westlichen Avantgarde verfestigt (diese Interessen waren sogar noch vor dem Auftauchen des Computers in der Musik vorherrschend), nämlich um algorithmische Komposition (eigentlich eine digitale Erweiterung der seriellen Musik) und die erweiterte Erforschung der Klangfarbe. Angesichts der 287 Werken, die in diesem Jahr für den Prix Ars Electronica eingereicht wurden, ist es bemerkenswert, daß sich der Schwerpunkt der Computermusik im Laufe der Jahrzehnte nur sehr wenig von diesen ursprünglichen Interessen entfernt hat. Dies wird umso deutlicher, wenn man bedenkt, daß, formal gesprochen, der Großteil jener Werke, bei denen der Computer auf Live-Instrumentalmusiker reagiert, lediglich Variationen algorithmischer Komposition darstellt. (Obwohl ein Faktor – zumindest in manchen Fällen – auch das durch die Verbreitung der westlichen Avantgarde gesteigerte Interesse an Improvisation ist.)*

2. Soziales Eigeninteresse. *Die Entstehung einer Computermusik als etwas, das wir zu Betrachtungszwecken isolieren, wofür wir akademischen Würden Preise verleihen verleihen, worüber wir Fachzeitschriften veröffentlichen und Konferenzen organisieren, ist natürlich eng verbunden mit den Karrieren, Gehältern und dem Prestige jener Individuen und Institutionen, die davon profitieren. Hier hat die Logik dieser inversen Entwicklung – zunehmender Einsatz des Computers in der Musik versus zunehmender Eingrenzung der Anliegen der Computermusik – zumindest eine klare und rationale Grundlage in den Eigeninteressen der Beteiligten. Es handelt sich dabei um ein in der akademischen Welt immer wieder zu beobachtendes Phänomen: Je größere öffentliche Verbreitung ein bestimmtes Wissensgebiet erfährt, desto lauter werden die Behauptungen der Bewohner des Elfenbeinturms, exklusives Fachwissen auf diesem Gebiet zu besitzen, und desto enger werden die Kriterien gefaßt, die bestimmen, wer die wirklichen „Experten" sind.*

Die Sackgasse, in die diese Tendenzen die „Computermusik" manövriert haben, ist nicht gerade ein sehr gemütlicher Ort, denn eine technologische Barriere wird immer deutlicher: Trotz der wachsenden Leistungsfähigkeit der betreffenden Technologien ist die klangfarbliche Raffinesse der meisten dieser avancierten Techno-

logien nicht wesentlich besser als die der gewöhnlichsten und gebräuchlichsten Systeme.

Nachdem wir die 287 Einreichungen für den Prix Ars Electronica angehört haben, würde ich sogar sagen, daß die Werke, die mit der allerneuesten Technologie erzeugt wurden (Spectral Resynthesis, ausgeklügelte Phase-Vocoding-Abläufe usw.), einen noch einheitlicheren Klang aufweisen als jene, die mit MIDI-Modulen erzeugt wurden, wie sie in jedem Musikgeschäft erhältlich sind – ein Faktum, das während der Jurysitzung noch einmal auffiel, als entdeckt wurde, daß ein Stück, das der Jury wegen seiner klangfarblichen Innovation besonders aufgefallen war, hauptsächlich mit einer alten Buchla Analog-Ausrüstung geschaffen wurde.

Die Tatsache, daß eine größere technologische Leistungsstärke nicht unbedingt mehr interessante klangfarbliche Resultate bedingt, wäre nicht von derart zentraler Bedeutung, wenn sich nicht die Computermusik nicht – wie oben beschrieben – ganz der Erforschung der Klangfarbe verschrieben hätte. Um es ganz kraß auszudrücken – je mehr Technologie, desto langweiliger die Ergebnisse. Menschen machen sich auf die Suche nach neuen timbralen Dimensionen, verirren sich beim Codeschreiben, Systemeinrichten und beim Geldauftreiben und übersehen dabei, daß die Resultate den Aufwand gar nicht rechtfertigen.

Es ist interessant, daß die Jury für Computeranimation einem gegenteiligen Schluß kam: Zumindest in der Animation ist der Qualitätsunterschied zwischen Werken, die mit hochentwickelter Technologie produziert wurden, und solchen, die mit herkömmlicher Technologie produziert wurden, auch für den unbedarften Betrachter sofort erkennbar — sogar für ein achtjähriges Kind. Darauf beruht der Erfolg von „Toy Story". In der Computermusik hingegen ist die relative Wertigkeit von Werken, die mit hochentwickelter bzw. herkömmlicher Technologie produziert wurden, den Uneingeweihten keineswegs einsichtig und wird oft nur von denen erkannt, die sehr viel Zeit und Energie dafür aufgebracht haben, sich ein Fachwissen bezüglich dieser speziellen Technologie anzueignen.

(Allerdings muß man auch festhalten, daß aufgrund des riesigen finanziellen Umsatzes, der von der visuellen Innovation abhängt, wesentlich mehr Ressourcen in Computeranimation als in High-End-Musiksysteme investiert werden. Wer weiß, was herauskommen könnte, wenn die Ressourcen, die für die Entwicklung der zwei Stunden „Toy Story" aufgewendet wurden, in zwei Stunden Musik investiert würden?)

technology is not significantly greater that of the most mundane and commonplace systems.

In fact, after listening to the 287 pieces submitted to Ars Electronica, I would venture to say that the pieces created with today's cutting edge technology (spectral resynthesis, sophisticated phase vocoding schemes, and so on) have an even greater uniformity of sound among them than the pieces done on MIDI modules available in any music store serving the popular music market. This fact was highlighted during the jury session when it was discovered that a piece whose timbral novelty was noted by the jury as being exceptional was discovered to have been created largely with old Buchla analog gear. The problem of greater technological power failing to produce more interesting timbral results would not be so central were it not for the fact discussed above that Computer Music has made timbral exploration its central concern. To put the matter in its bluntest form, it appears that the more technology is thrown at the problem, the more boring the results. People set out for new timbral horizons, get lost along the way in the writing of the code, the trouble-shooting of the systems, and the funding to make the whole thing possible, then fail to notice that the results do not justify the effort. It is interesting to note that the jury for computer animation found an opposite result: in animation at least, the difference in quality between work done with cutting edge versus commonplace technology is immediately apparent to even the untrained observer. Even, in fact, to an 8-year old. Thus the success of "Toy Story". In Computer Music, on the other hand, the merits of the works done with cutting edge versus commonplace technology are certainly opaque to the uninitiated, and often discernible only to those who have invested time and effort in acquiring expertise in the very same technology.

(It must be said, however, that due to the enormous financial returns which hinge on visual innovation, the resources thrown at computer animation dwarf those involved in even the most high end music systems. Who knows what might result if the resources put into developing the two hours of "Toy Story" animation were put into two hours of music?) If, however, we leave the confines of the Computer Music tower and look at what is happening outside in the rest of world, what do we see? Computers are revolutionizing the way music is made.

Take dance club music, for example. Techno, hip-hop, trip-hop, trance, etc. Here we have genre upon sub-genre upon micro-genre of music which is based almost entirely upon, and impossible to conceive of without, the absolute regularity of tempo computers are capable of producing.

But this development is not limited to music with the regularity of beat of those I just mentioned. The funkiness of almost every groove on every Prince record would not have been possible without the timing re-solution offered by computers. Or to go to a different extreme, the drum machine extra-vaganza's of Ikue Mori, with their almost absurdly complex tempo and meter juxta-positions, usually determined on the fly, are unthinkable without computers.

Or to take yet another development: automated mixing consoles and effects processors have brought a sea of change in the subtlety and nuance possible in the mixing of popular music, as immediately becomes apparent upon comparing recor-dings made before and after their emer-gence. This has opened up a whole new range of studio artistry.

All these developments and more are cases in which the introduction of computers has revolutionized the way music is conceived, played, recorded, and appreciated, creating new genres, new fields of expertise, new forms of experiencing a performance, and so on. All of it is unimaginable without com-puters. And none of it is Computer Music. And up to now we have not even added sampling into the discussion. Of all the ways that computers have been applied to music, sampling has had the most radical

Was sehen wir aber, wenn wir die engen Grenzen der akademischen Computermusikwelt verlassen und das betrachten, was in der restlichen Welt passiert? Compu-ter revolutionieren die Art und Weise, wie Musik produ-ziert wird.

Nehmen wir Tanzclubmusik, zum Beispiel. Techno, Hip-Hop, Trip-Hop, Trance usw. Hier finden wir Gattungen und Subgattungen und Mikrogattungen einer Musik, die fast ausschließlich auf dem absolut regelmäßigen Tempo aufbaut, das Computer produzieren können, und ohne diese spezielle Fähigkeit des Computers un-denkbar wäre.

Doch diese Entwicklung beschränkt sich nicht allein auf Musik mit einem so regelmäßigen Rhythmus wie die oben angeführte. Ohne die von Computern gebotene Timing-Auflösung gäbe es die „Funkiness" der Aufnah-men von Prince nicht. Ein anderes Extrem: die phanta-stischen Drum-Machine-Kompositionen von Ikue Mori mit ihren fast absurd komplizierten Tempo- und Takt-gegenüberstellungen, die meistens spontan festgelegt werden, wären ohne Computer undenkbar.

Oder nehmen wir noch eine andere Entwicklung: Auto-matisierte Mischpulte und Effektprozessoren haben unüberschaubare Veränderungen in der Herstellung po-pulärer Musik bewirkt, was die Möglichkeiten der Fein-einstellungen und Nuancen betrifft. Die Tragweite die-ser Veränderungen wird sofort klar, wenn wir Aufnah-men vergleichen, die vor bzw. nach der Entstehung dieser Technologie gemacht wurden. Eine ganz neue Palette künstlerischer Studio-Aktivitäten hat sich da-durch eröffnet.

Bei allen diesen und noch vielen anderen Entwicklun-gen haben Computer eine Revolution in Gang gebracht, was die Art und Weise betrifft, wie Musik konzipiert, gespielt, aufgenommen und gehört wird; neue Gattun-gen, neue Fachgebiete, neue Erfahrungsformen bei Per-formance u. v. a. wurden dadurch geschaffen. Alles da-von ist ohne Computer unvorstellbar. Und nichts davon ist Computermusik.

Und bis jetzt haben wir Sampling noch gar nicht berücksichtigt. Von allen möglichen Computeranwen-dung im Bereich der Musik hat Sampling den radikal-sten Effekt bewirkt. Sampling hat die Musique Concrète hergenommen, in die Luft gesprengt und die Trümmer auf die ganze Musikwelt herunterregnen lassen. Neue Gattungen wurden geboren und die bisherigen für im-mer verändert. Neuland in der Zusammenarbeit und der Aneignung wurden betreten. Und was noch wichtiger ist: Grundsätzliche Vorstellungen von Urheberschaft und künstlerischem Eigentum wurden zertrümmert, und derzeit gibt es dafür noch keine eindeutigen Erben.

Es wäre vielleicht nicht einmal übertrieben zu behaupten, die gesamte „postmoderne" Ästhetik wurde in wesentlichen Punkten durch diese Technologie geformt. Aber Sampling ist auch nicht Computermusik. Warum nicht? Gerade weil Sampling allgegenwärtig ist. Wenn Sampling zum legitimen Betätigungsfeld eines jeden Teenagers gehört, der zu Hause am Macintosh arbeitet, kann niemand den Anspruch erheben, ein Monopol auf dieses Wissen zu besitzen. So fällt Sampling von den vergeistigten Höhen der Computermusik herab, und zwar trotz der weitreichenden Konsequenzen, die es hat.

Hier will ich nicht mißverstanden werden: Ich plädiere nicht dafür, daß der Markt, in dem populäre Musik ge- und verkauft wird, sich zum Richter über künstlerische Leistung aufspielt. Als Komponist, der seit Jahren ohne institutionelle Verbindungen oder Förderung arbeitet und am Rande des Musikmarktes überlebt, ist es mir deutlich bewußt, wie der Markt seine eigene Beschränkungen aufstellt und gerade die Art von Kreativität behindert, die mich am meisten interessiert. Und weil gerade diese Marktschranken so schwer zu durchbrechen sind, ist es mein besonders Anliegen, daß jene musikalischen Gebiete, die sich nicht an Marktkriterien orientieren, so offen und flexibel wie möglich sein sollen.

Die Tatsache, daß es Kids gibt, die mit Sampling auf ihrem eigenen Macintosh herumtoben, hat dazu beigetragen, daß das Interesse an neuen Musikformen im allgemeinen und an mit Computern hergestellter Musik im besonderen jetzt größer ist als je zuvor.

Ist das nicht eine Ironie? Auf der einen Seite sehen wir, wie die Schranken des Marktes populäre Musik mehr als je zuvor unter Druck setzen, auf der anderen Seite haben wir ein Publikum, das mehr als je zuvor von Computern und deren Möglichkeiten fasziniert ist. Und trotzdem gelingt es der Computermusik nicht, ein Publikum außerhalb des Kreises jener Menschen zu finden, die an ihrer Herstellung beteiligt sind.

impact. Sampling has taken musique concrete, blown it open, and showered the debris down on the entire musical world. New genres been spawned and existing ones changed forever. New terrains of collaboration and appropriation have been opened. Even more profoundly, fundamental notions of authorship and artistic ownership have been shattered, leaving for the moment no clear heir in their place. It may not even be an exaggeration to say that the entire "post-modern" aesthetic has been shaped in important ways by this technology. Yet sampling is not Computer Music. Why? Precisely because sampling is everywhere. If sampling is the legitimate domain of any teenager working on the family Macintosh, no one can claim a monopoly on its knowledge. Thus it falls from the rarefied heights of Computer Music, its vast impact and consequences notwithstanding.

I wish to be very clear here: I am not arguing that the market in which popular music is bought and sold is a valid arbiter of artistic excellence. As a composer who has worked for years with no institutional connection or support, surviving on the fringes of the music market, I am acutely aware of how the market imposes its own constraints, and discourages the kinds of creativity that interest me the most. It is the weight of these very market contraints that make it so important that those musical arenas which operate according to non-market criteria be as open and flexible as possible.

The very existence of all those kids goofing around with sampling on the family Macintosh has helped to stir an interest in novel musical approaches in general and music made with computers in particular that is broader than ever.

Isn't it ironic? On the one hand we find market contraints squeezing popular music with an unprecedented vigour, and on the other hand we have a public with an equally unprecedented fascination with computers and their possibilities. And yet Computer Music can find no audience beyond those who make it.

THE COMPUTER ANIMATOR
AS SORCERER'S APPRENTICE

Animation is difficult work. It demands ofits practitioner a variety of skills, working in concert, that are, if not antithetical, at least derived from a number of disciplines.

Animation ist eine schwierige Aufgabe. Von denen, die sie praktizieren wollen, verlangt sie eine Vielfalt harmonisch funktionierender Fähigkeiten, die—wenn sie sich schon nicht gegenseitig ausschließen— zumindest aus verschiedenen Bereichen stammen.

LISA FISHER

Computer animation asks of those who would choose it as a vocation the artistic talent of a designer, the fluency with three-dimensional space of an architect, the narrative skills of a storyteller, the grasp of computer technology of a scientist, and the appreciation of the emotive power of sound of a composer, combined in an amalgam of richness that aspires to great film making. It is no wonder, really, that so few people do it well.

It is also a very young art form. As compared to any of the more traditional arts, animation, except in its simplest executions, is a twentieth century development. And computer animation, barely a quarter century old, has only been an accessible medium for the last ten years. Prior to that, computer animation was a kind of black art: a bit of witchcraft and a bit of alchemy practiced by a few Merlin-like magicians who poured digits into keyboards, cast spells on huge, smoking rendering engines, and out came ... pictures. Nearly all of this work was done under the auspices of universities, large corporations, or one of the pioneering animation produc-

Computeranimation verlangt von denen, die sich dazu berufen fühlen, das künstlerische Talent eines Designers, die Versiertheit eines Architekten im Umgang mit dem dreidimensionalen Raum, die erzählerischen Fähigkeiten eines Märchenerzählers, die Beherrschung der Computertechnologie eines Wissenschafters, das Verständnis eines Komponisten für die affektvolle Kraft des Klangs, und all das in einer Fülle kombiniert, die es ermöglicht, großartige Filme zu machen. Eigentlich soll es uns nicht wundern, daß nur wenige Menschen diesen Erfordernissen gerecht werden.

Computeranimation ist außerdem ist eine sehr junge Kunstform. Im Gegensatz zu traditionelleren Kunstformen ist die Animation, abgesehen von ihren einfachsten Spielarten, eine Entwicklung des 20. Jahrhunderts. Und die Computeranimation, die kaum 25 Jahre alt ist, ist erst in den letzten zehn Jahren zu einem zugänglichen Medium geworden.

Vorher war die Computeranimation so etwas wie moderne schwarze Magie: eine Prise Hexerei und eine Prise Alchemie, zusammengemischt von ein paar Merlin-artigen Zauberern, die Zahlen in Tastaturen gossen, riesige, rauchende Rendering-Engines mit Zaubersprüchen belegten, und daraus entstanden ... Bilder. Der Großteil dieser Arbeit entstand unter der Obhut von Universitäten, Großkonzernen oder von einer der wegbereitenden Animationsfirmen der späten 70er Jahre.

Und wo stehen wir heute? Wo steht die Computeranimation in diesem Jahr, was können wir für die nächste Zukunft erwarten? Wird die Computeranimation dank der Entwicklung, die sie durchmacht, reifer? Betreten wir jetzt ein Animations-Neuland, wie es vor der Einführung des Computers in diesen Bereich noch nicht möglich gewesen wäre?

Durch den Prix Ars Electronica wurde mir und meinen Kollegen Gelegenheit geboten, viele Arbeiten zu sehen – ganze zweihundertundvierzehn Stück an der Zahl – und diese in Bezug auf ihren relativen künstlerischen Wert zu begutachten. Sämtliche Einreichungen durchzuarbeiten hat viel Zeit in Anspruch genommen und war oft auch ermüdend. Doch da wir diese große Anzahl an Arbeiten ohne Vorauswahl ansahen, sahen wir einen sehr großen Ausschnitt jener Arbeiten, die zumindest in den Augen ihrer Erzeuger für bewertungswürdig befunden wurden.

Wenn das Spektrum der Einreichungen, die der Jury vorgelegt wurden, für die Entwicklungen im Bereich der Computeranimation im letzten Jahr repräsentiv ist (was zumindest teilweise in Frage gestellt wird, da die Einreichungen natürlich von den Künstlern selbst selektiert wurden), dann sind die darin erkennbaren Tendenzen interessant, wenn auch beunruhigend. Auch wenn es bemerkenswerte Ausnahmen gab, konnte der größte Teil der Arbeiten in zwei klare Kategorien eingeteilt werden:

1) gut ausgeführte Animationen, hergestellt von kommerziellen Produktionsfirmen, und

2) Arbeiten mit mangelhaftem Konzept von freischaffenden Animatoren.

Das soll auf keinen Fall bedeuten, daß alle kommerziellen Arbeiten brilliant, originell, gut geplant und gut ausgeführt waren, auch nicht, daß die studentischen und anderen unabhängigen Arbeiten durchgehend mangelhaft waren. Doch die Unterschiede waren so markant, daß ich mich zum Schluß fragte, wieso.

Die naheliegendsten Antworten sind natürlich Geld und die Verfügbarkeit der Technologie. Wenn ein kommerzielles Produkt, wie z. B. ein abendfüllender Film oder ein Musikvideo, aufgrund der zu erwartenden Einspielergebnisse finanziert wird, haben die Produzenten Interesse daran, daß das Produkt möglichst professionell ausgeführt wird. Umgekehrt fehlen unabhängigen oder studentischen Projekten per definitionem fast immer die benötigte Förderung und die Mittel. Doch wir soll-

tion companies of the late 1970's.

So where are we today? Where has computer animation arrived this year, and what do we have to look forward to? As it develops, is it maturing? And are we breaking ground in animation that we couldn't prior to the introduction of the computer into the field?

The Prix Ars Electronica has afforded me and my colleagues on the animation jury the opportunity to see a lot of work – two-hundred and fourteen pieces in all – and to evaluate their relative merits. The process of sifting through the roster of entries was time consuming, and often tiresome. But the size of the sample, and the policy of viewing selections from all entries without an initial screening for merit, meant that we saw a very broad sampling of the work that, at least to its creators, was thought worthy of evaluation.

If the roster presented to the jury is an accurate reflection of the computer animation work produced over the last year (the efficacy of this claim being at least partially in question as the entries were a self-selected sample), the trends evinced are interesting, if unsettling. Though there were notable exceptions, the vast majority of the work shown fell into two distinct categories:

1) Well-crafted animations created by commercial production companies, and

2) ill-conceived work of independent animators.

This is not to say that all the commercial work was brilliant, clever, well-designed, and well-executed. Nor that the student and other independent work was uniformly lacking. But the split was marked and left me asking why.

Of course, money and access to technology are the most obvious answers. If a commercial product, such as a feature film or a music video, is being financed for its anticipated return on investment, it benefits, its producers to want to make it polished. Conversely, independent or student projects, by definition, are almost always under-supported and under-financed. But we need to look beyond the obvious to get closer to the real issues causing this division in the field of computer animation.

The evolution of computer animation in the last several years has been driven by the availability of faster, more interactive technology at increasingly lower costs. The good news is that, in the right hands, this means better animation. "Toy Story", directed by John Lasseter and produced by Pixar, the winner of this year's computer animation Golden Nica, is groundbreaking. Developments in computer character animation have brought us a full-length feature that moves beyond novelty into real filmmaking. It's well-conceived, designed, and executed, and works as a piece of entertainment. So too, the contributions to the field made by BUF Compagnie, winner of both second prizes, show a breadth of creativity and grasp of the technology that, while more subtle than Pixar's work, is nonetheless stellar. And the honorable mentions awarded by this year's jury all show a high level of excellence.

The majority of the work presented to the panel, however, fell off very rapidly from the heights achieved by the honored pieces. As is apparent with simpler applications like word processing, the ability to sit down at a computer and type a sentence doesn't make one Shakespeare. So too, having access to computer animation software and hardware doesn't make every animation student an animator. Creating enduring, or even interesting, computer animation requires a vision that is both stylish and substantial. The consumer market may not care how the work is done, but it recognizes in "Toy Story" something that it wants to see. Conversely, as consumers, we know what we don't want to see. And a lot of flash, without substance, falls short very quickly.

But where is the root of the problem? Without wishing to sounding too antediluvian, I would suggest that both the education and the expectations of computer animators are being misdirected. Students, it seems, aren't being taught thoroughly about the disciplines involved in the craft of animation. The

6/96
ONAL
ILFORD
1
1A
2
2A
ILFORD
7 7 8
5
5A
6
6A
ILFORD
7 7 8 2
1238/15/1

7 7 8 2
400 DELTA PROFESSIONAL
3
3 A
4
4 A
400 DELTA PROFESSIONAL
7
7 A
8
8 A
400 DELTA PROFESSIONAL

STATEMENT OF THE
WORLD WIDE WEB JURY

Fast magisch angezogen fühlte sich die Jury von dem, was wir „echte" Netz-Seiten nannten: Homepages, die Technologie und narrative Strukturen verwenden, die nur im Netz zur Verfügung stehen und auch nur dort sinnvoll angewendet werden können und versuchen, damit einen Schritt weiterzugehen. Etwas enttäuscht waren wir von den Homepages der Künstler, denen nichts anderes einfiel, als die Sachen, die normalerweise an der Wand hängen, ins Netz zu stellen. So werden nur Dinge verschoben, das heißt aber noch lange nicht, das so etwas wie „Webness" („Webtauglichkeit") geschaffen wird. Diese Erkenntnis ermutigte uns, den „echten" Netz-Seiten treu zu bleiben. Andererseits strotzen diese „echten" Netz-Seiten nur so vor neuester Netztechnologie, obwohl die Produzenten der Seiten noch gar nicht so genau wissen, was sie mit dieser Technologie überhaupt alles machen können.
Nachdem wir Kunst um der Kunst willen und Tech um des Techs willen ausgeschlossen hatten, versuchten wir jene Seiten auszuwählen, die sowohl den spezifischen Anforderungen des Netzwerkes als auch dem künstlerischen Anspruch gerecht wurden. Im Endeffekt konzentrierten wir uns auf diejenigen Seiten, die einen gewissen Sinn für Selbstreflexion ausstrahlten, die erkennen ließen, daß sie das, was rund um sie im Netz passiert, wahrnehmen und mit einbeziehen – als Bereicherung, als Anspielung oder Gedankenanstoß.

The jury found, that we were magically attracted to what we dubbed "true" Net pages: homepages that use technology and narrative structures that are only available and only meaningful on the Net, and try to take those a step further. And we were a bit disappointed by artist's homepages that did nothing but put on the Net what would usually be on a wall. That's just moving things around, not creating "webness". That realisation strengthened our loyalty to the "true" Net pages. On the down side, these true Net pages sometimes gorge themselves on new Net-technologies, in spite of the fact that they don't yet know what to do with it. Having thus ruled out both art for art's sake and tech for tech's sake, we tried to make a selection that contained both Net and art. We ended up focussing on pages that had a special smell of self-reflectiveness, that somehow showed that they were aware of what else was happening on the Net and used that as a treasure, as a joke, or as something to dwell upon.

GOLDEN NICA

„etoy" (The Hijack Project)
http://www.hijack.org oder http://www.etoy.com

Imagine travelling on what everybody calls the Information Highway, looking for information about your preferred subject: for instance, Madona, Psion, Fassbinder movies or Playboy nudies. You find an underground site that promises you the best on your favourite subject, and eagerly, you click the link. POW! A screen flashes at you: "Don't fucking move. This is a digital hijack." There's not a thing you can do, there's a script running somewhere. A new page appears: "You are hostage no. 421705 hijacked by the organisation etoy." An audio file offers some explanation. It tells you about the dire conditions of Kevin Mitnick and requests his release. A voice explains to you that you've been digitally hijacked, just as the Internet itself has already been hijacked – not by "etoy", but by Internet mogul Netscape. When you at last find the button to exit this strange and upsetting Website and press it, it turns out that there's

GOLDENE NICA

„etoy" (The Hijack Project)
http://www.hijack.org oder http://www.etoy.com

Stell dir vor, du bist auf dem vielzitierten Informations-Highway unterwegs und suchst nach Infos zu deinen Lieblingsthemen, z. B. Madonna, Psion, Fassbinder-Filmen oder Playboy-Nackten. Du findest eine Underground-Seite, die dir das Beste zu deinem Lieblingsthema verspricht, und du klickst schnell auf den Link. PAFF! Der Bildschirm leuchtet auf: „Beweg dich nicht, du Hosenscheißer! Dies ist eine digitale Entführung!" Du kannst überhaupt nichts machen, irgendwo läuft ein Skript. Eine neue Seite erscheint: „Du bist jetzt Geisel Nr. 421705, entführt von der Organisation etoy." Eine Audiodatei liefert die vorläufige Erklärung. Sie sagt dir, daß Kevin Mitnick unter furchtbaren Bedingungen festgehalten wird, und fordert seine Freilassung. Eine Stimme erklärt dir, daß du soeben digital entführt worden bist, genauso wie das Internet selbst entführt wurde – allerdings nicht von „etoy", sondern vom Internetmagnaten Netscape. Endlich findest du den Button, um aus dieser seltsamen und beunruhigenden Webseite aussteigen zu können. Du klickst darauf – aber Erlösung gibt's immer noch keine: jetzt befindest Du dich innerhalb „etoys" eigener Seite.

„etoy" ist eine leicht anarchistische Webseite. Die visuelle Ästhetik kommt bei manchen Leuten nicht gut an, andere sehen darin ein sicheres Zeichen für eine blühende Gegenkultur. Und „etoy" propagiert eine Gegenkultur. Hier gibt es keine glatten, linear angeordneten Homepages, sondern eher eine Geisterbahn, in der man sich leicht verirren kann. Manchmal hilft es, auf den Down-Button zu klicken; manchmal hilft es aber auch nicht. Es gibt eine Seite, wo man seine Identität einfrieren lassen kann – im digitalen Eis: Man muß nur Namen, Alter und die Lieblingsabschiedsworte eintragen. Der Haken daran ist, daß man seinen Beruf nur aus einer ziemlich eingeschränkten Liste möglicher Berufe aussuchen darf; keiner davon ist sonderlich ansprechend, die Vorauswahl ist auf „Dieb" eingestellt. Eine andere Seite bietet einen Schnellkurs im Netz-Terrorismus: Da kann man eine Adresse eingeben, die Ziel einer Mailbombe sein soll. Man kann auch Schießübungen machen, indem man auf ein Ziel klickt (das Pech ist nur, daß man immer daneben trifft).

Und „etoy" hat tatsächlich bereits an verschiedenen Stellen Chaos angerichtet. Wir haben alle möglichen Geschichten gehört. Böse Geschichten. Nach einer solchen Geschichte haben sie sich in eine Hochsicherheits-Mailingliste eingetragen und dann die dort gesammelte Information in verschiedenen Newsgroups verbreitet, sehr zum Unmut der anderen Listenmitglieder. Einer anderen Geschichte zufolge kaperten sie den V_2-Server und vertauschten dort beliebige Nachrichten mit an „etoy" geschickten Mails.

Es ist anscheinend „etoys" Ziel, das Internet zu zerschlagen. Die Chance, dieses Ziel zu erreichen, ist natürlich gering, auch wenn sie möglicherweise schon einiges durcheinandergebracht haben. (Und um ehrlich zu sein, wünschen ihnen die Jurymitglieder auch nicht unbedingt Erfolg mit ihren Netz-Terrorismus-Versuchen, weil wir alle das Netz zu sehr brauchen). Ein Grund dafür ist, daß ihre Gegner zur stark sind: Regierungen sind derzeit darum bemüht, das Netz zu säubern; geschützte, „familienfreundliche" Räume wie in den America-Online-Angeboten sprießen überall; und Netscape hat tatsächlich, wie von „etoy" behauptet, das Web schon vor Jahren entführt, und weder Begründungen noch Argumente oder gutes Zureden oder Mailbombing und Geiselnahme werden diese Entwicklung aufhalten können. Das Verhältnis ist allerdings ein zwiespältiges, denn „etoy" liebt das Netz, auch wenn es so scheint, als wollte „etoy" das Netz sprengen. Die Webseiten wurden sorgfältig gestaltet. Auf einer Seite werden Rei-

no relief. You're inside "etoy's" own site now. "Etoy" is a slightly anarchistic site. Its visual aesthetics rub some people the wrong way; to others, this is a sure sign of full-fledged counterculture. And indeed it is a counterculture that "etoy" promotes. No smooth linearly arranged homepages, but a merry-go-round one tends to get lost in. Sometimes clicking the down-button helps; sometimes it doesn't get you anywhere. There's a page where you can have your identity frozen, in digital ice: all you need to do is enter your name, age and your preferred last statement. The only trouble is that your profession can only be selected from a very small range of vocations, none of them too appealing, and the pre-selected one is thief. Another page offers you a short course in net-terrorism: you can enter an address that you want to have mailbombed, or you can practice shooting by clicking on a target (only trouble is that you'll always miss).

And "etoy" has indeed created havoc in various places. We've heard stories. Nasty stories. In one, they subscribed to a high security mailing list and disseminated the information found there to various newsgroups, much to the distress of the other list subscribers. In another, they captured V2's server, and randomly swapped messages sitting there for mail "etoy" had received.

What "etoy" seems bent on doing is disrupting the Internet. The chances that they'll manage to do so are of course slight, although they may indeed have caused some trouble. (And, to be perfectly honest, none of the jurors would like them to succeed in their shot at net-terrorism, because we need the Net too badly). One reason of course is that their opponents are too strong: governments are currently trying to cleanse the Net; shielded, "family supporting" spaces such as those offered by AOL flourish; and Netscape has, as "etoy" states, indeed hijacked the Web years ago, and neither reasoning, arguing, pleading, mailbombing nor keeping people hostage will stop it.

Yet, ambiguously, "etoy" loves the Net even though they seem bent on disrupting it. Their pages have been carefully designed. One of their pages warns the traveller of the risks of the outside world: a desolate and grungy picture of the world as seen through a window is shown, with the caption "... and it's cold too". Instead, "etoy" offers a page where you can get a tan. A solarium flashes rays at you. Please stay inside, locked behind your computer, is their message; the Net ist a much more fun world.

And it's a real piece of Gesamtarbeit. "Etoy" is a hybrid, a multimedia-crew working in various fields and trying to tie them together in a new way. They aim at "a new way of playing the soundtrack for a new travelling generation. We play this soundtrack with different instruments like graphics, infoseek-flooding-robots, c-animation and ascii-txt as part of the show. Our stage is the web," as they put it.

What we liked, and what got to us, is that "etoy" fools around with preconceived notions about the Net and turns these upside down. Using the Internet intensively, one tends to grow familiar with a whole set of notions: that homepages contain what their indices say they contain, that mail cannot be read, that mailing lists can not be infiltrated, in short: that we are safe behind our computers. "Etoy's" irony, that is all-pervasive, is funny but also necessary. They poke fun at the Net and teach us a well-needed lesson as well. Regarding their hijack page, they state: "With this action, etoy demonstrates the 'room' behind popular interfaces of the world wide web. Weak points and twilight-zones of this medium are the place of action..." The Net can indeed be used in other ways than is expected; there is a space behind the obvious that can be used, reverted and changed into something completely different.

One of the jurors had severe doubts about "etoy". Seeing that one of their pages contained an ad for a flexi-disk, he thought they might just be a hype, an ad for a band. He hesitantly agreed to their nomination. He

Alles in allem ist „etoy" ein Gesamtkunstwerk. Es ist ein „Hybrid", ein Multimediateam, das in verschiedenen Bereichen arbeitet und versucht, sie auf neue Art und Weise miteinander zu verbinden. Ihr Ziel im O-Ton: „Wir wollen den Soundtrack anders spielen, für eine neue Generation auf Achse. Wir spielen ihn mit verschiedenen Instrumenten: mit Graphik, Info-seek-flooding-robots, C-Animation und ascii-txt, alles als Teil der Show. Unsere Bühne ist das Web."

Was uns gefiel und was uns überzeugte, ist, wie „etoy" mit den vorgefaßten Vorstellungen, die man vom Netz hat, spielt und sie auf den Kopf stellt. Wenn man das Internet intensiv nutzt, tendiert man dazu, sich gewisse Vorstellungen davon zu machen: daß Homepages das beinhalten, was im Index steht, daß Mails nicht gelesen werden können, daß Mailing-Listen nicht unterwandert werden können – kurzum, daß wir hinter unseren Computern sicher sind. Ironie ist bei „etoy" allgegenwärtig, sie ist lustig und auch notwendig. „etoy" macht sich lustig über das Netz und bringt uns damit etwas Wichtiges bei. In bezug auf ihre Hijack-Seite behaupten die „etoy"-Leute: „Mit dieser Aktion zeigt „etoy" den „Raum" hinter den beliebten Interfaces des World Wide Webs. Schwachstellen und Twilight-Zones sind der Veranstaltungsort für Aktion ...."

Es stimmt: Das Netz kann auf andere, unerwartete Weise genützt werden; es gibt einen Raum hinter dem Vordergründigen, und dieser Raum kann so genützt, verkehrt und verrückt werden, daß etwas ganz anderes daraus wird.

Ein Jurymitglied meldete ernsthafte Zweifel in bezug auf „etoy" an. Er bemerkte eine Werbung für ein Flexidisk auf einer Seite und meinte, daß Ganze könnte, bloß hype sein, ein Werbegag für eine Band. Er stimmte der Nominierung von „etoy" für die Goldene Nica nur zögerlich zu. Vielleicht hat er recht. Vielleicht ist „etoy" wirklich bloß ein Hype. Wenn schon, dann aber wirklich gut gestaltet, und im Netz ist das schließlich so gut wie wirklich. Wenn man es genau nimmt, glänzt das Netz mit Zwergen, und keiner weiß daß du ein Hund bist. Solange du nicht bellst.

may be right. "Etoy" might be a hype. But it's a well-designed one, and surely on the Net that is as good as the real thing. After all, the Net excells in trolls and nobody knows that you're a dog. As long as you don't bark.

AUSZEICHNUNGEN

„HyGrid"

http://www.sito.org/synergy/hygrid/

„HyGrid" ist eine Kunstseite: ein Joint Venture. Als Ausgangspunkt bietet es nichts als ein kleines Bild. Jeder kann mittun und sein eigenes Bild gestalten, das dann eingepaßt wird, wenn man es auf den Server gestellt hat. Was daraus entsteht, ist kein Flickwerk, sondern ein sich stets verwandelndes Gitter. Die Bilder wachsen aus den vorhergehenden Bildern heraus; das erste Bild liefert Ideen für die Gestaltung des nächsten Bildes. Die aus diesen Bildern bestehenden Gitter können in verschiedenen Anordnungen abgerufen werden. Jedes Bild ist mit der Homepage seines Erzeugers verknüpft, so daß eine virtuelle Künstlergemeinschaft entsteht. Es hört sich zwar sehr einfach an, aber die Software dahinter muß ziemlich kompliziert sein, denn die einzelnen Bilder erscheinen in immer anderer Position in den sich verschiebenden Gittern und sind auch noch miteinander und mit den relevanten Homepages verknüpft. Die Seite ist sehr einladend gestaltet und motiviert einen dazu, ein eigenes Bild hinzuzufügen.

VVV-Journey as an Exile

http://193.170.97.45/vvv/

Eingefaßt in einzelne, doch miteinander verknüpfte Rahmen zeigen vier Künstler ihre Arbeit und geben Kommentare zu den Arbeiten der anderen ab. Zunächst ruft ein Rahmen AltaVista ab und sucht in der Datenbank dort nach dem Satz „Reisen ist nützlich, es stärkt die Phantasie". Und AltaVista findet tatsächlich etwa 20.000 Links; etwas später wird das Suchprogramm dazu verwendet, nach der Phrase „Alles andere bedeutet Enttäuschung und Müdigkeit, unsere ganze Reise ist eine Illusion" zu suchen. Währenddessen hört man Engelsmusik und eine Stimme, die aus einem Buch von H.G. Ballard vorliest.

Wenn man auf einen Rahmen klickt, werden neue Bilder und Texte in einem anderen Rahmen aufgerufen. Die Rahmen – sogenannte „mind frames" – werden dazu verwendet, um – wie sie sagen – „aufeinander zu zielen

DISTINCTIONS

"Hygrid"

http://www.sito.org/synergy/hygrid/

"Hygrid" is an art site: a joint venture. It offers you a starting point in the shape of a small picture. People may join in and design their own pictures that, once they are uploaded, will be fitted next to it. What evolves is not a patchwork, but a shape-shifting grid. The pictures grow from one another; the image of the original supplying ideas for the one that is to go next to it. The grids that are formed with these pictures can be selected from a variety of arrangements. Each picture is linked to the maker's homepage. In this way, this virtual artist community connects.

Easy as this may sound, the software that keeps track of the position of the various pictures that reappear in a number of grids and their respective links both to each other and to related homepages, must be rather complicated. The page looks very inviting and spurs you on to submit a picture of your own.

VVV – Journey as an Exile

http://193.170.97.45/vvv/

Fitted within seperate but linked frames, four artists present their work, and their comments on each other's work. While one frame checks into AltaVista and searches their database for the phrase "Travel is useful, it exercises the imagination" (and indeed, AltaVista comes up with some 20.000 links; later on the search engine is used to retrieve instances of the phrase "All the rest is disappointment and fatigue. Our journey is entirely imaginary.") All the while, angelic music can be heard and a voice that read's from an H.G. Ballard book.

Clicking one frame brings up new images and texts in another. The frames – mind frames – are used to, as they put it, "'target' on each other and build so together a kind of parallel processing HyperMedia Tool." There's a weird dreamlike – or nightmarish – feel to the page, perhaps emphasized by the humming angels. The makers themselves state that their frames of mind relating to each other present "a kind of slow scan chat – or a other possibilty of creating mindcrap conferencing".

HONORARY MENTIONS

Web Collider
Supercollider
http://audio.apana.org.au/collider/
collider.html
The "Web Collider" is another pun on the Net. Considering the Net to be an endless stream of electric particles, it attempts to find out what happens if you crash them together at high velocity. It takes random parts of homepages and fires those at each other. Sometimes beautiful things come out of this collision, sometimes it's hilarious, sometimes it's just dadaist shambles. The funny thing is that you suddenly find yourself visiting the homepages from which the collider took a particle. On the down side, many pictures it snatches from other people's homepages are not retrievable in this way, so there are too many broken gifs.

Use of VRML
Webearth
http://tcc.iz.net/we/
"Web Earth" makes beautiful and meaningful use of VRML (which a bit too many people use just to prove that they're up to date on the technical side). "Web Earth" presents you with a globe, on which real-time satellite photographs of the earth are mapped. Various degrees of detail may be configured. Using your mouse, you can then spin the earth and zoom in or out. The notion is that this technique presents you with a real-time picture of the earth, and that you can see

und so gemeinsam eine Art parallelverarbeitendes HyperMedia-Tool aufzubauen." Die Seite ist von einer sonderbaren traumähnlichen – oder auch alptraum-ähnlichen – Atmosphäre gekennzeichnet, die von den summenden Engeln womöglich noch verstärkt wird. Die Köpfe dahinter behaupten, die Art und Weise, wie ihre *„mind frames"* sich aufeinander bezie-hen, stellt eine Art *„slow scan chat"* dar – *„eine andere Möglichkeit, Mindcrap-Conferencing herzu-stellen".*

ANERKENNUNGEN

Web Collider
Supercollider
http://audio.apana.org.au/collider/collider.html
„Web Collider" ist ein weiteres Wortspiel im Netz. Wenn man sich das Netz als einen endlosen Strom elektri-scher Teilchen vorstellt, kann man auch versuchen her-auszufinden, was passiert, wenn man diese Teilchen bei hoher Geschwindigkeit aufeinander aufprallen läßt. Diese Seite nimmt beliebige Auszüge von anderen Homepages und feuert sie aufeinander ab. Was bei dem darauffolgenden Aufprall herauskommt, ist manchmal wunderschön, manchmal furchtbar komisch, und manchmal entsteht lediglich ein dadaistisches Chaos. Interessanterweise ertappt man sich dann plötzlich dabei, daß man die Homepages, von denen „Supercollider" einen Teil entnommen hat, besucht. Der Nachteil ist, daß viele der Bilder, die „Supercolli-der" von anderen Homepages herausnimmt, in dieser Form nicht aufrufbar sind; aus diesem Grund gibt es zu-viele beschädigte GIF-Dateien.

VRML-Verwendung
Webearth
http://tcc.iz.net/we/
„Web Earth" verwendet VRML auf ansprechende und sinnvolle Art und Weise (im Gegensatz zu vielen, die VRML nur verwenden, um zu beweisen, daß sie sich in der neuesten Technologie auskennen). „Web Earth" präsentiert einen Globus, auf den Echtzeit-Satelliten-photos der Erde gemappt sind. Den Detail-Maßstab kann man selbst festlegen. Die Maus verwendet man, um die Erde drehen zu lassen und um Nah- oder Groß-aufnahmen einzustellen. Das Beindruckende an „Web Earth" ist, daß man hier ein Bild der Erde in Echtzeit

sieht und erkennt, wo es auf der Welt z. B. bewölkt oder stürmisch ist.

Global Clock
http://www.flab.mag.keio.ac.jp/GClock/
Wie „Web Earth" präsentiert uns „Global Clock" eine Echtzeitwelt. „Web Earth" zeigt, welche Erdteile gerade von der Sonne beleuchtet werden. Es gibt schon einige Meßstellen – aber bei weitem noch nicht genug –, die für diese Webseite installiert wurden. Das Sonnenlicht wird mit längeren und kürzeren Balken dargestellt, die auf die Erde fixiert werden.

Neue Dokumentationsform
Mc Spotlight
http://www.mcspotlight.org/ oder
http://www.mcspotlight.org.media/tour_top.html
Diese Seite bezieht sich auf eine Verleumdungsklage, die von der Firma McDonald's gegen zwei Personen vorgebracht wurde, weil diese die Politik McDonald's kritisierten. Diese Klage ist inzwischen als die „McLibel Suit" berühmt geworden, und in der Folge machte eine Unterstützungsgruppe von Kritikern regen Gebrauch, um via Mailinglisten diesbezügliche Information zu verbreiten. Daraus ist nun diese riesige Webseite geworden. Das Interessanteste an dieser Seite ist die Verwendung der Technologie als eine neue Form der Kritikdarstellung. Mit der Frames-Option, die Netscape zur Verfügung stellt, verwenden die Erhalter McDonald's konzerneigene Webseite als eine der Quellen. Auf einer Seite des Bildschirms sieht man die teure Hochglanz-Webseite von McDonald's, auf der atderen sieht man sie in dekonstruierter Form sowie die entsprechende Kritik von „McSpotlight". Es gibt sogar eine Audiodatei, die eine Führung durch McDonald's bietet. Auf den gegenübergestellten „McLibel"-Seiten wird die sorgfältig zusammengestellte Öffentlichkeitsarbeit von McDonald's Wort für Wort zerpflückt. „McSpotlight" beinhaltet 25 MB detaillierte Information über McDonald's sowie Links, die auf wissenschaftliche Berichte und Zeugenaussagen verwiesen.

Ron Newman's Homepage
(Der Konflikt mit Scientology)
http://www.cybercom.net/~rnewman/sientology/home.html
Der Streit zwischen dem Internet und Scientology ist bereits in die Geschichte des Netzes eingegangen.

which parts of the world are clouded or stormy at this very moment, and it makes "Web Earth" an impressive site.

Global Clock
http://www.flab.mag.keio.ac.jp/GClock/
Just like "Web Earth", "Global Clock" presents one with a real-time world. This one shows which parts of the earth are exposed to the sun. There are a few measuring points installed for this project, but unfortunately , the project has not yet been able to install all those that it needs. Sunlight is represented by longer or shorter pillars, which are appended to the earth,

New Documentary Form
Mc Spotlight
http://www.mcspotlight.org/ or http://www.mcspotlight.org/media/tour_top.html
In relation to a lawsuit McDonald's started against two people they accused of libel when they criticised McDonald's policy – a lawsuit now becoming famous as the "McLibel suit" – and in the aftermath of an extensive use of mailing lists by a group of supporting critics, a huge Website has now been created. The most interesting feature of this site is how they use technology as a new way to present criticism. Using the frames option that Netscape has, they use McDonald's own corporate Website as one of their sources. On one side of your screen you have McDonald's shiny, expensive Website, and on the other you have a detailed deconstruction and criticism from "McSpotlight". There's even an audio file that will help you along this guided tour of McDonald's. In the opposing "McLibel" pages, McDonald's carefully constructed PR is taken apart word by word. McSpotlight contains 25 Mb of detailed information about McDonald's and add links to scientific reports and witness statements.

Ron Newman's Homepage
(The Scientology Conflict)
http://www.cybercom.net/~rnewman/scientology/home.html

The fight between Internet and Scientology has already made it to Net-history. Scientology tried to remove the discussion group devoted to debating them (alt.religion. scientology), has tried to kill the newsgroup with endless bouts of spams, has investigated people who use pseudonyms and posted their personalia to the Net, used a private detective to observe posters from this newsgroup, has raided anon.penet.fi, Dutch ISP XS4all and the homes of various (US) citizens. Some of these actions are inspired by what Scientology calls copyright violation. The fight between a.r.s. and Scientology is in many ways formative for what one can and cannot do on the net in the very near future: for rules and regulations, for law and netiquette.

Ron Newman's homepage is devoted to this fight. Beginning in early 1995, he has kept a homepage on this Internet fight. The page has been updated nearly every day for fourteen months at a stretch, and now contains 5,5 Mb of data. It fullfills the needs of many who what to know what exactly is going on.

Irony
DigiCrime

http://www.digicrime.com

A major spoof. "DigiCrime" educates us on the hazards of the Net by presenting a collection of weird but true stories, and persuades us to do things we'd better not do. Also, they use Netscape's technical innovations to trick you.

They claim to offer a variety of electronic crime services with the professional attitude of a serious company. However, "DigiCrime" retains the right to be corrupt, to cheat their potential customers. Somehow they remind us of the fact, that privacy today is no more than a question of power and money.

Workshop
Coded Messages: CHAINS – "Cultural Ecology from Ghana to the World Wide Web"

http://found.cs.nyn.edu/andrvid/chains.html

"Chains" is more than just a documentation of a real life performance. It aims to achieve

Scientology versuchte, die sich kritisch mit Scientology auseinandersetzende Newsgruppe ‹alt.religion.scientology› aufzulösen. Zu deren Methoden zählten z. B. endloses Spamming dieser Liste, Ausforschen der Menschen, die Pseudonyme verwenden, und die Verbreitung deren persönlicher Daten im Netz, Beauftragung eines Privatdetektivs mit der Beobachtung von einigen an dieser Newsgroup Beteiligten, Überfälle auf ‹anon.penet.fi›, den holländischen Serviceanbieter (XS4all) und Privathäuser verschiedener (US-)Staatsbürger. Einige dieser Aktionen werden mit dem begründet, was Scientology „Urheberrechtsverletzungen" nennt. In vielen Hinsichten ist der Streit zwischen ‹alt.religion.scientology› und Scientology richtungsweisend für das, was man in nächster Zukunft im Netz tun und nicht tun darf: für Vorschriften und Regeln, für Gesetze und Netiquette.

Die Homepage von Ron Newman ist diesem Streit gewidmet. Seit Anfang 1995 dokumentiert er diesen Internet-Streit. Seine Seite wird seit über vierzehn Monate fast täglich aktualisiert und beinhaltet inzwischen eine Datenmenge von 5,5 MB. Diese Seite kommt dem Bedürfnis von vielen Menschen entgegen, die genau wissen wollen, was los it.

Ironie
Digicrime

http://www.digicrime.com

Eine riesige Persiflage. „Digicrime" informiert uns mit einer Ansammlung seltsamer, doch wahrer Geschichten über die Gefahren des Netzes und überredet uns, Dinge zu tun, die wir eigentlich lieber nicht tun sollten. Außerdem verwenden sie die technischen Innovationen von Netscape, um uns zu auszutricksen.

Angeblich bieten sie mit dem professionellen Auftreten einer seriösen Firma eine Vielzahl an elektronischen Verbrecherdiensten an. „Digicrime behält sich jedoch das Recht vor, korrupt zu sein und potentielle Kunden zu betrügen. Doch irgendwie erinnern sie uns an die Tatsache, daß Geheimhaltung heute nicht mehr ist, als eine Frage der Macht und des Geldes.

Workshop

Coded Messages: CHAINS – „Kulturelle Ökologie von Ghana zum World Wide Web".

http://found.cs.nyu.edu/andruid/chains.html

„Chains" ist mehr als nur die Dokumentation einer echten Performance. Es ist das anspruchsvolle Ziel dieser Seite, den Begriff „kulturelle Ökologie" zu definieren

und mittels Technologie, dem World Wide Web, unterschiedliche Kultursysteme miteinander zu verbinden und zu vergleichen. Mit der echten Performance „Coded Messages" wird die Beziehung zwischen den unterschiedlichen semiotischen Systemen der Trommelsprache aus Ghana und der Sprache amerikanischer Werbeeinschaltungen gezeigt. Diese Beziehung wird zu einer „respektvollen Beteiligung an interkultureller Arbeit" erweitert, indem die Technologie in die schöpferische Arbeit integriert wird.

Ein neuer „Code" für das World Wide Web entwickelt sich daraus. Schließlich werden gegenseitige Links zwischen dokumentarischem

Material und „coded messages" der Industrie gelegt, wodurch die „wirkliche" Bedeutung der Letztgenannten plötzlich zu Tage tritt; die Random Links in den Collagen/Imagemaps von „CHAINS" habe dieselbe Wirkung. Die Grafitti-Wand bietet jedem eine Gelegenheit, sich einzubringen, wie dies auch bei den Trommel-Performances in Ghana der Fall war.

Doch die Lücke, die Kette – "CHAIN" –, welche die Netzanwender von der restlichen Welt trennt, bleibt trotzdem erhalten, wie dies ein Link auf die „Virtual Tourist Map of Africa" zeigt.

Metazine
SUCK

http://www.suck.com
SUCK ist ein schnelles Magazin.

Es ist schnell und es kennt sämtliche Links. SUCK stellt sie alle in einem ganz anderen als dem ursprünglich beabsichtigten Kontext zusammen. So findet man einen Link auf die Seite von Camille Paglia auf derselben Seite wie einen Link auf die Bibelauslegung eines Managers – eine SUCK-Ausgabe über die Trendanalystin Faith Popcorn.

Als die Idee eines Metazin bietet SUCK dem Publikum ein täglich neues Web und führt von einem bestimmten Thema zu einer offenen Integration anderer Gedanken durch die Auswahl seiner Links.

Netverse
Electro Magnetic Poetry

http://prominence.com/java/poetry
Eine schön gestaltete Seite, die sehr einfach, aber einladend wirkt. Mit einem Cursor, einer Handvoll Wörter und einem eleganten Javaskript kann man Gedichte – ja, was denn? Zusammenstellen?

a highly valuable goal by inventing the term "cultural ecology", integrating and contrasting different cultural systems by means of technology, the World Wide Web. The real life performance "Coded Messages" attempts to show the relationship between different semiotic systems of a language of drums in Ghana and American magazine ads. They extend that to a "respectful participation in intercultural work" by integrating technology into creative work. A new "code" for the World Wide Web is being developed. Finally, they cross-link documentary material with "coded messages" from industry, wich suddenly reveal their "real" meaning, as do the random links from CHAINS' collages and imagemaps. The Graffiti Wall offers everyone an opportunity to participate, as in the drumming performance in Ghana. However, the gap, the "CHAIN" that "separates" the connected from the rest of the world remains, illustrated by a link to the Virtual Tourist map of Africa.

Metazine
SUCK

http://www.suck.com
SUCK is a "fast" magazine. It's fast and it knows all the links. SUCK puts them together in quite a different context from where they were originally supposed to be. Thus you may find a link to Camille Paglia's site on the same page as a link to a manager's interpretation of the bible – a SUCK issue about the trend analyst Faith Popcorn. SUCK, as the idea of a Metazine, daily brings a new Web to their audience, leading from one specific topic to an open minded integration of other thoughts through the selection of their links.

Netverse
Electro Magnetic Poetry

http://prominence.com/java/poetry
A page that ist very well done, simple to behold but very inviting. With a cursor, a few handful of words and an elegant Java script, poetry can be – well, what? Assembled?

Hypernarrative
Variety is...

http://art-slab.ucsd.edu/ARTSLAB/LisaHutton/LLHpage.html

A page which tells many stories. One of the most interesting ones is the story about "Cyberbabes", that shows you what harm the Telecommunications Decency Act might do to the Net. Hutton links to many outside places in order to let her story develop; that is a way to go about things that the jury liked.

Hegirascope

http://raven.ubalt.edu/staff/moulthrop/hypertexts/hgs/

A story presented in parts, which are retrieved by following various hyperlinks. There is, however, the possibility that the pages are retrieved according to an underlying script: when you don't click a link, the script will automatically present one to you.

Home
Timothy Leary

http://www.leary.com

Leary's page is indeed a home. Clicking your way through his house – his living room, his library, his computer – one can access much of the stuff that he has written, read stories about his friends, see some cherished possessions. A video of his death may soon be accessible via this page.

Hypernarrative
Variety is ...

http://art-slab.ucsd.edu/ARTSLAB/LisaHutton/LLHpage.html

Diese Seite erzählt viele Geschichten. Eine der interessantesten ist die Geschichte der „Cyberbabes", die zeigt, welchen Schaden der der „Telecommunications Decency Act" im Netz anzurichten imstande ist. Hutton hat viele Links auf andere Stellen außerhalb ihrer Seite angelegt, um die Geschichte entstehen zu lassen. Diese Vorgehensweise hat der Jury besonders gut gefallen.

Hegirascope

http://raven.ubalt.edu/staff/moulthrop/hypertexts/hgs

Eine Geschichte wird in verschiedenen Teilen präsentiert, die durch das Verfolgen von diversen Links abgerufen werden. Es besteht jedoch die Möglichkeit, daß die Seiten nach einem Skript im Hintergrund abgerufen werden; wenn man auf keinen Link klickt, wird eine Seite automatisch vom Skript abgerufen.

Home
Timothy Leary

http://www.leary.com

Learys Seite ist tatsächlich ein Zuhause: wenn man durch sein Haus klickt – sein Wohnzimmer, seine Bibliothek, seinen Computer – kann man die Sachen, die er geschrieben hat, betrachten, Geschichten über seine Freunde lesen, einige seiner Schätze sehen. Möglicherweise wird bald ein Video von seinem Tod über diese Seite zugänglich.

etoy

etoy. BRAINHARD	1972	PUBLIC RELATIONS / WORDS	VIENNA
etoy.GOLDSTEIN	1974	MODEL / SHOW / VOCALS	MANCHESTER
etoy.KUBLI	1973	DEALER / LAW	ZUERICH
etoy.GRAMAZIO	1971	ARCHITECT / CODER	ZUERICH / MONZA
etoy.UD	1973	CODER / DIGITAL EFFECTS	PRAHA / VIENNA
etoy.ESPOSTO	1973	SOUNDCODER	ZUERICH
etoy.ZAI	1974	STYLE / CORPORATE IDENTITY	VIENNA

always online - sometimes lost

✪ DER NAME: etoy

Mit einem Zufallsgenerator wurden 2000 Four-Letter-Words aufgrund bestimmter Vorgaben auf Listen ausgegeben. Attraktive Silben / Buchstaben / Wörter dienten als Grundlagematerial zur Bildung der Namensvorschläge. In einer 15-stündigen I.R.C. Konferenz selektionierte die Crew aufgrund ästhetischer Gesichtspunkte. electronic-toy, endo-toy, energy-toy: Assoziationen, die sich automatisch ergeben.

✪ DIE CORPORATE IDENTITY:

Das programmäßige Auftreten der sieben etoy.AGENTS im selben Look und die Verwendung derselben Tools ist ein Prinzip zur Unterstreichung der Austauschbarkeit der etoy.MEMBERS. everyone is everyone. everywhere. everything. leaving reality behind ...
Die Zusammenarbeit innerhalb der etoy.CREW orientiert sich an der Ästethik und Funktionsweise eines Formel-1-Teams.

✪ THE NAME: etoy

A random output generator was used to list 2000 four letter words according to certain criteria. attractive syllables / letters / words provided the basic material for creating name suggestions. In a 15-hour IRC conference, the Crew made a selection based on aesthetic features. electronic-toy, endo-toy, energy-toy: automatically resulting associations.

✪ CORPORATE IDENTITY:

In keeping with the program, the seven etoy.AGENTS make their appearance in the same look, and the same tools are always used: this principle emphasizes how the etoy.MEMBERS are interchangeable. everyone is everyone. everywhere. everything. leaving reality behind ...
Collaboration within the etoy.CREW is oriented to the aesthetic and working methods of a Formel-1 team.

✪ THE LOOK / ACCESSOIRES:

The orange crew jacket is the identifying
feature No.1. Standard overalls and a black
suit are required items in the luggage of all
etoy.AGENTS, just like the hand-held computer Psion, Serie 3a for ensuring minimal
communication (etoy.DUTYCHECK —›
http://www.etoy.com/dutycheck) and the
etoy.BUSINESSCARDS (plastic cards with a
magnetized strip for identification).

✪ THE PROGRAM:

run / jump / shoot and shout ... for the
"digital generation" !
communication and production via Internet.
reality emigration. digitale existence.

flashing into the future!

The limitations of the digital world are
scanned and extended through the
excessive and associative use of technology.

always online – sometimes lost

✪ "DIE HEIMAT": http://www.etoy.com/

The etoy.TANKSYSTEM, which consists of
containers and connecting pipelines,
illustrates the spatial paradox (the complete
elimination of intermediate spaces) in web
space and thus becomes a metaphor, which
may be used to establish (alleged)
orientation. Our immaterial communication
environment on the web provides the basis
for the transmission, transformation,
destillation and exposition of originating
and existing data.

✪ DER LOOK / ACCESSOIRES:

*Die orange Crew-Jacke ist Erkennungszeichen
No.1. Standard-Overalls und schwarze Anzüge
gehören genauso ins Reisegepäck des
etoy.AGENTS wie der Handheld-Computer Psion,
Serie 3a, zur Sicherung der minimalen Kommunikation (etoy.DUTYCHECK —›
http://www.etoy.com/dutycheck) und die
etoy.BUSINESSCARDS (Plastik-Karte mit Magnet-
streifen zur Identifikation).*

✪ DAS PROGRAMM:

*run / jump / shoot and shout ... for the „digital
generation" !
Kommunikation und Produktion via Internet. Rea-
lity-Emigration. Digitale Existenz.*

flashing into the future!

*Durch exzessive und assoziative Technologie-An-
wendung werden die Grenzen der digitalen Welt
gescannt und ausgedehnt.*

always online – sometimes lost

✪ *DIE HEIMAT: http://www.etoy.com/*

*Das etoy.TANKSYSTEM, bestehend aus Gefäßen
und Verbindungs-Pipelines, thematisiert das räumliche Paradoxon (gänzliche Aufhebung der Zwi-
schenräume) im Webspace und wird somit zur Metapher, mit deren Hilfe eine (vermeintliche) Orientierung erst möglich wird. Unsere immaterielle
Kommunikationsumgebung im Web dient zur
Transmission, Transformation, Destillation und Exposition der darin be- und entstehenden Daten.*

DER TANK WIRD DURCH SEINEN INHALT DEFINIERT.

„Digital-Entertainment-Actions" sollen die Grundstruktur sowie die besonderen Tools des TANKSYSTEMS (www.etoy.com) nutzen und die Entwicklung weitertreiben. Die erfolgreiche Verknüpfung der verschiedenen Streams in digitalen Environments ist das Ziel: Sounds, Visuals, Archtitecture und Software-Roboter kollaborieren mit Disco-Triphop, Image-Streams und ASCII-Codes.
Eine nicht-materielle Plattform: the virtual stage for the new travelling generation!

THE TANK IS DEFINED BY ITS CONTENTS.

"Digital Entertainment Actions" are designed to use the basic structure and the special tools of the TANKSYSTEM (www.etoy.com) and to further their development.
The aim is to successfully link different streams in digital environments: sounds, visuals, architecture and software robots collaborate with disco-triphop, image streams and ASCII codes.
A non-material platform: the virtual stage for the new travelling generation!

"the digital hijack" *etoy* 1996

http://www.hijack.org

[der Rezipient als Geisel]

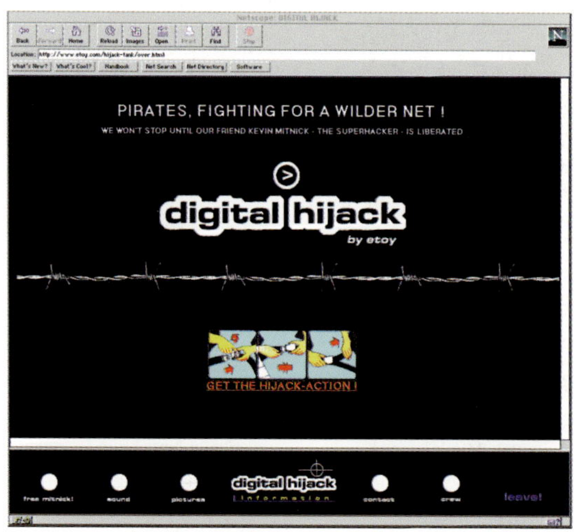

etoy inszenierte mit dieser vier Monate dauernden Aktion den „Raum" hinter der populären Oberfläche des World Wide Web. System-Schwachstellen und Grauzonen des Mediums bildeten den Handlungsrahmen. Suchserver-Datenbanken wurden zur Selbstdarstellungsbühne. etoy.SOFTWARE-AGENTS steuerten die systematische Täuschung und Entführung von ahnungslosen Netzreisenden: 250.000 Art-Hostages im März 1996.

With an action lasting four months, etoy demonstrated the "space" behind the popular interfaces of the World Wide Web. The weak points in the system and the twilight zone of the medium formed the place of action. Search-server databases became a stage for self-presentation. etoy.SOFTWARE AGENTS controlled the systematic illusion and hijack of hapless net-travellers: 250.000

leaving reality behind...

✪ The soundtrack for the new travelling generation by etoy on flexi-disc: 10.000 units distributed worldwide.

art-hostages in March 1996. "The technology-tourist is evasively assimilated into a trap configured by the etoy.GANG. In this labyrinth, the fascination of manipulating and hacking the search systems becomes The Story." The "digital hijack" project was terminated after the 600.000th hijacking, because the etoy.486-WEBSERVERS could no longer cope with the extreme amount of traffic (as many as 17.000 users every day). The software agents were officially withdrawn from the search engines at the end of July 1996 ... some of them could not be rescued ...The scene of the crime is open to the public and is still frequently visited by many inquisitive users:

http://www.hijack.org/

smashing the boring style of established electronic traffic channels, changing directions...

www.etoy.com
www.hijack.org

mailme@etoy.com

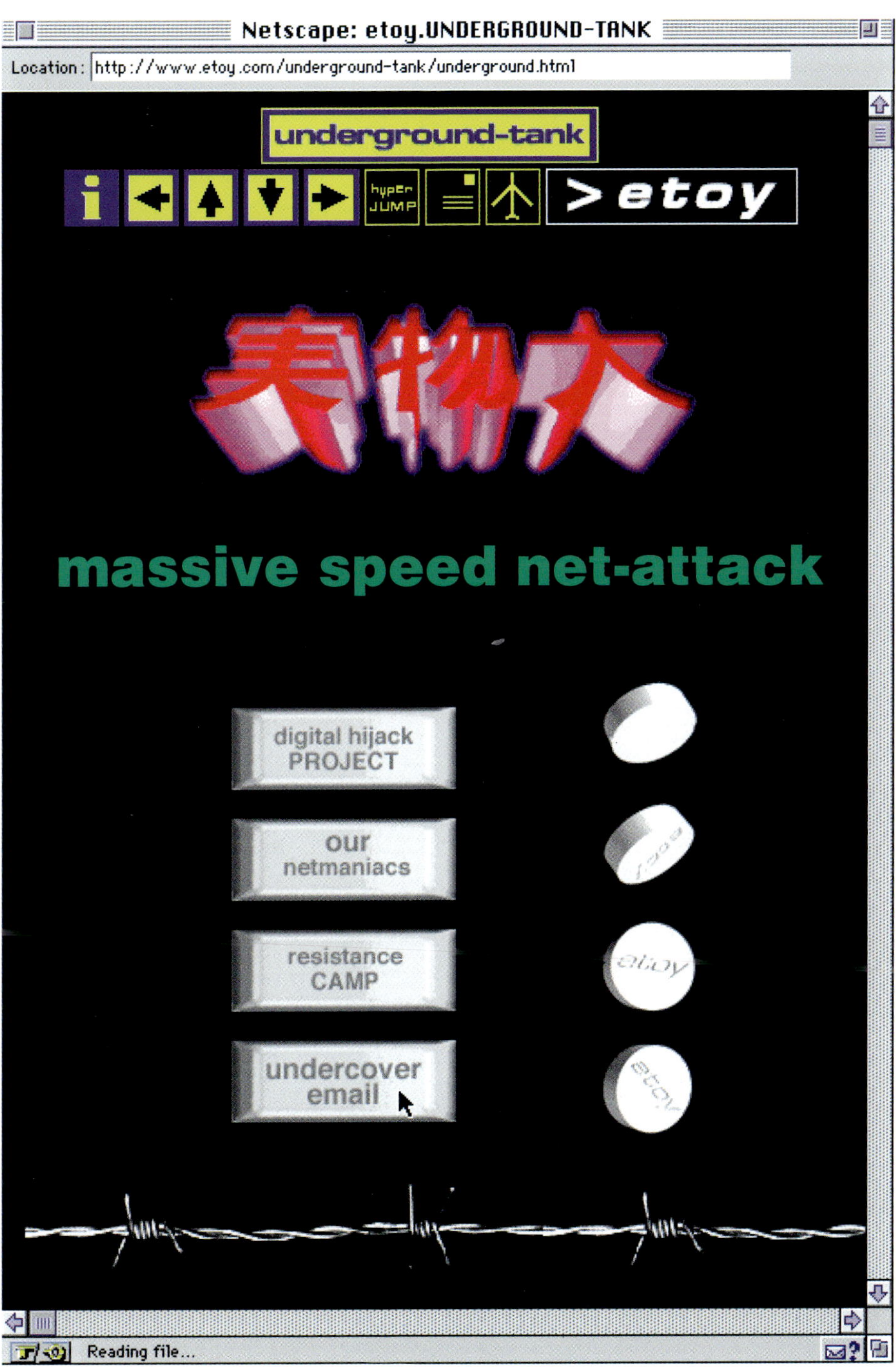

KISSES TO: Ruth Schnell, Claudia Kenan, Andreas Radlmayr, Caroline Webb, Florian Wenz, Marc Hell, Michael Huber, Viola Zimmermann, Oskar Obereder, Coco, Manfred Fassler, XXX-emotion, archzai, Frank Odgen, Doris Keller, Hochschule fuer angewandte Kunst Wien, Isabel Kirsch, Sabotage, Peter Weibel, Roger Schneider, Rita Palanikumar, Maya Küng, Nicolas Scharnagl, Anarres Rec & Org, SUB-Rec, Anja Catregn, Res Zangger, Regula Bochsler, Cassinelli-Vogel-Stiftung, Pop-Kredit Zürich, www.jodi.org DANKE!

ED STASTNY

*Ed Stastny (USA), geb. 1972,
war als Teenie Herausgeber der Zeit-
schrift „Dark Chaos", in der Kunst, Glos-
sen und Kritiken veröffentlicht wurden;
produzierte eine zweiwöchentliche
Kabelfernsehsendung, „DDT-TV".
Entdeckte Internet 1990
und tauchte ein in den
„reinen und ungehinderten
Informationsfluß".*

**Ed Stastny (USA), born 1972.
Ed published a fanzine in his teens
called "Dark Chaos", full of art, rants
and reviews. He produced a
biweekly public-access cable
television show called DDT-TV.
Discovered Internet in 1990
and became engulfed in the
"pure and unhindered flow
of information".**

WORLD WIDE WEB

*Geboren wurden „HyGrid" eines Nachts in einem Kaf-
feehaus in der Stadt Omaha, Nebraska, USA, während
ich in mein Skizzenheft kritzelte. Die grundlegende Idee
war, ein dynamisches, wachsendes, lineares, navigier-
bares, gemeinschaftliches Kunstwerk mit ineinander-
greifenden Quadraten zu schaffen. Jedes Quadrat sollte
auf einer Seite eines anderen Quadrats aufgebaut werden, und dann sollten weitere drei Quadrate auf den
Seiten des neuen Quadrats aufgebaut werden. Das
Resultat wäre nach nur wenigen Generationen ein
hypertextartiger Bilderweg, durch den man navigieren
könnte.*

*Anfangs wurde der Prozeß „tri-linear gridding" genannt:
„tri-linear", weil der Prozeß sequentiell und teilweise
linear in Sets von jeweils drei Zweigen ist, und „gridding", weil die Idee eines Basisquadrats aus einigen
meiner anderen Gemeinschaftsprojekten „GRID" und
„Infinite Grid" entwickelt wurde. Ich setzte alles daran,
„HyGrid" automatisch, lustig, einfach, flexibel und Web-
spezifisch zu machen.*

*Ein CGI-Perlskript bildet den Motor für „HyGrid". Seine
Seele besteht aus einer wachsenden Zahl begeisterter
Künstler/Mitwirkenden aus der/dem ganzen Welt(-wei-
ten Web). Im Dezember 1995 begann ich mit dem
Skript. Nachdem ich angefangen hatte, über das Projekt
nachzudenken, ließ mich die Idee überhaupt nicht mehr
los. Jede Nacht schlief ich ein, während ich noch nach-
dachte, welche Methoden und Formen „HyGrid" annehmen könnte. Wichtig war mir „HyGrid" so zu gestalten,
daß es einfach sei, dabei mitzumachen, daß das Brow-*

The "HyGrid" was born one night at a coffee
shop in the city of Omaha, Nebraska, USA,
as I scribbled in my sketchbook. The basic
idea was to create a dynamic growing linear
navigateable collaborative artwork with inter-
locked squares. Each square was to build off
of the side of another square and, in turn,
three more squares were to be built off of the
new square. After only a few generations,
the result would be a strange hypertextual
path of images that you could navigate.
The process was initially called "tri-linear
gridding". "Tri-linear" because it was se-
quential and semi-linear in sets of three
branches, and "gridding" because the base-
square idea was built off of some of my
other collaborative projects, "GRID" and
"Infinite Grid". The hope was to make the
"HyGrid" automatic, fun, simple, flexible and
web-specific.
"HyGrid's" engine is a CGI Perl script. It's
soul consists of a growing roster of eager
artist participants from around the world-
(wideweb). I started the script in December
of 1995. Once I began to think about the
project, I couldn't get the idea out of my
head. I would think myself to sleep every
night trying to envision the methods and
forms the "HyGrid" could manifest. It was
important for the "HyGrid" to be easy to

participate in, a pleasure to browse and easy to maintain. These factors, more than anything, shaped the project.

Browsing the "HyGrid" is fairly simple. Presented with one of the many display patterns available, you will see a set of 5 or more squares. Each square is created by a separate artist and all squares are intended to flow as seamlessly as possible into their neighbors. By clicking on any square, you will be presented with a new pattern of squares, this time with the square you clicked on as your center, or base, square. You will notice that going "up and right" doesn't present you with the same square as going "right and up". This is the hyperdimensionality of the project rearing it's beautiful head. Each square exists on its own "plane", so to speak. It is impossible to easily represent the HyGrid in any other medium. It is built for the World Wide Web. While browsing, you'll run across a few different types of squares. The art-squares, of course, are the focus of the project. These are squares submitted by participating artists. The "unreserved" marker square indicates that that specific square on the "HyGrid" has not been reserved and is open for creation. To reserve that square, a participant needs merely click on it and fill out the short reservation form supplied. Once a square is reserved, it will be marked as such and browsers will see a "reserved" square in its place. The final type of square on the "HyGrid" is the "void" square. A "void" square is used to mark a segment of the "HyGrid" that, by its location behind an unfinished square, isn't active. These "void" squares are used only to fill out unrepresented squares on the bigger pattern configurations.

On a purely artistic level, the patterns provide the altered perspective that's needed to appreciate the "HyGrid's" sprawling chaos. The "HyGrid" grows itself. For the first two months, participants could only ADD a square to an open space on the "HyGrid", effectively adding three new sides from which others could build. As the program

sen Spaß macht und daß es leicht zu warten sei. Diese Aspekte bestimmten mehr als andere das Projekt.

Es ist relativ einfach, durch „HyGrid" zu browsen. Sobald eines der vielen verfügbaren Ausgabemuster erscheint, sieht man ein Set von fünf oder mehr Quadraten. Jedes Quadrat wird von einem einzelnen Künstler geschaffen, und alle Quadrate sollten so fließend wie möglich in die angrenzenden Quadraten übergehen. Wenn man ein Quadrat anklickt, erscheint ein neues Quadratmuster; dieses Mal ist aber das angeklickte Quadrat das Mittel- oder Basisquadrat. Man merkt dabei, daß Bewegung „nach oben und rechts" ein anderes Quadrat hervorbringt als Bewegung „nach rechts und oben". Genau das ist das Schöne daran – die Hyperdimensionalität des Projekts. Jedes Quadrat existiert quasi auf einer eigenen Ebene. Es ist unmöglich, „HyGrid" in irgendeinem anderen Medium darzustellen. Es wurde für das World Wide Web kreiert.

Beim Browsen findet man einige verschiedene Arten von Quadraten. Die künstlerisch gestalteten Quadrate bilden natürlich den Mittelpunkt des Projekts. Das sind jene Quadrate, die von den mitwirkenden Künstlern beigesteuert wurden. Das als „nicht reserviert" gekennzeichnete Quadrat markiert jeweils ein „HyGrid"-Quadrat, das noch nicht reserviert ist und daher noch gestaltet werden kann. Um sich dieses Quadrat zu reservieren, muß man es nur anklicken und ein kurzes Reservierungsformular ausfüllen. Wenn ein Quadrat schon reserviert ist, wird es auch dementsprechend gekennzeichnet, und Besucher sehen auf dieser Stelle ein „reserviertes" Quadrat. Die letzte Art der „HyGrid"-Quadrate ist das leere („void") Quadrat. Ein leeres Quadrat wird verwendet, um ein Segment von „HyGrid" zu markieren, das nicht aktiv ist, weil es hinter einem unvollständigen Quadrat liegt. Diese leeren Quadrate werden nur verwendet, um die nicht-repräsentierten Quadrate in den größeren Musteranordnungen auszufüllen.

Rein künstlerisch gesehen, bieten die Muster die veränderte Perspektive, die man braucht, um das ausufernde Chaos von „HyGrid" schätzen zu können.

„HyGrid" wächst selbständig und aus sich heraus. In den ersten zwei Monaten war es den Mitwirkenden nur möglich, ein Quadrat an einem freien Platz im „HyGrid" hinzuzufügen, wodurch drei neue Seiten entstanden, auf denen andere ihre Quadrate aufbauen konnten. Als das Programm ausgereift war, entstand dann die Möglichkeit, „weirdlinks" oder „wormholes" zu erzeugen. Diese „weirdlinks" erlaubten es einem Benutzer, unter

bestimmten Bedingungen eine beliebige Anzahl seiner reservierten Quadrate in einem zu kombinieren. Dadurch können Benutzer ein neues Quadrat erzeugen, das als eine Brücke zwischen zwei, drei oder sogar vier Quadraten funktioniert. Dadurch wurde es noch unmöglicher, „HyGrid" in irgendeinem anderen Medium darzustellen. Aber dadurch wurde „HyGrid" auch sterblich. Es bestand nun keine Aussicht mehr, daß es kontinuierlich bis in alle Ewigkeit weiterwachsen würde. Es besteht die Möglichkeit, daß „HyGrid" sich in sich schließen könnte, indem sämtliche noch verfügbaren freien Quadrate geschlossen werden. „HyGrid" könnte zu einer phantastischen digitalen Möbiusschleife werden. Meiner Meinung nach wird das nie passieren, solange die Mitwirkenden immer wieder neue Einzel-Link- und Doppel-Link-Quadrate gestalten können. Einzel-Links erzeugen drei neue Seiten, auf denen man aufbauen kann (sie blockieren eine Seite und erzeugen drei). Doppel-Links erzeugen zwar keine neue Seiten, doch sie nehmen auch keine Seiten weg (sie blockieren zwei Seiten, erzeugen dafür zwei andere Seiten).

Die Gestaltung der „HyGrid"-Quadrate kann man ohne weiteres als eine eigene Kunstform betrachten. Die Techniken und Stilrichtungen der Mitwirkenden sind sehr unterschiedlich. Manche Künstler gehen dabei äußerst akribisch vor und verfolgen „HyGrid"-Stücke über fünf Generationen zurück, oft sogar bis zum Ursprungsquadrat; visuelle Elemente dieses Quadrats werden dann in das neue Quadrat miteinbezogen.

Im Dezember 1995 trat „HyGrid" an die Öffentlichkeit. Bis 30. April 1996 gab es über 30 Mitwirkende und fast 400 Einzelstücke. Ich bin sehr stolz auf „HyGrid" und auf das, was es geworden ist. „HyGrid" ist ein wachsendes Projekt und wird sicher nicht so schnell aufhören.

Unter anderem sind folgende Verbesserungen für die Zukunft geplant: Drumloop-Musik, die mit jedem Quadrat so verknüpft ist, daß man neue Melodien und Rhythmen bloß beim Navigieren durch „HyGrid" erzeugen kann, auch eine VRML-Ausgabe kommt in Betracht, damit man sich einigermaßen vorstellen kann, wie eine „HyGrid"-artige Struktur in drei Dimensionen aussehen könnte.

Und wenn es auch sonst nichts erreichen sollte – „HyGrid" zeigt die geheimnisvollen Regeln der Relation, der Evolution und des Perspektivischen auf eine Art und Weise, daß sie sogar ein Künstler kapiert.

matured, the ability to create "weirdlinks" or "wormholes" on the "HyGrid" was installed. These "weirdlinks" allowed a user to combine any number of their reserved spaces into one, provided the conditions were right. In this way, they could create a new square that acted as a bridge between two, three or FOUR squares. The "HyGrid" was now MORE impossible to render in any other medium. This also gave the "HyGrid" mortality. No longer was it destined to go on into infinity, constantly growing. There now exists the possibility that the "HyGrid" can cinch itself off by using up all available open squares. The "HyGrid" can become closed, like some fantastic digital moebius strip. It is my opinion that this will actually never happen as long as participants are able to create single-link and double-link squares. Single-links create 3 new sides from which to build (they plug-up one and provide three). Double-links don't create any new sides, but they don't take away any either (they plug-up two, but provide two more). Creating "HyGrid" squares is easily an artform unto itself. Techniques and styles vary greatly among participants. Some like to be extremely vigilant in their referentiality, they will go back to "HyGrid" pieces more than five generations back, often to the origin square, and include visual elements from that square into their new piece. The "HyGrid" became public in December of 1995. As of April 30, 1996, there are over 30 participants and nearly 400 individual pieces. I'm very proud of "HyGrid" and what it's become. "HyGrid" is a growing project and has no intention of stopping any time soon. Future upgrades include drumloop music linked to every square, allowing new songs and beats to be created by merely cruising through the "HyGrid". VRML output is also being looked at, to allow some idea of how a HyGriddish structure would look in three-dimensions.

If nothing else, "HyGrid" illustrates the mysterious rigors of relation, evolution and perspective in a way that even an artist can understand.

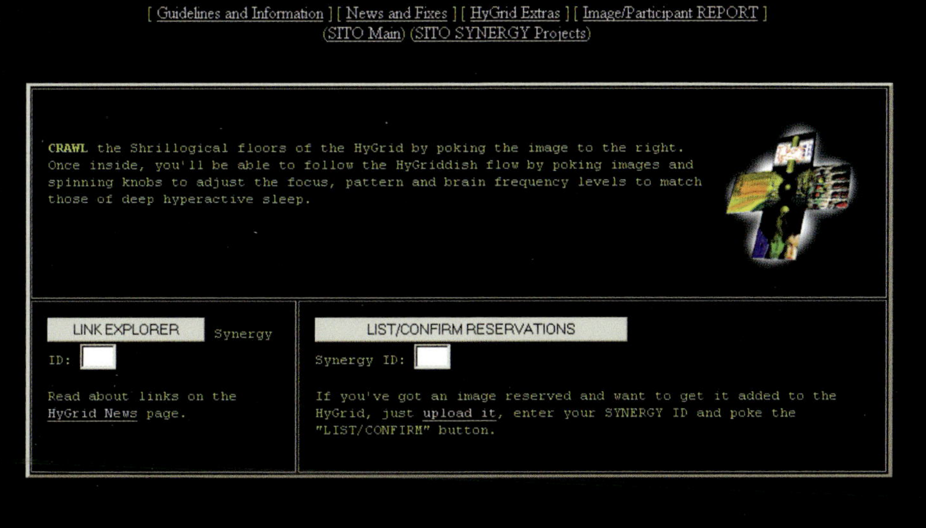

Ed Stastny, "HyGrid", 1996

http://www.sito.org/synergy/hygrid/

MANUEL SCHILCHER

Manuel Schilcher (A), geb. 1966, diplomierte mit einem Projekt im Internet an der Hochschule für künstlerische und industrielle Gestaltung in Linz. Seit 1990 diverse Ausstellungen und Organisation artifizieller Situationen. Gründete 1994 Relais-digital office, beschäftigt sich mit Wahrnehmungskonzeption und Informationsdesign.

Manuel Schilcher (A), born 1966, graduated from the Hochschule für künstlerische und industrielle Gestaltung in Linz with an Internet project as his diploma work. Various exhibitions and organization of artificial situations since 1990; in 1994 he founded Relais – digital office. He is interested in conceptions of perception and information design.

WORLD WIDE WEB

KUNST ALS METHODE

Es ist obsolet geworden, der Welt zu erklären, wie sie ist oder wie sie sein wird. Wenn die Kunst zu glauben denkt, sie könnte als Mittler der neuen Zeit, die sie selbst nicht versteht, ihrem Publikum erklären, was die Technologie bringen möge, und das Feld einfach nur in Verherrlichung und Mißtrauen spaltet, zeigt sie nur die Unfähigkeit, sie zu benutzen. Die Dinge brauchen keine Kanalisation in den Köpfen durch Vorwegwisser, sie existieren, ohne initiiert zu werden, entstehen aus sich selbst, aus ihren Zusammenhängen und verschwinden auch in diesen. Es geht nicht um eine Ablöse realer durch virtuelle Wirklichkeiten, sondern um eine Erweiterung und vor allem um eine mediale, kommunikative Selbstverwaltung.

Das Projekt „A Journey as an Exile" verborgt Wahrnehmungen an seine Benutzer, welche sich so ihre eigenen Assoziationsfelder aufbauen.

Unter Zuhilfenahme aller notwendigen Konditionierungstechniken entwickelt sich die „Reise als Exil" zu einer Suche nach einer dialektischen Organisation vorübergehender, teilweise vorhandener Wirklichkeiten, die den Zufall nicht ausschließt, sondern im Gegenteil „wiederfindet".

Die Teilnehmer benutzen die verschiedenen Interpretationen von Material und Situation, um gegenseitige Impulse zu generieren, welche weitergeführt, verworfen oder archiviert werden.

Die eigenen Impressionen werden durch die Erfahrung und Wahrnehmung der anderen filtriert und in neue Zusammenhänge gesetzt.

ART AS METHOD

Explaining the world as it is or as it will be has become obsolete. If art thinks it can act as an intermediary for a new age it does not understand and explain to its audience what technology may be capable of, while merely splitting the field into glorification and distrust, then this only serves to show that art itself is incapable of using this very technology. These things need not be channeled into minds by the prescient; they exist without being initiated, emerge from themselves, from their contexts, and then disappear back into where they came from. It is not a question of replacing real reality with virtual reality, but rather of an expansion and especially of media-based, communicative self-administration. The project "A Journey as an Exile" lends perceptions to its users, who may then use them to construct their own fields of associations.

With the assistance of all the necessary techniques of conditioning, "Journey as an Exile" evolves into a search for a dialectical organization of provisional, partially existing realities. This search does not exclude chance, but rather "rediscovers" it. Participants use the various interpretations of material and situations to generate mutual impulses, which may be continued, abandoned or archived. The participants' own impressions are filtered through the experience and perception of the others and placed in new contexts.

MISSING ACCOMODATION

On the constructs in our own heads and memories. The starting point for wanting to set out on a journey is not only missing accomodations, but also a lack of conformity. But inner thoughts and the ways in which they are intertwined lead to hesitation. The boundary and the abutment – both should be understood as heterotropes – are among the few points where communication with other travellers may be established. Perception, enabled by recollection and recognition, is shifted, destroyed and thus no longer comprehensible in our own minds.

MISSING ACCOMODATION

Über die Konstrukte im eigenen Kopfe und im Gedächtnis. Nicht nur die vermißte Unterkunft, sondern auch die mangelnde Anpassung werden als Ausgangspunkt genommen, sich auf eine Reise begeben zu wollen. Doch die inneren Gedanken und deren Verflechtungen halten davon ab. Die Nahtstelle und das Widerlager – beide seien als Heterotope zu verstehen – als die wenigen Punkte, von denen aus die Mitteilung zu den anderen Reisenden noch zustande kommen kann. Die Wahrnehmung, die erst die Erinnerung und das Wiedererkennen ermöglicht, wird verschoben, zerstört und so im eigenen Kopfe nicht mehr nachvollziehbar.

"Trace an inner thought as an arch (Noah's ark) in your mind. But the traces are zerolines and manipulated."

Manuel Schilcher
"VVV – A Journey as an Exile", 1996

http://193.170.97.45/vvv/

TREVOR BLACKWELL

Trevor Blackwell ist Graduate Student der Informatik, arbeitet bei Aiken G9, Harvard University; sein Hauptforschungsgebiet ist schnelle SVC´s für ATM-Netze und Flow Control in ATM-Netze.

Trevor Blackwell is a graduate student of Computer Science, working at Aiken G9, Harvard University; his main research interests involve fast SVCs for ATM Networks and Flow Control in ATM Networks.

WORLD WIDE WEB

Von überall aus dem Internet werden Elementarteilchen der Information bis auf Lichtgeschwindigkeit beschleunigt. Sie bewegen sich in entgegengesetzten Richtungen um den riesigen Fiberring herum und treffen sich in der Kollisionskammer. Durch den Zusammenprall werden kleine, aber massive Informationsteilchen freigesetzt und in alle Richtungen zerstreut. Manche werden vom Informationsdetektor eingesammelt und für spätere Betrachtung gespeichert. Wenn man beim „Supercollider" auf „Reload" drückt, kommt es zu einer neuen zufälligen Kollision. Man sollte das aber öfter probieren, da es auch vorkommt, daß manche Durchgänge eher langweilig sind. [Anmerkung: Kollisionen beinhalten häufig viele Bilder. Die Bilder kommen von jener Webseite, in der sie ursprünglich gefunden wurden.] Im Detail: Ein Trawler-Daemon fischt im Web mit einer Tiefensuche nach allen HTML-Seiten. (Um die Leistung zu steigern, wird zunächst bei einer einzelnen Seite eine Tiefensuche durchgeführt; dadurch wird die Anzahl der DNS-Abfragen begrenzt, wenn das Programm läuft.) Sobald eine Seite gelesen wird, werden die Links in eine „zu erledigen"-Warteliste von URLs eingetragen, und die Inline-Bilder werden einer Gruppe von Bildern hinzugefügt. Die Seite wird einem „Interessant-Test" unterzogen, und wenn sie diesen Test besteht, wird sie in einer großen Datei, die alle verketteten Dokumenten enthält, aufgenommen. Mit dem „Interessant-Test" wird überprüft, ob das Dokument nicht zu lang oder zu kurz ist und ob das Bild/Text-Verhältnis einigermaßen ausgewogen ist. Jeder HTML-Text mit dem Wort „copyright" wird abgelehnt, obwohl der Trawler Links auf Bilder, die auf Seiten mit einem „Copyright" gefunden werden, aufnehmen kann. Ich glaube nicht, daß das eine Urheberrechtsverletzung darstellt, da ich die Bilder nicht kopiere, sondern nur Verweise anlege. Wenn du anderer Meinung bist, kannst du dich bei mir melden.

From across the Internet, elementary particles of information are accelerated to nearly the speed of light. They travel in opposite directions around the giant fiber ring, meeting in the collision chamber. The collisions release small but massive information particles, scattered in all directions. Some of them are collected by the information detector and stored for later viewing. Pressing "reload" will get you a new random collision. Be sure to try it a few times, because on any given run you might get something really boring. Note: collisions tend to be image-rich. Images come from whatever web site they were originally found on.

Details: A daemon trawls the web, doing a breadth-first search of all HTML pages. When it reads a page, it adds all the links to a 'to do' queue of URLs, and adds all the inlined images to a set of images. If the page passes an interestingness test, the text is added to a large file containing all the html documents concatenated together. The interestingness test requires that the document not be too long or trivially short, and that it has a reasonable proportion of pictures to text. Any HTML with the word "copyright" is discarded, although the trawler may add links to pictures found on copyrighted pages. I don't think this is a violation of anyone's copyright, as I don't make any copies, just create references. If you think differently, let me know.

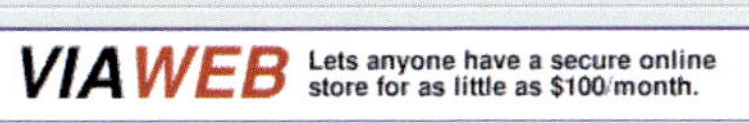

Or go directly to the infamous Acme Catalog.

k on the antenna to **send** your **message** into **space** with **20 Megawatts** EIRP!

Document: Done

Trevor Blackwell
"Supercollider"

MARK PESCE

Mark Pesce (USA) is a cyberspace researcher and theorist, he is currently working on his third book, Why in the World Wide Web?, which focuses on contextual examination of the rapidly unfolding developments in the human Noosphere, vis-a-vis Internet and interface. Lives and works in Los Angeles.

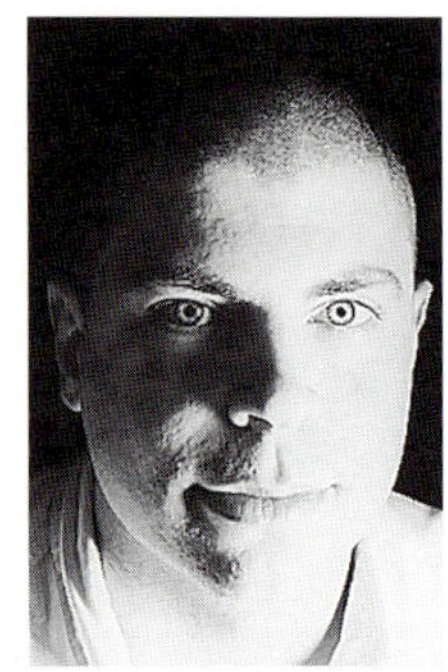

Mark Pesce (USA) ist Cyberspace-forscher und -theoretiker; derzeit arbeitet er an seinem dritten Buch „Why in the World Wide Web?" mit Schwerpunkt auf einer kontextbezogenen Untersuchung der rasanten Entwicklungen in der menschlichen Noosphäre im Wechselspiel von Internet und Interfaces. Er lebt und arbeitet in Los Angeles.

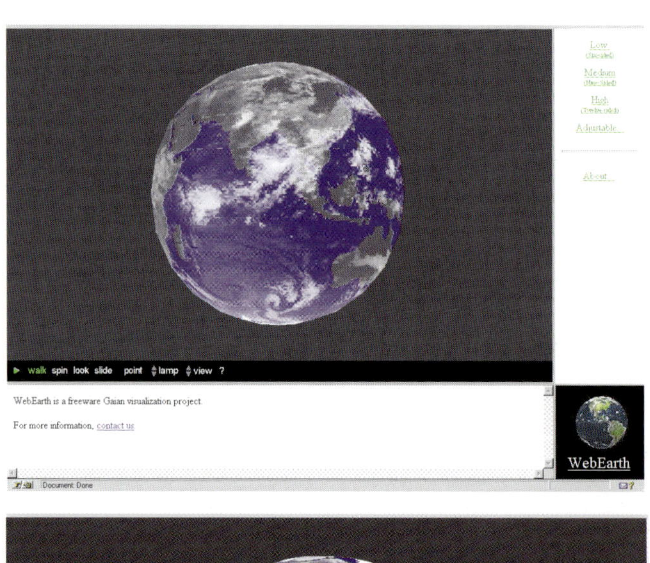

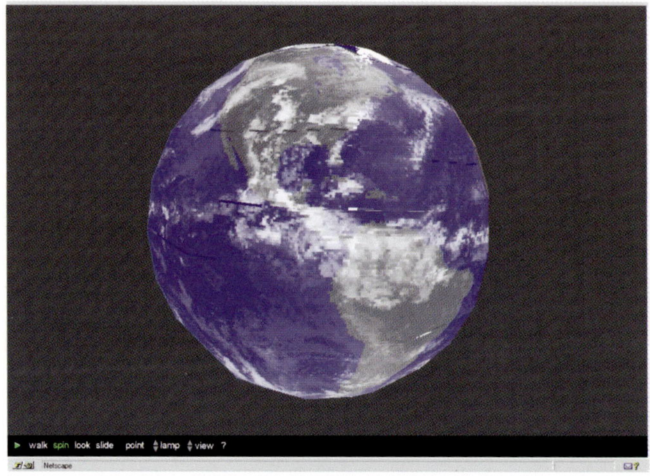

Mark Pesce
"WebEarth", 1996

While Aristophanes measured the curvature of the Earth's surface over two thousand years ago, until the Apollo astronauts photographed the "big blue marble", we had no visible – hence apprehendible – model of the body of the planet. From the moment the first photograph taken by Apollo 8 reached Earth, the image – captivating and curiously seductive – supplanted all other models of the Earth, until, thirty years later, we think of this image as synonymous with Earth.

In the generation between Project Apollo and NASA's Mission to Planet Earth, we have moved from static imaging to interactive simulation; our models respond to us, coupling us to their projections of reality through a coupling that binds interface and intelligence to representation. Suddenly we have found ourselves in possession of the ultimate tool for planetary management; we can focus our perceptions in any quadrant of Earth's surface. Through this we can come to an understanding of the deep precesses of ecology – how the different systems in the biosphere interrelate, and how our own actions directly affect them. While this may be the ecologist's dream come true, it's equally the Orwellian nightmare of absolute surveillance.

As Foucault noted in "Discipline and Panish", greatest danger of such panoptic technologies lies in their concentration within any locus of power; such a situation confronted the nation-states at the birth of the spy satellite. This resulted in the adoption of an "Option Skies" policy, which allow the nation-states to spy on each other freely; the presumption that unrestricted observation would engender a more comprehensive security has been proven the efficacy of this policy. "WebEarth" seeks to extend this enfranchisement to the individual, and the desktop.

Obwohl Aristophanes die Kurve der Erdoberfläche schon vor mehr als zweitausend Jahren vermessen hatte, hatten wir kein sichtbares — und somit greifbares — Modell des Planetenkörpers, bis die „große blaue Kugel", die Erde, von den Apollo-Astronauten fotografiert wurde. Von dem Moment an, als die erste Aufnahme von Apollo 8 die Erde erreicht hat, hat dieses Bild — das ansprechend und seltsam verführerisch ist — sämtliche andere Modelle der Erde so vollständig ersetzt, daß wir heute, dreißig Jahre später, meinen, dieses Bild sei mit der Erde an sich gleichzusetzen.

In der Generation zwischen Projekt Apollo und der Mission zum Planeten Erde der NASA ist aus den statischen Bildern interaktive Simulation geworden; unsere Modelle reagieren auf uns, verbinden uns mit ihren Projektionen der Wirklichkeit durch eine Koppelung, die Interface und Intelligenz mit deren Repräsentation verbindet.

Wir stellen plötzlich fest, das wir das höchstentwickelte Werkzeug zur Verwaltung des Planeten in der Hand haben. Wir können unsere Wahrnehmungen auf jeden beliebigen Quadranten der Erdoberfläche einstellen. Dadurch verstehen wir die tieferen Prozesse der Ökologie besser — wie die verschiedenen Systeme in der Biosphäre ineinander übergreifen und wie diese von unseren Handlungen direkt betroffen sind. Und wenn das die größten Wünsche der Ökologen erfüllt, bedeutet es gleichzeitig eine absolute Überwachung im Orwell'schen Sinn.

Wie Foucault in „Discipline and Panic" bemerkte, besteht die größte Gefahr solcher panoptischen Technologien in deren Verdichtung an jedem beliebigen Ort der Macht; mit einer ähnlichen Situation sah sich die internationale Staatengemeinschaft bei der Erfindung der Spionagesatelliten konfrontiert. Die Folge war die Vereinbarung einer Politik der „Open Skies", die es den verschiedenen Staaten erlaubt, gegenseitige Spionage zu betreiben. Die Annahme, daß unbeschränkte Beobachtung zu umfassenderer Sicherheit führen würde, beweist die Wirksamkeit dieser Politik. „WebEarth" will dieses politische Recht auf jeden einzelnen und auf jeden Desktop erweitern.

MASAKI FUJIHATA

*Masaki Fujihata (J), geb. 1956; BA
1979 und MA 1981 an der Tokyo University of Arts/Design Course;
1982–1990 Karriere in der Wirtschaft;
Vorstandsmitglied der Japan Animation Film Association, seit 1987 Mitglied von ASIFA; seit 1990 Associate
Professor an der Fakultät für Umweltinformation an der Keio University.*

*„The Global Clock Project" ist eine Visualisierung der
Erde als Uhr mit Hilfe von Lichtsensoren, die durch das
Internet mit beliebig vielen Webseiten irgendwo auf der
ganzen Welt verbunden sind.*

*Die Lichtsensoren in den verschiedenen Teilen vermit-
teln die Echtzeit-Helligkeit am jeweiligen Ort. Der
„Global Clock"-Server empfängt Echtzeit-Parameter von
den Lichtservern und mappt sie auf ein Bild des Globus.
Das natürliche Phänomen der graduellen Verschiebung
der hellen und der dunklen Bereiche auf dem Globus
passiert, weil der Globus sich dreht. Vielleicht erkennt
man, daß darin der Ursprung der „Uhr" lag.*

*Ideen teilen und zusammenarbeiten, um neue Schwer-
punkte zu setzen – das sind natürliche Merkmale
des Internets als Medienraum.*

*Das Internet an sich baut auf einem Konzept des „glo-
balen Bewußtseins" auf. Ohne die Zusammenarbeit von
Webseiten überall auf der Welt kann „The Global Clock
Project" nicht umgesetzt werden. Man könnte behaupten, das Projekt sei eine Art „Visualisierung der Zusammenarbeit".*

*Das Ansprechende an diesem Projekt ist, daß es eine
Tatsache ins Bewußtsein ruft: daß wir alle nur dadurch
leben, daß wir diesen Ort, den wir „die Erde" nennen,
miteinander teilen, und daß wir gemeinsam daran
arbeiten müssen, um auf diesem Planeten leben
zu können.*

The "Global Clock Project" is a visualization
of the earth as a clock, using light sensors
connected through the Internet to any other
site anywhere in the world. The light sensors in various parts of the world transmit
the real-time brightness of that specific
location. The "Global Clock" server receives
real-time parameters from the light servers
and maps them onto an image of the globe.
The natural phenomenon of the gradual
shifting of the light area on the globe and
the shadow area on the globe occurs
because of the rotation of the globe itself.
People may recognize that this was the
origin of the "clock". Sharing ideas and
collaborating to create new emphases are
natural characteristics of the Internet as a
media space. The Internet itself is based on
a concept of "global conciousness". The
"Global Clock Project" cannot be realized
without collaboration from sites all over the
world. We could say the project is a form of
"visualization of collaboration". This project
is appealing, because it calls attention to
the fact that we all live by sharing this place
called "The Earth", and we must all work
together to live on this planet.

Masaki Fujihata (J), born 1956,
BA in 1979 and MA in 1981 at Tokyo
University of Arts/design course;
1982–1990 business career, Board
Member of Japan Animation Film
Association, since 1987 Member of
ASIFA, since 1990 Associate
Professor, Faculty of Environmental
Information at Keio University.

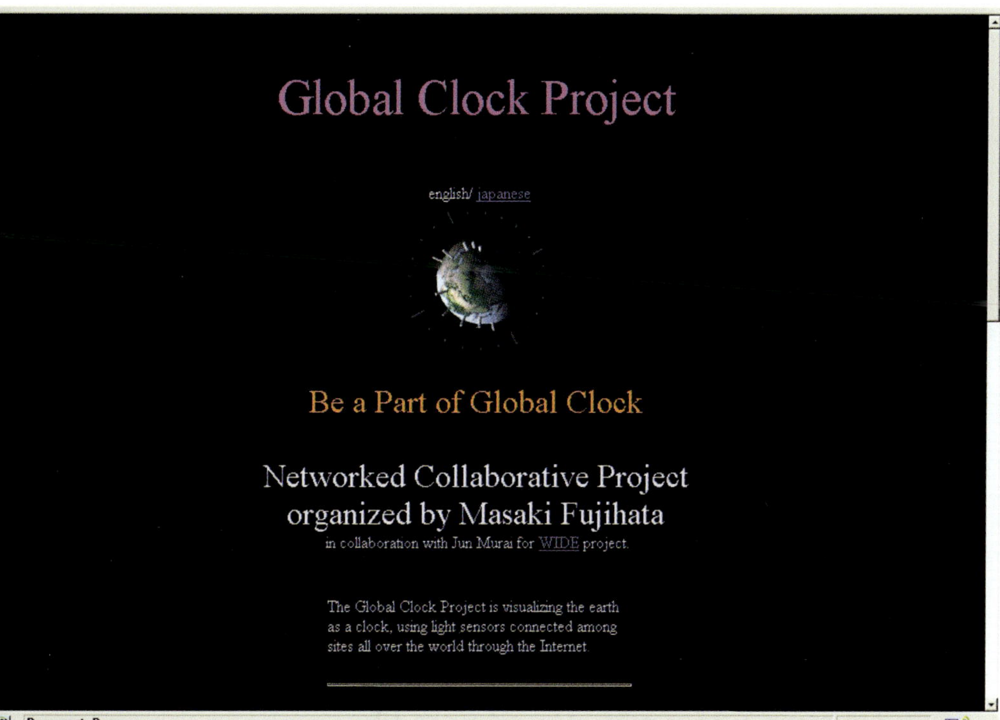

Masaki Fujihata
"The Global Clock Project", 1996

http://www.flab.mag.keio.ac.jp/GClock

MC SPOTLIGHT

McDonald's stellt nur ein Beispiel eines Phänomens des 20. Jahrhunderts dar – die progressive Übermacht der Weltökonomie und die Veränderungen im alltäglichen Leben, die von transnationalen Konzernen verursacht werden.

Aufgrund seiner prominenten Stellung in der Öffentlichkeit, die McDonald's mit großem Aufwand erreicht hat, ist dieser Fast-Food-Riese zu einem Symbol des aggressiven und sich immer weiter ausdehnenden Kapitalismus geworden, der die letzten Winkel des Globus und immer mehr Aspekte unserer Gesellschaft kolonisiert. Obwohl McDonald's eigentlich nur ein kleiner Teil im gesamten Puzzlebild ist, ist es zum Symbol geworden – sowohl für diejenigen, die dieses System unterstützen, als auch für diejenigen, die es ablehnen und Widerstand leisten wollen.

Doch Nestle, PepsiCo und Coca Cola, Unilever, Shell Oil, BP und Exxon, ICI, Sony, Gereal Motors, Murdoch's News International, IBM, Boeing, Dupont, Union Carbide und hunderte andere Konzerne und Finanzinstitutionen wie die Weltbank haben bereits ihre Herrschaftsgebiete abgesteckt und ihre Kontrolle über die Weltressourcen abgesichert. Gemeinsam und mit Unterstützung von politischen Institutionen bilden sie ein Netzwerk der Ausbeutung und der Unterdrückung, das die wenigen begünstigt, die von den Profiten leben und an den Hebel der Macht sitzen. Die Folgen kennen wir alle – Lohnsklaverei, Hunger, die Zerschlagung der Unabhängigkeit und Selbsterhaltung lokaler Gemeinschaften, Mißbrauch der Ressourcen, Umweltschäden und die Unterdrückung der echten Bedürfnisse und Wünsche vieler Menschen.

Doch überall, wo es Unterdrückung gibt, gibt es auch Unzufriedenheit, Kritik und Widerstand. Hier leuchtet „McSpotlight" auch andere Konzerne aus und hebt diejenigen hervor, die Widerstand leisten: einige der Bewegungen und Kämpfe rund um die Welt.

Wenn also diese Seite sich in erster Linie mit McDonald's auseinandersetzt, so gelten die angesprochenen Anliegen doch in gleichem Maß für alle anderen großen Konzerne bzw. selbst ganze Industriezweige.

McDonald's is just one example of a 20th century phenomenon – the progessive takeover of the world's economy and the transformation of people's everyday lives by Transnational Corporations. The fast food giant, because of its carefully and expensively manufactured public prominence, has become a symbol of an aggressive and continually expanding capitalism colonising all corner of the globe and ever more aspects of our society. McDonald's is a small part of the whole jigsaw but a symbol both for those who advocate such a system and for those who oppose and resist it. But Nestle, PepsiCo and Coca Cola, Unilever, Shell Oil, BP and Exxon, ICI, Sony, General Motors, Murdoch's News International, IBM, Boeing, Dupont, Union Carbide and hundreds of other corporations and financial institutions like the World Bank have each carved out their spheres of domination and control over the world's resource. Together, backed by governmental institutions, they constitute a fabric of exploitation and oppression to benefit those few who live off the profits and control the levers of decision-making. We all know the results – wage slavery, hunger, break up of the independence and self-sufficiency of local communities, abuse of resources, despoliation of the environoment and the suppression of people's genuine needs. But wherever there is oppression, there is dissatisfaction, criticism and resistance. Here we put the McSpotlight on other corporations, and also highlight those who stand up to them: some of the campaigns and struggles around the world. So although this site is primarily devoted to McDonald's, the issues raised can equally be applied to any of the other big corporations, or even to entire industries.

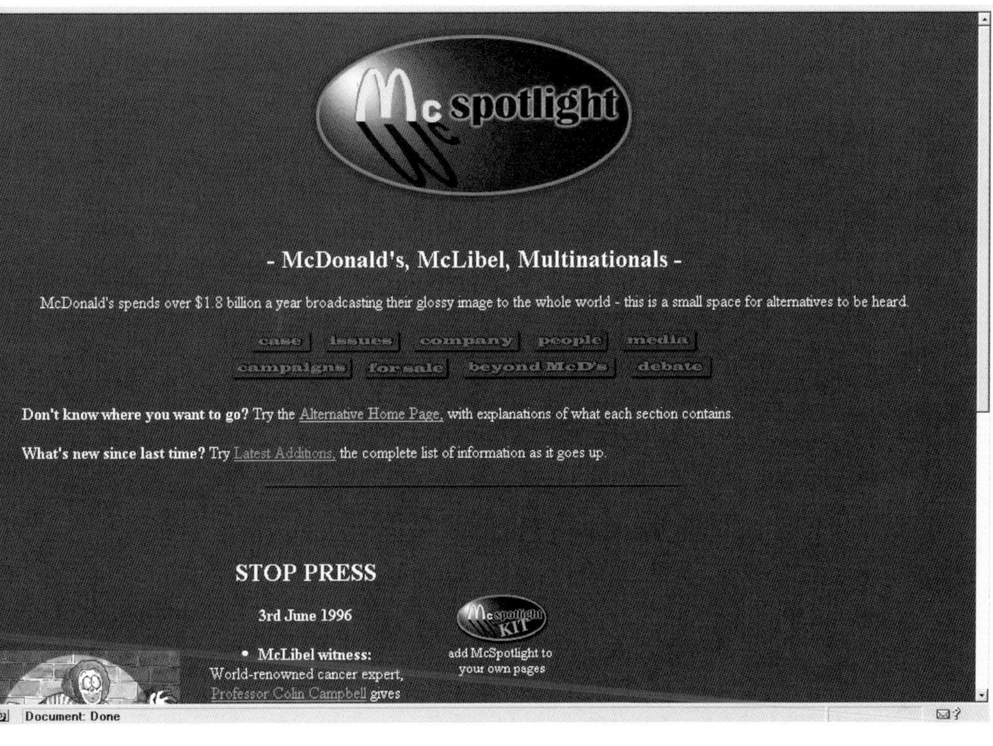

"McSpotlight"

 99

RON NEWMAN

Ron Newman arbeitete als Programmierer beim MIT Media Lab; seit Oktober arbeitet er bei New Frontiers Information Corporation. Versucht, gewisse Standards in Form von „The Good Net-Keeping Seal of Approval" für das Schreiben von Usenet-Newreaders, die mit dem Rest der Usenet-Gemeinschaft kompatibel sind, zu verbreiten.

Ron Newman worked as a computer programmer in the MIT Media Lab, now he is working for New Frontiers Information Corporation, doing World Wide Web work. The Good Net-Keeping Seal of Approval for Usenet Software is a set of standards he is trying to promote for writing Usenet news readers that are friendly to the rest of the Usenet community.

Die Scientology-Kirche ist eine Vereinigung, die unvernünftigerweise beschlossen hat, der Usenet- und Internetgemeinschaft den Krieg zu erklären. Seit Dezember 1994 haben die Anhänger dieser Kirche mehrmals Aktionen durchgeführt, die sich mit dem Prinzip der Redefreiheit im Netz nicht vereinbaren lassen. Es ist das Ziel dieser Webseite, diese Aktivitäten zu dokumentieren. Von Dezember 1994 bis jetzt haben Mitglieder und Anhänger dieser Kirche versucht, Nachrichten, die diese Kirche kritisieren, aus der Usenet-Diskussionsgruppe ‹alt.religion.scientology› zu entfernen, und zwar mittels unautorisierten Stornierbefehlen. d. h. mit speziell formatierten Nachrichten, die den Usenet-Server anweisen, eine bereits abgeschickte Nachricht zu löschen. Viele dieser Stornierbefehle enthielten die Behauptung, sie würden deswegen abgeschickt, um Mails zu löschen, die „Urheberrechts- und Firmengeheimnisverletzungen" enthielten. Schließlich organisierte sich eine Gruppe von „Netzbürgern", die als „Rabbit Hunters" bekannt wurden, um jene Personen, die diese Stornierbefehle abschickten, ausfindig zu machen und aufzuhalten. Im Winter 1995 ergingen Rechtsdrohungen von Anwälten der Scientology-Kirche mit der Forderung, die Remailer sollten den Zugang zu ‹alt.religion.scientology› und einer verwandten Newsgroup ‹alt.clearing.technology› blockieren, an viele anonyme Remailing-Dienste. Update, April 1996: Es scheint, das Scientology die Attacken auf die Remailers wieder aufgenommen hat.

The Church of Scientology is a religious cult which has unwisely decided to declare war against the Usenet and Internet communities. Since December of 1994, this Church and its followers have committed numerous acts that are hostile to the spirit of free speech on the Net. This web page is intended to document these activities.

Starting in December 1994 and continuing up to the present time, members or allies of the Church have tried to remove messages critical of the Church from the Usenet discussion group ‹alt.religion.scientology›. They did this by sending unauthorized cancels, which are specially-formatted messages instructing Usenet servers to delete a previously posted message. Many of these cancels contained a sentence claiming that they were issued to remove "copyright and trade secret violations." Eventually, a group of Netizens known as the "Rabbit Hunters" organized to find and stop the people who were sending these cancels.

During the winter of 1995, the Church of Scientology's lawyers sent legal threats to the operators of numerous anonymous-remailing services, demanding that the remailers block access to ‹alt.religion. scientology› and another related newsgroup ‹alt.clearing. technology›. Update, April 1996: Scientology appears to be renewing its attack on the remailers.

This page created by Ron Newman. The opinions expressed here are solely those of the author, and are not necessarily shared by CyberAccess Internet Communications, Inc.

Last revised Friday, May 31, 1996.

Massive spam attack hits alt.religion.scientology

Since May 19, 1996, the newsgroup alt.religion.scientology has been bombarded with thousands of spam postings from at least ten different accounts or pseudonyms. The spam consists of verbatim excerpts from copyrighted material found on the Church of Scientology's official web site. For more information on the spam, please visit Keith Spurgeon's web page entitled "Scientology ® Materials Posting Attack", and Frank Copeland's web page alt.religion.scientology Spam Attack.

NOTE TO READERS
from the editor of this web site

For at least the month of May, I am taking a much-needed break from tracking day-to-day happenings in the battle between Scientology and the Net. My friend Marina Chong is now maintaining a separate "update page" with the latest news. Please visit her page at http://www.icon.fi/~marina/rnewman/index.htm .

Thanks for all of your support over the past 14 months. -- Ron Newman

The Church of Scientology is a religious cult which has unwisely decided to declare war against the Usenet and Internet communities. Since December of 1994, this church and its followers have committed numerous acts that are hostile to the spirit of free speech on the Net. This web page is intended to document these

Document: Done

Ron Newman
"Scientology", 1994-1996

KEVIN McCURLEY

Kevin McCurley ist Informatiker, das Hauptinteresse seiner Forschungstätigkeit gilt Verschlüsselungssystemen, Netzwerksicherheit, parallelem Computing und rechnerischer Zahlentherorie. Er meint, Informationssicherheit müsse viel tiefgreifender in den gesamten Lehrplan der Informatik integriert werden, wenn sie Wirkung zeigen soll.

Kevin McCurley (USA) is a computer scientist whose primary research interests are in cryptology, network security, parallel computing, and computational number therory. He believes that information security needs to be more tightly integrated into the entire computer science curriculum in order for it to have any impact.

Wo ist die Zentrale von „DigiCrime"?

Wir haben kein physisch existentes Büro. Außerdem haben wir keine eigenen Computersysteme, da es einfacher ist und uns viel billiger kommt, wenn wir die Computer von anderen verwenden.

Sucht „DigiCrime" zur Zeit Mitarbeiter?

Nein, wir haben beschlossen, die Kohle für uns zu behalten.

Welche Fähigkeiten werden bei einer solchen Firma benötigt?

Diejenigen, die du wahrscheinlich nicht hast. Qualifikationen sind u. a. ein blühender Zynismus in bezug auf Informationssicherheit und messerscharfe Schlagfertigkeit.

Welche Auszeichnungen und Preise hat „DigiCrime" bereits gewonnen?

Nach einem Gutachten einer Jury der Nicht-Gleichwertigen erschien „DigiCrime" im „CNN International World, Business Today" am 12. Oktober 1995 und in „InfoWeek" am 20. November 1995. Es wurde außerdem am 1. November 1995 als „Cool Site of the Day" ausgewählt und gehört zu den „obersten 5 % aller Webseiten".

Was ist „DigiCrime" genau?

Wenn du noch nicht draufgekommen bist – „DigiCrime" ist ein Witz. Es ist ein verrückter Versuch unsererseits, uns über die Verletzbarkeit, an der unsere Gesellschaft auf dem Weg ins Informationszeitalter leidet, lustig zu machen. Auf der anderen Seite ist es kein Witz, daß die Zukunft unserer Gesellschaft von der Fähigkeit, Information zu schützen, abhängt. Daran arbeiten wir im wirklichen Leben.

Fördert oder betreibt „DigiCrime" kriminelle Aktivitäten?

Auf keinen Fall. Für wie blöd hältst du uns? Uns liegt nichts daran, dem FBI in die Quere zu kommen.

Where is the headquarters of DigiCrime?
We have no physical offices. We also do not maintain our own computer systems, since we find it cheaper and easier to use other people's computers.
Is DigiCrime hiring at this time?
No, we've decided to keep the wealth to ourselves.
What kind of skills are required for such a company?
Probably the kind you don't have. Qualifications include a healthy cynicism about information security, and a rapier wit. What recognition and awards has DigiCrime won?
Having been judged by a jury of non-peers, DigiCrime has appeared on CNN International World Business Today on October 12, 1995, and InfoWeek on November 20, 1995. It has been selected as "Cool Site of the Day" on November 1, 1995, and has also been selected among the "top 5% of all web sites".
What exactly is DigiCrime?
In case you have not figured it out yet, DigiCrime is a joke. It is our twisted attempt to poke fun at the vulnerability that our society suffers from as we move into the information age. On the other hand it's not a joke in the sense that the future of our society depends on the ability to protect information. That's what we're working on in real life.
Does DigiCrime encourage or engage in criminal activity? Certainly not. What kind of fools do you take us for? We have no desire to cross the FBI.

Welcome from file:///C|/Program Files/Website/htdocs/prixdi/wwwwin.htm. So much for privacy.

DigiCrime, Inc.

A full service criminal computer hacking organization.

Reporter: *Why do you rob banks?*
Willie Sutton: *That's where the money is.*

Now with Java and JavaScript. Be afraid. Be **very** afraid.

NEWS FLASH: DigiCrime obtains <u>interesting digital IDs</u> from VeriSign.

Some of us working on information security issues have noticed that there are many vulnerabilities of information systems that can easily be exploited by a technologically advanced criminal element. We don't advocate doing this, but we often find it both amusing and alarming to ponder the possibilities. Therefore...

We are pleased to offer the following products and services to our customers:

- <u>Internet Shoplifting Network</u> **NEW!**
- <u>New products</u>: Escrowed fax document shredder and Affinity credit card program. **NEW!**
- <u>stolen computational services at wholesale prices</u>. SALE!
- an <u>airline rerouting service</u> (NOTE: we bear no responsibility for <u>this incident</u>).
- a <u>wealth redistribution service</u> (NOTE: we bear no responsibility for <u>this incident</u>).
- a <u>phone rerouting service</u> (NOTE: we bear no responsibility for <u>this incident</u>).
- a <u>telephone wiretap service</u> (NOTE: we bear no responsibility for <u>this incident</u>).
- <u>Free legal opinions on ITAR</u>.
- a <u>custom pornographic blackmail service</u> (NOTE: we bear no responsibility for <u>this incident</u>).
- a <u>password generation service</u> (NOTE: we do not endorse <u>Bob</u>, but we admire the design).
- <u>Electronic money laundering service</u>.

Document: Done

Kevin McCurley
"DigiCrime"

ANDRUID KERNE

Andruid Kerne (USA) studierte unter Anthony Braxton und Alvin Lucier zeitgenössische Musikkomposition und Performance; Forschungstätigkeit am International Centre for African Music and Dance an der University of Ghana. Untersucht derzeit Mensch/Maschine-Interface als Sichtbarmachung der Kultur am Center for Digital Multimedia an der New York University.

ANDRUID KERNE (USA), studied with Anthony Braxton and Alvin Lucier, two pioneers in contemporary music composition and performance. Research affiliation with the International Centre for African Music and Dance at the University of Ghana, currently doing research investigating human-computer interface as a manifestation of culture at MYU's center for Digital Multimedia.

In den letzten zwei Jahren wurde das World Wide Web als befreiendes Medium gefeiert, das die Macht hat, alle Menschen zusammenzubringen. Doch eine Karte der Internet-Serviceanbieter in Afrika zeigt, daß dieser Kontinent nur eine geringe Beteiligung aufweist. In beiden Zusammenhängen – sowohl in der traditionellen Kultur der Ewe als auch in der Cyberkultur – bedeutet das einen wesentlichen Verlust. Mit einer gewissen Ironie werden diese Verluste durch „Coded Messages: CHAINS" ins Gegenteil verkehrt. Mit dieser Installation wird zum ersten Mal die immens reiche Kultur des Ewe-Volkes aus Ghana ins World Wide Web gebracht; doch die Menschen, die hier dargestellt werden, haben diese Installation noch nie gesehen, und solange das Internet ein Medium der technologisch Priviligierten bleibt, werden sie sie möglicherweise auch nie sehen können.

Den Ausgangspunkt für diese Web-Installation bildeten die gleichnamigen interkulturellen Performances, die 1994 in Ghana stattfanden.

In „Coded Messages: „CHAINS" begegnet der Besucher Darstellungen aus einer anderen Kultur, die eine Deutung seines eigenen „Codes" beinhalten. Mit unseren „Guerilla"-Links zu multinationalen Seiten im World Wide Web konfrontieren wir den Beobachter mit dem Code, der diese Kultur fördert. Die Teilnehmer an „Coded Messages: CHAINS" überqueren interaktiv die Grenzen jener Kontexte, die wir präsentieren.

In the last two years, the World Wide Web has been espoused as a liberating medium which has the power to bring all people together. Yet a map of Internet service providers in Africa shows that this continent participates marginally. In both contexts – traditional Ewe culture and cyberculture – the loss is paramount. In a twist of irony, "Coded Messages: CHAINS" reverses those losses. This installation brings the immensely rich culture of the Ewe people of Ghana to the World Wide Web for the first time; yet, the people who are being represented have never seen this installation, and, as long as the Internet remains a medium for the technologically privileged, may never do so.

This Web-installation is based on the 1994 intercultural performances of the same name that were held in Ghana.

In "Coded Messages: CHAINS" the visitor meets perfomances from another cultural world, with an interpretation of their code. In our "guerilla" links to multinational sites on the World Wide Web, we bring the viewer face to face with the "code" that this culture promotes. Participant/visitors of "Coded Messages: CHAINS" interactively cross the boundaries between the contexts we present.

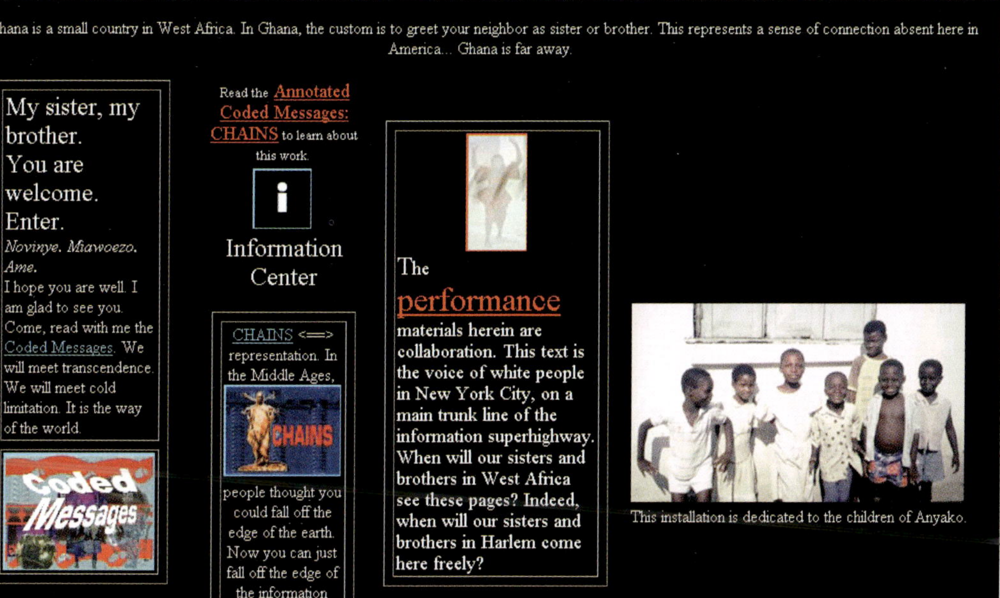

Andruid Kerne
"Coded Messages: CHAINS"

JOEY ANUFF

Joey Anuff gibt sich gerne als „Duke of URL“ aus, ist ehemaliger Produktionsassistent von „HotWired“. Ana Marie Cox ist Chefredakteurin von „Suck“. Die „Society of Stucksters“, die „Suck“ zusammenstellt, besteht aus T. Jay Fowler, Heather Havrilesky, Sean Welch, Carl Steadman und Brady Clark .

Joey Anuff masquerades as the Duke of URL, was formerly a Production Assistant at "HotWired". Ana Marie Cox is Senior Editor of "Suck". Jay Fowler, Heather Havrilesky, Sean Welch, Carl Steadman and Brady Clark form "The Society of Sucksters" putting together "Suck".

Unsere Mission:

Aus Scheiße wird großartiges Düngemittel, aber nur ein Bauer kann daraus eine Mahlzeit machen.

Mit diesem Gedanken im Hinterkopf präsentieren wir nun „Suck“, ein Experiment – wir provozieren, betreiben ätzenden Dekonstruktionismus und Kreissägenjournalistik. Kathodenverwirrte Netsurfer strömen in Scharen zu den seichten Wassern – „Suck“ ist die schmutzige Nadel, die im Sand versteckt ist. Wolltest du Feedback? Halte die Ohren zu und schütze deinen Rücken ... es will dich auch. Doch „Suck“ ist mehr als nur ein Medienstreich. Viel mehr. Bei „Suck“ verfolgen wir das Prinzip, wonach jemand sich immer so positioniert, daß er alles Wertvolle in dieser Welt systematisch für sich einstreift, um damit zu Geld, zu Macht und/oder zur Erfüllung seines Egos zu gelangen.

Wir wollen dieser „Jemand“ sein.

Our Mission:
Shit makes great fertilizer, but it takes a farmer to turn it into a meal. With that thought in mind, we present Suck, an experiment in provocation, mordant deconstructionism, and buzz-saw journalism. Cathode-addled netsurfers flock to shallow waters – Suck is the dirty syringe@hidden in the sand. You wanted feedback? Cover your ears and watch your back ... it wants you too. But Suck is more than a media prank. Much more. At Suck, we abide by the principle which dictates that somebody will always position himself or herself to systematically harvest anything of value in this world for the sake of money, power and/or ego-fulfillment.
We aim to be that somebody.

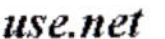

Suck.

"a fish, a barrel, and a smoking gun"
for 3 June 1996. Updated every WEEKDAY.

use.net

They ride into town, pitch a

tent, and fill it up with

hard-luck country folk at two

dollars a head. They sell 'em

big words and the promise of a

better place. And then, after a

night of miracles and a whole

86% of 8K (at 487 bytes/sec)

Joey Anuff
"Suck"

MARIA WINSLOW

Maria Winslow has a background in computer science from the University of North Carolina, and founded an Internet software company, Prominence Dot Com, in 1995. She is among a core group of early Java developers, and is currently co-authoring two books on Java for Prentice-Hall.

Maria Winslow (USA) studierte Informatik an der University of North Carolina; gründete 1995 eine Internet-Softwarefirma, Prominence Dot Com. Sie gehört zum Kreis der ersten Java-Entwickler und schreibt derzeit mit an zwei Bücher über Java für Prentice Hall.

„Electro Magnetic Poetry" wurde im September 1995 geschrieben, es ist mein erstes Experiment mit der Java-Programmiersprache von Sun Microystems. Es ist eine interaktive Web-Anwendung, mit der ein Anwender eigene Gedichte mittels „Drag & Drop" aus einer Wörtersammlung kreieren kann. Den Quellcode habe ich zur Verfügung gestellt, um zu demonstrieren, wie man in Java Graphiktechniken verwenden kann, um ein gleitendes „Drag & Drop" zu erreichen. Diesen Quellcode darf auch jeder kopieren, der ihn haben will. Dieses Applet wurde von „The Magnetic Poetry Kit", einer kunstvollen Sammlung von Kühlschrankmagneten, die von Dave Kapell stammen, inspiriert.
Als nächstes werde ich eine Galerie mit den Gedichten, die mit diesem Applet hergestellt wurden, zusammenstellen.

Electro Magnetic Poetry was my first experiment with the Java programming language from Sun Microsystems, and was written in September of 1995. It is an interactive Web application that allows the user to drag and drop custom poems from a collection of words. I have made the source code available to demonstrate graphics techniques to achieve smooth drag and drop in Java, and anyone who wishes to do so is free to copy it. This applet was inspired by the Magnetic Poetry Kit by Dave Kapell, an artful collection of refridgerator magnets.

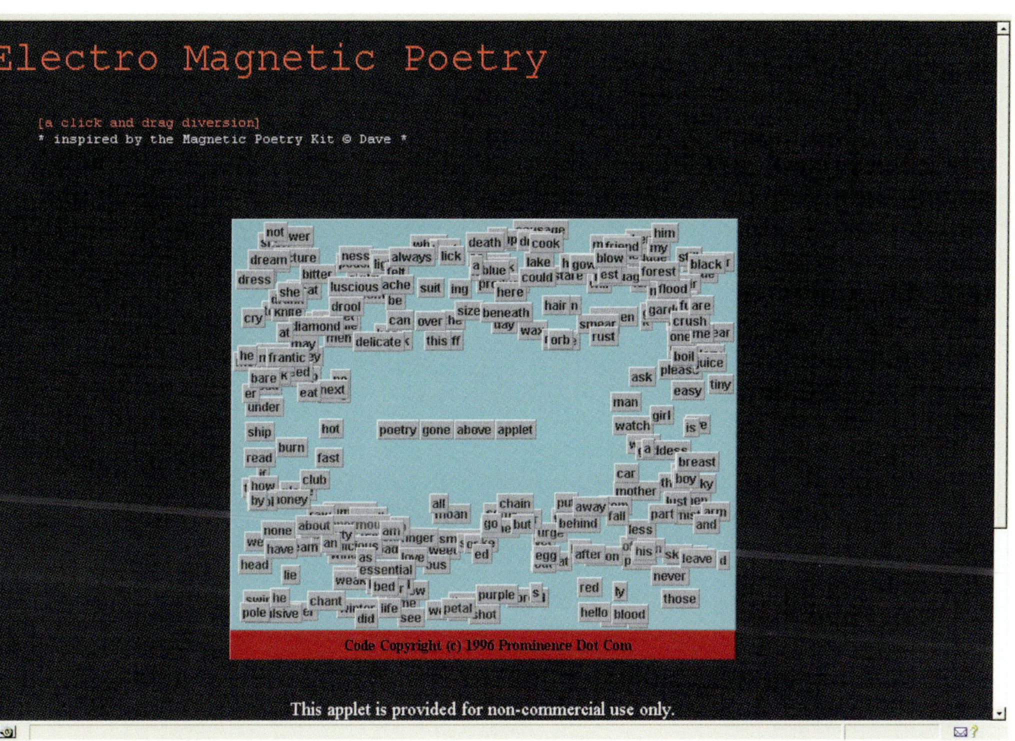

Maria Winslow
"Electro Magnetic Poetry"

http://prominence.com/java/poetry

LISA HUTTON

Lisa Hutton (USA), geb. 1959, Studiumabschluß 1979 mit Schwerpunkt Illustration an der Ivy School of Professional Art, Pittsburgh; 1996 BA in Visueller Kunst mit Schwerpunkt Computermedien, Nebenstudium der Literatur an der University of California, San Diego.

Lisa Hutton (USA), born 1959, degree specializing in illustration at Ivy School of Professional Art, Pittsburgh in 1979, currently at University of California, San Diego. BA in Visual Art with Computer Media Emphasis and a minor in Literature Writing (graduation June 1996).

Die Webseite „Variety is ..." beinhaltet derzeit fünf Module:
*„Cyber*babes (A Fan Dance for Adults)": Cyber*babes setzt sich mit den jüngsten vom US-Kongreß verabschiedeten Regelungen zum Telecommunications Act von 1996 auseinander. Inhaltlich beschäftigt sich diese Arbeit mit der Grundidee der Zensur. Bilder von „Cyberbabes" und URL-Links zu anderen Webseiten kombinieren männliche und weibliche Körper in einem anregenden Fächertanz, wobei „obszöne" Nacktheit kurz gezeigt und gleich wieder verdeckt wird. Die WWW-Links außerhalb meiner Seiten wählte ich aus zwei Kategorien aus. Die erste Kategorie untersucht Inhalt und Kommentare des Telecommunications Act – eine Sammlung empfohlener Literatur. Die zweite Kategorie beinhaltet Links zum gegenteiligen Kontext, indem der Besucher zu anderem „obszönen" Material im Internet verwiesen wird. Dazu gehören Themen wie die konsumeristische Motivation des Internets, die amerikanische „Political Correctness", Foto-Kriegsdokumentation, die Suche nach Pornographie im Internet und die Ausbeutung von Wildtieren.*
„Poems from the Fishwrap": Dieser Teil beinhaltet Zufallsgedichte und Bilder. Die Zufallsgedichte werden mit einer Methode erzeugt, die Motive aus dem frühen 20. Jahrhundert mittels Zeitungspapier oder „fishwrap" (da Fische am Markt in Zeitungspapier eingewickelt wurden) aufgreift.
„Having Trouble with Maria": Dieser Teil setzt sich mit dem Konflikt zwischen den USA und Mexico am Tijuana-Grenzübergang auseinander.
„Dada Boom Boom": Dieser Teil beinhaltet drei Module auf Basis der Dada-Prinzipien.
„Hot Links": In diesem Modul findet man Links zu jenen anderen Webseiten, die mir gefallen.

The web site, "Variety is ..." currently contains five modules:
"Cyber*babes (A Fan Dance For Adults)" explores the recent laws promulgated by congress in the Telecommunications Act of 1996. The content of the piece explores the notion of censorship by using changeable imagery of "cyberbabes" and URL links combining male and female bodies in a titillating fan dance where "obscene" nudity is flashed and then covered. The links to the WWW outside my site are chosen from two categories. The first category explores the content and commentary surrounding the Telecommunications Act – a collection of suggested readings. The second categroy provides links of an opposing context by sending the visitor to some of the other "obscene" material available on the Internet. These include the Internet's consumerist motivations, American "political correctness", photographic war documentation, the search for pornography on the Internet, and the exploitation of wild animals.
Poems from the Fishwrap: This piece contains random poetry and images created by a method derived from early 20th century motifs using a newspaper, or "fishwrap".
Having trouble with Maria ...: This piece explores the conflict of America and Mexico at the Tijuana border crossing.
Dada Boom Boom: This piece contains three modules based on the principles of Dada.
Hot Links: This module provides links to sites I've enjoyed.

VARIETY IS...

by lisa

CYBER*BABES (a fan dance for adults)

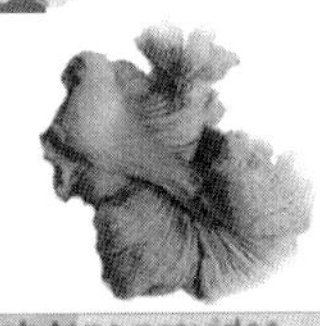

DADA BOOMBOOM

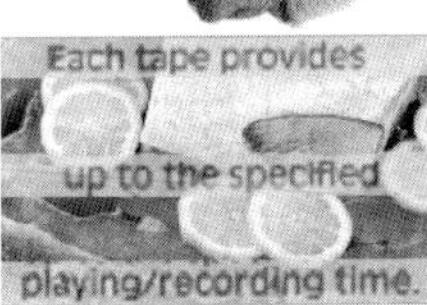

Poems From The Fishwrap

My Life As A Clock

Reading file...Done

Netscape - [Electro Magnetic Poetry]

Lisa Hutton
"Variety is ..."

STUART MOULTHROP

Stuart Moulthrop ist Associate Professor an der School of Communications Design, University of Baltimore: „Die Paranoia, die bei den Anwendern dieser Technologie oft festgestellt wird, ist nicht weiter bemerkenswert. Es ist nicht anders als der Anfang, der Vorstoß zur Entdeckung, daß alles mit allem verbunden ist, alles in der Schöpfung ...“

Stuart Moulthrop is Associate Professor at the School of Communications Design, University of Baltimore: "About the paranoia often noted in users of this technology, there is nothing remarkable. It is nothing less than the onset, the leading edge, of the discovery that everything is connected, everything in the Creation ..."

„Hegirascope" ist ein Werk der Hypertextfiktion, das für das World Wide Web konzipiert ist. Es ist kein Roman, und es wird auch nicht unbedingt deinen Erwartungen in Bezug auf interaktive Fiktion entsprechen. Ich erforsche die Formen des narrativen Schreibens – und die Geschichten –, die aus dem Web-Hypertext entstehen und gut in diese Umgebung passen. Im Moment ist das jedenfalls meine Flucht, mein „Hegira". Was man bei „Hegirascope" sieht, ist eigentlich nur die Hälfte eines anderen Projekts, auf das ich mich langsam hinbewege (Herbst 1995). Was als Experiment begonnen hat, sieht jetzt eher nach einer Studie aus, obwohl ich deren Gegenstand noch nicht klar benennen kann. Die Netscape-HTML-Umgebung gefällt mir, und vom Web als Liefersystem bin ich fest überzeugt. Doch die Schranken, die sowohl Netscape als auch das Web auferlegen, sind nicht leicht zu durchbrechen. Während ich jetzt schreibe, setzen die Netscapees an, mit den Ketten des Daseins wieder zu rasseln. „Hegirascope" verwendet den „META"-Tag von Netscape, um „client pull" zu ermöglichen. Das bedeutet, das ein Wort nicht still bleibt. Jede Seite in diesem Text ist so programmiert., daß sie nach einer Verzögerung von nur weniger Sekunden automatisch der nächsten Seite Platz macht (es gibt natürlich Ausnahmen). Diesen zeitlich festgelegten Übergang kann man umgehen, indem man eines der Links auf der Seite verwendet: nach der Öffnungssequenz gibt es fast auf jeder Seite Links. Um zu verstehen, worum es hier eigentlich geht, sollte man es am besten einfach ausprobieren. Solvitur ambulando, caveat lector, gute Reise.

"Hegirascope" is a work of hypertext fiction intended for the World Wide Web. This is not a novel, nor will it necessarily meet your expectations about interactive fictions. I am trying to explore forms of narrative writing – and stories – that emerge from Web hypertext and seem well suited to that environment. For the moment anyway, that is my hegira. What you're seeing is at most half of something else toward which I'm presently slouching (Fall, 1995). What started as an experiment now looks more like a study, though for what I can't yet say. I like the Netscape-HTML environment and believe strongly in the Web as a delivery system. Yet the constraints of both are heavy, and at this writing the Netscapees are about to rattle the chain of being yet again. "Hegirascope" employs the Netscape "META" tag to enable "client pull," which means that the word does not keep still. Almost every page in this text is programmed to yield automatically to another page after a delay of some seconds (with exceptions, of course). You may override this timed transition by using one of the links on the page: after the opening sequence, almost every page has links. To understand what this is all about, you really have to go and do. Solvitur ambulando, caveat lector, have a nice trip.

Stuart Moulthrop,
"Hegirascope" 1995

TIMOTHY LEARY

Die Timothy Leary Homepage heißt nicht nur so; sie wird ihrer Bezeichnung ganz und gar gerecht. Neben den bewährten Informationseinheiten einer „Homepage" ließ der Guru sich tatsächlich online in seine Privatgemächer schauen. Ließ insofern, weil die Timothy Leary Homepage seit Anfang Juni zu einem Ausstellungsambiente der besonderen Art geraten ist: Timothy Leary hat Anfang Juni seinen letzten „Trip" angetreten. Im September soll seine Asche in einer Kapsel ihre Reise in den Orbit antreten. In eine Umlaufbahn der Erde gebracht, wird „Leary" einige Erdumdrehungen drehen, bevor die Kapsel in der Erdatmosphäre verglühen wird. Für Timothy Learys Homepage haben seine Gestalter eine Videodokumentation seines Todes angekündigt, ein letztes Home-Video, das in Learys Sinn die Untersuchung über die Soziologie (genauer: den Voyeurismus) der Netzgemeinde wohl fortsetzen wird.

The Timothy Leary Homepage is not only the name of this Website, it is also a complete and accurate description of the contents. In addition to the information a homepage commonly provides, the guru actually permitted an on-line glimpse of his private home. "Permitted", in this case, refers to the fact that the Timothy Leary Homepage has become a special type of exhibition environment since the beginning of June this year: in early June, Timothy Leary set out on his last "trip". In September, his ashes are to be sent into orbit around the earth in a capsule, where "Leary" will circle the earth several times before the capsule burns up in the earth's atmosphere. The makers of Timothy Leary's Homepage have announced a video documentation of his death: the ultimate home video intended to continue the study of the sociology (or to be more precise: the voyeurism) of the Net community in keeping with Leary's intentions.

Timothy Leary
"Timothy Leary Homepage", 1996

http://www.leary.com

5 3 3
ILFORD
13   13A   14   14A
ILFORD
17   17A   18   18A
FORD   400 DELTA PROFES
21   21A   22   22 A

400 DELTA PROFESSIONAL 4 5 3 3
15 15A 16 16A
DELTA PROFESSIONAL 4 5 3 3
19 19A 20 20A
NAL 4 5 3 3 ILFORD
23 23A 24 24A

STATEMENT
OF THE INTERACTIVE ART JURY
Jurybegründung Interaktive Kunst

Die Jury wählte für die Goldene Nica „Global Interior Project" von Masaki Fujihata, ein vernetztes Skulptur-werk, das eine Beziehung zwischen virtuellen und physischen Räumen und Gegenständen herstellt. Für die zwei Auszeichnungen wählten wir „Motion Phone" von Scott Sona Snibbe, ein Software-Werk für zwei Teilnehmer, das ein neues Medium für persönliche Gespräche in nicht-verbaler Form bietet, und „Scaven-gers" von Louis-Philippe Demers und Bill Vorn, ein robotisches Werk, das unsere Beziehung zu unseren jüngst autonom gewordenen Schöpfungen provokant in Frage stellt.

Unter den prämierten Werken waren einige mit einer Internet- bzw. Netzwerkkomponente („Global Interior Project", „Dialog with the Knowbotic South", „sense:less", „where I can see my house ...", „Paral-lel Mesmerization ..." und „Eye to Eye"). Fasziniert haben uns außerdem Werke, die Kanäle zwischen zwei („Motion Phone", „Eye to Eye", „Cross-active Sy-stem" und „Inter Dis-communication Machine") oder mehreren Teilnehmern („Global Interior Project", „where i can see my house ..." und „Three Men Three Legs") öffneten.

Viele Werke betonten die physische Installation („Glo-bal Interior Project", „Scavengers", „Resident", „Par-allel Mesmerization...", „where i can see my house ...", „sense:less" und „Dialogue with the Knowbotic South"), und setzten sich oft mit dem Verhältnis der Installation zum virtuellen bzw. vernetzten Raum aus-

For the Golden Nica, the Jury chose "Global In-terior Project" by Masaki Fujihata, a networked sculptural work which builds a relationship bet-ween virtual and physical spaces and objects. For the second prize, we chose "Motion Phone" by Scott Sona Snibbe, a soft-ware work for two participants which offers a new medium for in-timate conversation in a nonverbal form; and "Scavengers" by Louis-Philippe Demers and Bill Vorn, a robotic work which poses provocative questions about our relationship to our newly autonomous creations.

Among the winners and honorable mentions were a number of works with an Internet or network component ("Global Interior Project", "Dialog with the Knowbotic South", "sense: less", "where i can see my house ...", "Parallel Mesmerization..." and "Eye to Eye"). We were also attracted to works that opened channels between two ("Motion Phone", "Eye to Eye", "Cross-active System" and "Inter Dis-communi-cation Machine") or more participants ("Global Interior Project", "where I can see my house..." and "Three Men three legs").

Many of the works emphasized physical instal-lation ("Global Interior Project", "Scavengers", "Resident", "Parallel Mesmerization", "where I can see my house...", "sense:less" and "Dialog with the Knowbotic South"), often investigating the relation of the installation to virtual or networked space. There were works that represented varying kinds of immersion ("sense:less", "Dialog with the Knowbotic South", "Inter Dis-communication Machine", "Cross-Active System" and "In Corpus"). Many works, including the immersive works just mentioned, fell into the categories of virtual reality and telepresence ("Global Interior Project", "where I can see my house..." and "Virtual Wheelchair"). Works dealing with robotics ("Scavengers", "where I can see my house..." and "Parallel Mesmerization..." and "Three men three legs") and artificial life forms and agents ("Resident", "sense:less" and "Dialog with the Knowbotic South") were well represented. There were also a number of works with unusual or innovative interfaces ("Virtual Wheelchair", "Eye to Eye" and others already mentioned). These works also dealt with issues of the body and notions of the "normal" (as did "Rehearsal of Memory"). More generally, a number of these works treat interactivity on many levels, often including critical and conceptual approaches. We can also see a high degree of humor (and some irony) in a many of them. And most importantly, all of these works take an open, expansive approach to the interaction and participation of their users and audiences.

einander. Unterschiedliche Arten der Immersion waren ebenfalls vertreten („sense:less", „Dialogue with the Knowbotic South", „Inter Dis-communication Machine", „Cross-active System" und „In Corpus"). Viele Werke, u. a. die erwähnten immersiven Werke, gehörten zu den Kategorien der virtuellen Wirklichkeit und Telepräsenz („Global Interior Project", „where i can see my house..." und „Virtual Wheelchair"). Stark vertreten waren Werke, die Robotik („Scavengers", „where i can see my house...", und Parallel Mesmerization ...") und Formen und Agenten Künstlichen Lebens („Resident", „sense:less" und „Dialogue with the Knowbotic South") behandelten. Außerdem waren einige Werke mit ungewöhnlichen oder innovativen Interfaces dabei („Virtual Wheelchair", „Eye to Eye" und andere, bereits erwähnte Werke). Diese Werke setzten sich auch mit dem Thema "Körper" oder der Vorstellung des „Normalen" auseinandersetzten (wie auch „Rehearsal of Memory").

Generell wird Interaktivität von einigen dieser Werken auf vielen Ebenen behandelt, wobei die Künstler oft einen kritischen und konzeptuellen Zugang zeigen. Außerdem entdeckten wir in vielen Werken ein hohes Maß an Humor (und manchmal Ironie). Und am wichtigsten ist, daß all diese Werke einen offenen, expansiven Zugang zur Interaktion und Beteiligung der Teilnehmer und des Publikums aufweisen.

MASAKI FUJIHATA

Masaki Fujihata (J), geb. 1956; BA 1979 und MA 1981 an der Tokyo University of Arts/Design Course; 1982–1990 Karriere in der Wirtschaft (SEDIC Inc., FROGS Inc.); Vorstandsmitglied der Japan Animation Film Association, seit 1987 Mitglied von ASIFA; seit 1990 Associate Professor an der Fakultät für Umweltinformation an der Keio University.

Masaki Fujihata (J), born 1956; BA in 1979 and MA in 1981 at Tokyo University of Arts/design course; 1982–1990 business career (SEDIC Inc., FROGS Inc.), board member of Japan Animation Film Association, since 1987 Member of ASIFA, since 1990 Associate Professor, Faculty of Environmental Information at Keio University.

INTERACTIVE ART

„Global Interior Project" ist ein vernetztes Environment für mehrere Anwender, in dem Menschen einander begegnen, miteinander reden und die Metaphysik der Wirklichkeit entdecken können.

Als Beispiel für eine Gestaltung der Kommunikationsmedien zeigt das Projekt Möglichkeiten, wie Menschen auf eine neue Weise zusammenkommen können. Das Projekt will den Metamechanismus einer elektronischen Vernetzung von Raum und Kommunikation visualisieren, wobei ein Wechsel zwischen virtuellem und realem Raum stattfindet. „Real" bezieht sich hier auf den eigenen Wohnraum, wo man mit einem Gerät, wie z. B. einem Trackball, eine virtuelle Welt manipulieren und die errechneten Bilder auf dem Bildschirm sehen kann. Die Möglichkeit, ein Modell als greifbaren Gegenstand aufzustellen, der die Architektur/Konstruktion des virtuellen Raums repräsentiert, ist ein besonderes Merkmal dieses Projekts. Konstruiert wird das Modell aus computergesteuerten Schachteln mit je einer eigenen Tür. Der Status der Tür signalisiert die Anwesenheit eines anderen Menschen im virtuellen Raum. So ist es möglich, eine außerordentliche Verbindung zwischen dem Virtuellen und dem Realen herzustellen.

"Global Interior Project" is a networked multiuser virtual environment where people can meet, talk and discover the metaphysics of reality.

It is an example of communication media design, which demonstrates new possibilities of connecting people in a new way. The aim of this project is to visualize the meta-mechanism of electronically networked space and communication, while moving back and forth between "real" and virtual space. Hence, the word real means your living space, where you can manipulate a virtual world with a device such as a trackball and see the calculated image on your screen. A remarkable feature of this project is the possibility of setting up a model as an actual object to represent the architecture/construction of virtual space. It is constructed with computer-controlled boxes that have an actual door. The status of this door signals the existence of someone in virtual space. As a result, it is possible to make an extraordinary link between the virtual and the real.

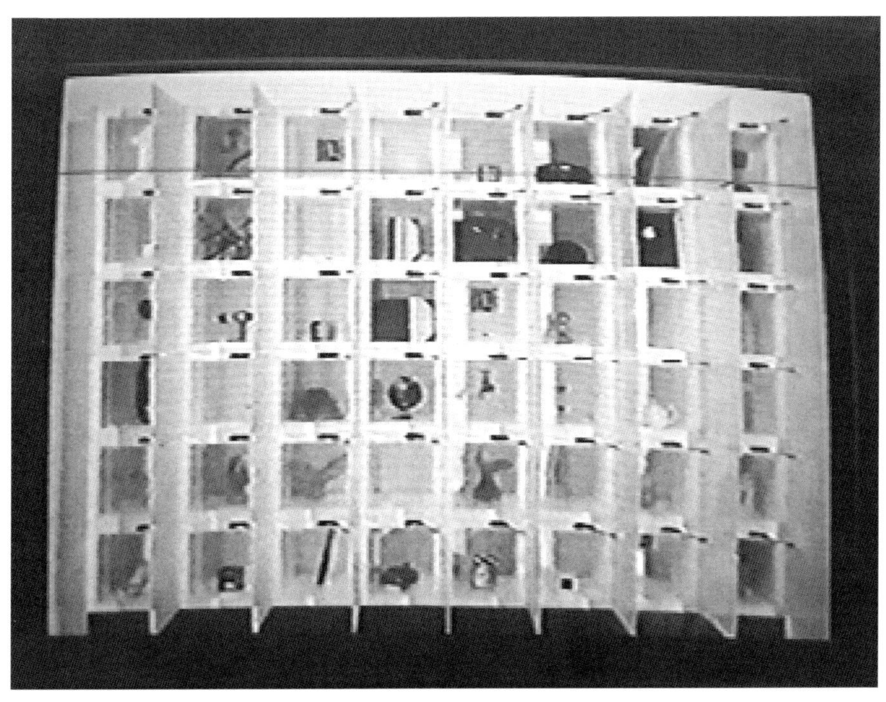

Masaki Fujihata
"Global Interior Project", 1995

Das Projekt im Detail

Die vom virtuellen Raum errechneten Bilder werden an einem Terminal, dem „Cubical Terminal", dargestellt und manipuliert; die Schachteln, die den virtuellen Raum repräsentieren, sind die „Matrix Cubes". Am „Cubical Terminal" können die Mitwirkenden das eigene virtuelle Selbst im virtuellen Raum manipulieren, während ihre Körper in der realen Welt bleiben. Der virtuelle Raum wird bei diesem Projekt mit einer gewissen Anzahl kubischer Räume gestaltet, die alle miteinander verbunden sind. Die Inneneinrichtung der Räume ähnelt dem Inneren des „Cubical Terminal". Vom „Cubical Terminal" aus navigierend können sich die Mitwirkenden von einem Raum zum anderen bewegen.

„Matrix Cubes" bestehen aus gestapelten Schachteln mit Türen. Diese stellen die Verbindungen zwischen virtuellen Räumen, zwischen aufgestapelten Terminals oder zwischen Stapeln in der realen Welt dar. So fungieren die „Matrix Cubes" als eine Miniatur/ Metapher/ Karte des virtuellen Raums. Ein Mitwirkender kann in diesem System dreifach existieren: als reales Ich, als virtuelles Ich und als virtuelles Ich in der realen Welt. Zum Beispiel bewirkt eine Handlung, die mit dem Bild des realen Ichs durch den virtuellen Raum ausgeführt wird, eine Reaktion des virtuellen Ichs: Wo bist du? Was bedeutet deine Adresse? Wo befindest du dich? Wovon lebst du? Die gesamte Topologie der eigenen Existenz wird durcheinandergebracht.

Der „Cubical Terminal"

Mitwirkende können mit dieser virtuellen Welt mittels eines „Cubical Terminal", das aus einer 3D-Graphikworkstation und einem Projektor besteht, interagieren. Das Terminal ist mit dem Server verbunden. Menschen können einander in dieser virtuellen Welt begegnen und miteinander reden, selbst wenn sie von getrennten Orten aus Zugang dazu haben.

Ein in Echtzeit übersetztes Bild, das auf die Bewegungen, die der Teilnehmer mit dem Trackball ausführt, reagiert, wird auf den Bildschirm im „Cubical Terminal" projiziert. Der Teilnehmer sieht das Bild durch das Fenster des „Cubical Terminal". Ein Bild eines kubischen Raumes mit einem Fenster auf jeder Seite wird im Inneren des „Cubical Terminal" projiziert. In jedem Raum befindet sich ein Gegenstand, wie z. B. ein

Details of the Project

The terminal for displaying and manipulating calculated images of virtual space is called the "Cubical Terminal", and the boxes representing virtual space are called "Matrix Cubes". At the "Cubical Terminal", participants can manipulate themselves in virtual space, while their bodies remain in a real world.

Virtual space is designed in this project with a certain number of cubical rooms, and all the rooms are interconnected. The interior design of each room resembles the interior of the "Cubical Terminal". Participants can move from room to room by navigating from the "Cubical Terminal".

"Matrix Cubes" are made up of stacks of boxes with doors. These represent the links between virtual rooms or stacks of "Terminal Cubes" or stacks in the real world. The "Matrix Cubes" thus function as a miniature/metaphor/-map of the virtual space. In this system, it is possible for a participant to have a threefold existence: Real Me, Virtual Me, and Virtual Me in the Actual World. For example, an action conducted with the image of Real Me through virtual space causes a reaction on the part of Virtual Me: Where are you? What is the meaning of your address? Where is your location? How is your existence supported? The whole topology of your existence will be shaken up.

The Cubical Terminal

A participant may interact with this virtual world through a "Cubical Terminal" containing a 3D graphics workstation and a projector. The terminal is connected to the server. People can meet and talk to one another in this virtual world, even when they access it from different locations.

A realtime rendered image, which interacts with the participant's trackball movement, is projected onto the screen inside the "Cubical Terminal". The participant can see the image through the window of the "Cubical Terminal". The image of a cubic room with a window on each side is projected inside the "Cubical

Terminal". There is an object, such as an apple, a hat, a doorknob, etc., in each room, which indicates that room's identity.

By manipulating the trackball, participants can change the perspective of themselves and can go through the room and even dive into objects. To leave a room, you simply go out one of the windows in the room. The view from the virtual window has an earth texture reflecting the concept of the project. When you go out a window you will hear a warp sound, and then the location changes to another room that has a different object. If there is more than one person in a room, their faces are mapped on a cubic avatar, so they can see and talk to each other.

Virtual Cubic Rooms

The Virtual World consists of a certain number of virtual cubic rooms. Each of the interactive images in the picture here has been extracted from projected images inside the Cubical Terminal and may be explored through manipulation on the part of the participants. Each room contains a symbolic 3D image that identifies it. Participants can move around in a virtual room by manipulating Virtual Me with the trackball mounted on the "Cubical Terminal" and may also go to a different virtual room by going through the window (each of the four sides of a virtual room has a square window, and each window is linked to a different room). The "Cubical Terminal" has a similar window on the side as well, which imitates the window of a virtual room. People accessing this space from different sites may use audio devices to talk to one another as through a telephone. If more than two participants are in the same virtual cubic room, the other participants will appear as an avatar with a video image of the participant's face mapped on it.

Matrix Cubes

Each box of the "Matrix Cubes" reflects the state of the virtual rooms, which means that each box corresponds to a particular virtual

Apfel, ein Hut, eine Türklinke usw., der auf die Identität des Raumes hinweist.

Wenn die Mitwirkenden den Trackball manipulieren, können sie die Perspektive ihres dargestellten Selbst verändern, im Raum herumgehen und sogar in die Gegenstände eintauchen. Um einen Raum zu verlassen, geht man einfach durch irgendein Fenster. Der Ausblick aus einem virtuellen Fenster hat eine Erdtextur, die dem Konzept des Projekts entspricht. Wenn man durch ein Fenster geht, hört man einen verzerrten Klang; danach befindet man sich in einem anderen Raum mit einem anderen Gegenstand. Falls sich mehr als eine Person in dem Raum befinden, werden die Gesichter auf einem quadratischen Avatar dargestellt, damit sie sich sehen und miteinander reden können.

Virtuelle Kubische Räume

Die virtuelle Welt besteht aus einer gewissen Anzahl virtueller kubischer Räume. Jedes der in der Abbildung dargestellten interaktiven Bilder wurde aus den im „Cubical Terminal" projizierten Bildern extrahiert, und die Mitwirkenden können sie durch ihre Manipulationen erforschen. Jeder Raum beinhaltet ein symbolisches 3D-Bild, das den Raum identifiziert. Mitwirkende können sich in dem jeweiligen virtuellen Raum herumbewegen, indem sie das virtuelle Selbst mit dem am „Cubical Terminal" montierten Trackball manipulieren. Außerdem können sie in einen anderen Raum gehen, wenn sie durch das Fenster hinausgehen (jeder virtuelle Raum hat auf jeder Seite ein quadratisches Fenster und jedes Fenster ist mit einem anderen Raum verbunden). Das „Cubical Terminal" hat ebenfalls auf jeder Seite ein Fenster, das eines der Fenster der virtuellen Räume imitiert. Mitwirkende, die diesen Raum von unterschiedlichen Orten aus ansteuern, können mittels Audiogeräten genauso wie am Telefon miteinander kommunizieren. Wenn sich mehr als zwei Mitwirkende in demselben virtuellen kubischen Raum befinden, erscheinen die anderen Mitwirkenden in der Form eines Avatar, auf den ein Videobild des Gesichts des jeweiligen Mitwirkenden gemappt ist.

Matrix Cubes

Jede Schachtel der „Matrix Cubes" spiegelt den Status der virtuellen Räume wider, das heißt, jede einzelne Schachtel entspricht einem bestimmten virtuellen

Project's Installation Overview:

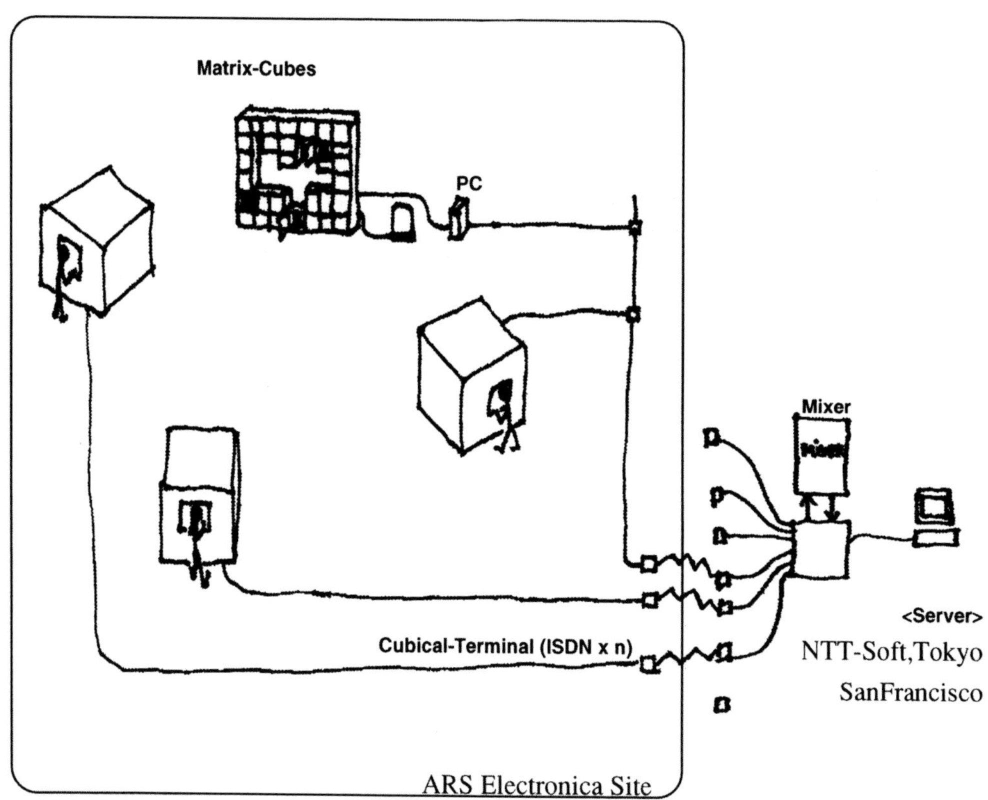

room. For instance, if someone accesses the virtual room X from one of the "Cubical Terminals", the door of the box X opens on the "Matrix Cubes". These cubes show the real-time activity of the virtual environment and provide a visualization model of the networked virtual world. The essential idea here is that the Real World is ONLY a map of the Virtual World for the Virtual Me.

Background Infrastructure

The first prototype was implemented using "InterSpace", which was developed by NTT Human Interface Laboratories. The InterSpace server runs at an NTT software corporation in Tokyo and also at the San Francisco branch. This server has numerous ISDN connection ports, and it is currently linked with Stanford University, Golden Gate College, Cal Arts and others. We are now trying to coordinate a connection with MoMA in New York, V_2 organization in Rotterdam and ICC in Tokyo. The server consists of a UNIX workstation and a special sound mixing console. The UNIX workstation is used for coordinating the users' behavior in virtual space. It requires special hardware specifically designed for the console to be able to mix various sounds from different places. The boards of this hardware convert analog/digital signals and then send these signals back to the user's terminal. The sounds are mixed according to parameters determined by the user's position in virtual space.

Raum. Wenn zum Beispiel jemand den virtuellen Raum X von einem der „Cubical Terminal" ansteuert, öffnet sich die Tür der Schachtel X an den „Matrix Cubes". Diese Würfel zeigen die Aktivitäten im virtuellen Environment in Echtzeit und ermöglichen auf diese Weise ein Visualisierungsmodell der vernetzten virtuellen Welt. Der springende Punkt dabei ist, daß die reale Welt NUR eine Karte der virtuellen Welt für das virtuelle Selbst darstellt.

Entwicklungsstand

Der erste Prototyp wurde mit „InterSpace", das von NTT Human Interface Laboratories entwickelt wurde, verwirklicht. Der InterSpace-Server läuft in einem NTT-Softwarekonzern in Tokio sowie in einer Filiale in San Francisco. Dieser Server verfügt über zahlreiche Verbindungsanschlüsse und ist bereits mit der Stanford University, dem Golden Gate College, Cal Arts und anderen verbunden. Wir bemühen uns außerdem, eine Verbindung mit dem Museum of Modern Art in New York, mit der Organisation V_2 in Rotterdam sowie mit ICC in Tokio herzustellen.
Der Server besteht aus einer UNIX-Workstation und einer speziellen Konsole zur Klangaufbereitung. Durch die UNIX-Workstation wird das Anwenderverhalten im virtuellen Raum koordiniert. Dazu wird spezielle Hardware benötigt, damit die Konsole die verschiedenen Klänge unterschiedlicher Herkunft aufbereiten kann. Die Karten dieser Hardware konvertieren Analog-/Digitalsignale und übermitteln dann diese Signale zurück zum Anwenderterminal. Die Parameter, die die Aufbereitung der Klänge bestimmen, werden von der Position des Anwenders im virtuellen Raum definiert.

LOUIS-PHILIPPE DEMERS / BILL VORN

Louis-Philippe Demers (CDN) ist Lichtspezialist, Softwaretechniker und freischaffender elektronischer Künstler. Er ist Präsident von Kunst Macchina Production, einer Firma, die sich auf Steuerungssoftware für Live-Performances spezialisiert hat.
Bill Vorn (CDN), geb. 1959, arbeitet seit über zehn Jahren als Komponist und Sound-Designer.

Louis-Philippe Demers (CDN) is a lighting designer, software engineer and independent electronic artist. He is the president of Kunst Macchina Production, a company specialized in control software for live performance. Bill Vorn (CDN), born in 1959, has worked as a music composer and sound designer for over ten years.

Die Installationen werden an düsteren, dunklen Orten aufgestellt, an architektonisch ungewöhnlichen Orten, und der Betrachter wird eingeladen, über ein erfundenes Habitat zu reflektieren, das ausschließlich für Roboterorganismen geschaffen wurde.
Jede Installation repliziert elementare Roboterorganismen und bildet eine fiktive Gesellschaft, ein "Roboterökosystem". Wenn die Besucher diese Environments mit ihrem ganzen Körper erleben, wenn sie ganz in diese simulierte Welt eintauchen, werden sie mehr denn je von den Simulakra überzeugt.

No Man's Land

Mittels verschiedener Roboterspezies evoziert "No Man's Land" das fiktive Verhalten eines noch größeren Roboterökosystems. Hier werden Roboterorganismen sowohl der Anzahl als auch dem Geschlecht nach repliziert. Das Geschlecht der Roboterorganismen wird entsprechend ihrem Verhalten in diesem Lebensraum gestaltet, und es gibt außerdem Metaphern für natürliche Gesellschaften: Parasiten, Aasfresser, Überbevölkerung, Scharen usw.
Die Maschinen werden auf ihre grundlegendsten Eigenschaften reduziert, damit das beabsichtigte Verhalten überhaupt realisiert werden kann. Eine Hammermaschine ist so zugleich rhythmisches Instrument und Parasit, wenn sie gezielt auf einen anderen Roboterorga-

The installations are deployed in dark hazy spaces, in unusual architectural sites where the viewer is invited to consider an invented habitat created solely for the robotorganisms. Each installation replicates elementary robot-organisms, thereby building a fictious society or robotic ecosystem. By experiencing these environments with the entire body, immersed in this simulated world, the audience is more convinced of the simulacra.

No Man's Land

Through various robotic species, "No Man's Land" especially "The Scavengers" evokes fictitious behaviors of an even larger robotic ecosystem. Here the robot-organisms are replicated in number and also in gender. The robotic genders are designed on the basis of their behaviors in the habitat, and there are metaphors of natural societies: parasites, scavengers, overpopulation, flocks, etc. The machines are reduced to their most nominal expression to implement their intended behaviors. A simple hammer machine becomes a rhythmic element at the same time and a parasite when installed judiciously on another robot-organism. The behaviors are seen as a common thread for the design of each of the robot-organisms. Here we present our interpretation of these domains in respect to our intentions of producing an aesthetic media out of machines.

Real Artificial Life as Invented Robotic Ecosystems

Real artificial life is robotics. The hyperreal simulacra of the robot world goes beyond the unreachable simulation of life on a computer screen. Robots are not only a virtual model (a pattern in space and time) but also a dynamic and evolving phenomenon embodied in matter.
As far as we can observe in the architecture of living things, the whole is always greater than the sum of the parts. In "Out of Control," Kevin Kelly wrote: "An ecology of machines enhances the limited skills of dumb machines." Following this assumption, the installations evoke fictitious behaviors of a global robotic ecosystem through local inter-

Reales Künstliches Leben als erfundene Roboterökosysteme

Reales Künstliches Leben ist Robotik. Die Reichweite der hyperrealen Simulakra der Roboterwelt ist größer als die nicht greifbare Simulation des Lebens am Bildschirm. Roboter stellen nicht nur ein virtuelles Modell (ein Muster in Zeit und Raum) dar, sondern auch ein dynamisches und sich entwickelndes, materiell verkörpertes Phänomen.
Soweit wir überhaupt die Architektur von Lebewesen beurteilen können, ist die Gesamtheit immer größer als die Summe der Einzelteile. In "Out of Control" schrieb Keven Kelly: "Eine Ökologie der Maschinen verbessert die begrenzten Fähigkeiten nicht-sprechender Maschinen." Ausgehend von dieser Annahme evozieren die Installationen fiktive Verhaltensweisen eines globalen Roboterökosystems durch Interaktion zwischen minimalen mechanischen Organismen auf lokaler Ebene. Das dem Gesamtsystem zugrundeliegende Design (ein Orga-

Louis-Philippe Demers / Bill Vorn
"Scavengers", 1996

nismus aus Organismen) baut dementsprechend auf den Merkmalen der Verhaltensweisen natürlicher Gesellschaften auf: Kettenreaktionen, Verhaltensweisen zur Vermehrung und Versammlung, Herden und Schwärme usw.

Die Maschinen können also als virtuelle Organismen verstanden werden, die sich bewegen und Geräusche und Licht als Produkt ihres künstlichen Stoffwechsels erzeugen. In diesem Sinne ist es nicht unsere Absicht, echte Tiere zu simulieren oder physisch nachzubilden. Statt dessen beschäftigen wir uns mit einfachen Verhaltensweisen, die von primitiven mechanischen Animaten verkörpert werden. Diese Metapher speist sich von organischen Geräuschen und Bewegungen, um eine hybride Welt zwischen der Natur und dem Künstlichen zu erzeugen.

In diesen Installationen geht es um die Verschiebung bestehender Artefakte und erwarteter lebensähnlicher Verhaltensweisen. Unsere Wahrnehmung natürlicher Verhaltensweisen wird auf eine aus mechanischen, hörbaren und visuellen Elementen bestehende Gemeinschaft projiziert.

Die Replikation von Maschinenorganismen stellt ein Grundprinzip dar und impliziert eine große Anzahl von Maschinenorganismen. Die Grundlage von Ökosystemen ist klarerweise die Population (Geschlecht und Anzahl), und ihre Komplexität ist eine Folge der Vielschichtigkeit der sich ergebenden Interaktionen. Außerdem wäre die Illusion der Lebendigkeit weniger überzeugend, wenn es nur wenige Einheiten gäbe: dadurch wären die möglichen Zustandskombinationen des Systems, die folglich als Verhaltensweisen wahrgenommen werden, beschränkt.

Diese Maschinen erlauben es, hypnotische und sich wiederholende Bewegungen leicht vorauszusehen.

Selbst die kinetische Kunst weist darauf hin, daß reale (im Gegensatz zur virtuellen) Bewegung eine Reaktion in uns hervorruft und daß jede Bewegung außerhalb unseres Körpers hypnotisch wirkt. Potentielle Verhaltensweisen, die die Installationen aufweisen können, sind Rituale, Hierarchien, Chaos, Aggregation und der Gegensatz zwischen dem Kollektiven und dem Individuellen.

Unsere These ist, daß keine vorbedingte oder notwendige Äquivalenz über die Grenzen zwischen Leben und dessen maschineller Darstellung hinweg existiert. Da es eine der vordringlichsten ästhetischen Absichten dieser Arbeit ist, den Eindruck von Leben durch abstrakte,

actions of minimal mechanical organisms. The underlying design of the whole system (an organism of organisms) is then based on the characteristics of natural societies' behaviors: chain reactions, propagation and aggregation behavior, herds and swarms, etc.

The machines can then be seen as virtual organisms that move and produce sound and light as the output of their invented metabolisms. In this sense, we do not intend to simulate or physically reproduce real life animals, but rather we deal with simplistic behaviors engendered by primitive mechanical animats. This metaphor feeds on the organic sounds and movements in order to create a hybrid world between nature and the artificial.

Our installations are about displacement of existing artifacts and expected life-like behaviors. Our own perception of natural behaviors is imposed on a society of mechanical, audio and visual elements.

The concept of replication is fundamental to these projects, which involve a large number of machine-organisms. Ecosystems are obviously based on population (gender and number), and their complexity is obtained from the multiplicity of the inherent interactions. Furthermore, the illusion of life would not be as convincing if there were only a few units, limiting the combinations of possible states of the system which are consequently perceived as behaviors.

Hypnotic and repetitive movement are easily foreseen with these machines. The kinetic art itself suggests that real (as opposed to virtual) movement generates a response in us and that any movement outside our body is hypnotic. Rituals, hierarchy, chaos, aggregation, the collective versus the individual, are among the potential behaviors addressed by the installations.

We can suggest that no prerequisite or imposed equivalence exists across the boundaries of life and its machine represenation. Since one of the forefront aesthetic choices of these works is the evocation of life through an abstract, even displaced, bare inorganic skeleton, the machines are kept deliberately simplistic. Shapes move from primitive abstract objects (spheres, cylinders, sound, light) to kinetic and complex organisms (polymorphic patterns).

The installations also convey a displacement of sensations, perceptions and expectations: duality, ambiguity and contradiction are part of the sculptures. The aesthetics of the societies are continuously in conflict when they are not animated. For instance, if the objects are lying still in a particular pattern, the viewer perceives the specific image of this pattern. As they move and react, the initial perception is destroyed. What was first seen as the external inert perception, the known experience of the objects, is continuously transformed.

Behaviors – No Man's Land

In the "No Man's Land" installation, the robot-organisms' species are classified by their shapes, functions and behaviors. One out of the indicative list of targeted behaviors is: "Scavengers" seem to fight for a large chunk of a dead animat; they are large and make a lot of noise. The dead animat is depicted by a steel cube (2' x 2' x 2') simultaneously pushed around by four pneumatic actuators. The scraping surfaces of the cube and the floor will generate a uncomfortable rhythmic pitch. Light sources are embedded into the cube to underline sudden movements of the cube and the scavengers.

Summary through these installations, we pursue our research on intelligent environments and life embodiment into matter.

We intend to present robotic machines not as specialized and virtuoso automata, but rather as expressive artworks. We also explore the reformulation of sound and light applications by simulating metabolism functions and by creating dynamic virtual architectures.

In fact, real artificial life is more than an immersive media, it is a world of its own.

wenn nicht sogar verlagerte, nackte, anorganische Skelette hervorzurufen, sind die Maschinen bewußt möglichst einfach gehalten. Die Formen reichen von primitiven abstrakten Objekten (Kugeln, Zylinder, Klang, Licht) bis hin zu kinetischen und komplexen Organismen (polymorphe Muster).

Die Installationen vermitteln auch eine Verlagerung der Empfindungen, der Wahrnehmungen und der Erwartungen: Dualität, Zweideutigkeit und Widerspruch sind Teil der Skulpturen. Die Ästhetik der Gesellschaften, wenn sie nicht animiert sind, ist widersprüchlich. Wenn zum Beispiel die Objekte nach einem speziellen Muster angeordnet still liegen, nimmt der Betrachter ein bestimmtes Bild dieses Musters wahr. Wenn die Objekte sich dann bewegen und reagieren, wird diese ursprüngliche Wahrnehmung zerstört. Was zunächst als äußere, unveränderliche Wahrnehmung gesehen wurde – die erlebte Erfahrung der Objekte – ist einem steten Wandel begriffen.

Verhaltensweisen — "No Man's Land"

In der Installation "No Man's Land" werden die Spezies der Roboterorganismen nach Form, Funktion und Verhaltensweisen klassifiziert. Eine der beabsichtigten Verhaltensweisen sind die „Aasfresser". Die "Scavengers" kämpfen scheinbar um ein großes Stück eines toten Animaten; sie sind groß und sehr laut. Das tote Animat wird von einem Stahlwürfel (2' x 2' 2') dargestellt, der gleichzeitig von vier pneumatischen Stempeln herumgestoßen wird. Wenn die Würfelflächen auf den Boden scharren, entsteht ein unangenehmer rhythmischer Ton. Im Würfel eingebetteten Lichtquellen verstärken die plötzlichen Bewegungen des Würfels und der Aasfresser.

Mit diesen Installationen setzen wir unsere Forschungen über intelligente Environments und die Verkörperung von Leben in Materie fort.

Unsere Roboter sollen keine spezialisierten und virtuosen Automaten sein, sondern ausdrucksvolle, belebte Kunstwerke. Außerdem setzen wir uns mit neuen Möglichkeiten der Anwendung von Klang und Licht auseinander, indem wir metabolische Funktionen simulieren und dynamische virtuelle Architekturen schaffen.

Reales Künstliches Leben ist mehr als ein immersives Medium; es ist eine Welt für sich.

SCOTT SONA SNIBBE

Scott Sona Snibbe (USA) ist Filme-macher und Informatiker. Er konzen-triert sich darauf, Gesten und das menschliche Element in Computer-animation miteinzubeziehen. Die Schwerpunkte seiner Projekte reichen von neuen Techniken der Keyframe-Animation bis zu interaktiver abstrakter Live-Animation im Internet.

Scott Sona Snibbe (USA) is a filmmaker and a computer scientist. He has focused on incorporating gesture and the human element into computer animation. His projects range from new techniques for keyframe animation to live interactive abstract animation over the Internet.

„The Motion Phone" ist ein Experiment in reiner visuel-ler Kommunikation. Es ist ein Versuch, die Sprache der abstrakten Kommunikation einem breiteren Publikum zugänglich zu machen, und zwar dadurch, daß die spontanen menschlichen Gesten in all ihren Nuancen eingefangen werden. Das Programm wurde vom ab-strakten Film inspiriert und verwendet dessen Sprache der zweidimensionalen animierten Formen und Farben. Die Qualität der Arbeit, die mit diesem Werkzeug ge-schaffen wird, ist auffallend menschlich – und unter-scheidet sich dadurch stark vom Großteil der heutigen Computerkunst und Animationsprogramme.

„The Motion Phone" ist ein Programm, das auf einer graphischen Workstation läuft. Bei der ersten Annähe-rung präsentiert das Programm Farb- und Formpaletten und eine breite, leere Leinwand. Wenn der Benutzer auf diese Leinwand zeichnet, werden die Geschwindigkeit und die Stelle der Markierungen in eine digitale Anima-tionsschleife eingetragen. Wenn der Benutzer auf die Tastatur oder auf ein Graphiktablett drückt, kann er Form, Größe und Farbe der Markierungen gleichzeitig verändern. Wenn er weiterzeichnet, werden die neuen Markierungen derselben Animationsschleife hinzuge-fügt, wodurch er sequentiell vielschichtige Form- und Farbrhythmen auftragen kann.

Selbst die unerfahrensten Benutzer können innerhalb nur weniger Minuten eine originelle und visuell faszinie-

The "Motion Phone" is an experiment in pure visual communication. It is an attempt to open up the language of abstract animation to a general audience by allowing spontane-ous human gestures to be captured in all their subtlety. The program draws its inspira-tion from abstract film and uses its language of two-dimensional animated shape and color. The quality of work created with this tool is strikingly human – in stark compari-son to the work created with most computer art and animation programs today.

The "Motion Phone" is a program which runs on a graphics workstation. When first appro-ached, the program presents palettes of colors and shapes and a wide blank canvas. When a user draws upon this canvas the speed and location of his marks are entered into a digital animation loop. By pressing on the keyboard or on the graphics tablet, the shape, size and color of the marks can be simultaneously changed. As he continues to draw, her marks are added into the same animation loop, allowing him to sequentially layer multiple rhythms of form and color. Even the most naive of users can create uni-que and visually fascinating animation within

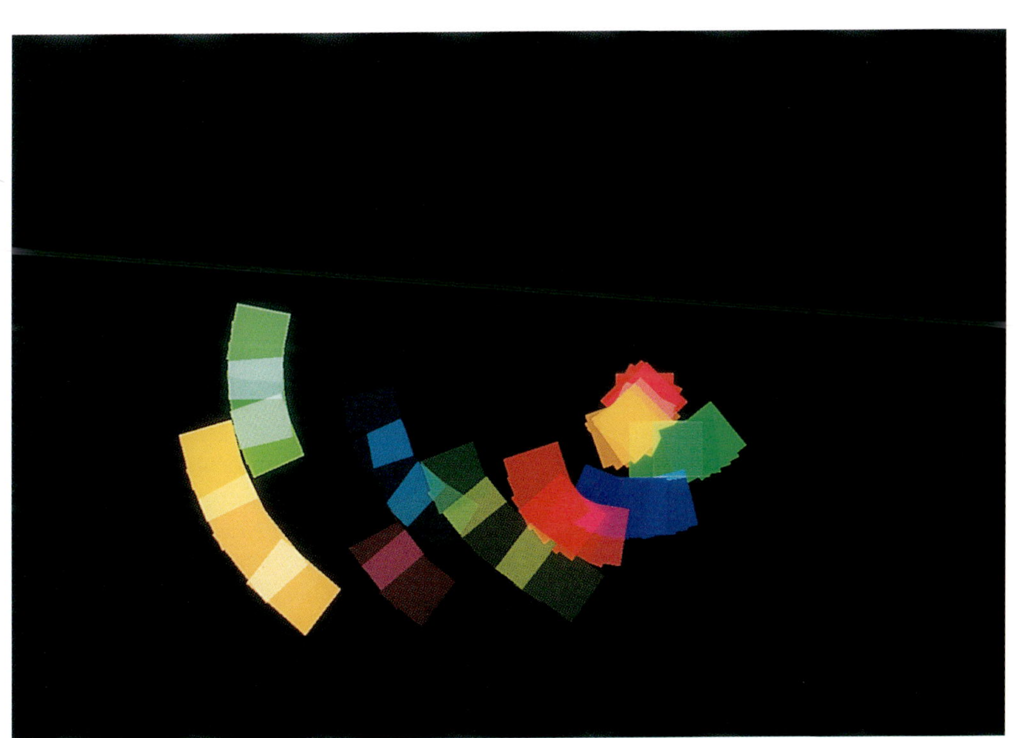

Scott Sona Snibbe
"Motion Phone", 1995

a few minutes. Once users make the connection between their hand gestures and the motion on the screen, they quickly learn to control the subtleties of their motion. By building on earlier visual themes and combining prior motions into complex rhythms, the user creates a rich animated composition. People are astounded by the beauty of their natural motion when they see it sampled over time, rather than the instantaneous slice of reality we are used to.

The inspiration for the two-dimensional language of the "Motion Phone" comes from the history of abstract film. In the 1920's, several European filmmakers sought to expand the new abstract language of painting into animation. These first pioneers included Oskar Fishinger, Walter Ruttman and Hans Richter. They created films which expanded on the abstract languages being developed by Kandinsky, Klee and others. By adding a temporal element to abstract forms, they believed that they could create "visual music". The temporal structures developed in their films were often direct visual analogs to existing musical structures, expressed with shape and color rather than tone and rhythm. These films were painstakingly created over the course of years by creating successive drawings and photographing them onto film. This process, by its nature, lacked a key element of music – the spontaneous nature of live performance.

The users of the "Motion Phone" can collaborate over a network to create animation on the same shared plane. Each individual can zoom in and out of the shared world to an arbitrary degree. With this capability, improvisations and visual conversations can take place in many locations and scales at once. One can zoom out and have a god's eye view of the complexity of many different animations. One also can zoom in on what appears to be a single dot and find a complex abstract dance in progress.

KEN FEINGOLD

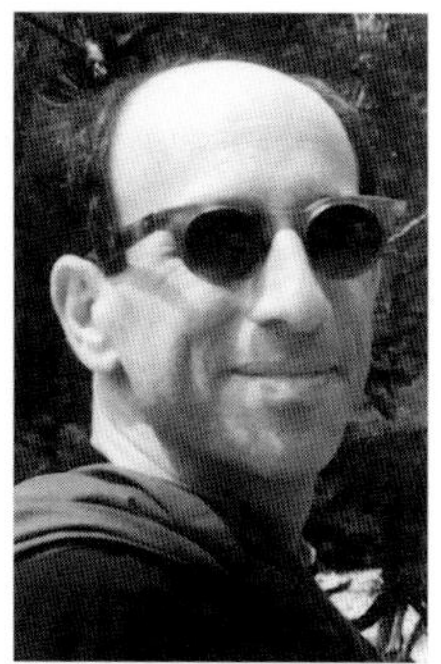

Ken Feingold (USA), geb. 1952; 1976 MA für Post-Studio Art am California Institute of the Arts, School of Arts, Valancia, Kalifornien; seit 1993 Lehrauftrag am Graduate Computer Art Department an der School of Visual Arts, New York. Feingold lebt in New York City.

Ken Feingold (USA), born 1952; MA in Post-Studio Art at California Institute of the Arts, School of Art, Valancia, CA, in 1976; since 1993 teacher at the Graduate Computer Art Department at the School of Visual Arts, NYC; lives in New York City.

INTERACTIVE ART

Ein virtuelles Maskenfest, ein ferngesteuertes Puppentheater, eine Welt, eine unerträgliche Hölle oder der Anfang einer neuen Form des öffentlichen Raums? Solche Ideen mögen auftauchen, wenn man an „Where I can see my house from here so we are" denkt: Der unvorstellbare Raum zwischen „Hier" und „Dort" kollabiert in der audiovisuellen Materialisierung des Dazwischen. Alle, die sich an diesem Ort begegnen, „verlieren" unterwegs ihren Körper, bewohnen einen anderen, wenn sie ankommen.

Drei kleine Roboterpuppen mit Videokameraauge und mit Mikrophonohren befinden sich gemeinsam in einem gespiegelten Raum. Die Wände sind gerade so hoch, daß die Roboterpuppen nicht direkt hinübersehen können. Über das Internet sind die Roboterpuppen mit einem anderen Raum irgendwo verbunden, in dem das, was sie sehen und hören, von einem entfernten Betrachter/Bauchredner als projiziertes Video gesehen bzw. gehört wird. In jedem entfernten Raum gibt es ein Steuergerät, das aus einem sichtbaren, offenen, aktentaschenähnlichen Objekt besteht, in dem sich ein Joystick und ein Mikrophon befinden. Mittels Tools und der Fernsteuerungssoftware kann der Betrachter/Bauchredner die Roboterpuppe, mit der er verbunden ist, in dem Spiegelraum herumbewegen. Wenn der Besucher/Bauchredner spricht, wird seine Stimme in der Roboterpuppe verstärkt und durch sie „projiziert", wobei sich der Mund der Roboterpuppe bewegt. Auf diese Weise können sich drei Besucher/Bauchredner von drei verschiedenen Orten aus in einem vierten (gespiegelten) Raum begegnen. Der Raum setzt jeder Roboterpuppe physische Grenzen, die sie, wie nationale Grenzen, nicht überqueren können ...

Würde man eine Videoconference unter drei Bauchred-

A virtual masquerade party, a remote-control puppet-theater, a world, one of the unbearable hells, or the beginning of a new form of public space? These spin off at the thought of "Where I can see my house from here so we are ..." The inconceivable space between „here" and „there" collapses in an audiovisual materialization of the connection, and those who meet in that place „lose" their body along the way, inhabiting another when they arrive.

Three small robot-puppets, each with a video camera-eye, and microphone ears, are together in a mirrored space in an exhibition site; its walls are high enough so that the robot-puppets can't see directly over them. Each robot-puppet is connected, via the Internet, to another space, elsewhere, in which their sight and hearing is seen and heard by a distant viewer-ventriloquist as projected video and amplified sound. In each remote space, there is a control device, consisting visibly of an opened attaché-case-like object, revealing a joystick and a microphone. Utilizing these tools and remote-control software that I have put together, the viewer-ventriloquist may drive around the robot-puppet to which they are connected in the mirrored space, and when the remote viewer-ventriloquist speaks, their voice is "projected" through the robot-puppet, amplified within it, and moves the robot-puppet's mouth. In this way, three viewer-ventriloquists may meet in the fourth (mirrored) room. The space has

physical limits for each robot-puppet, like
national borders which they cannot cross ...
Creating a videoconference among three
ventriloquist puppets would be enough to
ask the guest ventriloquists – "What is there
to say? Does it make a difference that you are
not seen, but only your projection – which
sees and speaks and hears in your place? Is
it the 'I' saying 'Me' to 'It-You' (or its reflection)? That the one who stands in your place
is not free to go where they wish, and that
even as you move them 'freely' in their mirrored infinity theater, that there are borders?
That they can see their wires but know not
where they lead? And that in the space of the
'art exhibition' there is also a meeting of those
who see but are not seen and those who learn
to play the game with their projections?"

nerpuppen herstellen, wäre es dann genug, die Besu-
cher/Bauchredner zu fragen: „Was kann man überhaupt
sagen? Macht es etwas aus, daß nicht du, sondern nur
deine Projektion gesehen wird – deine Projektion, die
an deiner Stelle sieht und spricht und hört? Handelt es
sich um das „Ich", das zu dem „Es/Dich" (oder dessen
Spiegelbild) „Mich" sagt?
Macht es etwas aus, daß die Gestalt, die an deiner
Stelle steht, sich nicht so bewegen kann, wie sie will,
daß es Grenzen gibt, selbst wenn du diese Gestalt in
einem gespiegelten endlosen Theater „frei" bewegen
kannst? Macht es etwas aus, daß diese Gestalten ihre
eigenen Drähte sehen können, aber nicht wissen, wo
sie hinführen? Macht es etwas aus, daß im Raum einer
„Kunstausstellung" eine Begegnung zwischen denen,
die sehen, aber nicht gesehen werden, und denen, die
gelernt haben, das Spiel mit den eigenen Projektionen
zu spielen, stattfindet?

HONORARY MENTION

Ken Feingold
"Where I can see my house from here so we are ...", 1993–1995

ELISABETH GOLDRING

Elizabeth Goldring (USA), geb. 1945 in Forest City, Iowa; seit 1975 Fellow am Center for Advanced Visual Studies (CAVS), Massachusetts, seit 1989 Lehrauftrag am Department of Architecture, MIT; 1994–1995 Co-Direktor CAVS/MIT.

Elizabeth Goldring (USA), born 1945 in Forest City, Iowa; Fellow at the Center for Advanced Visual Studies (CAVS), Massachusetts since 1975, Lecturer at the Department of Architecture, MIT since 1989, acting Co-Director, CAVS/MIT 1994–1995.

Ziel des SLO-Internetprojekts „Eye to Eye: Interactive Cybervision Environments for the Visually Challenged" ist es, sehbehinderte Menschen zu ermutigen, via Internet mit anderen Menschen visuell zu kommunizieren. Durch das Internet wird eine Live-Kommunikationsverbindung zwischen einer SLO-Mac-Site am Center for Advanced Visual Studies am MIT in Cambridge, Massachusetts, und einer Mac-SLO-Site am Ausstellungsort hergestellt. Jede beteiligte Station ist mit einer Videokamera ausgerüstet. Zusätzlich zur Teleconferencing-Verbindung, die SLO („Scanning Laser Ophtalmoscope") verwendet, können sowohl sehbehinderte wie auch sehende Besucher an Gedicht-Animationen und Environments teilhaben, die für dieses Projekt mit Silicon Graphics Imaging Systemen am Media Lab des MIT gestaltet wurden. Diese Kunstwerke können sowohl über das Internet mit SLO wie auch durch das SLO-Mac-Interface am jeweiligen Ort gesehen werden. Außerdem können Besucher Live-Videoaufnahmen von der Netzhaut der anderen Besucher sehen, während sie Bilder, Texte, Gesichter und die Gedicht-Animationen und Environments durch SLO betrachten.

The goal of the SLO-Internet "Eye to Eye: Interactive Cybervision Environments for the Visually Challenged" project is to encourage people who are visually challenged to communicate visually over the Internet. The Internet will provide a live communication link between a SLO-Mac site at CAVS, MIT in Cambridge, MA, and a Mac-SLO site at the exhibition location. Each participating station will be outfitted with a video camera. In addition to the teleconferencing link using the SLO, visually challenged as well as fully sighted visitors to each location will be able to enjoy Poem Animations and Environments recently created for this project employing Silicon Graphics Imaging systems at MIT's Media Lab. These artworks may either be seen through the SLO over the Internet or via the SLO Mac interface at each location. Visitors will also be able to view live video images of people's retinas as they look at images, texts, faces and Poem Animations and Environments through the SLO.

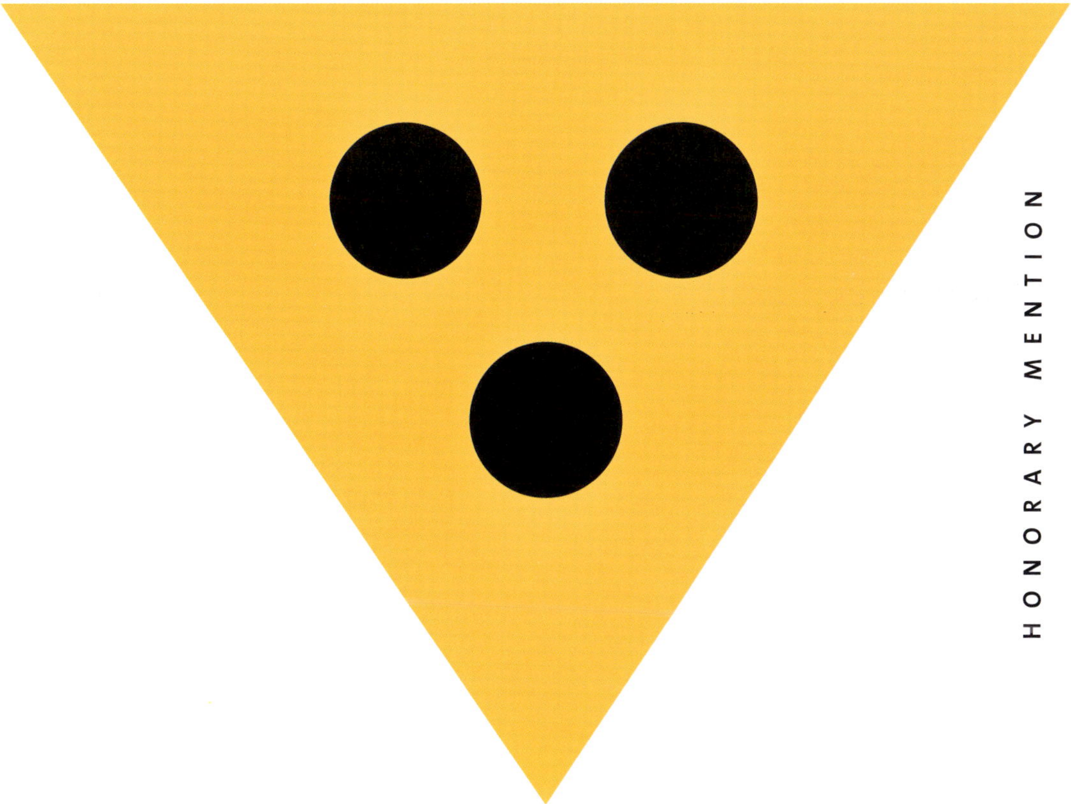

Elisabeth Goldring
"Eye to Eye: Interactive Cybervision Environments for the Visually Challenged"

KAZUHIKO HACHIYA

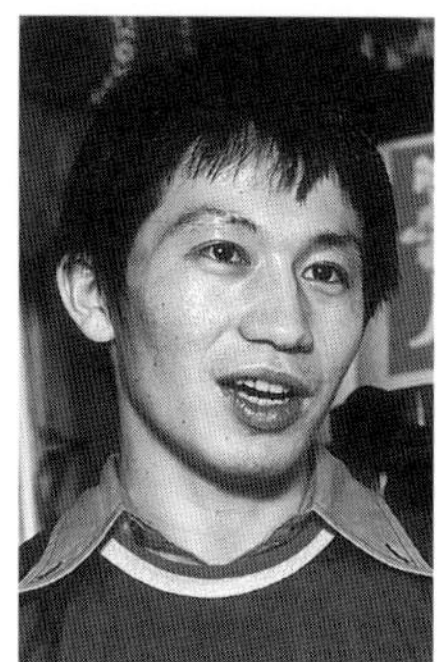

Kazuhiko Hachiya (J), geb. 1966 in Saga, Japan; Studiumabschluß 1989 am Kyushu Institute of Design (Visual Communication Design); verschiedene Ausstellungen in Tokio und anderswo, die letzte war „Empty Entity – Maga Diary Mix" im Juni/Juli im Hiroshima City Museum of Contemporary Art.

Kazuhiko Hachiya (J), born 1966 in Saga, Japan. Graduated from Kyushu Institute of Design (Visual Communication Design) in 1989; several exhibitions in Tokyo and elsewhere, the last one, "Empty Entity – Maga Diary mix" during June and July at the Hiroshima City Museum of Contemporary Art.

Mit der „Inter Dis-communication Machine" können zwei Teilnehmer ihre jeweiligen visuellen Perspektiven tauschen, wodurch sie gezwungen werden, alles aus dem Blickwinkel des anderen zu betrachten. Ich bin nicht du, und du bist nicht ich. Doch oft werden wir verwirrt und glauben dann, der andere denke ähnlich. In Wirklichkeit existiert diese reale Welt nur im Gehirn eines einzelnen Menschen, und so sieht jeder eine andere Welt. „Hier bin ich." In diesem Fall ist „hier" der Ort, wo meine Augen sind; es ist der Mittelpunkt der Welt. Nun, was passiert dann, wenn ich meine Augen dir gebe? Und wenn ich deine Augen bekomme? Dann werden wir miteinander zu einer Person verschmelzen. Stellen wir uns außerdem vor, „ich bin du und du bist ich".

Diese Ideen sind die Grundsätze meiner Arbeit. Diese Maschine ist so konzipiert, daß sie von zwei Menschen benutzt wird. Ich versuche, die Situation einer „doppelten Identität des Selbst" und einer „gegenseitigen Identität" herzustellen. Die kann man mit dem Phänomen vergleichen, daß man den eigenen „Doppelgänger" sieht.

Jede Maschine ist mit einem HMD (Head Mounted Display) und einem Rucksack ausgerüstet. Jedes HMD hat zwei Monitoren und eine Videokamera. Im HMD sieht man ausschließlich die Sicht des anderen. Der Rucksack ist mit einer Batterie (7,5 V), einem TV-Einstellungsgerät und einem Transmitter ausgerüstet. Eine TV-Antenne ist in den Flügeln installiert. Die Maschine verwendet Radiowellen, um das Videobild zu senden. Die Maschine wurde so gestaltet, daß auch Küssen und Beischlaf möglich sind.

Through the device of the "Inter Dis-communication Machine", two participants exchange their visual perspectives, which forces them to see things the other person's way. I am not you, and you are not me. Yet we are often confused and think that the other person thinks in a similar way. This real world actually only exists in the brain of any one person, so everyone sees a different world. "Here, I am." In this case, "here" is the place where "my" eyes exist; it is the center of the world. Well then, what happens if I give my eyes to you ? And if I receive your eyes ? Then we will fuse to become one person. Furthermore, let's imagine "I am you and you are me." These are the ideas my work is based on. This machine is designed to be used by two people. The situation I have tried to create is that of a "double identity self" and "mutual identity". It may be compared to the phenomenon of seeing one's own doppelganger. Each machine is equipped with a HMD (Head Mounted Display) and a backpack. Each HMD has two monitors and a video camera. The HMD shows only the other person's view. The backpack is equipped with a battery (7.5 V), a TV tuner and a transmitter. A TV antenna is installed inside the wings. The machine uses radio waves to send the video image. The machine was designed to allow for the possibility of kissing and making love.

Kazuhiko Hachiya
"Inter Dis-communication Machine", 1993, 1995

HARWOOD

Harwood (GB) ist ein international tätiger Multimediakünstler und Mitbegründer von „The Working Press" und „Underground Press". Harwood wirkt oft bei internationalen Konferenzen über elektronische Kunst mit. Harwood arbeitet bei Artec mit Langzeitarbeitslosen.

Harwood (GB) is an international multi- media artist who previously co-founded "The Working Press" and "Underground Press" and is a regular contributor to conferences on the electronic arts. Harwood works at Artec with the long term unemployed.

INTERACTIVE ART

Harwood
"Rehearsal of Memory", 1996

During the winter of 1994 to 1995, Harwood worked with a group of people from Ashworth Maximum Security Hospital to produce an interactive programme that embodied their life experiences. The skins of those taking part were scanned to assemble physical traces of their lives, defined by notions of insanity. These were then made to form a composite individual through which the programme user can make close contact with significant events in the lives of those involved.

Ashworth Mental Hospital is both home and prison to six hundred and fifty people of whom seventy percent are mentally disordered "offenders". These patients are admitted to Ashworth Hospital on the authority of the British courts or from other prisons at the direction of the Home Secretary.

Thirty percent of patients at Ashworth, however, have not offended and are referred to the hospital by social service departments and health authorities. The average length of stay at Ashworth is eight years, but a minority of patients will spend the rest of their lives at the hospital.

This artwork is about recording the lives of the patient/staff group that act as a mirror to ourselves (i.e., "normal" society) and to our amnesia when confronted with our society's excesses. This forgetting is a dark shadow cast by plenty, a nightmare for some that reconstitutes misinformation and fear about insanity.

"Rehearsal of Memory" simultaneously challenges our assumptions of normality and confronts us with a clean comfortable machine, filled with filth, with the forbidden and with the demented, its hygienic procedures contaminated by the effluent of excluded human relations. For a long time we have assigned machines our dirty laundry while maintaining the image of their enamelled white veneers. Now is the time for filth.

Im Winter 1994/95 arbeitete Harwood mit einer Gruppe von Menschen vom Ashworth Maximum Security Hospital, um ein interaktives Programm herzustellen, das die Lebenserfahrung dieser Menschen beinhaltet. Die Haut der Teilnehmer wurde gescannt, um physische Spuren ihres Lebens, das von der Vorstellung der Unzurechnungsfähigkeit bestimmt ist, zu sammeln. Aus diesen Bildern wurde eine zusammengesetzte Person gebildet, durch die der User mit den bedeutendsten Erlebnissen aus dem Leben der beteiligten Menschen in Kontakt kommen kann.

Das Ashworth Mental Hospital ist zugleich Heimat und Gefängnis für die 650 Insassen, wovon siebzig Prozent unzurechnungsfähige „Verbrecher" sind. Diese Patienten wurden auf Anordnung britischer Gerichte in Ashworth Hospital aufgenommen oder von anderen Gefängnissen auf Empfehlung des Innenministers dorthin überstellt. Dreißig Prozent der Ashworth-Patienten haben jedoch kein Verbrechen begangen und wurden von Sozialämtern und Gesundheitsbehörden an das Krankenhaus verwiesen. Die durchschnittliche Dauer eines Aufenthalts in Ashworth beträgt acht Jahre, doch ein geringer Prozentsatz der Patienten wird den Rest seines Lebens in Ashworth verbringen.

In „Rehearsal of Memory" geht es um die Aufzeichnung des Lebens der Patienten-/Mitarbeitergruppe, es hält uns (d. h. der „normalen" Gesellschaft) einen Spiegel vor; es geht um den Gedächtnisverlust, der immer dann auftritt, wenn wir mit den Exzessen unserer Gesellschaft konfrontiert werden. Dieses Vergessen ist ein dunkler Schatten des Überflusses, für eine kleine Anzahl von Menschen wird es zum Alptraum, weil es den Nährboden für Fehlinformation und Angst vor Wahnsinn bildet. „Rehearsal of Memory" stellt unsere Ideen in bezug auf Normalität in Frage und konfrontiert uns gleichzeitig mit einer sauberen, bequemen Maschine, die mit Dreck, dem Verbotenen und dem Wahnsinn gefüllt ist, deren Hygienebestrebungen mit dem Ausfluß dieser ausgeschlossenen menschlichen Beziehungen kontaminiert worden sind. Schon lange haben wir unsere Schmutzwäsche den Maschinen übergeben, während wir die Vorstellung eines weißen, emaillierten Äußeren aufrechterhalten haben.

Nun ist die Zeit des Drecks gekommen.

HIROO IWATA

Hiroo Iwata (J), geb. 1957, Doktorat von der University of Tokio, ist Associate Professor am Institute of Engineering Mechanics an der University of Tsukuba, unterrichtet Human Interface und betreibt Forschungsprojekte zu Virtual Reality. Tätig im Bereich der Kraftrückkoppelung in virtuellen Environments. Er entwickelte verschiedene Vorgaben für 3D-Formmodulierung und wissenschaftliche Visualisierung.

Hiroo Iwata (J), born in 1957, is an Associate Professor at the Institute of Engineering Mechanics at the University of Tsukuba, where he teaches human interface and conducts research projects on virtual reality. MS and PhD in engineering from the University of Tokyo; is active in research on force feedback in virtual environments. He has developed various force displays and applied them to 3D shape modelling and scientific visualization.

„Cross-active System" ist ein modifiziertes Virtual-Reality-System, das es ermöglicht, die Bewegungseingabe eines anderen Teilnehmers als Sinnesfeedback wahrzunehmen. In einem normalen interaktiven System erhält ein Teilnehmer Sinnesfeedback als Rückantwort auf die eigene Bewegungseingabe. Die Kommunikation zwischen zwei Teilnehmern wird bei „Cross-active System" jedoch anders erlebt, da das Sinnesfeedback auf die Bewegungseingabe zwischen den beiden aufgeteilt wird.

Die Installation „Cross-active System" besteht aus einer beweglichen Plattform, die sich bis zu sechs Grad in jede Richtung bewegen kann, einer großen Leinwand und aus einer Mikrovideokamera mit einem Positionssensor. Ein Teilnehmer sitzt auf der beweglichen Plattform, und der andere hält die Mikrovideokamera. Das Bild der Kamera wird auf die große Leinwand projiziert, während der Bewegungssensor die Bewegungen der Mikrovideokamera verfolgt. Da die bewegliche Plattform von Daten des Positionssensors gesteuert wird, bewirkt eine kleine Bewegung mit der Mikrovideokamera eine große Bewegung der Plattform. Die Sinneserfahrung des Teilnehmers auf der Plattform wird in einem Verhältnis 1:100 vom anderen Teilnehmer gesteuert.

"Cross-active System" is a modified virtual reality system, in which the motion input from one participant provides sensory feedback to the other participant. In an ordinary interactive system, a user obtains sensory feedback in response to his/her own motion input. In "Cross-active System", two participants experience unusual communication by dividing the sensory feedback from their motion input.

The "Cross-active System" installation consists of a motion platform capable of moving up to six degrees in any direction, with a large screen in front of it, and a micro-video camera with a position sensor. One participant sits on the motion platform and the other participant holds the micro-video camera. The image from the camera is displayed on the big screen, while the motion from the micro-video camera is tracked by the position sensor. Since the data from the position sensor controls the motion platform, a slight motion of the micro-video camera results in a large motion on the part of the motion platform. The sensory experience of the participant on the motion platform is controlled by the other participant in a ratio of 1/100.

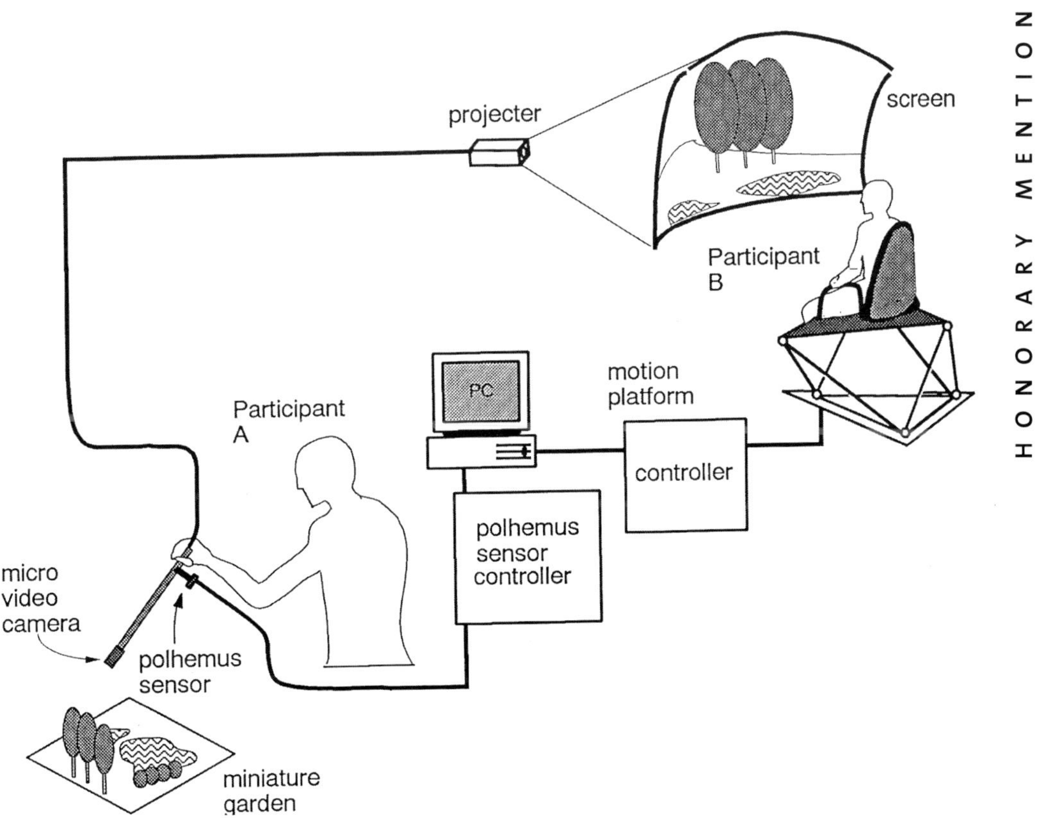

Hiroo Iwata
"Cross-active System", 1996

KNOWBOTIC RESEARCH

Knowbotic Research (KR+cF) – Yvonne Wilhelm, Alexander Tuchacek, Christian Huebler – ist in Köln angesiedelt. Mit Westbank Industries und Tactile Technology als Partner sowie mit Unterstützung der Academy for Media Arts hat KR+cF „Mem_brane", ein Laboratorium für Medienstrategien, gegründet. KR+cF wurde bereits mit wichtigen internationalen Medienkunstpreisen ausgezeichnet.

Knowbotic research (KR+cF) – Yvonne Wilhelm, Alexander Tuchacek, Christian Huebler – is based in Cologne. With the partners of Westbank Industries and Tactile Technology and the support of Academy for Media Arts, KR+cF has founded Mem_brane, a laboratory for media strategies. KR+cF has received major international Media Art Awards.

Knowbotic Research
"Dialogue with Knowbotic South", 1996

KR+cF devises a dynamic infrastructure for a Public Knowledge Space in which a dialogue about a potenial nature can take place. Here knowbots as hypothetical elements equipped with generative algorithms incorporate scientific, economic and political forces within the Antarctic Research and expose a confrontation with the dynamic complexities of Computer Aided Nature.

Recorded series of measured values represent natural conditions in the form of digitally coded data structures. For the purpose of these transformation processes, Antarctica is surveyed (in the deep sea as in the orbit, in its pack ice as in volcanic craters) by a formidable array of automatic measuring instruments which, installed and maintained by scientists, observe and record natural phenomena as an extension of perceptual organs. These measuring instruments divide the entirety of nature into processable information units. Their sensory capacities are highly specialised and focused on individual phenomena which are additionally broken down into space and time fragments to generate information output.

Natural scientists transform exterritorialized nature into models, formulating functional mathematical equations to reflect system effects as they might take place in the reference nature. Nature becomes a concept.

The current scientific dialogue relies increasingly on reconstructed form of nature. Answers are no longer supplied by reference nature via the experiment, but by the medium, i. e. the computer. At the same time, the dialogue is popularied in the sense that it becomes generally accessible through public data networks. The circle of participants in the dialogue widens. Reconstructed nature detaches itself from its technological synthesizing process. It becomes emancipated form its reference basis and assumes the role of an autonomous partner in the dialogue emerging as Computer Aided Nature.

KR+cF konstruiert eine dynamische Infrastruktur für einen öffentlichen Diskurs über eine mögliche Natur. In ihr verbinden „knowbots" als hypothetische Elemente, die mit „Zeugungsalgorithmen" ausgestattet sind, wissenschaftliche, wirtschaftliche und politische Kräfte innerhalb der Antarktis-Forschung und konfrontieren sie mit der dynamischen Komplexität einer „Computer Aided Nature".

Aufzeichnungen über Untersuchungsreihen spiegeln die natürlichen Begebenheiten in Form von digital kodierten Datenstrukturen. Im Sinne dieses Transformationsvorhabens wurde Antarktis durch und durch (Meer wie Weltraum, Packeis und Vulkankrater) von einer spezifischen Anordnung automatischer Meßgeräte vermessen, die – von Wissenschaftlern installiert und gewartet – die Naturphänomene als voranschreitender organischer Ausdruck beobachten und aufzeichnen. Diese Meßgeräte zerlegen die Gesamtheit der Natur in verfahrenstauglichen Informationseinheiten. Ihre sensorische Kapazität ist hochspezialisiert und auf Einzelphänomene gerichtet, welche zusätzlich in Raum- und Zeitfragmente zerlegt werden, um einen höheren Informationsoutput zu evozieren.

Naturwissenschaftler transformieren so extraterritoriale Natur in Modelle, indem sie funktionale mathematische Gleichungen schaffen, um jene systematischen Effekte zu reflektieren, die in diese referentiellen Natur Platz greifen könnten. Natur wird zum Konzept.

Der laufende wissenschaftliche Diskurs baut immer mehr auf dieser rekonstruierten Form der Natur. Forschungsresulate werden nicht länger durch Experiment mit der referentiellen Natur beschafft, sondern per Medium, also per Computer. Zugleich erreicht der Dialog insofern eine breite Öffentlichkeit, als daß er über öffentliche Datennetze zugänglich ist. Der Kreis jener, die an ihm teilhaben, wird immer größer. Die rekonstruierte Natur löst sich vom technologisch-synthetischen Prozeß ab. Sie emanzipiert sich von ihrer referentiellen Ausgangsbasis und wächst in die Rolle eines autonomen „Gesprächspartner", in der sie eben als „Computer Aided Nature" auftritt.

MINTZ / DITMARS / DUGGAN

Ronen Mintz (USA), der ein Studium an der University of California San Diego abgeschlossen hat, ist kinetischer Bildhauer in der Tradition eines Jean Tinguely oder Italo Scanga. Jason Ditmars (USA) hat sich als kinetischer Bildhauer auf computergesteuerte interaktive Installationen spezialisiert.
Brian Duggan (USA), entwickelt Software für 2D- und 3D-Graphik am San Diego Supercomputer Center.

Ronen Mintz (USA) graduated from the University of California San Diego. He is a kinetic sculptor in the tradition of Jean Tinguely and Italo Scanga. Jason Ditmars (USA) is a kinetic sculptor who specializes in computer-controlled, interactive installations. Brian Duggan (USA) was born in Washington, DC., has been developing 2D and 3D graphics software at the San Diego Supercomputer Center.

INTERACTIVE ART

Ronen Mintz / Jason Ditmars / Brian Duggan
"Virtual Wheelchair", 1995

The "Virtual Wheelchair" is a project that interfaces any wheelchair with a computer-generated virtual space. The user rolls up the ramp until the wheels of the wheelchair are positioned and lowered onto two sets of rollers. Optical encoders and an interface box translate the motion of the wheels to the computer, allowing wheelchair navigation through a computer modelled environment.

The wheelchair alone represents mobility for the physically challenged. As an interface, it becomes a metaphor for a new kind of mobility – one in which the physical world is left behind.

By making an interface specifically for wheelchairs, the experience is accessible to the entire public. People who are bound to wheelchairs are often considered handicapped in our society. With this interface, they become the expert navigators – able to maneuver around the space with ease. People who do not normally use a wheelchair will need to sit in a wheelchair, roll up the ramp, and navigate through the space by rotating the wheels.

The next stage of the project will be to incorporate force-feedback motors into the ramp. These motors will be used to reflect real-world gravity and friction. Thus, when you are on a virtual hill, the wheels of your wheelchair begin to coast forwards. To stop yourself, you will have to brake the wheels with your hands, just as you would normally. With this system installed, the wheelchair ramp will be one of the most submersive physical interfaces to date.

In dem Projekt „Virtual Wheelchair" wird ein Interface zwischen einem beliebigen Rollstuhl und einem computergenerierten virtuellen Raum hergestellt. Der Benutzer rollt die Rampe hinauf, bis die Rollstuhlräder auf zwei Rollen in Position gebracht und eingerastet sind. Optische Umkodierer und eine Interface-Box übertragen die Bewegungen der Räder so zum Computer, daß der Benutzer im Rollstuhl durch ein computermodelliertes Environment navigieren kann.

An sich bedeutet der Rollstuhl Mobilität für körperbehinderte Menschen. Als Interface wird der Rollstuhl zur Metapher für eine neue Art der Mobilität – für eine Mobilität, die die physische Welt hinter sich läßt. Dadurch, daß das Interface speziell für Rollstühle eingerichtet ist, ist diese Erfahrung tatsächlich allgemein zugänglich. Menschen, die einen Rollstuhl brauchen, werden in unserer Gesellschaft als behindert betrachtet. Mit diesem Interface werden sie die Experten im Navigieren – sie können sich mit größerer Leichtigkeit in diesem Raum bewegen. Menschen, die normalerweise keinen Rollstuhl brauchen, werden sich zunächst auf einen Rollstuhl setzen müssen, die Rampe hinaufrollen und dann durch den Raum navigieren, indem sie die Räder drehen.

In der nächsten Phase des Projekts werden Kraftrückkoppelungs-Motoren in die Rampe eingebaut. Durch diese Motoren werden Schwerkraft und Reibung, wie sie in der wirklichen Welt wirken, nachempfunden. Wenn man sich auf einem virtuellen Hügel befindet, werden die Räder vorwärts gleiten, und man muß die Räder mit den Händen bremsen, wie es auch normalerweise der Fall ist. Sobald dieses System eingebaut wird, wird die Rollstuhlrampe eines der umfassendsten physischen Interfaces sein, die es bis jetzt gibt.

MORK / PENDRY / STENSLIE

Knut Mork (N) ist Softwaretechniker, Schriftsteller und elektronischer Künstler. Er hat bei der norwegischen Telecom im Bereich der VR-Entwicklung gearbeitet. Kate Pendry ist Schauspielerin mit einer klassischen Ausbildung und verfügt über 15 Jahre Bühnenerfahrung. Ståle Stenslie ist Künstler und Mediendesigner; er arbeitet mit VR- und Kommunikationssystemen. Marius Watz ist Graphiker, war Ausstellungskoordinator der elektronischen Kunstausstellung Electra 96 am Henie-Onstad Art Center.

Knut Mork (N) is a software engineer, writer and electronic artist. He has worked on VR development at Norwegian Telecom. Kate Pendry is a classically trained actress, with 15 years performance experience in the UK and Europe. Ståle Stenslie is an artist and media designer working with VR and communication systems. Marius Watz is a graphic designer. He was the exhibition coordinator for the electronic art exhibition Electra 96 at the Henie-Onstad Art Center.

INTERACTIVE ART

"sense:less" is a place for humans to experience a strange alternate reality. Through VR technology and a custom-made body suit, "sense:less" puts the user in a multi-sensory environment. This is a dramatic space, influenced by theatre, and the users' journey through the world is an exploration of multiple personalities. People watching the installation can see the users' travels as they are projected onto the walls of the "sense:less" egg, a five metre high construction of plastic and steel.

The user stands inside the semi-transparent plastic egg, which is inflated by a cool air fan and suspended by metal arms over a steel platform. Video images of the virtual world are projected onto the egg's walls, and these images are seen by both the user and the spectators outside the shell. A speaker system broadcasts everything the user hears to the audience.

Five creatures live in the virtual world of "sense:less". The creatures have human voices, alien bodies and distinct personalities. They are based on real people and personal experience, and each has a story they need to tell. The virtual world the creatures live in, is a constantly changing network structure based on realtime data derived from a World Wide Web server. In this way, users on the Net become points on this network, indicating Net activity and the virtual presence of other human users. These human users are represented by mechanoid "agents" who constantly roam the virtual world, changing shape and direction depending on the users' behaviour in the hypertext structure of the World Wide Web server.

„sense:less" ist ein Ort, an dem Menschen eine seltsam veränderte Wirklichkeit erleben können. Mittels VR-Technologie und eines speziell angefertigten Bodysuit stellt „sense:less" den Besucher in ein multisensorielles Environment. Es ist ein dramatischer, vom Theater beeinflußter Raum, in dem die Reise des Besuchers durch die Welt eine Auseinandersetzung mit verschiedenen Persönlichkeiten darstellt. Zuschauer der Installation können die Reise des Benutzers als Projektionen an den Wänden des „sense:less"-Eis, einem fünf Meter hohen Gebilde aus Kunststoff und Stahl, mitverfolgen.

Der Benutzer steht in einem halbdurchsichtigen Kunststoffei, das von einem Kühlgebläse aufgeblasen und mit Metallarmen über einer Stahlplattform aufgehängt wird. Videobilder der virtuellen Welt werden auf die Wände des Eis projiziert und können sowohl vom Benutzer drinnen als auch von den Besuchern draußen gesehen werden. Über ein Lautsprechersystem wird alles, was der Benutzer drinnen hört, an das Publikum draußen übermittelt.

In der virtuellen Welt von „sense:less" leben fünf Wesen. Sie haben menschliche Stimmen, fremdartige Körper und eigenständige Persönlichkeiten. Diese Wesen sind alle nach wirklichen Personen und persönlichen Erfahrungen modelliert, und jedes Wesen hat eine Geschichte, die es unbedingt erzählen will. Die virtuelle Welt, in der diese Wesen leben, besteht aus einer sich stets verändernden Netzwerkstruktur, die auf Echtzeitdaten eines World-Web-Servers aufgebaut ist. Auf diese Weise werden Netzbenutzer zu Punkten im Netzwerk, wodurch Netzwerkaktivität und die virtuelle Anwesenheit anderer menschlicher Benutzer angezeigt wird. Menschliche Benutzer werden von mechanoiden „Agenten" dargestellt, die pausenlos in der virtuellen Welt umherwandern und ihre Gestalt und Richtung je nach Verhalten der Benutzer in der Hypertextstruktur des WWW-Servers verändern.

Knut Mork / Kate Pendry / Ståle Stenslie
"sense:less", 1996

NOBUYA SUZUKI

Nobuya Suzuki (J), geb. 1969 in Houya-City, Tokio. 1994 Studiumabschluß an der Faculty of Environmental Information, Keio University, Japan; 1996 Abschluß der Graduate School of Media and Governance, Keio University, Japan, derzeit Assistent an der International Academy of Media Arts and Sciences.

Nobuya Suzuki (J), born 1969 in Houya-City, Tokyo; graduated from the Faculty of Environmental Information, Keio University, Japan, in 1994; completed Graduate School of Media and Governance, Keio University, Japan in 1996. Now assistant at the International Academy of Media Arts and Sciences.

INTERACTIVE ART

Mit meiner Arbeit „Three Men Three Legs" will ich einen dreidimensionalen Raum herstellen, in dem Menschen Computernetzwerke verwenden können, um einander bei der Erreichung ihrer Ziele zu unterstützen. Ende 1993 hatte sich im Internet der WWW-Browser „Mosaic" durchgesetzt. Daraus erfolgte eine Verschiebung von textorientierter zu graphikorientierter Kommunikation. Was bei dieser Art der Kommunikation aber fehlte, war ein Konzept zur Zusammenarbeit. Das grundlegende System für die Arbeit „Three men three legs" wurde noch getestet, bevor „Mosaic" allgemein verfügbar wurde.

Masaki Fujihata hatte eine Vorstellung davon, wie Menschen miteinander Zeit und Raum innerhalb eines begrenzten Informationsfelds teilen könnten. Diese Idee wurde ursprünglich im Sommer 1993 entwickelt und bis Frühjahr 1994 verfeinert. Zu diesem Zeitpunkt wurde ein Experiment mit dem „Twister-Game on Network" durchgeführt, wobei eine Konferenz in Monte Carlo (IMAGINA) mit der Keio Universität in Japan verbunden wurde.

In „Three men three legs" verwenden drei Spieler drei vernetzte Computer. Jeder der Spieler sieht nur eine Figur im virtuellen Raum, die einen Kugelkörper und drei Beine hat. Jeder Spieler darf ein Bein dieser Figur manipulieren, doch hält die Figur automatisch das Gleichgewicht. Um die Figur in eine bestimmte Richtung zu bewegen, müssen alle Spieler zusammenhelfen, damit sie die Beinbewegungen im virtuellen Raum koordinieren können.

The aim of my work "Three Men Three Legs" is to create a three-dimensional space, in which people can use computer networks to help one another achieve their goals. The World Wide Web browser „Mosaic" came into wide use on the Internet at the end of 1993. A result of this was a shift from text-based communication to graphical communication. However, one thing that was lacking from this style of communication was the concept of collaboration. The system for this work, "Three men three legs", was tested before "Mosaic" was made available to the public.

Masaki Fujihata had an idea of how people could share time and space within a limited scope of information. This idea was initially developed in the summer of 1993 and work continued until the spring of 1994. At that time, an experiment was conducted with the "TwisterGame on Network", which connected a conference in Monte Carlo (IMAGINA) and Keio University in Japan. Three players use three networked computers. Each individual player can see only one figure, which has a spherical body and three legs in a virtual space. Players are allowed to manipulate only one leg each, but the figure keeps itself balanced automatically. In order for the figure to move in one direction, all the players must work together in this virtual space to coordinate the movement of the legs.

Nobuya Suzuki
"Three Men Three Legs", 1996

ERWIN REDL

*Erwin Redl (A), MFA Computer Art
(School of Visual Arts, New York)
Diplom in Tonsatz und Elektro-
akustische Musik (Hochschule für
Musik und darstellende Kunst Wien)
Preise und Ausstellungen in Europa
und den USA. Arbeitsbereich:
synästhetische
Computerinstallationen*

**Erwin Redl (A),
MFA Computer Art (School
of Visual Arts, New York)
BA Composition / Electronic
Music (Music Academy, Vienna).
Awards and exhibitions in
Europe and USA. Focus on
synaesthetic computer
installations**

*Die Installation „Parallel Mesmerization of Eleven Blon-
des and Eleven Brunettes by Two Computers" interagiert mit dem Organismus des Dow Jones Industrial
Average. Der Dow Jones stellt eine organische virtuelle
Spezies dar, die aus reiner Quantität besteht: die
Börsenkurse der 30 größten amerikanischen Firmen.
Die Lebenszeichen des Dow Jones sind auf der ganzen
Welt verteilt und leicht zugänglich, weil man die Kurse
vom Internet einfach runterladen kann. (Fast) jeder
kann an diesem System teilhaben und dessen Verhalten beeinflussen, doch nur bis zu einem gewissen Grad
– die Investition.*

*Dieses Werk simuliert nicht die Börse, sondern
ver(ent)wendet die Lebenszeichen des Dow Jones als
Auslöser für audio-visuelle Geschehnisse oder – etwas
allgemeiner gesagt – Masseverhalten als Inspiantion für
die Kunst.*

*Zwei aus Puppen bestehende Teams werden auf das
Fußballfeldmodell gestellt (Team der Blondinen/Team
der Dunkelhaarigen). Das Verhalten der Teams wird von
einem Computer gesteuert. Jede Puppe ist mit den
Bewegungen eines bestimmten Dow-Jones-Kurses
gekoppelt. Alle fünfzehn Minuten loggt sich der Computer bei einem Internet-Börsenkurs-Provider ein und fragt
die Kurse ab. Je nach Kurswertveränderungen ändert
sich auch das Verhalten der Puppen: Brüste leuchten
auf, sie sprechen (Samples aus Kindergeschichten und
pornographischen Aufnahmen) und singen usw. Durch
kleine Motoren werden die Figuren in willkürlichen
Mustern kreuz und quer über das Feld bewegt – eine
seltsame Ballettruppe aus singenden Blondinen und
Dunkelhaarigen mit aufleuchtenden Brüsten führt ein
hybrides Theaterstück auf, das vom virtuellen Organismus des Dow Jones dirigiert wird.*

The installation "Parallel Mesmerization of
Eleven Blondes and Eleven Brunettes by Two
Computers" interacts with the organism of
the Dow Jones Industrial Average. The Dow
Jones represents an organic virtual species
made up of pure quantity: the stock quotes
of the 30 largest American companies.
Dow Jones' life signs are distributed all over
the world and easily accessed by download-
ing the quotes from the Internet. (Almost)
everyone can be part and influence the behavior of this being, but only to a small
degree – the investment.

The piece does not simulate the stock market but (ab)uses the life signs of the Dow
Jones as a trigger for audio-visual events, or
in a more generic sense – mass behavior as
an inspiration for the arts.

Two teams of dolls are placed on the soccer
field model (blonde team/brunette team). A
computer controls the behavior of the teams.
Each doll is linked to the actions of a particular Dow Jones' stock. Every 15 minutes the
computer logs into a stock quote provider
on the Internet and downloads quotes. Changes in the stocks' values cause the dolls'
actions: breasts flash, they speak (samples
from kids tales and pornographic tapes) and
sing, etc. Little motors move the figures in
random patterns across the field – a strange
ballet of singing blondes and brunettes with
flashing breasts performs a hybrid theater
piece conducted by the the Dow Jones' virtual
organism.

Erwin Redl
**"Parallel Mesmerization of Eleven Blondes and
Eleven Brunettes by Two Computers"**

MICHEL REDOLFI / LUC MARTINEZ

Michel Redolfi (F), geb. 1951 in Marseille, seit 1986 Direktor des Centre International de Recherche Musicale (CIRM) in Nizza, 1968 Mitbegründer der Groupe de Musique Expérimentale de Marseille (GMEM). Luc Martinez (F), geb. 1962, beschäftigt sich mit interaktiven Musiksystemen und leitet die Forschungsabteilung am CIRM.

Michel Redolfi (F), born 1951 in Marseille, Director of the Centre International de Recherche Musicale (CIRM) in Nice since 1986, co-founder of the Groupe de Musique Expérimentale de Marseille (GMEM) in 1968. Luc Martinez (F), born 1962, is working on interactive music systems; he is in charge of the Research Department at CIRM.

Grundlage des Projekts „In Corpus" bildet die musikalische Interaktivität zwischen den Zuhörern – die bei Schwerkraft Null schweben – und dem dreidimensionalen Raum. Das Wasser ermöglicht es den Zuhörern, sich in jede beliebige Richtung zu bewegen und die Musik in einem echten 3D-Raum nach Wunsch zu steuern. Sie erfahren eine Verschmelzung mit/Verwechslung von virtueller Wirklichkeit und reiner Wirklichkeit, während sie buchstäblich durch die Komposition fliegen.

Ihre Bewegungen interagieren mit den Echtzeit-Musikinstrumenten mittels einer Reihe digitaler Kameras, die jede Sekunde verfolgen: die Position jedes einzelnen Zuhörers (Unterwasserkamera), die Gruppenentwicklung (Kamera über dem Schwimmbecken) und Farbentsprechungen mit den MIDI-Zonen (alle Kameras). Jeder Zuhörer-Navigator wird durch die Farbe des Badeanzugs oder der Badehaube, die er trägt, individualisiert. Manche Navigatoren sind dann an bestimmten Stellen aktiv, manche nicht; alle haben aber Körperkontrolle über ein MIDI-Parameter und spielen auf dem System über Fernsteuerung. Für jede Gruppe der Aquanauten hat die dadurch entstehende Musik ihren eigenen Stil und eigene Originalität.

Im Wasser wird Musik viermal so schnell wie in der Luft übermittelt, und man kann sie nur dann hören, wenn man mit dem Wasser Kontakt hat. Indem sie ins Wasser gehen, können die Teilnehmer das Zuhören durch Knochenübermittlung erfahren (direkte Resonanz im inneren Ohr). Die Lokalisierung im Raum wird vollständig neu definiert. Das Spektrum wird anders wahrgenommen, und Low-End und High-End werden auf spektakuläre Weise ausgeglichen.

The project "In Corpus" is based on a musical interactivity between listeners – floating in zero gravity – and 3D space. Water enables the listeners to move in any direction and pilot music as they wish in a real 3D space. They experience a (con)fusion between Virtual Reality and pure reality as they literally fly through the composition. Their motion interacts with real-time musical instruments, thanks to a set of digital cameras which track every second: each listener's position (underwater camera), group evolution (above the pool camera), and color matching with MIDI zones (all cameras). Each listener-navigator is individualized by the color of the bathing suit or the cap (s)he is wearing. Thus, some navigators are active in certain locations. Some are not; but everyone has the body control of a MIDI parameter and remotely plays on the system.

The resulting music has it's own style and originality for each group of aquanauts. Music in the water travels four time faster than in the air and can be heard only by being in contact with the surface. By entering into the water, participants experience bone conduction listening (direct inner ear resonance). Space locating is completely redefined. Spectra is perceived differently, with a spectacular equalization of low and high ends.

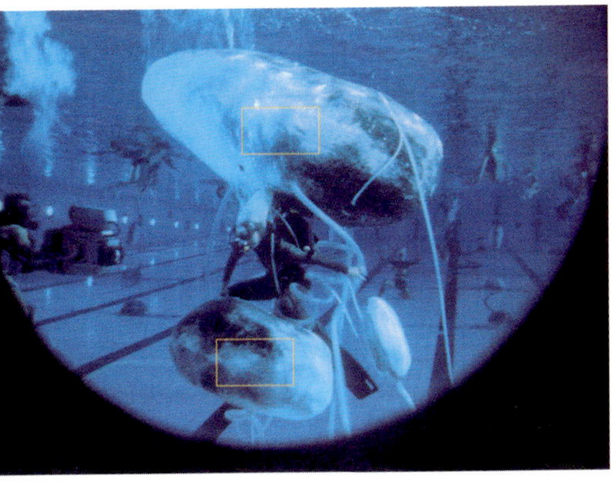

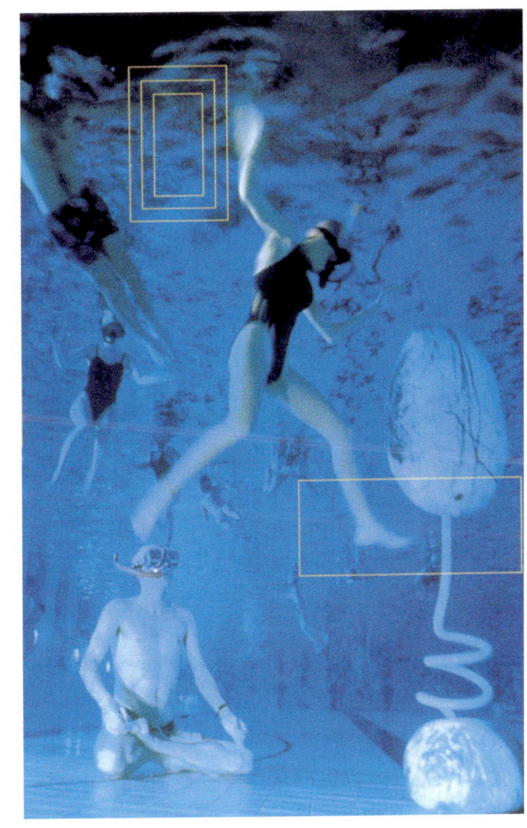

Michel Redolfi / Luc Martinez
"In Corpus", 1994

SILVER

Silver (CZ) ist virtueller Künstler, lebt und arbeitet hauptsächlich in Tschechien. Interessiert sich für interaktive Kunst und VR. Ausstellungsbeteiligung in Brünn, Prag und Plasy seit 1994.

Silver (CZ) is a virtual artist, living and working mostly in the Czech Republic. Interested in interactive art and virtual reality. Has participated in exhibitions in Brno, Prague and Plasy since 1994.

Das virtuelle Wesen: aus der VR-Technologie erzeugt, eingeschlossen in einem weißen Behälter, der an einen Brutkasten oder Sarkophag erinnert. Auf menschliche Sprache reagiert es mit Bewegungen, Geräuschen oder einer Veränderung seiner Gestalt. Man kann es durch die enge Öffnung eines Beobachtungsgeräts, unter dem auch ein Mikrophon montiert ist, betrachten.

Die Installation „RESIDENT" bezieht sich auf die Mythen und Legenden rund um die Erschaffung künstlichen Lebens. Inspiriert wurde das Design von alchemistischen Praktiken. Die Form des Körpers, das immaterielle Lichtfeld und das Verhalten des Wesens werden von Zahlen exakt festgelegt (Schlüsselzahlen sind: eins, zwei, vier und sieben).

The virtual being: created by virtual reality technology, enclosed in a white container reminiscent of an incubator or sarcophagus. It responds to human speech with movement, sounds, or by changing its shape. It may be observed through a narrow viewing device with a microphone mounted below it.

The installation "RESIDENT" relates to myths and legends about the creation of artificial life. Its design was inspired by methods of alchemy. The body form, the immaterial field of light, and the behaviour of the creature are precisely defined by numbers (key numbers are: one, two, four and seven).

"

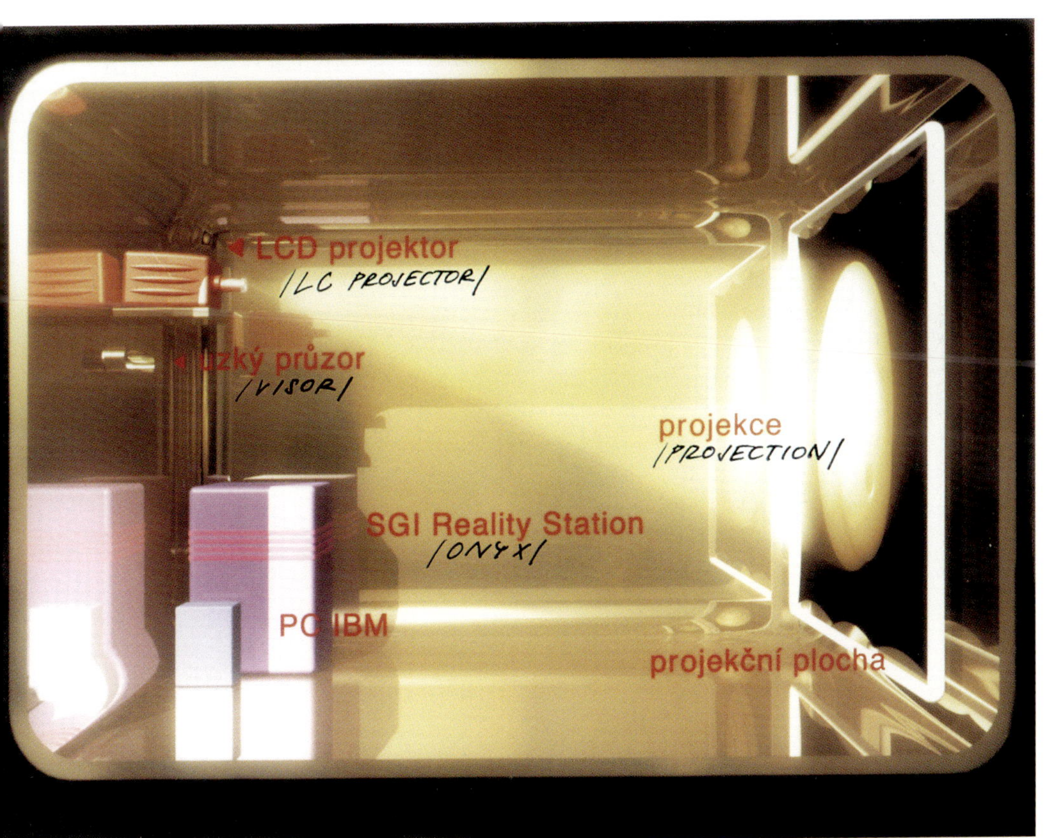

Silver
"RESIDENT", 1995

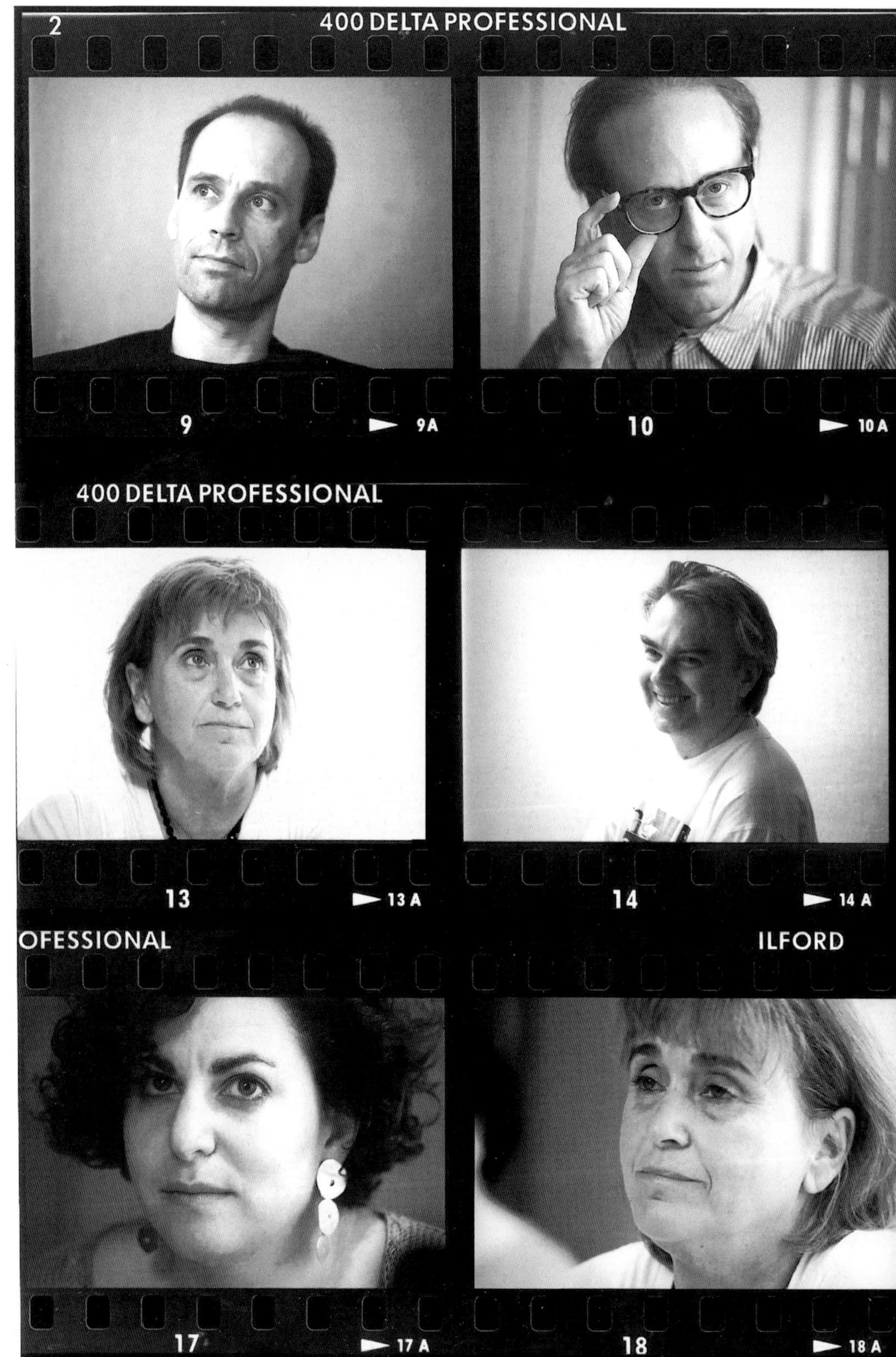
2
400 DELTA PROFESSIONAL
9
9A
10
10 A
400 DELTA PROFESSIONAL
13
13 A
14
14 A
OFESSIONAL
ILFORD
17
17 A
18
18 A

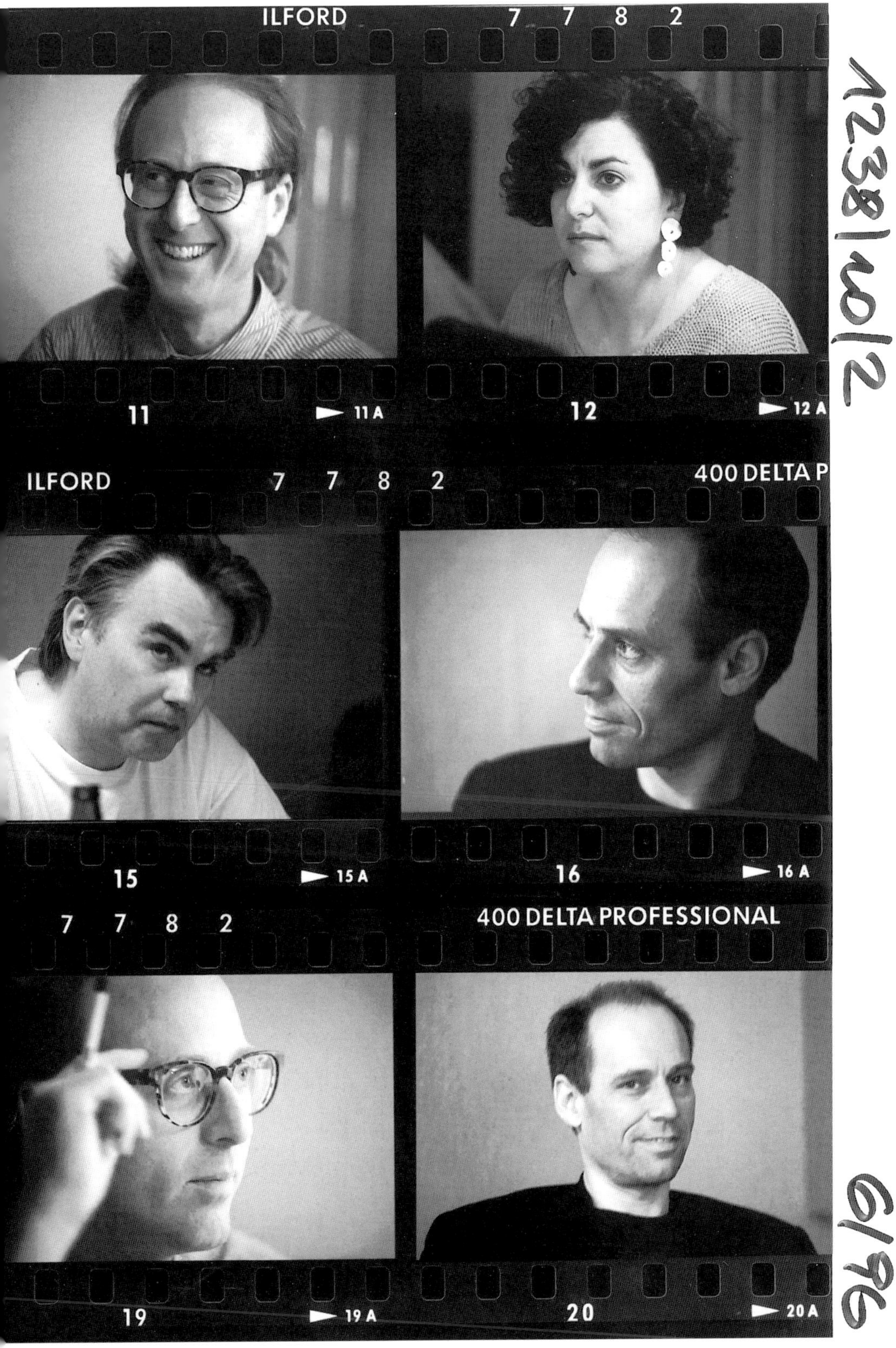

ILFORD
7 7 8 2
11
11 A
12
12 A
ILFORD
7 7 8 2
400 DELTA P
15
15 A
16
16 A
7 7 8 2
400 DELTA PROFESSIONAL
19
19 A
20
20 A

STATEMENT OF THE COMPUTER ANIMATION JURY
Jurybegründung Computeranimation

Wir haben uns entschieden, den ersten Preis an John Lasseter und sein Team bei Pixar zu vergeben, die gemeinsam „Toy Story", den ersten abendfüllenden Film, der ausschließlich im Computer hergestellt wurde, geschaffen haben. Dieser Film ist nicht nur von enormer Wichtigkeit für den Gesamtbereich der Computeranimation, sondern auch zweifellos ein Meilenstein in der Filmgeschichte überhaupt. Nach der erfolgreichen Produktion von „Toy Story" ist 3D-Animation jetzt endgültig erwachsen geworden. In Zukunft wird 3D-Animation genauso ein Werkzeug der herkömmlichen Filmproduktion werden, wie es 2D-Animation bisher gewesen ist. Eine ähnliche Veränderung in der Filmgeschichte wurde durch den Schritt Walt Disneys hervorgerufen, als er den Bereich der Kurzfilmanimation verließ, um den ersten abendfüllenden Animationsfilm zu erzeugen: „Schneewittchen" („Snow White").

An „Toy Story" geht der erste Preis nicht nur wegen der hervorragenden technischen Leistungen und der ganzen Arbeit, die hinter der erfolgreichen Fertigstellung dieses ambitionierten Projekts steckt; der Preis gilt ebenso der originellen und vielschichtigen Geschichte, der ausgezeichneten dramatischen Struktur und nicht zuletzt dem Können, das in jedem noch so kleinsten Detail der Erschaffung und der technischen Umsetzung der Bilder dieses Films sehr deutlich erkennbar ist, selbst in den kurzen Auszügen des Films, die hier eingereicht wurden.

BUF Compagnie spielte die Rolle des Aschenputtels beim Prix Ars Electronica 96. Ihre drei großartigen Projekte zeichnen sich sowohl durch Kreativität, Phantasie, Stil, Spaß als auch durch technische

Our decision to award the Golden Nica to John Lasseter and his team at Pixar, the makers of "Toy Story", the first entirely computer generated feature film, is not only on based on the film's extraordinary importance for the entire area of computer animation, but also because this film is undoubtedly one of the milestones in the history of movie making as a whole. The successful completion of "Toy Story" will forever mark the growing-up of 3D computer animation. Henceforth it will be considered as a mainstream production tool in the same way that 2D animation established itself as such in the past. A similar transition happened in film history when Walt Disney decided to move beyond animated shorts to make the first feature animated film: Snow White. Indeed, "Toy Story" does not deserve the prize soley on the basis of the significant technical achievements and the immense amount of work which were required for the successful completion of this ambitious project. It also deserves the prize because of its unique and multifaceted story, its extraordinary dramatic structure and, finally, because of the enormous talent which went into every minuscule detail of the creation and technical realization of its images, which is clearly evident in the submitted selected short excerpt from the whole work.

BUF Compagnie was the Cinderella company at the Prix Ars Electronica 96. Creative imagination, style, fun, and technical virtuosity and innovation were all combined into three great projects. Two of them won the awards of distinction, one an honory mention.

The awards of distinction go to "City of lost children" and to "Like a Rolling Stone". They clearly represent the highest level of excellence that has been be achieved today with respect to the integration of computer generated effects into traditional film. Where "Toy Story" is entirely made by using computer graphics, the pieces from BUF each use it in a unique and fascinating way to bolster up conventional production.

At first, "Like a Rolling Stone" appears to be a straightforward morph piece. But as it proceeds, it becomes clear that this is an excellent short film on top of technique that appears deceptively simple. We felt that this piece captured the essence of the song that it was portraying. It really illustrates the disorientation and the world view in every respect of the main character of the Rolling Stones' song where everything is increasingly out of normal perspective.

"City of Lost Children" demonstrates similar excellence in the more traditional domain of 3D computer animation and visual effects for a landmark feature film. The rendering and overall integration of computer animation with live action is defining the current state of the art. The effects of "City of Lost Children" are almost invisible as effects, but they are highly visible in terms of the affect that they produce in the audience. Both in techni-

Hochleistungen und Innovation aus. Zwei dieser Projekte verdienen eine Auszeichnung, eines davon eine Anerkennung.

Die Auszeichnungen gehen an „City of Lost Children" und „Like a Rolling Stone". Sie zeigen, welch hohes Niveau bei der Integration computergenerierter Effekte in den traditionellen Film erreicht werden kann. Während „Toy Story" ausschließlich mit Mitteln der Computergraphik erstellt wurde, verwenden die Arbeiten von BUF Compagnie die Computergraphik auf originelle und faszinierende Art und Weise, um die herkömmliche Filmproduktion zu ergänzen.

Beim ersten Blick scheint „Like a Rolling Stone" ein unkompliziertes Morph-Werk zu sein. Im Laufe der Zeit wird es allerdings klar, daß es sich hier um einen ausgezeichneten Kurzfilm handelt, der auf einer nur scheinbar einfachen Technik beruht. Mit einem unserer Meinung nach sehr klaren Bezug zum Song. Dieses Werk illustriert eindringlich den Orientierungsverlust und die Weltsicht der Hauptfigur dieses Rolling-Stones-Liedes, in dem alles zunehmend aus den Fugen der normalen Perspektiven gerät.

„City of Lost Children" zeigt in einem hervorragenden Spielfilm eine ähnlich hohe Qualität auf dem eher traditionellen Gebiet der Computeranimation und der visuellen Effekte. Das Rendering und die Verbindung der Computeranimation mit Live-Action stecken auf beeindruckende Weise die Grenzen der derzeitigen Möglichkeiten der Computeranimation ab. Die Effekte in „City of Lost Children" sind als solche fast unsichtbar, machen sich aber in der Wirkung, die sie auf das Publikum haben, äußerst bemerkbar. Sowohl was die technische Qualität als auch was den Produktionswert be-

trifft, sind diese zwei Werke den anderen Einreichungen, die die Jury gesehen hat, weit voraus.

Mit Absicht beschloß die Jury, die Auswahl jener Werke, denen eine Anerkennung zuerkannt wird, auf solche zu beschränken, die letztendlich nicht einen der ersten drei Preise gewonnen haben, jedoch durchaus dafür in Betracht gezogen wurden. Aus diesem Grund wurden nur acht der zwölf möglichen Anerkennungen vergeben:

„The Visible Human Project" ist ein Beispiel einer wissenschaftlichen Anwendung, deren Bedeutung sich nicht nur auf die reine Leistung der Herstellung beschränkt. Es stellt eine Datenbank zur Verfügung, die noch viele Jahre und hoffentlich zum Vorteil der Menschheit verwendet wird. Heuer präsentierte James Duesing in „The Law of Averages" eine Art Erzählung, die wie ein visuelles „Stream-of-Consciousness" wirkt. Obwohl der Streifen eine vollständige komplexe Geschichte erzählt, wurde er mit einem sehr niedrigen Budget und mit einer relativ einfachen technischen Ausrüstung hergestellt. Außerdem zeigt dieser Film sehr gut, wie sich auch begrenzte Ressourcen auf raffinierte Weise positiv auf Inhalt und Stil eines Werkes auswirken können. Das an sich ist schon eine beachtliche Leistung. „The Boxer Trailer" von Pierre Lachapelle zeigt Animation und Rendering in einer Qualität wie der von „Toy Story", doch unterscheidet er sich im Stil deutlich von den meisten Hollywoodproduktionen – ein hoffentlich gutes Zeichen für die zukünftige Entwicklung. Welche Möglichkeiten die 3D-Animation hinsichtlich Stil und Technik bieten, zeigt auch „Period" von Philippe Billion/Ex Machina.

cal quality and in production value these two works are way ahead of almost anything else the jury has seen. The Jury deliberately decided to restrict the group of works that should be awarded an honorary mention to those high quality pieces that were not awarded the first three prizes, but were of close enough quality to have been considered. Therefore, only a total of eight rather than the possible twelve submissions were finally selected. "The Visible Human Project" is an example of a scientific application being of extraordinary usefulness beyond the moment of its creation. It provides a database hat can be used for many years and hopefully to the advantage of humanity. This year, James Duesing presented with "The Law of Averages" a visual stream of consciousness type of narration. Although the film tells a complete and complex story, it was produced on a very low budget with fairly simple technical epuipment. Furthermore, it was accomplished with a high degree of sophistication in employing its limitations for the sake of the story and the unique style of the work. This in itself represents a major achievement. The "Boxer Trailer", made by Pierre Lachapelle, shows animation and rendering of the quality of "Toy Story", but with a style which is different from mainstream Hollywood and that hopefully bodes well for the future. Another significant exercise in 3D animation style and technique is "Period" by Philippe Billion from Ex Machina. The overall visual quality which was achieved in this draft clearly deserves an honorary mention. Christian Boustani's "Cities of the Past" is a wonderful example of the way in which atmosphere can be created using computers. It has a painterly sense which illustrates another amazing direction in which computers can take us. "Homer Simpson" is as great as a comment on computer graphics as it is in making use of it. We particularly like the way the 3D computer graphics catch the feelings and personalities of the two-dimensional conventional animation. It also shows how you can again, as in "Toy Story", use computer graphics to be funny, although in a more subversive way. "Jumanji", coming from ILM-Studios, is a stunning technical exercise. If there had not been "Toy Story" we would certainly have seen it up in the top three. The integration of the effects and the using of the effects to create otherwise impossible situations is truly fantastic and professional. Finally, the "Amnesty International" piece done by Arnauld Lamorlette of BUF Compagnie, is an amazing integration of computer graphics into live action. It is used to extend and comment on live action, real footage, for a political purpose. It is awarded an honorary mention not only for its technical excellence, but also as an example for the use of computer graphics in a more intellectual context, rather than for purely visual or entertainment purposes.

JOHN LASSETER

John Lasseter, geb. 1957 in Los Angeles; erhielt seine künstlerische Ausbildung am California Institute of the Arts in Valencia. John Lasseter kam 1984 zur Pixar Computer-animations-Gruppe, nachdem er 5 Jahre als Animator in den Walt Disney Studios gearbeitet hatte. Mit der Computergraphik kam John Lasseter erstmals während der Produktion von „Wild Things Test" in Kontakt. John Lasseter arbeitete in der Folge auch an der ersten volldigitalen Disneyproduktion „Tron" mit. Bei Lucasfilm, dem jetzigen Pixar, verfeinerte er die Verschmelzung von Trickfilm und Computeranimation und entwickelte im Pixar Team ein 3D-Computer-animations-System, das eine interaktive Figurenanimation ermöglicht.

Born 1957 in Los Angeles, got his artistic training at the California Institute of the Arts in Valencia. In 1984, John Lasseter joined the Pixar computer animation group after having worked for five years at the Walt Disney studios. John Lasseter's first contact with computer graphics occured when working at the production of "Wild Things Test". Consequently, John Lasseter took part in the production of Disney's first all-digital production "Tron". At Lucasfilm now Pixar, he refines the merging of animated cartoon and computer animation and develops a 3D-computer animations system with the Pixar Team, allowing an interactive animation of the character.

John Lasseter
"Toy Story", 1996

COMPUTER ANIMATION

"To infinity and beyond!" – That is where Walt Disney Pictures and the northern Californian computer graphics specialists from Pixar Animation Studios have gone, taking the art of animation to previously unknown dimensions with "Toy Story". "Toy Story" is the first animated feature film to be created not on the drawing board, but entirely in the computer. It took four years to complete the pictures and sounds of the adventures of Woody and Buzz.

The Genesis of the Characters. If you compare the production of a computer animated cartoon with that of a feature film with real actors, you could say that the computer technicians are like the film team and the animators are like the actors. "I define the animation of a character so that you have to think this character," says Lasseter. "Every single movement or feeling this character shows has to look as though it has come right out of the animator's mind." Once the story has been written and separated into individual sequences, once the cameras are rolling and the scene starts, it is the animators' job to breathe life into the characters. The characters' expressions and movements are key-controlled by means of so-called "avars" (articulated variables) integrated in the model forms, which may be compared with the strings on a marionette. This allows the animator to separately determine certain gestures or movements like raising an eyebrow or twitching the corner of the mouth, and the computer puts that together with the rest of the face or body. For instance, Bill Reeves, the technical director, provided Woody with more than 700 control functions of this type, with 212 of them just for his face. The program that Pixar developed especially for computer animation is called "Menv" (Modeling Environment), and it has been continuously improved and rewritten over the past nine years. This program allows animators to construct three-dimensional figures from scanned drawings and to move

„In die Unendlichkeit und noch weiter!" – dorthin dringen Walt Disney Pictures und die nordkalifornischen Computergrafik-Spezialisten von den Pixar Animation Studios vor, die mit „Toy Story" die Kunst der Animation in bislang ungekannte Dimensionen tragen: „Toy Story" ist der erste Animationsfilm in Spielfilmlänge, der von den Kreativen nicht auf dem Zeichenbrett, sondern komplett im Computer geschaffen wurde. Vier Jahre dauerte es, bis die Abenteuer von Woody und Buzz in Bild und Ton fertiggestellt waren.

Die Genesis der Figuren. *Wenn man die Produktion eines computeranimierten Trickfilms mit der eines Spielfilms mit echten Schauspielern vergleichen wollte, könnte man die Computertechniker mit dem Team am Set und die Animatoren mit den Schauspielern gleichsetzen. „Ich definiere die Animation einer Figur so, daß man diese Figur denken muß", sagt Lasseter. „Jede einzelne Bewegung oder Gefühlsregung, die diese Figur macht, sollte so aussehen, als entstamme sie der Gedankenwelt des Animators selbst." Sobald die Story geschrieben und in einzelne Sequenzen untergliedert ist, sobald die Kameras laufen und die Klappe gefallen ist, ist es die Aufgabe des Animators, den Figuren Leben einzuhauchen. Mimik und Bewegungen der Charaktere werden über Tastendruck gesteuert, durch sogenannte „Avars" (Articulated Variables), die, vergleichbar den Schnüren an einer Marionette, in die Modellformen eingearbeitet sind. Dadurch kann der Animator bestimmte Gesten oder Bewegungen wie das Hochziehen einer Augenbraue oder das Verziehen der Mundwinkel isoliert bestimmen, und der Computer setzt das Ganze dann in Beziehung zum Rest des Gesichtes oder Körpers. Woody zum Beispiel erhielt von Bill Reeves, dem technischen Leiter, über 700 solcher Kontrollfunktionen, allein 212 davon für sein Gesicht. Das Programm, das Pixar eigens für die Computeranimation entwickelt und während der vergangenen neun Jahre ständig verbessert und umgeschrieben hat, nennt sich „Menv" (Modeling Environment). Es erlaubt den Animatoren, eingescannte Zeichnungen dreidimensional aufzubauen und innerhalb dieser virtuellen Modelle bestimmte Teile mit den Avars zu bewegen. Das Menv-Programm und ein weiteres, seinerzeit von Pixars Programmierern geschriebenes 3D-System namens „RenderMan" (das die vollständige Information einer digitalen Szenerie zu einem perfekten dreidimensionalen Bild unter Berücksichtigung von Licht,*

Oberflächenstruktur und Farbschattierungen montiert) liefen auf den von Pixar entwickelten und produzierten PIC-Rechnern (Pixar Image Computer).

Im Gegensatz zu traditionellen Arbeitsweise bei Disney, wo jeder Zeichner für eine Figur zuständig ist, arbeiten die „Toy Story"-Animatoren auch an allen Charakteren gemeinsam, wobei sie jeweils komplette Sequenzen von drei bis sieben Sekunden Länge fertigstellten. Täglich wurden die Ergebnisse dem ganzen Team vorgeführt, jeder konnte so seine Arbeit im Gesamtzusammenhang sehen und sich mit Kritik und Verbesserungsvorschlägen einbringen. Bei Buzz wiederum mußten die Animatoren auf andere Bewegungsabläufe achten, denn schließlich ist er aus Plastik und sollte sich deshalb steif und methodisch bewegen. Der Computer-Modellbauspezialist Eben Ostby baute an die 800 Animationskontrollen in den Space Ranger ein. Eine der aufwendigsten und schwierigsten, aber auch lohnenswertesten Sequenzen für die Animatoren war die Erkundungsmission der „Green Army Men" auf Andys Geburtstagsparty. Um ein Gefühl dafür zu bekommen, wie diese Plastiksoldaten sich mit ihren auf einer kleinen Konsole verschweißten Stiefeln bewegen würden, nagelte Pete Doctor ein Paar alte Joggingschuhe auf einem Sperrholzbrett fest. Er und sein Team wechselten sich anschließend dabei ab, mit der Konstruktion über die Studioflure zu hopsen und die jeweils gewagtesten Schritte zu analysieren.

Wie man eine Welt der Karikaturen erschafft

Art Director Ralph Eggleston fiel die Aufgabe zu, den Schauplätzen von „Toy Story" ein „betont realistisches" und glaubwürdiges Aussehen zu geben. Das Ergebnis ist eine von Karikaturen bevölkerte Welt, in der die Figuren selbst künstlich sind, ihre Gestalt und Oberflächenstruktur aber extrem realistisch.

Zu den Haupt-„Drehorten", die Eggleston designte, gehören die beiden unterschiedlichen Welten von Andys und Sids Kinderzimmern, das spacige Interieur des „Pizza Planet" und die mondlichtbeschienene Tankstelle, an der sich Woody und Buzz zusammentun müssen, um zurück zu Andy zu finden. Trotz der hochtechnisierten Produktionsstandards, mit denen Eggleston sich zurechtfinden mußte, beeindruckte er Lasseter mit „seinem einigartigen Sinn für Farbe und seinem Talent, den designten Oberflächen Tiefe und Gestalt zu verleihen". Nach langen Diskussionen mit dem Regisseur entwarf der Art Director eine Farbpalette für die 28 wichtigsten Sequenzen des Films, auf der er die vor-

certain parts of these virtual models with the avars. The Menv program and also a special 3D-system originally written by programmers at Pixar, called "RenderMan" (which mounts the complete information of a digital setting to a perfect three-dimensional image, including lighting, surface structures and color shading) were run on PIC computers (Pixar Image Computer), which were developed and produced by Pixar. Unlike the traditional working methods at Disney, where each animator is responsible for one particular character, for "Toy Story" all the animators worked on all the characters together to produce individual complete sequences of three to seven seconds in length. The results were presented to the whole team each day, so that each person could see their work in the overall context and add criticisms and suggestions for improvement. For Buzz, the animators had to consider a different series of movements than for Woody, because, of course, Buzz is made of plastic and thus needs to move more stiffly and methodically than Woody. Eben Ostby, the specialist for computer model construction, integrated roughly 800 animation con-trols into the Space Ranger. "Our mottos for thinking about the main characters' motoric were 'Think in snake-like dangling movements for Woody!' and 'Think in daring angles for Buzz!'", remembers Ostby. One of the most complicated and difficult sequences for the animators, which also turned out to be one of the most rewarding, was the "reconnaissance mission" of the "Green Army Men" at Andy's birthday party. In order to get a feeling for the way these plastic figures would move with their boots attached to these little plastic bases, Pete Docter nailed a pair of old jogging shoes to a plank. He and his team took turns hopping around the studio halls with this construction, analyzing the movements and each of the most daring steps.

How to create a world of caricatures

Art Director Ralph Eggleston was assigned the task of providing the settings in "Toy

Story" with a "decidedly realistic" and plausible appearance. The result is a world populated by caricatures, in which the figures themselves are artificial, but whose form and surface structure appears entirely realistic. Among the main "shooting sets" that Eggleston designed are the two different worlds of Andy's and Sid's rooms, the spacey interior of "Pizza Planet" and the moonlit gas station, where Woody and Buzz must join forces to get back to Andy. Despite the high tech production standards that Eggleston had to deal with, he impressed Lasseter with "his unique sense of color and his talent for providing the surfaces he designed with depth and form." Following long discussions with the director, the art director designed a color palette for the 28 most important sequences of the film. For this he composed the main color shadings for each scene according to the atmosphere and lighting. He was inspired in his work by paintings by Maxfield Parrish, which are characterized by saturated colors and strong contrasts. Andy's room was intended to be a safe harbor, a pleasant and comfortable environment in which the toys come to life. Everything is bright and sunny and full of warm pastel colors; even the blue wallpaper with the white clouds on it conveys a feeling of openness. Sid's room, on the other hand, is a dreadful torture chamber for toys, where hard rock posters glow on the walls and there is rusty barbed wire wrapped around the bed that has no comfortable blanket or sheet on it. The only light in the room comes from a bare light bulb hanging above Sid's workbench.

The Gigantic Pipeline: Every creature, every toy, accessory and every landscape in "Toy Story" exists soley in a virtual space. Absolutely everything. It is a world that no one can touch or even see directly. From the violent storms to the enchanting sunsets, from every single blade of grass to the 1.2 million leaves on the trees in Andy's neighborhood, from the telephone poles and pebble paths to the flickering of a burning match - they are all artificial pictures.

Andys Kinderzimmer war gedacht als sicherer Heimathafen, eine angenehme und gemütliche Umgebung, in der die Spielzeuge zum Leben erwachen. Alles ist sonnendurchflutet und voll warmer Pastelltöne, und auch die blaue Tapete mit ihren weißen Wölkchen vermittelt ein Gefühl von Weite. Sids Zimmer dagegen ist eine schreckliche Folterkammer für Spielzeuge, in der Hardrock-Poster im Schwarzlicht an den Wänden glühen und das Bett mit rostigem Stacheldraht umwickelt ist und keine gemütlichen Decken oder Lacken hat. Das einzige Licht kommt von einer nackten Glühbirne, die über Sids Werkbank hängt. Augenmerk gilt auch den Details: Die Türleiste wurde mit Staubflocken geschmückt, der Fußboden in Andys Zimmer hat schon ein paar Kratzer und Schrammen vom Spielen, und in Sids Zimmer steht eine Kommode voller Schmutzwäsche. Wegen der organischen Beschaffenheit von Haaren, Haut und Kleidung gehören menschliche Figuren zu den Dingen, die am allerschwierigsten im Computer zu erzeugen sind. Die menschliche Haut weist eine der komplexesten Oberflächenstrukturen überhaupt auf. Um ein einigermaßen natürliches Aussehen hinzukriegen, müssen bis zu zehn verschiedene Programme, die jeweils eine bestimmte Oberflächeneigenschaft simulieren, übereinander gelegt werden. Erst so können Details wie Sommersprossen, Härchen, Fettglanz, Falten oder Erröten geschaffen werden.

Die gigantische Pipeline. *Jedes Wesen, jedes Spielzeug, Accessoire und jede Landschaft von „Toy Story" existiert ausschließlich in einem virtuellen Raum. Absolut alles. Es ist eine Welt, die nie jemand anfassen oder direkt wird sehen können. Vom heftigen Gewittersturm über den bezaubernden Sonnenuntergang, vom einzelnen Grashalm bis zu den 1,2 Millionen Blättern an den Bäumen in Andys Viertel, von den Telegrafenmasten und Kieswegen bis zum Flackern eines brennenden Streichholzes – künstliche Bilder. Dabei ist der Prozeß der Computeranimation von dem der klassischen Zeichentrickproduktion gar nicht so verschieden, und doch ist er gleichzeitig völlig anders. Zehn Stadien durchläuft jedes Bild, ähnlich wie beim Zeichen- oder Stop-Motion-Animations-Trick: Storyboards, Szenenschnitt, Produktionsdesign, Modellieren, Layout, Animation, Shading, Ausleuchtung, Rendering und Filmaufnahme.*

As with any other animation, the artists begin with hand-drawn storyboards that are then joined to create action sequences. The working texts or the finished dialogues of the speakers are written into each of the pictures. Then action sequences are developed bit by bit to form a patchwork of storyboards, individually drawn details and series of movements, and partially animated computer files until they become completed images. Since most of the work at Pixar is done digitally on different computers, video proved to be the most helpful medium at this stage for the two cutters, Robert Gordon and Lee Unkrich: it is very easy to call up a video on the screen, and individual pictures can be frozen and worked on. All the animated objects and characters are "modelled" three-dimensionally in the computer to attain a complete 3D image of their surface. To do this, the computer follows steps similar to those of a classic model builder: first a 3D framework is made from the scanned drawing – this is somwhat like a skeleton of bones and it can be moved the same way, then this framework is covered with "skin". A total of about 2,000 models were made this way for "Toy Story". Scenes (rooms, hallways, streets, etc.) and furniture or other room furnishings were modelled with computer supported design programs. These "model packages", which may be compared with an architect's blueprints, arrange the size and features of each object in relation to everything else in this artificially created world. After that, the layouters are responsible for the cinematographic resolution of a scene and the camera movements. They pay their respects to traditional cinema by consciously adopting the camera settings of film directors. When the animators finally receive a scene from the layout department, the outlines of the characters are usually indicated by rough polygon shapes ("polys") or by frame-like figures. This simplified representation allows the computer to work much faster than it could if it had to construct the complete 3D image, and the animators can concentrate on the characters' "acting". Once a scene has been animated, it is given depth focus, lighting and finally the complete coloration with the shadows and all the fantastic lighting effects. "Shaders" are mathematical programs that the computer uses to determine the surface structures: color, texture, reflection and roughness. For instance, there is a copper "shader", a wooden floor "shader", and one for the wallpaper in Andy's room. This kind of "shader" program provides the rendering program, which composes the completed image, with information about how the various surfaces reflect light. In the final step, the color artists give these shiny, perfect surfaces a final touch to achieve the used, worn out, dirty or dull appearance they are supposed to have. Many of the surfaces used were not created directly in the computer, but rather from scanned photos or pictures. The spread on Andy's bed, for example, was designed on the basis of an actual piece of material that was scanned in. And the carpet in the hall of Sid's house was taken directly from Stanley Kubrick's thriller "The Shining". Every one of these images was processed as a separate surface file. All in all, there are over 2,000 of these files for "Toy Story". A scene is given its dramatic visual effects by the lighting, the last process of the computer graphics. Here the "lighting crew" designs the appropriate atmosphere by using every imaginable light source that an ordinary film team would use – including a virtual sun and a virtual moon.

The process of constructing the final details and color highlights of a three-dimensional picture is called rendering. Here the information of every single component of the image is collected and composited. The computer composites a 3D image by compiling all the available information about the outlines of all the occurring objects (models), their positions (animation), their surface structures (shader) and their lighting and renders this information graphically.

MARC CARO / JEAN-PIERRE JEUNET

Marc Caro (F) begann seine Karriere als Comics-Zeichner für französische und amerikanische Magazine, wechselte das Metier und produziert seit 1981 Kurzfilme, Videoclips und Jingles, u. a. gemeinsam mit Jean-Pierre Jeunet (z. B. Buch und Regie für den Spielfilm „Delicatessen"). Caro erhielt beim Prix Ars Electronica 1994 eine Goldene Nica für „K. O. KID".

Marc Caro (F) began his career as a comics artist for French and American magazines, subsequently changed profession and has been producing short films, music videos and jingles since 1981, some in collaboration with Jean-Pierre Jeunet (among others screenplay for the feature film ÑDelicatessenì). Caro has been awarded the Golden Nica at Prix Ars Electronica 94 for "K.O. Kid".

In Frankreich hatte noch niemand einen abendfüllenden Film mit so vielen verschiedenen Special Effects – direkt, CGI und digital – gemacht: 144 von 800 Aufnahmen, siebzehn Minuten, ein Fünftel des gesamten Filmes. BUF Compagnie übernahm die CGI für „The City of Lost Children". Im Laufe ihres zehnjährigen Bestehens hat sich BUF Compagnie einen guten Ruf im Bereich der 3D-computergenerierten Special Effects erworben und bereits seit langem mit Jean-Pierre Jeunet und Marc Caro zusammengearbeitet. Beide sind bekanntlich abenteuerlustig, und in „Die Stadt der Verlorenen Kinder" bewiesen sie sich neuerlich.

No one in France had made a full length film with so many different kinds of special effects ever before – direct, CGI and digital: 144 out of 800 shots, seventeen minutes, one fifth of the entire film. BUF Compagnie did the CGI of "The City of Lost Children". In its ten years of existence, BUF Compagnie has gained a solid reputation in the creation of 3D computer generated special effects and had a long record of professional contact with Jean-Pierre Jeunet and Marc Caro. They both have a taste for adventure, and they both had it for "The City of Lost children".

Floh

Pulex irritans, ein rötlich-bräunliches Insekt, das sich als Parasit von Menschenblut ernährt, jede Größe – bis zu 4 mm – erreichen kann und fröhlich durch die Szene hüpft und gierig seinen Stachel in die zufällig Vorbeigehenden sticht. Woraus besteht dieser Floh überhaupt? Er ist weder ein elektronisches Modell noch ein digitalisiertes Photo, sondern eine hübsche kleine, in CGI gebastelte Chimäre, die von ihren Erzeugern bei BUF Compagnie modelliert, gefürchtet und animiert wurde. Dazu wurde eine mythologische Methode der Mathematik angewendet, wofür Hunderte von Stunden am Computer benötigt wurden.

Flea

Pulex irritans, a reddish brown insect that lives as a parasite on human blood, growing to all lengths – up to 4 mm – and merrily jumping all over the set, hungrily sticking its stinger into anyone who happens to cross its path. What's this flea made of anyway? It's not an electronic model, not a digitized photo, it's a cute little chimera concocted in C. G. I., modelled, dreaded, and animated by his creators at the BUF Compagnie, using a mythological method of mathematics that took hundreds of hours on

Marc Caro / Jean-Pierre Jeunet
"The City of Lost Children", 1995

*Zur Bildung der Oberflächenstruktur wurden verschie-
dene Schichten folgender schöner Materialen verwendet: Kieselsteine vom Strand, grüne Bohnen, Schlan-
genhaut, Schweinshaut, Leder usw. Die Animatoren
studierten stundenlang Dokumentarfilme, um heraus-
zufinden, wie Flöhe sich in der Natur verhalten. Sie
wissen inzwischen alles darüber, wie Flöhe hüpfen,
springen, landen, stechen, trinken und die unzähligen
gemeinen, juckenden Tricks vollziehen, mit denen sie
sich ihren weltweiten Verruf eingehandelt haben. Da
eine Vielfalt an Aufnahmen mit dem Floh im Mittelpunkt geplant waren, modellierten die Animatoren
eine Reihe von Flöhen mit einem unterschiedlichen
Definitionsgrad. Für den am feinsten definierten Floh
wurden nicht weniger als 800.000 Polygone verwendet. Und diese waren noch nicht die größten vom
Floh verursachten Komplikationen; ihn richtig aussehen und benehmen lassen, war ein Kinderspiel gegen
die Schwierigkeiten, ihn richtig ins Bild einzupassen.
Der Floh konnte noch so echt wirken, es wäre alles
umsonst gewesen, wenn er aussähe, als wäre er auf
einem künstlichen Dekor aufgeklebt. Wie könnte man
von einer Großaufnahme auf eine Nahaufnahme des
Flohs übergehen? Zu diesem Zeitpunkt gab es noch
kein Programm, das die Tiefe eines Feldes berück-
sichtigen konnte. Also schrieben die Techniker ein
neues – innerhalb von nur drei Monaten!*

Traum-Flaschen

*Für diese „Figur" stellte sich Caro ein grünfarbenes,
leicht leuchtendes Etwas vor, das wie Rauch aussieht, wie besorgte Gesichter, und sich in unterschiedlicher Geschwindigkeit von „langsam und
zögernd" bis „schnell" bewegen könnte. Es gab wieder keine Programme, die mit dieser Art Rauch arbeiten konnten. BUF Compagnie entwickelte wieder
innerhalb von drei Monaten ein eigenes Programm.
Es ist eine Art Teilchensystem, in dem jedes Teilchen
sich wie ein Teilchen Rauch verhält. Doch Rauch ist
kapriziös, und das Programm neigte dazu, auch echten Rauch zu produzieren. So mußten ungefähr
dreißig Parameter hinzugefügt werden, um diesen
Rauch einigermaßen zu zähmen. Für ein einziges Bild
des Rauchs werden ein oder zwei Stunden Rechenar-
beit benötigt, und das Endresultat kann man nur auf
Grund der Errechnungen für die Gesamtaufnahme*

the computer. The surface texture was obtained by using several layers of lovely materials
such as beach pebbles, green beans, snake
skin, pig skin, leather, etc. The animators
studied hours and hours of documentary films
to find out how fleas act out there in nature.
Now they know everything about how fleas
hop, skip, jump, land, sting and drink, and do
scores of dirty itchy tricks that have earned
them a worldwide reputation. Given the variety
of shots where the flea would star, the animators modelled a series of fleas with varying
degrees of definition. The most sharply defined had no less than 800.000 polygons. And
yet these were not the most serious compl-
ications caused by the flea; getting him to
look right and act right was nothing compared
to the difficulties of fitting him into the image.
No matter how real the flea looked, it would
all be spoiled if it seemed like it was stuck
onto an artificial decor. How could they go
from a wide shot to a closeup of the flea? At
that time there was no available program that
could take into account the depth of the field.
So the engineers wrote one – in the space of
three short months!

Dream Bottles

For this character Caro wanted a green-color-
slightly-luminous something that looked like
smoke, visions of troubled faces, and speeds
varying from "slow and hesitating" to "fast".
Again, there were no programs available that
could handle that kind of smoke. So BUF
Compagnie did a made-to-order program in
three months. It's a kind of particle system, in
which each particle acts like a particle of
smoke. But smoke is capricious and the
program had a tendancy to make real smoke.
So they had to add about thirty parameters to
domesticate that smoke. A single image of
smoke requires one or two hours of calculations and the final result can only be judged
on the basis of calculations for the whole
shot, so it's easy to understand why the
dream-as-a-character as the most difficult ele-

ment finally turns out to be the most delightful surprise.

Another problem with smoke is that you can see through it. Well, that dream in smoke goes past barred windows, skips across floors and puddles, etc. So the common solution of using a matte was excluded. To get the effect of smoke passing over all those different surfaces, they had to model the whole setting in three dimensions based on decorator's drawings and measurements made on the set and then do an image-by-image rotoscopy of all the shots where the dream would be cut in.

Metamorphosis of Krank and Miette

This touching scene where Miette grows old as Krank grows young took so much time to prepare that it was put at the very end of the shooting schedule. First the casting office tried to get doubles of the actors at different ages: younger and younger for Krank, older and older for Miette. Then BUF Compagnie took a try at morphing the doubles, going from one to the other, to pick out the most convincing combinations. Having the little girl grow old was no problem. But everything they tried for rejuvenating Krank was disastrous. So all through the metamorphosis, they had to keep some of the facial morphology and use the expression in the eyes of Emilfork, the actor who plays Krank. For this effect, his face was modelled in stereophotogrammetry. As Krank and Miette metamorphose, Krank's laboratory is distorted, although this is hardly noticed by viewers, because their attention is focussed on the changes in the characters. Nevertheless, this distortion required complete three-dimensional modelling of the laboratory, based on decorator's blueprints. The photos by the set photographer Eric Caro were scanned and flashed on to the model by mapping. So the set disorts without losing volume even when parts of it are invisible.

beurteilen. So wird es leicht verständlich, daß die Traum-"Figur" das schwierigste Element war, sich aber letztendlich als die schönste Überraschung zeigte.

Ein weiteres Problem beim Rauch ist, daß er durchsichtig ist. Der Traum-Rauch geht durch vergitterte Fenster hindurch, hüpft über den Boden und springt über Pfützen ... Dadurch war es unmöglic , eine Matte zu verwenden, was die übliche Lösung gewesen wäre. Um den Effekt zu erzielen, daß der Rauch über die vielen verschiedenen Oberflächen hinzieht, mußten 3D-Modelle des gesamten Bühnenbilds nach den Zeichnungen und Maßen des Bühnenbildners angefertigt werden; danach wurde Bild für Bild eine Rotoskopie aller Aufnahmen gemacht, in die der Traum eingearbeitet werden sollte.

Verwandlung von Krank und Miette

Die Vorbereitungszeit für die berührende Szene, wo Miette alt und Krank jung wird, war so aufwendig, daß die Szene ganz bis zum Schluß der Aufnahmen verschoben wurde. Zunächst versuchte das Besetzungsbüro verschiedenaltrige Doubles für die Schauspieler zu finden: jünger und jünger für Krank, älter und älter für Miette. Dann versuchte BUF Compagnie, die Doubles zu morphen, nahm zuerst einen, dann den nächsten, und versuchte, die besten Kombinationen zu finden. Es war kein Problem, das Mädchen älter werden zu lassen, aber alle Versuche, Krank zu verjüngen, schlugen fehl. Während der gesamten Metamorphose mußten sie einen Teil der Gesichtsmorphologie behalten und den Ausdruck in den Augen von Emilfork, dem Schauspieler, der Krank darstellt, verwenden. Für diesen Effekt wurde sein Gesicht in Stereophotogrammetrie modelliert. Während Krank und Miette sich verwandeln, wird Kranks Laboratorium verzerrt; diesen Vorgang bemerken die Zuschauer kaum, da sie sich auf die Veränderungen der Figuren konzentrieren. Trotzdem verlangte diese Verzerrung die vollständige dreidimensionale Modellierung des Laboratoriums nach den Plänen des Bühnenbildners.

Die Fotos des Bühnenbildphotographen Eric Caro wurden gescannt und mit Blitzlicht auf das Modell aufgezeichnet. So konnte die Szene verzerrt werden, ohne an Volumen zu verlieren, selbst wenn Teile davon unsichtbar sind.

MICHEL GONDRY / PIERRE BUFFIN

Michel Gondry (F), geb. 1964, Musiker und Videoclipregisseur, hat bereits eine steile Karriere mit einer Reihe anerkannter beeindruckender Videos hinter sich; Animation hatte er während des Kunststudiums begonnen, obwohl sie nicht sein Hauptfach war. Für die „Special Effects" für „Like a Rolling Stone" führte Pierre Buffin Regie.

Michel Gondry (F), born 1964, musician and director of video clips, has rocketed to international recognition with a series of dazzling, jaw-dropping videos; he began animation at art school although it was not his major subject for study. The special effects to „Like a Rolling Stone" were directed by Pierre Buffin.

Wir hatten bereits bei verschiedenen Projekten mit Michel Gondry zusammengearbeitet – z. B. bei den Videoclips für Björk, Lenny Kravitz und Terence Trent D'Arby. Als er bei BUF zu Besuch war, zeigten wir ihm die neuen Tools, die wir gerade entwickelten, und die Effekte, die damit erzeugt werden könnten. Eines Tages zeigten wir ihm jenes Tool, mit dem man aus zwei Bildern Objekte auf Basis der Stereophotogrammetrie modellieren kann. Ab und zu rief uns Michel an, weil er eine Idee für einen Film hatte und wissen wollte, ob es möglich wäre, diesen Effekt dafür zu verwenden. Zum Schluß führten wir dann mit Michel einen Test durch. Aus nur zwei Bildern, die mit zwei synchronisierten Standkameras aufgenommen wurden, modellierten wir Michel, wie er Luftsprünge vollführte, inmitten von Gebäuden. Nachdem das Environment mit unserem Tool modelliert und strukturiert wurde, war es möglich, eine Szene zu erstellen, in der eine virtuelle Computerkamera sich um einen in der Luft erstarrten Michel Gondry dreht. Ein weiterer Effekt war die Verwendung von nur einem Bild aus fünf auf einem Film, wobei der Übergang mittels „Image Warping" hergestellt wurde. Mit nur vier Bildern in der Sekunde (anstatt 24 für einen Film) wurde es möglich, einen nur leicht veränderten Film wiederherzustellen und verschiedene Elemente des Bilds zu betonen, um eine seltsame Atmosphäre zu schaffen. Die grundle-

We had already worked on different projects with Michel Gondry, such as video-clips like Björk, Lenny Kravitz or Terence Trent D'Arby. During his visits to BUF, we showed him the new tools we were developing and the new effects they could provide. One day we showed him our tool for modelling objects from two pictures, based on stereophotogrammetry. From time to time, Michel called us, because he had an idea for a film and wanted to know if it would be possible to use this effect. We finally did a test with Michel himself. From only two pictures taken from two synchronised still cameras, we modelled Michel jumping in the air, surrounded by buildings. Once the environment was modelled and textured with our tool, it was possible to create a scene where a virtual computer camera was turning around a frozen-in-the-air Michel Gondry. Another effect was to use one picture out of five from a film and do an image warping to do the transition. With four pictures per second (instead of 24 for a film), it was possible to recreate a film in slightly different way and play on the elements of the image to create a weired atmosphere. The basic ideas to do the „Rolling Stones" video-clip were there. Using only one or two still camera allows for great

Michel Gondry / Pierre Buffin
"Like a Rolling Stone", 1995

genden Ideen, die wir für das Rolling-Stones-Videoclip brauchten, waren also da. Wenn man nur eine oder zwei Standkameras verwendet, kann man sehr flexibel sein. Es wird dann unsinnig, große 35-mm- oder Videokameras zu verwenden. Für die „Party" im Videoclip wurde eine echte Party veranstaltet, und irgendwann später kamen, sehr zur Freude der Beteiligten, die Rolling Stones persönlich. Die Gruppe zerstreute sich schnell, um etwas von der Party zu haben. Michel mußte sie dann nur mehr suchen und Fotos schießen, wie ein echter „Paparazzo". Deswegen wirkt die Party auch so „echt". Die Fotos sind die Grundlage für den größten Teil des Videoclips, ansonsten wurden nur Teile des Konzerts gefilmt. Das bedauern wir am meisten. Das Konzert sollte nur gestellt sein, und die Rolling Stones sollten nur das eine Lied für den Videoclip spielen. Aber irgendwann beschloß dann die Band, ein improvisiertes Konzert zu spielen, und sie spielten dann die ganze Nacht. Für dieses einmalige Konzert waren wir natürlich nicht auf der Aufnahmebühne. Wir hatten nur drei Wochen Zeit, um sechs Minuten Effekte für über 1.000 Morphings und einige „Freeze"-Sequenzen fertigzustellen. Michel fertigte eine Animatic mit den Standbildern, und wir ersetzten die Bilder mit einem wiederhergestellten Film innerhalb der drei Wochen.

flexibility. It becomes useless to use big 35 mm or video-cameras. For the "party" of the video-clip, a real party was thrown, and after a while the Rolling Stones came, much to the pleasure of the participants. The group immediately split to enjoy the party. Michel then had only to look for them and take pictures, like a real "Paparazzo". That's one of the reasons why the party looks so "real". Most of the clip is based on pictures, only some parts of the concert have been filmed. That is what we regret most. The concert was supposed to be fake, and the Rolling Stones were only supposed to play the song of the clip. But after a while, the band decided to do an improvised concert that lasted until dawn.

And of course, we were not on the shooting stage for this unique concert. We only had three weeks to complete six minutes of effects from more than 1.000 morphings and several freeze sequences. Michel made an animatic with the still pictures, and during this three weeks we replaced the pictures with a reconstructed film.

Michel Gondry / Pierre Buffin
"Like a Rolling Stone", 1995

PHILIPPE BILLION

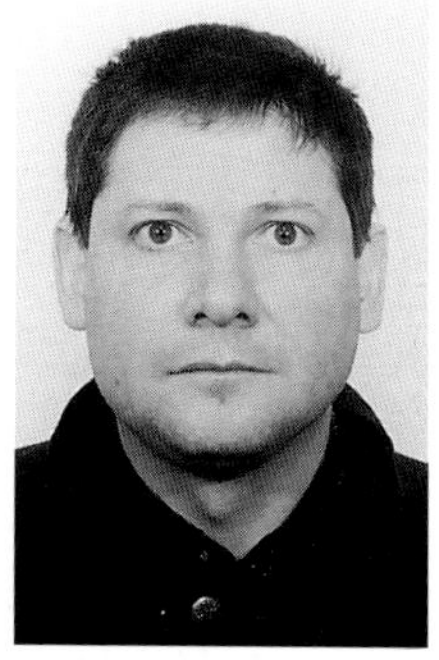

Philippe Billion (F), geb. 1954, schloß 1978 sein Studium der Wissenschaft und Technik an der ENSI (Ecole Nationale Supérieure den Ingéniers Electriciens) in Grenoble ab und kam 1988 zu ExMachina Paris. Sein Interesse gilt insbesondere der Verquickung von Ungewöhnlichem, Unerwartetem mit natürlichem Leben, was die Technik der Computergraphik heute immer stärker betont.

Philippe Billion (F), born 1954, graduated 1978 in Science and Engineering from ENSI (Ecole Nationale Supérieure des Ingénieurs Electriciens) in Grenoble, joined ExMachina Paris in 1988. He is especially interested in the blending of the unusual, the unexpected, with natural life in the way that this can be done increasingly well through computer graphics technology.

In einer dunklen, stürmischen Nacht schwebt ziellos und verlassen ein altes Luftschiff auf hoher See und versinkt langsam im Wasser. Noch bevor das Luftschiff Bekanntschaft mit der aufgewühlten See macht, merken wir, daß zwischen diesen beiden „Charakteren" etwas passiert – die See wird immer schillernder, während das Luftschiff angesichts seines langsamen Todes zunächst mit seinem Schicksal hadert und sich ihm dann doch überläßt.

Nebelbanken bewegen sich zwischen den Wellen und auf ihren Kämmen. Ein übernatürliches Licht beleuchtet das Geschehen. Das Luftschiff ist offenbar schon lange menschenleer. Auf seinem Segeltuch sieht man deutliche Zeichen der Abnützung durch Sonne und Unwetter. Das Gondel ist überall verrostet, trägt jedoch noch immer die zwei sich langsam drehenden, altmodischen Propellermotoren.

500 verschiedene Modelle der See wurden mit diesem Programm erstellt. Die Geschwindigkeit und Höhe der Wellen wurden für jede Aufnahme durch Interpolation und Skalieren angepaßt.

Vier verschiedene Nebelarten werden an der Wasseroberfläche und „in der Luft" verwendet. Der Filmtitel – „Period" – bezieht sich auf die paradoxe Doppeldeutigkeit des Wortes, das sowohl das Ende markiert („Period" – der Punkt am Satzende), wie auch eine Dauer beschreibt (wie die fließende Kontinuität einer Welle).

On a dark stormy night, on the high sea, an old dirigible, adrift, floats aimlessly and slowly sinks into the water. Even before the dirigible encounters the raging sea, we can tell that something is happening between these two "characters" – the sea gradually becomes irridescent while the dirigible agonizes over its slow death and seems to finally accept its fate.

Sheets of fog move around in between the waves and on their crests. A supernatural light illuminates the event. The dirigible seems to have been uninhabited for a long period of time. Its canvas bears clearly visible signs of wear and tear caused by the sun and the bad weather. The nacelle is extremely rusty, yet still supports two slowly turning, outdated propeller engines.

500 different models of the sea have been produced by this program. The speed and height of the waves are adapted to each shot using interpolation and scaling. Four different types of fog are used on the surface of the sea and „in the air".

The title of the film is based on the paradoxal correlation between the end of something (as the end of a sentence ...) and the idea of continuity (as the smooth continuity of a wave).

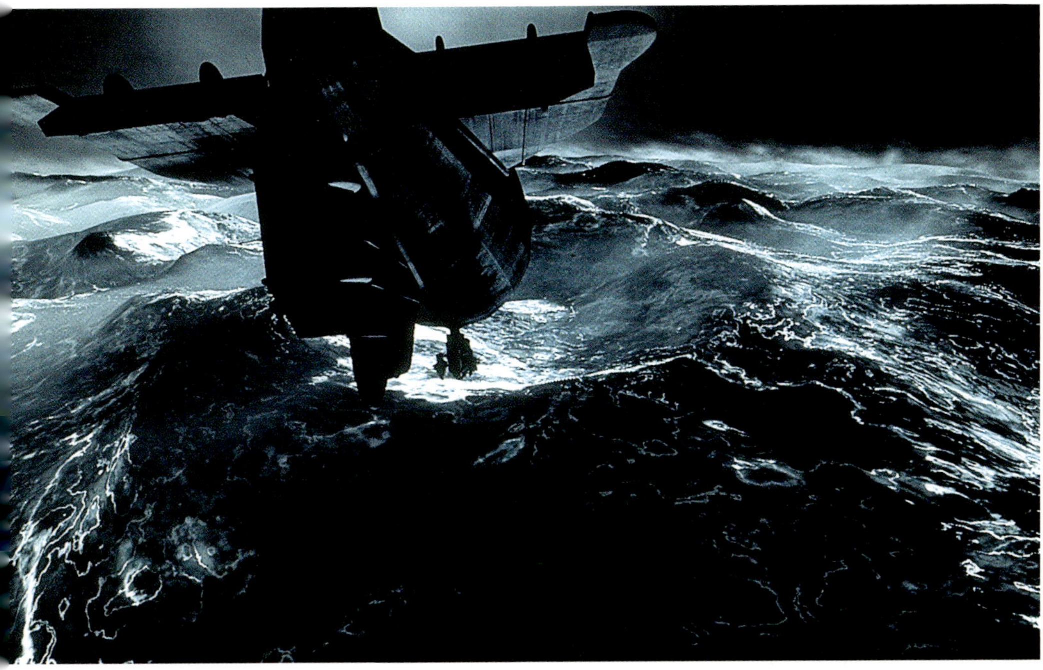

HONORARY MENTION

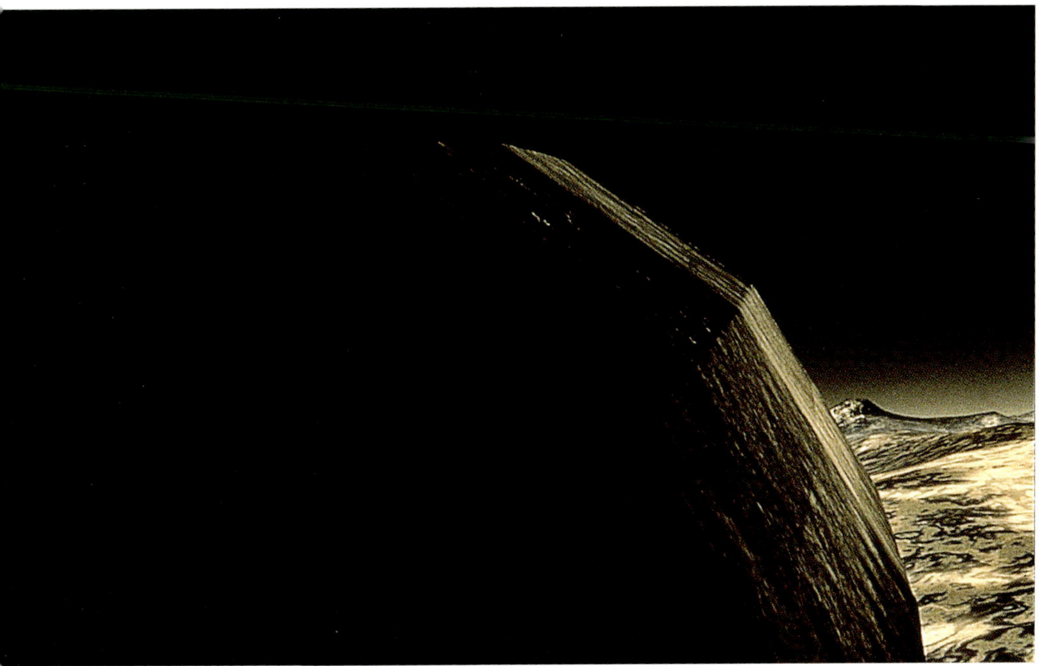

Philippe Billion
"Period", 1995

CHRISTIAN BOUSTANI

Christian Boustani (F) unterrichtet Video an der Université Paris I. Sein besonderes Interesse gilt der Beziehung zwischen Video und Malerei, was vor allem in seinem Zyklus „Citiés Antérieures" zum Ausdruck kommt.

Christian Boustani (F) teaches video at the Université Paris I. He is primarily interested in the relationship between video and painting, as is especially evident in his cycle "Cités Antérieures".

Brügge, die mittelalterliche Stadt des Nordens zwischen Land und See, ist den Schicksalsschlägen der Zeit ausgesetzt. Natürliche und endemische Katastrophen folgen aufeinander und trüben den Glanz der Stadt. Mitten im Untergang wartet die Stadt Brügge auf ihre Renaissance ...

Mitten in der Stadt lebt ein Maler, ein begnadeter Alchimist, der nach einer neuen Materie sucht. Er mischt Farbe und Öl mit seinem Atem, verdichtet Farbe und Licht, Durchsichtigkeit und Festigkeit. Wenn es ihm gelingt, das Geheimnis der Ölmalerei zu entdecken, kann er der Stadt eine Chance zum ewigen Leben bieten. Der Film „Cities of the Past – Brugge" zeigt anhand alter flämischer Gemälde, was das Mittelalter für uns bedeuten könnte, beschränkt sich dabei aber nicht auf eine streng historische Rekonstruktion. Diese Welt der Phantasie verbindet Legenden, Volks- und religiöse Rituale; sie entwickelt eine Geschichte und gibt ihr Bedeutung, indem sie Zusammenhänge zwischen Fälschung und Wirklichkeit wiederherstellt. Manche Figuren erscheinen wie Koordinaten in dieser Welt der Fälschung. Sie mischen sich unter Details aus Gemälden von Jan Van Eyck, Hans Memling, Pieter Bruegel und Hieronimus Bosch. Sie decken auf, was die Archive verbergen: das Geheimnis der Ölmalerei, das vor über 500 Jahren entdeckt wurde. Ein Geheimnis, das wahrscheinlich hinter der schweren Stille des Steins verborgen war.

Bruges, the northern and medieval city between land and sea, is exposed to the misfortunes of time. Natural and endemic calamities succeed one another, set upon the town to tarnish it. Aware of its decline, Brugges is waiting for its Renaissance ...

In the heart of the city, as an inspired alchemist, the painter is searching for a new material. He mingles pigment and oil with his breath, concentrates color and light, transparency and solidity. Finding the secret of oil-painting will allow him to offer a chance of eternity to the city. The film „Cities of the Past – Brugge" shows what the Middle Ages could represent for us through the primitive Flemish paintings without being restricted to a faithful historical reconstruction. This world of fantasy combines legends, popular and religious rituals, generating a story, finding a meaning, recreating connections between fiction and reality.

Some characters appear like points of reference in this ficticious world. They mingle in details from the paintings of Jan Van Eyck, Hans Memling, Pieter Bruegel and Hieronimus Bosch. They bring to light what archives hide: the secret of oil-painting discovered more than five hundred years ago. A secret that was probably hidden behind the heavy silence of stone ...

COMPUTER ANIMATION

Christian Boustani
"Cities of the Past – Brugge", 1996

JOHN CLYNE

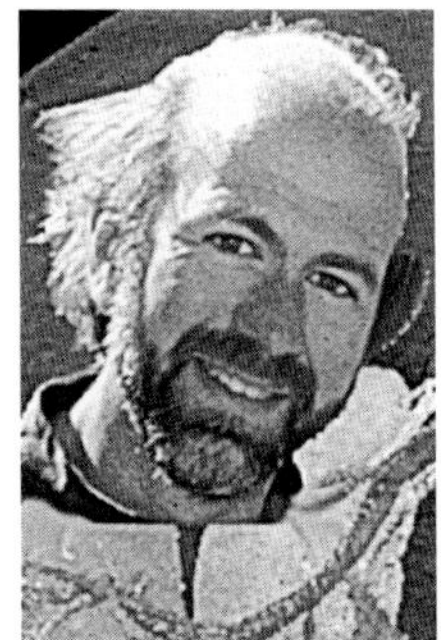

John Clyne (USA), BS und MS in Informatik an der University of Colorado, Boulder. Mitglied der Visualization Group der Abteilung für Scientific Computing des National Center for Atmospheric Research (NCAR). Interessiert sich u. a. für Volumenvisualisierung großer geowissenschaftlicher Datenmengen und Virtual-Reality-Anwendungen in wissenschaftlichen Visualisierungen.

John Clyne (USA), BS and MS in Computer Science from the University of Colorado, Boulder is a member of the Visualization Group in the Scientific Computing Division of the National Center for Atmospheric Research (NCAR). Clyne's professional interests include volume visualization of large geo-science datasets, and applications of Virtual Reality to scientific visualization.

1991 stellte die National Library of Medicine (NLM) Geldmittel für ein Projekt bereit, bei dem eine digitale Datenbank volumetrischer Daten entwickelt wurde, die einen erwachsenen Mann und eine erwachsene Frau darstellen. Dieser wissenschaftliche Versuch wurde „The Visible Human (TM) Project" genannt. Hauptziel war eine radiologische und fotografische Darstellung einer vollständigen männlichen Menschenleiche, und zwar in einer Auflösung von 1 mm in allen drei Dimensionen. Die weibliche Leiche sollte zu einem späteren Zeitpunkt erfaßt werden.

Es mußten dazu neue Techniken der Volumenvisualisierung entwickelt werden, die den einzigartigen Merkmalen der riesigen Datenmenge gerecht werden konnten. Höhepunkt dieser Zusammenarbeit war die Herstellung eines HDTV-Films, der diese Forschungsbestrebungen der Visualisierung in den Mittelpunkt stellte.

Ziel des Films war es einerseits, die medizinische Ausbildung zu fördern und den Medizinstudenten eine Vorstellung von virtueller Chirurgie zu vermitteln, andererseits wollten wir beim breiten Publikum das Bewußtsein für die Komplexitäten der menschlichen Anatomie stärken. Außerdem wollten wir mit dem Film das Publikum dazu anregen, sich Gedanken darüber zu machen, welche Entwicklungen der medizinischen Ausbildung und Technologie uns die Zukunft noch bescheren würde.

In 1991, the National Library of Medicine (NLM) funded a project to develop a digital database of volumetric data representing a complete adult male and female. This scientific effort was named the "Visible Human (TM) Project". A primary objective of the project was to provide the radiologic and photographic definition of a complete, human male cadaver at a resolution af 1 mm in all three dimensions. The female cadaver would be done at a later time.

This involved developing new volume-visualization techniques appropriate for the unique characteristics of the enormous dataset. The culmination of these collaborative efforts was the production of an HDTV movie which showcased these exploratory visualization efforts.

The movie's goals were to further medical education, stimulate the idea of virtual surgery for medical students, and to foster a stronger awareness of the complexities of human anatomy by the general public. It was also hoped that the movie would challenge people's imaginations about what the future might hold in the areas of medical science education and technology advancement.

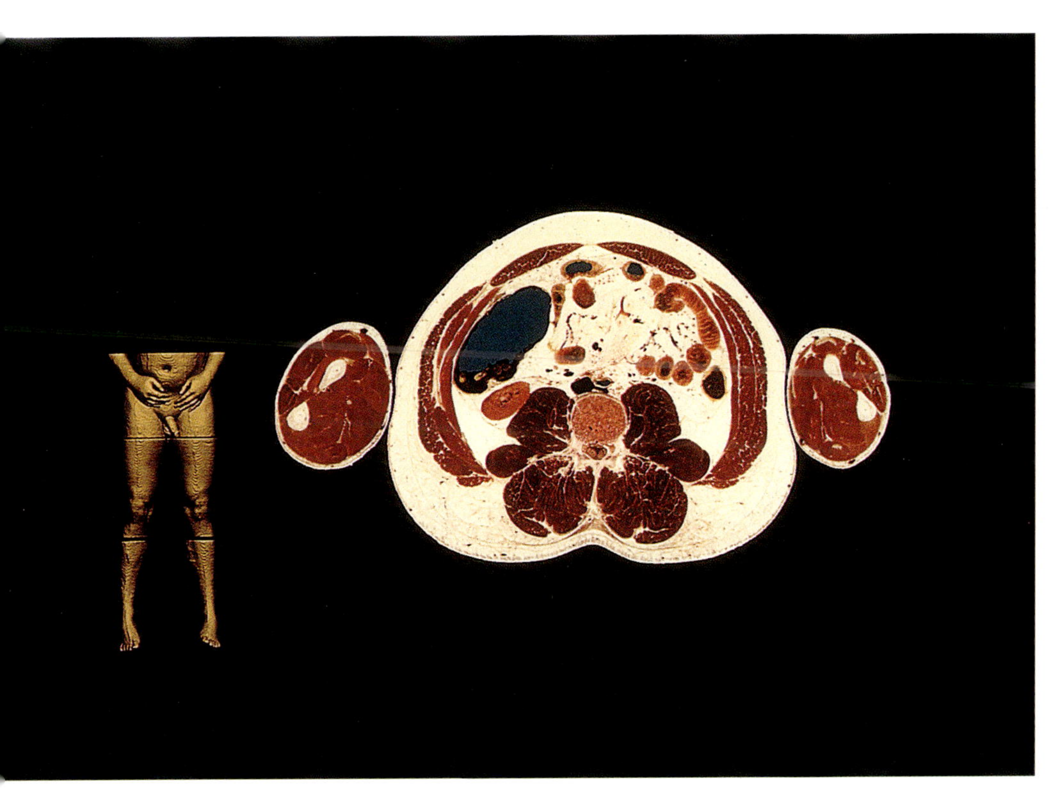

John Clyne
"The Visible Human Project", 1995

JAMES DUESING

James Duesing (USA), Animator und elektronischer Künstler mit Schwerpunkt Computeranimation. Seine Arbeiten wurden weltweit bei über einhundert Festivals und Ausstellungen präsentiert und bereits in den USA, in Europa, Asien und Australien im Fernsehen gezeigt. Ab Herbst nimmt er an einem artist-in-residence-Programm am Marin Headlands Center for the Arts in Kalifornien teilnehmen.

James Duesing (USA), animator and electronic artist, primary concentration in the area of computer animation. His work has been exhibited widely, in over a hundred festivals and exhibitions, and it has been televised in the United States, Europe, Asia and Australia. This fall he will participate in a residency program at the Marin Headlands Center for the Arts in California.

James Duesing
"Law of Averages", 1996

Industrial Light & Magic
***"Jumanji"**, *1995

PIERRE LACHAPELLE

*Pierre Lachapelle (CDN), motiviert
von einem starken Interesse an
Computergraphik und Film,
entwickelte Anfang der 8oer Jahre ein
vollständiges Computeranimations-
system für seine theoretischen und
praktischen Werke. 1985 war
er Produzent und Regisseur bei
seinem ersten computeranimierten
Kurzfilm, „Tony de Peltrie".*

**In the early 1980's, the theoretical
and practical works of Pierre
Lachapelle, driven by a strong
interest toward computer graphics
and cinema, have lead him to create
and develop a complete computer
animation system. In 1985,
Lachapelle produced and directed his
first computer animated short, "Tony
de Peltrie".**

*„The Boxer Trailer" präsentiert die Geschichte eines
humoristischen Ringkampfes zwischen Slim und
einem riesigen Muskelprotz namens Killer. Obwohl es
vom Anfang an klar ist, daß Slim überhaupt keine
Chance hat, verrät „The Boxer Trailer" nicht, wie es
ausgehen wird.*

"The Boxer Trailer" presents the story of a
humoristic boxing match between Slim and
a huge muscular fighter called Killer. It is
clear from the very offset that Slim doesn't
stand a chance, but the Trailer doesn't show
in any way how the match will end.

Pierre Lachapelle
"Boxer Trailer", 1996

ARNAULD LAMORLETTE

COMPUTER ANIMATION

Arnauld Lamorlette (F), geb. 1964, arbeitete bereits 1986, als er noch studierte (mechanische und Elektrotechnik), bei BUF. Aufgrund seiner Mathematikkenntnisse liegt der Schwerpunkt seiner Arbeit im technischen Bereich, obwohl er manchmal als Endverbraucher von Programmen auch Filme bearbeitet („So findet man die besten Ideen für die Erzeugung neuer Tools"). Die „Tian-An-Men"-Simulation produzierte er gemeinsam mit Pasquale Croce.

Arnauld Lamorlette (F), born 1964, began working at BUF in 1986 while he was still studying (mechanical and electrical engineering). Due to his background in mathematics, he works primarily on technical aspects, although he sometimes works on films as an end-user of the programs ("The only way to have good ideas for creating new tools"). He worked together with Pasquale Croce to create the "Tian-An-Men" simulation.

Als wir begannen, das Amnesty-International-Projekt zu analysieren, war es für uns eine Herausforderung, die Geschichte entsprechend der eigentlichen Bedeutung von Tian-An-Men zu verändern. Bis jetzt haben ausschließlich Diktatoren Geschichte verändert und sie ihren korrupten Zielen unterworfen, indem sie Bilder retouchiert oder gelöscht oder Figuren hinzugefügt haben. Zum ersten Mal wird nun Bildmanipulation dazu verwendet, gegen Diktatoren zu kämpfen. Wir glaubten, dieselben Waffen verwenden zu müssen, um die Freiheit zu verteidigen. Alle, die an diesem Film beteiligt waren, haben unentgeltlich gearbeitet.

Tatsache ist, daß der junge Chinese die Panzer nicht aufhalten konnte und daß die Tian-An-Men-Demonstration in der Nacht, als keine Kameras dabei waren, niedergeschlagen wurde. Deswegen bestand das Projekt darin, historische Originalaufnahmen vom Tian-An-Men wiederherzustellen und sie im Computerbild fortzusetzen und zu zeigen, wie der Panzer über den Student hinwegrollt. Die Arbeit mußte schnell fertiggestellt werden, da der chinesische Premierminister in Frankreich erwartet wurde, und der Film sollte vorher fertig sein. Das Endresultat war dermaßen überzeugend, daß der Film in Frankreich verboten wurde, weil er die „diplomatischen Beziehungen zwischen Frankreich und China" belasten könnte.

When we started to analyze the Amnesty International project, we were excited by the challenge of changing history to correspond to the real meaning of Tian-An-Men.

So far, only dictators have changed history to serve their evil purposes by retouching pictures to erase or add characters. For the first time, image manipulation is used here to fight dictatorship. We thought that we had to use the same weapons to defend freedom. All the people who worked on this film did it voluntarily.

In fact, the young Chinese man didn't stop the tanks, and the Tian-An-Men demonstration was repressed during the night when no camera was there. Thus, the project needed to retrieve the original, historical sequence of Tian-An-Men and to continue it with a computer image of the tank rolling over the student. The job had to be done very fast, because the Chinese prime minister was coming to France and we wanted the film to be ready. The final result is so convincing that this film has been forbidden in France, because it could compromise "diplomatic relationships between France and China".

Arnauld Lamorlette
"Tian-An-Men", 1996

DENISE MINTER / TIM JOHNSON

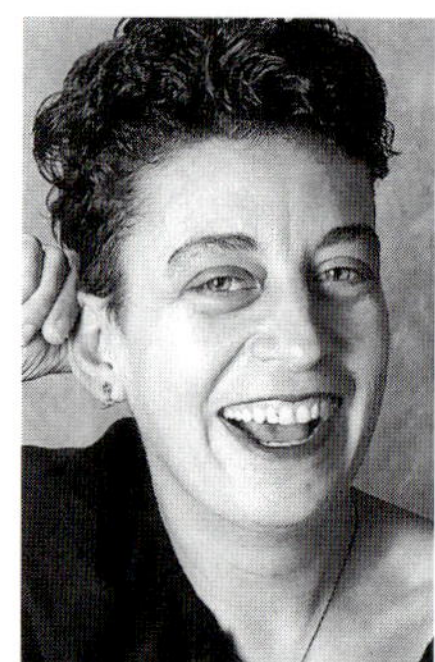

Denise Minter (USA) studierte Kommunikation und Computergraphik am New York Institute of Technology. Sie arbeitete zunächst mit Paintbox/Harry; seit 1993 ist sie bei PDI, wo sie „Homer3" produziert hat. Tim Johnson (USA), BA der englischen Literatur, freischaffender Cel-Animator und Regisseur; 1991 gründete PDI Character Animation Group.

Denise Minter (USA), studied Communication and Computer graphics at the New York Institute of Technology. After working as Paintbos/Harry artist, she joined PDI in 1993 where she produced „Homer3". Tim Johnson (USA), BA in English Literature at Northwestern University, freelance cel animatior and director. He founded the PDI Character Animation Group in 1991.

COMPUTER ANIMATION

Denise Minter / Tim Johnson
"Treehouse of Horror VI", 1996

"Treehouse of Horror VI", the latest installment in The Simpsons' popular Halloween specials, features Homer[3], a parody of a memor able episode of "The Twilight Zone" in which a young girl passes through a wall and is trapped in the 4th dimension. In the climatic moments of "Treehouse of Horror VI", Homer accidentally steps into the third dimension while desperately trying to avoid his sisters-in-law, Patty and Selma. Having lived his entire life in the 2D world, Homer enjoys his new depth until, through a minor mishap, he creates a black hole which threatens to engulf the entire universe. Bart alone is brave enough to cross over into this other world, in an attempt to save his father.

The story is replete with inside jokes poking fun at computer animation. Computer-generated backgrounds are filled with quirky mathematical equations, and historic CG references.

In the early stages of production, maquettes of Homer and Bart were used as reference, digitized into the computer and refined to create convincing 3D versions of the characters. A whole new set of movements were needed to capture the spirit of Homer and Bart in 3D. This included the development of several small hand gestures and nervous ticks that convey Homer's signature nervousness – and Bart's mischievous nature – even when the virtual camera and characters are standing still.

„Treehouse of Horror VI" ist die neueste der populären Halloween-Sondersendungen mit „The Simpsons" und bringt „Homer[3]", eine Parodie auf die denkwürdige Episode von „The Twilight Zone", in der ein junges Mädchen durch eine Mauer geht und dann in der vierten Dimension gefangen ist.

Am Höhepunkt von „Treehouse of Horror VI" tritt Homer, der verzweifelt versucht, seinen Schwägerinnen Patty und Selma aus dem Weg zu gehen, aus Versehen in die dritte Dimension ein. Nachdem er sein ganzes Leben in der 2D-Welt verbracht hat, macht ihm diese neue Tiefenerfahrung zunächst Spaß. Dann schafft er aber aufgrund eines kleinen Unfalls ein schwarzes Loch, und das gesamte Universum droht darin zu verschwinden. Nur Bart bringt den nötigen Mut auf, die Grenze zu dieser anderen Welt zu überqueren, wo er versucht, seinen Vater zu retten.

Die Geschichte ist mit unzähligen Insider-Witzen gespickt, die sich über Computeranimation lustig machen. Computergenerierte Hintergründe füllen sich mit wahnwitzigen mathematischen Formeln und historischen CG-Anspielungen.

In der Anfangsphase der Produktion wurden Maquetten von Homer und Bart verwendet; diese wurden in den Computer digitalisiert und bearbeitet, um getreue 3D-Versionen der Figuren zu schaffen. Gänzlich neue Bewegungsabläufe wurde benötigt, um das Wesen von Homer und Bart in 3D darzustellen. Dazu wurden u. a. einige kleine Handbewegungen und nervöse Ticks entwickelt, die Homers charakteristische Nervosität – und Barts schelmische Natur – auch dann sichtbar machen, wenn die virtuelle Kamera und die Figu-

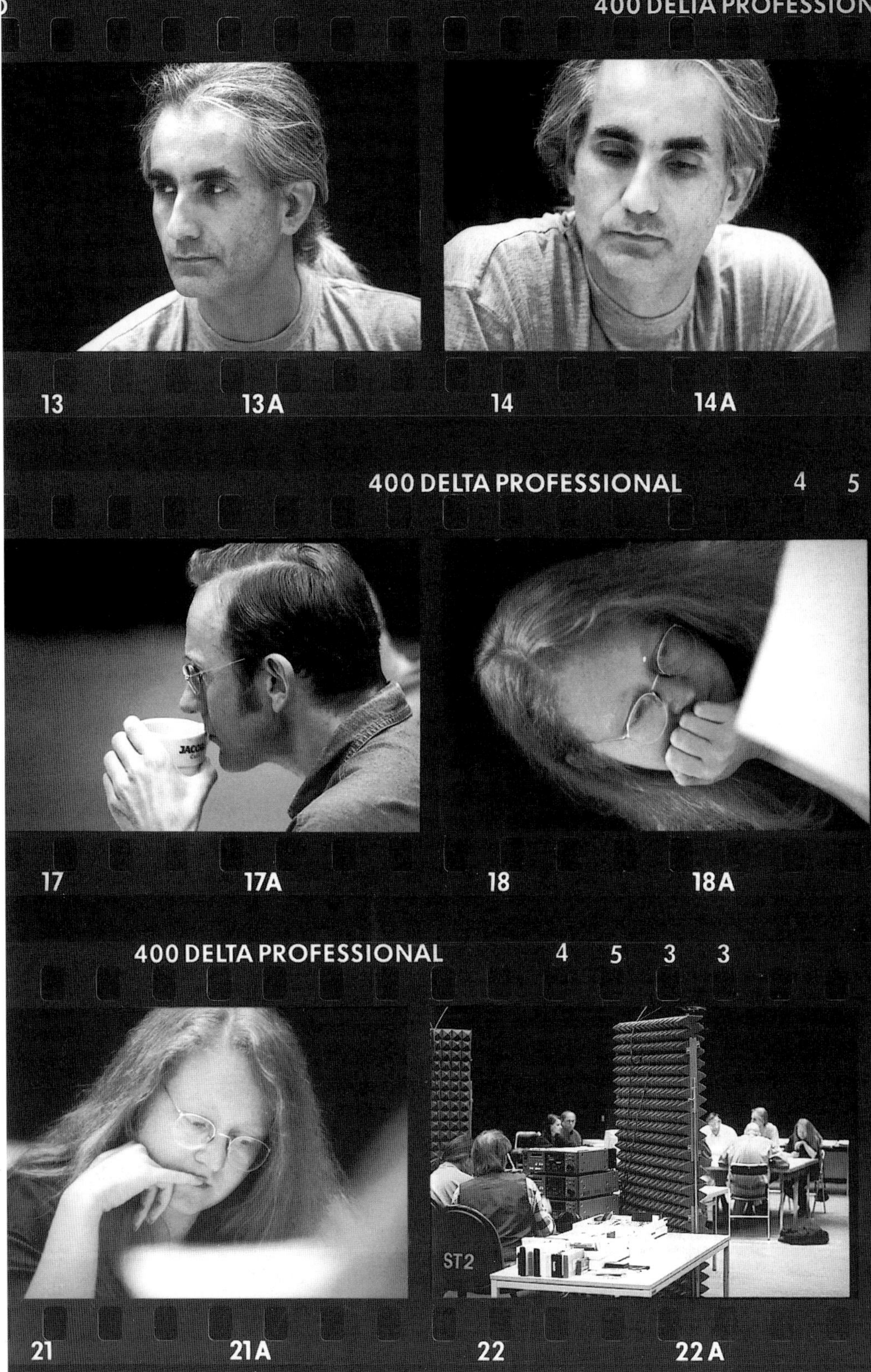
400 DELTA PROFESSION
13
13A
14
14A
400 DELTA PROFESSIONAL   4   5
17
17A
18
18A
400 DELTA PROFESSIONAL   4   5   3   3
21
21A
22
22A
ST2

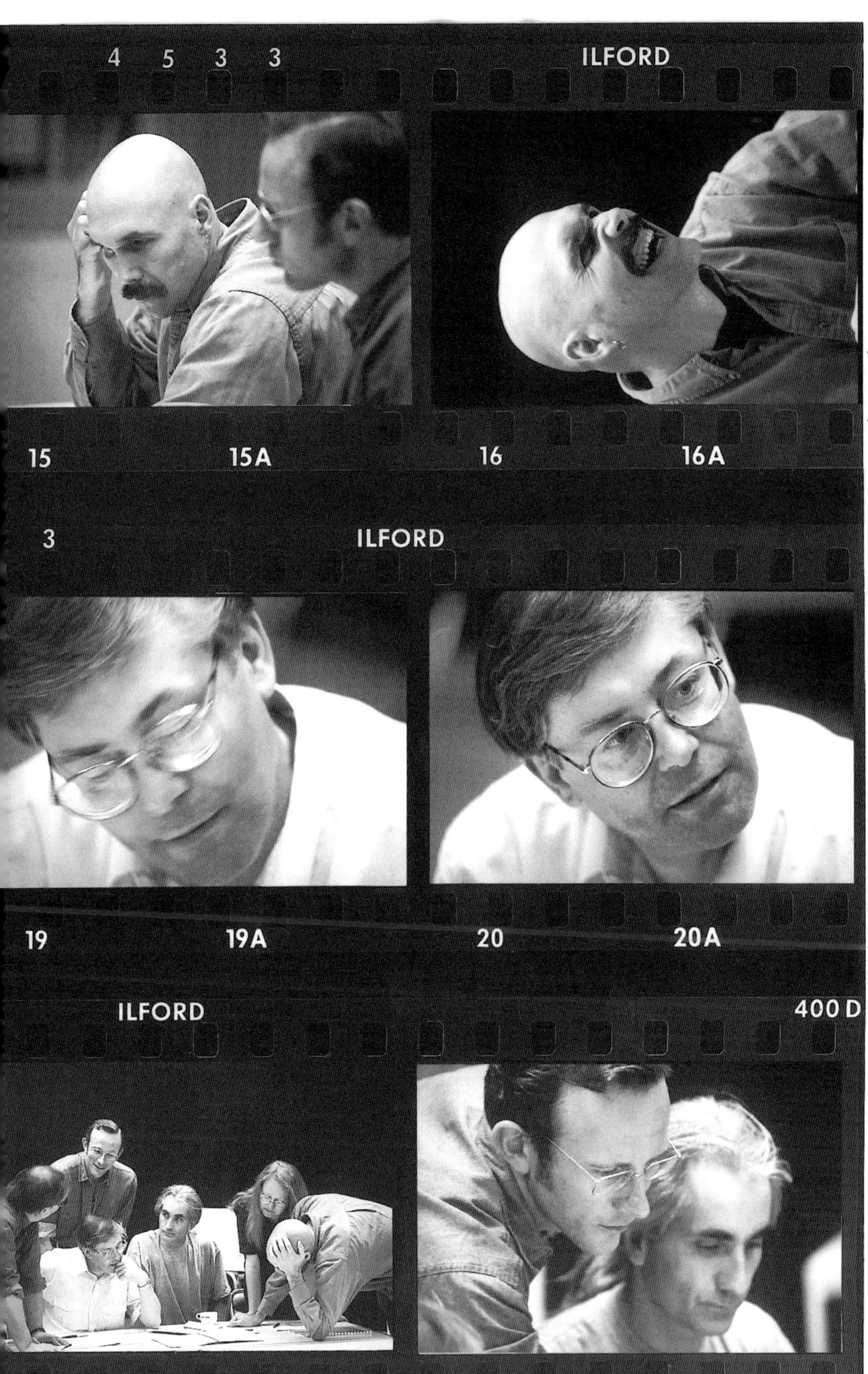

STATEMENT
OF THE COMPUTER MUSIC JURY
Jurybegründung Computermusik

Die Computermusik blickt inzwischen auf eine Geschichte von etwa dreieinhalb Jahrzehnten zurück und könnte deshalb als „erwachsen" betrachtet werden. Die Ergebnisse, die dieser Reifungsprozeß jetzt hervorgebracht hat, stellen keine einheitliche Sammlung von Vorgehensweisen dar, die durchgehende Zustimmung finden, und schon gar keine durchgehend akzeptierte Ästhetik.

Was sich uns jetzt präsentiert, ist ein Übermaß an kreativer und phantasievoller Anwendungen der Computertechnologie in verschiedenen Bereichen, z. B. bei der Synthese von Klang und Instrument, bei der Modifizierung von Klängen zu neuen Gebilden, bei der Entwicklung neuer formgenerierender Konzepte, die durch Computerbearbeitung ermöglicht werden, oder bei der computergestützten Präsentation von Musik, vor allem was die Gestaltung der räumlichen Umgebung betrifft. Der Begriff „Computermusik" scheint zu wenig aussagekräftig, um die vielen Gebiete abzudecken, die seit der ursprünglichen Verwendung des Begriffs entstanden sind (und man konnte sich am Anfang sicherlich kaum vorstellen, welche Bandweite der Begriff „Computermusik" noch abzudecken haben würde!) Neben geläufigen Beispielen wie der Tonbandmusik könnten wir anführen: Tonband mit akustischen Instrumenten, Live-Performance mit computergestützten elektronischen Instrumenten, interaktives und reaktives Computing in Echtzeit als Teil einer Performance, von Computern gesteuerte, nicht-elektronische „mechanische" Instrumente und Werke, die für einen Kontext außerhalb der Konzertpräsentation konzipiert werden, wie z. B. Klanginstallationen und Klangskulpturen. Gerade diese Vielfalt macht die Reife der Computermusik aus.

Im Kontext des Prix Ars Electronica möchte man neue Tendenzen aufspüren und durch die Anerken-

Computer Music has a history of some three and a half decades, and could therefore be said to have "matured". The present outcome of the maturation process is not a single, agreed collection of procedures, and certainly not an agreed aesthetic.

What one now encounters is a plethora of creative and imaginative applications of computer technology in areas such as sound and instrument synthesis, the modification of sounds into new entities, the development of new form-generating concepts enabled by computer processing, and the computer-assisted presentation of music, particularly with regard to the control of its spatial environment. The term "computer music" now seems under-powered, in that it has to embrace the many genres which have evolved since the expression was first coined (with little awareness, no doubt, of how hard it was going to have to work!). As well as straightforward examples such as the genre of tape music, one can cite tape-with-acoustic-instruments, live-performance on computer-aided electronic instruments, real-time interactive and reactive computing as part of performance, non-electric "mechanical" instruments controlled by computers, and works designed for contexts other than concert presentation, such as sound installations and sound sculptures. It is this diversity which is the defining characteristic of the maturity of computer music.

Within the context of the Prix Ars Electronica, one hopes to be able to identify and recognize, by means of the „honourable mentions", distinctive new trends, but, this year, the Music Jury found it impossible to do so from the collection of submissions before it. Computer music, in its maturity, is developing some of the less endearing aspects of middle age. For its own good, it needs, perhaps, to be leaner and fitter! Its ideas and their expression are in a bit of a rut. The same mannerisms are encountered in piece after piece – when the pieces are by different composers – suggesting an outbreak of the virus of cliche, even of epidemic proportions.

It is especially disappointing to realize that the infection has spread to the younger generation of composers. While it is understandable that student or young professional composers model their work on what has become established practice, since to do so is a valuable part of the learning process, it is disconcerting to observe the extent to which they are apparently content to bow down in front of the middle-aged icons set before them. Sometimes iconoclasm is the greater sign of respect!

The Music Jury encountered one or two examples of ichonoclasm, which engendered lively debate but ultimately a sense of disappointment that examples of new conceptual thinking did not manifest an aura of quality. The jury believes that better examples do exist, and hopes to be able recognize them on another occasion. One trend which was discussed at length was the emergence of „unskilled music". This is music, the composition and performance of which does not depend on acquiring traditional skills by undergoing formal training in those areas. This became a hypothetical possibility with the emergence of MIDI and the microcomputer in the early 1980s, and has since been increasingly realized (especially within the realm of popular music) as the power, sophistication and flexibility of computers and electroacoustic music equipment has developed. To be specific, the Music Jury would welcome a greater proportion of submissions:
– which experiment with modes of presentation other than the concert/recital paradigm

nungen explizit würdigen. Doch in diesem Jahr war es der Musikjury unmöglich, dieses Ziel angesichts der vorliegenden Einreichungen zu erreichen. Jetzt, wo die Computermusik „erwachsen" ist, treten einige der weniger vorteilhaften Aspekte des mittleren Alters in den Vordergrund. Zum eigenen Wohle sollte sie vielleicht wieder etwas schlanker und fitter werden! Die Ideen der Computermusik und deren Ausdrucksweisen treten gewissermaßen auf der Stelle. Stück für Stück begegnen uns immer wieder die gleichen Manierismen, wenn die Stücke von verschiedenen Komponisten stammen – so daß man sich des Eindrucks nicht erwehren kann, ein Virus des Klischeehaften sei ausgebrochen und nehme womöglich epidemische Ausmaße an.

Besonders enttäuschend ist, daß sich offenbar auch schon die jüngere Generation von Komponisten angesteckt hat. Mit allem Verständnis dafür, daß sich Studenten oder junge professionelle Komponisten die mittlerweile etablierte Praxis als Vorbild nehmen – diese Vorgehensweise ist ein durchaus wertvoller Bestandteil des Lernprozesses –, ist es jedoch befremdend zu sehen, wie groß die Bereitschaft der jüngeren Leute ist, sich vor den aufgebauten Ikonen mittleren Alters zu verbeugen. Eine etwas bilderstürmerische Haltung wäre eine größere Respektsbezeugung!

Die Musikjury fand ein oder zwei bilderstürmerische Beispiele, die lebhafte Debatten auslösten, uns jedoch schließlich doch enttäuschten, da ein neues konzeptionelles Denken sich nicht in hoher Qualität niederschlug. Die Jury ist überzeugt, daß bessere Beispiele existieren, und hofft, diese bei einer anderen Gelegenheit anerkennen zu können. Eine Tendenz, die ausführlich diskutiert wurde, ist das Aufkommen „untrainierter Musik". Damit ist die Art von Musik gemeint, für deren Komposition und Aufführung jene traditionellen Fähigkeiten, die durch formale Ausbildung auf diesen Gebieten erworben werden, keine Vorbedingung mehr sind. Diese theoretische Möglichkeit entstand Anfang der 8oer Jahre durch die Entwicklung von MIDI und dem Mikrocomputer. Sie wird seither zunehmend in demselben Maß umgesetzt (besonders auf dem Gebiet der Popmusik), in dem Stärke, Leistungsfähigkeit und Flexibilität der Computer und der elektroakustischen Musikgeräte weiterentwickelt werden. Um es präzis zu formulieren: Die Musikjury würde einen größeren Anteil an Einreichungen begrüßen,

Die Jury ist außerdem zu der Ansicht gekommen, daß es sinnvoll wäre, die Grenze der Kategorie „Computermusik" dahingehend zu erweitern, daß auch andere Artefakte – nicht nur Kompositionen – eingereicht werden könnten – z. B. neue und originelle technologiegestützte Strategien zur Förderung musikalischer Tätigkeit.

Was schließlich die Preise an sich betrifft, so spiegelt die Auswahl der Preisträger zumindest einige der oben genannten Anliegen wider. Zwei der Hauptpreise werden Komponisten zuerkannt, die in privaten Studios und nicht im Rahmen großer Institutionen arbeiten, und zwei von den drei Hauptpreisträgern haben die Soziologie des elektroakustischen Konzerts entweder neu erfunden oder zugunsten einer alternativen Präsentation verworfen. Alle ausgewählten Werke zeigen ein hohes Maß an Können, Phantasie und künstlerischer Integrität.

Einstimmig entschied sich die Musikjury, die Goldene Nica an Robert Normandeau für seine akusmatische Komposition „Le renard et la rose" zu vergeben. Das Werk zeichnet sich durch die nur scheinbar einfache Ausführung aus; es ist unmittelbar ansprechend, mit einem stark narrativen Element, das nicht nur durch den Text zum Ausdruck gebracht wird, sondern auch durch die durchgehend bearbeiteten oder dekonstruierten Formen, sowie durch die umgebenden und begleitenden Computer-„Instrumente". Die Verwendung der Periodizität als musikalische Quelle ist faszinierend. Das Werk ist Ausdruck der Bemühung, sämtliche konzeptionellen musikalischen Aspekte aus der dem digitalen Medium inhärenten Natur zu entwickeln. Beeindruckt war die Jury auch davon, mit welcher Sorgfalt der Komponist das Werk in die grundsätzliche konzeptionelle Gestaltung des Performance-Raums integriert hat. Die reichhaltige Klangwelt bietet das, was der Komponist ein „Kino für das Ohr" nennt: Zweifellos wird dies – wie auch der narrative Aspekt des

– which display high-quality examples of a still wider range of aesthetics
– by composers and sound artists with no institutional affiliations
– by women composers, who at present are seriously under-represented in submissions.

In addition, the jury felt that it would be worth expanding the scope of the Computer Music category to permit the submission of artefacts other than compositions – for example, new and original, technology-based strategies for supporting musical activity.

Turning finally to the awards themselves, at least some of the concerns outlined above are reflected in the choice of the award winners. Two of the major prizes go to composers who are working in personal studios rather than the large institutional context, and two out of the three have either reinvented the sociology of the electroacoustic concert or abandoned it in favour of an alternative presentation. All the works selected show very high degrees of skill, imagination and artistic intergrity.

The Music Jury was unanimous in its decision to award the Golden Nica to Robert Normandeau for his acousmatic composition, "Le renard et la rose". A work of deceptively easy accomplishment, it is immediately appealing, with a strong narrative element, articulated not only by means of text, but even by its most highly processed or deconstructed forms and by the surrounding and accompanying computer "instruments". it has an intriguing use of periodicity as a musical source and demonstrates a concern that all its conceptual musical aspects arise from the inherent nature of the digital medium. The jury was impressed by the careful consideration given to the integration into the fundamental conceptual design of the performance space. The richness of its sound world provides what the composer calls a "cinema for the ear": no doubt this, as well as the works narrative aspect, is helped by the work's origins in a radio play based on the same subject matter and musical sources.

One of the two second prizes awarded, coincidentally, goes to a radio programme, entitled "Media Survival Kit", a lyric satire by James Dashow, with a text by Bruno Ballardini, In spite of its diverse components – actors' voices, soprano, an instrumental ensemble and a human whistler, as well as a multitude of computer-processed and originated sounds – this vastly entertaining work comes across as a surreally unified view of the invasion of our lives and minds by the computer, its screen and the internet. The reality of everday personal existence is gradually supplanted by the attractive but insubstantial delights of the virtual world, to the point where everything becomes uncertain, including the reality of personal existence. "But as for us, are we really there?" Such dangerously deep and ancient philosophical questions are handled with the lightest of touches and with welcome wit and humour. From a musical point of view, the rhythmic handling of the spoken text is cunningly counterpointed with the synthetic and processed elements in a way which only the most aurally imaginative composers can achieve.

The other second prize was awarded to Régis Renouard Larivière for his work "Futaie" for an ensemble of loudspeakers. Another richly allusive work, where extra-musical symbology genuinely relates to musical materials and compositional un-folding, "Futaie" is a work of consciously extreme limitation of timbral, rhythmic and dynamic materials. It challenges common conceptions of how musical time should pass, and focusses attention on a distinctive, temporal dramaturgy, created in no small part by the careful attention given to the space between the sounds as the sounds themselves.

As previously noted, the award of "honorary mentions" does not acknowledge innova-tion so much as recognize works as being of inherent quality or representing one of the distinctive approaches to be found in the diverse world that is computer music.

ROBERT NORMANDEAU

Robert Normandeau (CDN), geb. 1955, Gründungsmitglied der Canada Electroacoustic Community (CEC) und von Réseaux, einer Gruppe zur Förderung der kreativen Zusammenarbeit zwischen Kunst und Medien. 1986–1993 Mitglied der Association pour la création et la recherche électroacoustique du Québec (ACREQ), seit 1988 Vorträge zur Akustik und Elektroakustik an der Musikfakultät der University of Montreal. Derzeitiger Arbeitsschwerpunkt ist akusmatische Musik (Anwendung ästhetischer Kriterien, um ein „Kino für das Ohr" zu schaffen).

Robert Normandeau (CDN), born 1955, founding member of the Canadian Electroacoustic Community (CEC) and of Réseaux, a group which promotes creative collaborations of art and the media. 1986–1993 member of the Association pour la création et la recherche électroacoustique du Québec (ACREQ), since 1988 lectures in acoustics and electroacoustics at the Faculty of Music of the University of Montreal. Current endeavors focussed on acousmatic music (employing a esthetic criteria to create a "cinema for the ear").

„Le renard et la rose" („Der Fuchs und die Rose") (1995) – es ist Odile Magnan gewidmet – ist eine Konzertsuite, die aus zwei Klangquellen komponiert wurde: aus der Musik, die von Radio-Canada für das Hörspiel nach „Der kleine Prinz" von Antoine de St. Exupéry (produziert 1994 von Odile Magnan) in Auftrag gegeben wurde, wovon wir hier die zwei Hauptthemen nehmen. Die zweite Klangquelle besteht aus den Stimmen der Schauspieler und Radiosprecher, die beim Hörspiel mitwirkten.

„Le renard et la rose" ist der dritte Teil eines 1991 begonnenen Zyklus („Éclats de voix" und „Spleen" waren die ersten beiden Teile), der ausschließlich mit Stimmen und insbesondere mit Lautmalerei arbeitet. Lautmalerei ist der einzige Fall in der menschlichen Sprache, in dem der Klang unmittelbar einen Gegenstand, eine Geste oder ein Gefühl beschreibt, anstatt das Gemeinte durch abstrakte Darstellungen – sprich: Wörter – mitzuteilen.

Die Themen der Geschichte „Der kleine Prinz" findet man nacheinander: den König, den Geschäftsmann, den Eitlen, die Vogelschar, die Quelle in der Wüste, die kleine Blume, die Rose, die Baobabs, den Laternenanzünder, den Wasserpillenhändler, den Fuchs und den Geograph.

Das Werk teilt sich in fünf Abschnitte, die fünf Zustände des Erwachsenenalters darstellen und mit

"Le renard et la rose" ("The Fox and the Rose", 1995) dedicated to Odile Magnan, is a concert suite composed from two sound sources: the music commissioned by Radio-Canada for the radio play adapted from "The Little Prince" by Antoine de St-Exupéry (produced by Odile Magnan in 1994), from which we will retrieve here the main themes, and the voices of the actors and radio speakers who participated to the radio play. "Le renard et la rose" is the third piece of a cycle started in 1991 ("Eclats de voix" and "Spleen" were the first two parts of that cycle) based exclusively on the use of the voice and more particularly on the use of onomatopoeia, considered as the only case in the human language where the sound describes directly the object, the gesture or the feeling that one wants to communicate, as opposed to their abstract representations, the words.

One will find successively the themes of "The Little Prince": The King, The Businessman, The Vain Person, the Flock of Birds, The Desert Well, The Little Flower, The Rose, The Baobabs, The Lamplighter, The Water Pills Tradesman, The Fox and The Geographer.

The work is divided into five sections which represent as many states of the adult age, and are associated with different sound parameters: chattering and rhythm; nostalgia and timbre; anger and dynamic; lassitude and space; and finally, serenity and texture. "Le renard et la rose" was composed for a 14 loudspeakers diffusion system. The original tape is intended to be played with one track directly assigned to one speaker. That means that in concert, the piece requires a multitrack tape recorder, a mixing board and 14 loudspeakers plus 2 sub-woofers.

The two tape recorders can be either 2 synchronized ADAT or 2 synchronized TASCAM DA 88 (one playing the first 8 tracks and the second one playing the last 6 tracks).

The mixing board should be as versatile as possible. With such a board, it would be possible to assign whatever tracks to any loudspeaker.

This might be useful in some concert halls, so that people who are at a distance from some speakers, do not lose any information. Playing the music from a multitrack recorder on which each track goes to a separate loudspeaker, without having to touch the levels or the equalizations, is a completely different way of composing music. The spatialization of the sounds becomes an integral part of the composition, and thusly the performance space serves to delineate the sonorous parameters as well as the height, the length, and the intensity. Mixing, therefore, is accomplished acoustically and not electronically.

"Le renard et la rose" was composed in the composer's personal studio in 1995 with the financial help of the conseil des arts et des lettres du Québec. The work was commissioned by the Banff Centre for the Arts with the financial help of the Canada Council for the 1995 International Computer Music Conference.

verschiedenen Klangparametern in Verbindung gebracht werden: Plappern und Rhythmus; Nostalgie und Klangfarbe; Zorn und Dynamik; Niedergeschlagenheit und Zwischenraum; und schließlich innere Ruhe und Struktur.

„Le renard et la rose" wurde für ein Diffusionssystem mit 14 Lautsprechern komponiert. Das Originalband sollte einspurig direkt über die Lautsprecher gespielt werden. Im Konzert heißt das, daß für das Stück ein mehrspuriges Tonbandgerät, ein Mischpult, 14 Lautsprecher und zwei Subwoofers benötigt werden.

Die zwei Tonbandgeräte können entweder zwei synchronisierte ADAT oder zwei synchronisierte TASCAM DA88 sein (eines davon spielt die ersten acht Spuren, das zweite spielt die letzten sechs Spuren). Das Mischpult sollte so vielseitig verwendbar wie möglich sein. Mit einem solchen Mischpult könnte man verschiedene Spuren beliebigen Lautsprechern zuordnen. In manchen Konzertsälen könnte dadurch vermieden werden, daß Zuhörer, die weit weg von einigen Lautsprechern sind, Information verlieren. Wäre dies der Fall könnten einige Spuren verdoppelt werden.

Es ist eine ganz andere Art, Musik zu komponieren, wenn die Musik von einem mehrspurigen Tonband gespielt wird, wobei jede Spur über einen anderen Lautsprecher gespielt wird, ohne daß die Tonregler oder die Balance eingestellt werden müssen. Die Verräumlichung des Klangs wird zu einem wesentlichen Bestandteil der Komposition. Von daher bestimmt der Aufführungsraum nicht nur die sonoren Parameter, sondern auch die Höhe, Länge und Intensität. Deswegen wird das Mischen akustisch und nicht elektronisch durchgeführt.

„Le renard et la rose" wurde 1995 im privaten Studio des Komponisten mit der finanziellen Unterstützung vom Conseil des arts et des lettres du Québec komponiert. Es ist ein Auftragswerk für das Banff Centre for the Arts, gefördert vom Canada Council for the 1995 International Computer Music Conference.

Robert Normandeau
"Le Renard et la Rose", 1995, 15:00 min

JAMES DASHOW

James Dashow (USA), geb. 1944 in Chicago, lebt in den Sabinischen Hügeln nördlich von Rom. Er war einige Jahre Direktor der Forum Players in Rom, einem Ensemble für zeitgenössische Musik. Am Centro di Sonologia Computazionale der Universität Padua ist er als Komponist und Lehrer tätig. 1985 bis 1992 Produzent der wöchentlichen Sendung für zeitgenössische Musik für das italienische nationale Radio (RAI), „Il Forum Internazionale".

James Dashow, (USA), born 1944 in Chicago and now living in the Sabine Hills north of Rome. For several years he directed the Forum Players in Rome, a contemporary music ensemble, and is now director of the Studio di Musica Elettronica Sciadoni. He has been associated as composer and Teacher with the Centro di Sonologia Computazionale of the University of Padua. From 1985 to 1992 Dashow was producer of the weekly broadcast of contemporary music for Italian National Radio (RAI), Il Forum Internazionale.

Unser Leben wird immer mehr durch die Interaktion mit irgendeiner Art von Bildschirm bestimmt: Zunächst gab es das Kino, dann den Fernseher und jetzt den Computer.

Der Computer nimmt uns weit mehr gefangen als seine Vorgänger, weil er uns einlädt, an einer Erfahrung teilzuhaben, die weit weniger passiv ist als die Einwegdarstellung der Videobilder. Doch diese Teilhabe ist bloß eine Illusion: Die Informationen und Methoden der Interaktion (die „Gebrauchsanleitungen") können von anderen leicht manipuliert werden. Dadurch findet eine kulturelle Anpassung statt, die viel heimtückischer ist als alle andere vorher ... Wir werden zu digitalen Lotosessern.

1. NICÒ

Unser Held, ein gewisser Nicò, erzählt von seinen frühen Erinnerungen; er ist bereits gefangen, hypnotisiert von seinem Computerbildschirm. Die Stimmen sind jene aus der Welt der Informatik, und sie werden immer halluzinierender, je weiter Nicó in die digitale Welt hineinfällt. Die Realität ruft ihn weiterhin, sie versucht, ihn aus dem Wirbel herauszuziehen, doch vergebens. Je weiter er vordringt, desto mehr erscheint ihm die Realität wie ein bloßes Lichtspiel.

2. CREMA (CREAM)

Hartnäckig wie ein Virus, erscheint dieser Werbespot

More and more, our lives are being determined by interactions with some sort of screen: first there was the cinema, then the TV, now the computer.

The latter captures us more than its predecessors by inviting us to take part in an experience much less passive than that based on merely the one-way presentation of video images. But this participation is only an illusion: the information and modes of interaction (the "instructions for use") are easily manipulated by others, producing a cultural conformism far more insidious than before ... we become digital lotus eaters.

1. NICÒ

Our hero, a certain Nicò, is recounting a few early memories; he is already captured, hypnotized by his computer screen. The voices are those of the world of informatics which become more and more hallucinatory as Nicò falls deeper and deeper into the digital world. Reality continues to call him, to pull him out of his vortex, but in vain; the further he gets inside, the more reality seems mere light-play.

2. CREMA (CREAM)

As persistent as a virus, the publicity spot

appears wherever there's a screen.
3. TUTTI COLLEGATI (Everybody Connected):
The ultimate triumph of the screen: its
universe is the Net. But as for us, are we
really there?
"Media Survival Kit" was produced for Audio
Box, a program of National Italian Radio
(RAI), Radio 3.
The voices, in order of their materialization:
Alfredo Lombardozzi, Bruno Ballardini,
Claudio Bianchi, Lucia Bova, Pinotto Fava.
The musicians: Lucia Bova, harp; Corrado
Canonici, contrabass; Paul Goldfield, percus-
sion; Barbara Lazotti, soprano; Paola
Buccian, cello; with the special participation
of whistler Nicholas Anagnostis.
Elaboration of recorded sounds and elec-
tronic sound synthesis was done using the
MUSIC30 system of digital sound synthesis,
on the Spirit30 accelerator board for per-
sonal computers by Sonitech International.
Digital editing by Giancarlo Grevi, Paolo
Antonini, Antonio Giordano.
With thanks to Roberto Carapellucci and
especially to Pinotto Fava, producer of Audio
Box.
P.S. The composer and the author of the
words, Bruno Ballardini, worked together
almost exclusively via the Internet;
nevertheless, towards the end of the project
each verified that the other really existed.

überall dort, wo es Bildschirme gibt.
3. TUTTI COLLEGATI (alle miteinander verbunden)
Der endgültige Sieg des Bildschirms: sein Universum
ist das Netz. Doch was uns betrifft, sind wir wirklich da?
„Media Survival Kit" wurde für „Audio Box", ein Pro-
gramm des italienischen nationalen Rundfunks (RAI)
Radio 3, produziert.
Die Stimmen (in der Reihenfolge ihrer „Verkörperung"):
Alfredo Lombardozzi, Bruno Ballardini, Claudio Bianchi,
Lucia Bova, Pinotto Fava.
Die Musiker: Lucia Bova, Harfe; Corrado Canonici, Kon-
trabaß; Paul Goldfield, Schlagzeug; Barbara Lazotti,
Sopran; Paola Buccian, Cello; mit besonderer Beteili-
gung des Pfeifers, Nicholas Anagnostis.
Die Ausarbeitung der aufgenommenen Klänge und die
elektronische Klangsynthese wurden unter Anwendung
des MUSIC30-Systems für digitale Klangsynthese auf
einem Spirit30 Accelerator-Board für PC von Sonitech
International durchgeführt.
Für die digitale Aufbereitung sorgten Giancarlo Grevi,
Paolo Antonini, Antonio Giordano.
Mit Dank an Roberto Carapellucci und beson-
ders Pinotto Pava, den Produzenten von „Audio
Box".
PS: Der Komponist und der Texter, Bruno Ballardini,
arbeiteten fast ausschließlich durch das Internet
zusammen; gegen Abschluß des Projekts verifizierten
allerdings beide, ob der andere auch tatsächlich
existiert...

James Dashow
"Media Survival Kit", 1995/96, 20:00 min

RÉGIS RENOUARD LARIVIÈRE

*Régis Renouard Larivière (F),
geb. 1959 in Paris. 1984 Praktikum für
elektroakustische Musik (ADAC-GRM)
bei den Komponisten Jacques Lejeune
und Philippe Mion. 1986 Gründung
eines eigenen Kompositionsstudios.
1987–1995 verschiedene Kompositionen in den Tonstudios des „Groupe
de Recherches Musicales". Larivière
lehrt seit 1990 elektroakustische
Musik in Poitiers (CFMI); seit 1995 ist
er Mitarbeiter der Vereinigung „Ars
Sonora", ihr Ziel: Verbreitung der
elektroakustischen Musik.*

COMPUTER MUSIC

*Die Art und Weise, wie sich das Stück „Futaie" –
auf deutsch „Hochwald" – über einen Zeitraum
erstreckt wie ein langer, langsamer, auf seine Zei-
chensetzung zusammengestrichener Satz, hat mehr
mit der Zeitfolge einer Beschreibung zu tun als mit
der Beschreibung eines bestimmten Gegenstandes.
Man wird dort kaum bildliche Darstellungen von
Baumgruppen, Häschen oder ähnlichem vorfinden
... Gleichmäßige Farbtöne stehen sich in bewe-
gungsloser Anhäufung einerseits, in sinn- und
zwecklosem Blitzen andererseits, gegenüber.
„Futaie" ist ein erweiterter, ausgedehnter Augenblick und versucht, durch das der Musik inhärente
Mittel der Zeitfolge ein Gefühl der Simultaneität zu
erzeugen, ein Gefühl „gemeinsamer Gegenwart"
(„Commune présence" – R. Char) der Dinge. Jene
erscheinen sowohl in ihren individuellen als auch
in den ihnen gemeinsamen Zeitfolgen, so wie die
einzelnen Bäume miteinander einen Hochwald bilden. Es ist wie ein aufgesplitterter Augenblick, dessen Einzelteile nacheinander vorgestellt werden.
„Futaie" kann auch wie Zeremonialmusik gehört*

The way in which the piece "Futaie", which
means "Mountain Forest", extends over a
period of time like a long, slow movement
reduced to its punctuation, has more to do
with the temporal structure of a description
than with a description of a certain thing.
Here, one will hardly find picturesque
representations of groups of trees, little
rabbits or other things of that nature ...
Smooth colorations are contrasted with one
another in motionless groups on one side
and senseless, random flashes on the other.
"Futaie" is an enlarged, extended moment,
and it attempts to create a feeling of simu-
ltaneity using the temporal structure inherent to the music: a feeling of the "com-
munal presence" of things. Everything is
intended to appear according to its own
temporal structure, as well as according to
the common temporal structure of things,
just as so many individual trees form a
forest together. It is like a shattered mo-

Régis Renouard Larivière (F),
born 1959 in Paris, studied electro-
acoustic music (ADAC-GRM) with the
composers Jacques Lejeune and
Philippe Mion, founded his own studio
for composition in 1986; 1987–1995
various compositions in the sound
studios of the "Groupe de Recherches
Musicales", has taught electro-acoustic
music in Poitiers (CFMI) since 1990.
Larivière has worked together since
1995 with the association "Ars Sonora",
which aims to spread electroacoustic
music more widely.

ment, where the separate pieces are presented one after another.

"Futaie" may also be heard as a kind of ceremonious music, but this is a ceremony without a cult; it is like a slow, extended procession of sound. My foremost concern in this piece, as in my previous work "Bromios", relates to the stillness that surrounds and traverses the music, that same stillness that both treatens and also evokes music. In both pieces, I focus on sudden emergence and on stillness.

It is possible that electro-acoustic music most strongly expresses this focus, in that it allows for the exploration of sounds separated from their causes and freed from their origins.

"Futaie" was composed in the sound studios of the Groupe de Recherches Musicales in the course of a few weeks, following a long period of preparation from July 1995 to January 1996.

werden; es geht um eine kultlose Zeremonie, gleich einer langsamen ausgedehnten Tonschleife. Meine Hauptsorge in diesem wie auch in meinem vorigen Stück, „Bromios", gilt der die Musik umgebenden und sie durchlaufenden Stille, jener Stille, welche die Musik sowohl bedroht als auch hervorruft. Hier wie dort ist mein Hauptanliegen das plötzliche Auftauchen und die Stille. Möglicherweise kommt die elektroakustische Musik diesem Anliegen besonders nahe, da in ihr die Klangtöne von ihrer Ursache losgelöst und von ihrer Herkunft befreit erarbeitet werden.

„Futaie" wurde in den Tonstudios der Groupe de Recherches Musicals (GRM) nach einer langen Vorbereitungszeit innerhalb einiger Wochen, zwischen Juli 1995 und Januar 1996, komponiert.

Régis Renouard Larivière
"Futaie", 1996, 14:00 min

FRANCESCO BOSCHETTO

*Francesco Boschetto (I),
geb. 1970 in Arezzo, studierte
Geige, Jazzgitarre und klassische
Komposition in Mailand. 1992
übersiedelte er nach Schweden, um
in Stockholm bei Erik M. Karlsson
(EMS Studios) elektronische
Komposition zu studieren. Seine
Musik wurde im schwedischen
Rundfunk und beim Stockholm
Electronic Music Festival aufgeführt.
1995 gewann er eine Anerkennung
beim Stockholm Electronic
Arts Awards.*

**Francesco Boschetto (I),
born 1970 in Arezzo, has been
studying violin, jazz guitar and
classical composition in Milan. In
1992 he moved to Stockholm
to study electronic composition
with Erik M. Karlsson at EMS
studios. His music has been
played by the Swedish Radio
and at the Stockholm Electronic
music festival. He has been
awarded an honourary mention at
the Stockholm Electronic Arts
Awards 1995.**

Diese Komposition ist dem vor zwanzig Jahren verstorbenen italienischen Dichter, Schriftsteller und Filmemacher Pier Paolo Pasolini gewidmet, der am Meer in der Nähe von Rom unter mysteriösen Umständen ermordet wurde.

Das Stück stellt eine Reise in vier kurzen Sätzen dar. Der Grund dieser Reise wird im Titel erklärt: das Wort wurde von Pasolini erfunden und als Name für eine späte Gedichtesammlung verwendet („Trasumanar e organizzar"). Es bedeutet, das Menschliche zu transzendieren, ein Objekt – ein geistiges oder ein gedachtes Objekt – zu ergreifen, um es dann mit Materie in Verbindung zu bringen und ihm eine Gestalt zu verleihen.

This composition is dedicated to the Italian poet, writer and filmmaker Pier Paolo Pasolini, who died twenty years ago, killed under unclear circumstances, near the sea near Rome.

The piece is meant to represent a journey in four short movements. The reason for this journey is explained by the title, a word invented by Pasolini and used to name a late collection of poems ("Trasumanar e organizzar"). It means to transcend the human, to grab an object, a spiritual, or mental object, in order to bring it in contact with the material and confer it a form.

Francesco Boschetto
"Trasumanar", 1995, 11:20 min

Chris Brown (USA), born 1953, San Francisco based composer, pianist, and electronic instrument builder, studied composition with William Brooks, electronic music with Gordon Mumma, and computer music with David Rosenboom. He is currently Co-Director for the Center for Contemporary Music (CCM) at Mills College in Oakland, where he also teaches Composition and Electronic Music.

Chris Brown (USA), geb. 1953, lebt in San Francisco. Er ist Komponist, Pianist und Instrumentenbauer elektronischer Instrumente; studierte Komposition bei William Brooks, elektronische Musik bei Gordon Mumma und Computermusik bei David Rosenboom. Derzeit Co-Direktor am Center for Contemporaray Music (CCM) an Mills College, Oakland, wo er auch Komposition und elektronische Musik unterrichtet.

"Talking Drum" is an interactive computer network piece based on cyclical rhythms. It expands on the idea of the drum-machine to enable much of what commercial instruments lack: performer interactivity, polyrhythmic complexity, temporal flexibility, and timbral variety. It extends these capabilities spatially to multiple-speaker installations, creating synchronized interlocking rhythms that exploit distance and resonance effects of the performance space, playing the environment like the membrane of a drum. "Talking Drum" runs on a local computer network of up to eight players installed outdoors or in a very large room.
The network ensemble is interactive with acoustic musicians, up to one player for every speaker/channel used in the performance. Each instrumentalist plays with rhythms generated by the computer, and the program responds to the player's feel (the emphasis placed on specific beats and patterns through subtleties of timing, loudness, density, and pitch) by continuously changing its music.
"Talking Drum" can take many different forms: it is an ongoing project that supports different collaborations at each perform-

„Talking Drum" ist ein Stück für interaktives Computernetzwerk auf Basis zyklischer Rhythmen. Es erweitert die Idee der Trommelmaschine, um das zu ermöglichen, wozu die meisten kommerziellen Instrumente nicht imstande sind: Interaktivität der Performer, polyrhythmische Komplexität, zeitliche Flexibilität und Vielfalt der Klangfarbe. Es erweitert diese Möglichkeiten räumlich auf Multi-Lautsprecher-Installationen, indem es synchronisierte, übergreifende Rhythmen schafft, die die Entfernung und die Resonanzwirkungen des Performanceraums ausnützen, indem das Environment wie das Fell einer Trommel bespielt wird.
„Talking Drum" wird auf einem lokalen aus bis zu acht Mitspieler bestehenden Computernetzwerk aufgeführt, das entweder im Freien oder in einem sehr großen Raum aufgebaut wird.
Das Netzwerkensemble interagiert mit akustischen Musikern, und zwar bis zu einem Musiker für jeden in der Performance verwendeten Lautsprecher/Kanal. Jeder Instrumentalmusiker spielt mit den vom Computer generierten Rhythmen, und das Programm reagiert auf die Stimmung des Musikers (wie z. B. spezifische Takte und Muster, durch die Feinheiten des Tempos, der Lautstärke, der Dichte und der Tonhöhe betont werden), indem er ständig die Musik verändert.
„Talking Drum" kann viele verschiedene Formen annehmen: Es ist ein offenes Projekt, das bei jeder Performance verschiedene Arten der Zusammenarbeit unter-

COMPUTER MUSIC HONORARY MENTION

Chris Brown
"Talking Drum", 1995, 14:20 min

KUI DONG

COMPUTER MUSIC HONORARY MENTION

Kui Dong (USA), geb. 1967 in Beijing, China, arbeitet derzeit am Doktorat in Komposition und Computermusik an der Stanford University. Unter ihren Kompositionen und Auftragswerken sind ein Ballett in drei Akten für Orchester, ein Tanz in einem Akt, verschiedene Kombinationen von Kammerwerken und Werke für Elektroakustik und Multimedia.

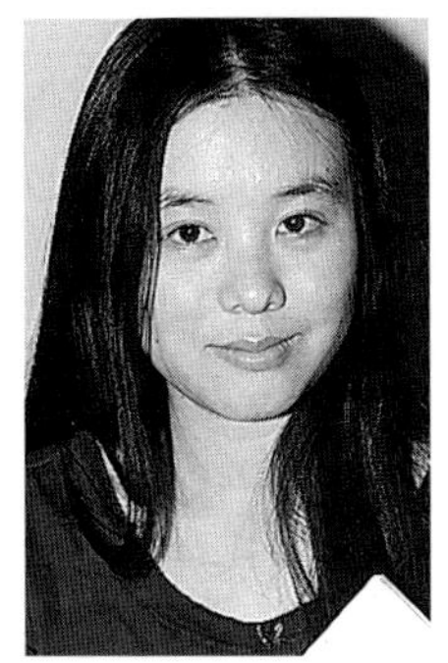

Kui Dong (USA), born 1967 in Beijing, China. She is currently completing her doctoral degree in composition and computer music at Stanford University. Her compositions and commissioned works include a 3-act ballet for orchestra, one act dance, different combinations of chamber works, and works for electroacoustics and multi-media.

Bei „Flying Apples" handelt es sich um einen unvollendeten Kindheitstraum; mit der unbegrenzten Phantasie eines Kindes spaziert man in diesem Traum durch eine bunte und unverdorbene Welt.

Diese algorithmische Komposition wurde auf DMIX, einer für Macintosch neu entwickelten Software, am CCRMA, Stanford University, komponiert. Programmiert wurde das Werk mit extremen Verschachtelungsmustern, die aus einer einfachen Idee ein komplexes Muster entwickeln.

Wenn ich komponiere, denke ich nicht übermäßig über mein Werkzeug und meine Technik nach. Statt dessen finde ich durch Zuhören, was am besten in das Gesamtkonzept des jeweiligen Musikstücks paßt. Jeder Klang hat auch eine Farbe und eine Gestalt, und danach suche ich beim Komponieren. Reinheit und Aufrichtigkeit sind die Wahrheiten, die mich leiten. In „Flying Apples" fange ich die durchsichtigen, leuchtenden Sterne auf, die aus der Ewigkeit herabfallen.

"Flying Apples" concerns an unfinished childhood dream where, with the unlimited imagination of a child, a walk is taken through a colorful and unspoiled world. This algorithmic composition was composed on DMIX, a newly developed software for a Macintosh, at CCRMA, Stanford University. It was programmed with extreme nesting patterns, forming a simple idea which then grows into a complex pattern.

I do not think excessively about tools and techniques while composing. Instead I listen for what best fits my overall concept for the piece of music. Each sound has a color and shape as well, which I am always looking for when I am composing. Purity and sincerity are truths that guide me. In "Flying Apples" I catch the transparent, brilliant stars falling from infinity.

Kui Dong
"Flying Apples", 1994, 10:00 min

JONTY HARRISON

Jonty Harrison (GB), born 1952, is Senior Lecturer in the University of Birmingham and director of the Electroacoustic Music Studios and BEAST (Birmingham Electro Acoustic Sound Theatre), currently Chair of Sonic Arts Network, the UK's national organisation for electroacoustic music and is on the Council of the Society for the Pomotion of New Music.

Jonty Harrison (GB), geb. 1952, ist Senior Lecturer an der University of Birmingham und Direktor der Electroacoustic Music Studios und BEAST (Birmingham Electro Acoustic Sound Theatre), derzeit Vorstand des Sonic Arts Network, der nationalen Organisation für elektroakustische Musik im UK und Mitglied des Council of the Society for the Promotion of New Music.

One of the principal source sounds for this work – balloons from children's parties – gave rise to a train of thought which, after linking "toy" balloons to "hot air" balloons, went on to draw in numerous other concepts of air (breath, utterance, natural phenomena) and heat (energy, action, danger). As work on the sound material progressed, other notions of air became important: motion through space; a certain fleeting quality; and air as the principal medium for the transmission of sound itself. The manner in which this happens became a model for the structure of the piece itself. Gradually, the aspects of the piece revealed the worrying image of the inflated balloon as a metaphor for the fragility of the Earth itself being manipulated, but not infinitely so. But beware! Danger! I run the risk of becoming too pompous, too "inflated" with the importance of my theme. If what someone says is "hot air", it means it lacks real substance, is rubbish, meaningless, bluff ... "Hot Air" was commissioned by the Groupe de Recherches Musicales and sound material was developed using the GRM's Syter and GRM Tools systems; later stages in the compositional process took place in the composer's private studio and in the Electroacoustic Music Studios of The University of Birmingham.

Eine der klanglichen Hauptquellen für dieses Werk – Luftballons von einem Kinderfest – führte zu einer Kette gedanklicher Assoziationen. Die Verbindung von „Spielzeug"- mit „Heißluft"-Ballons ließ eine Reihe anderer Konzepte auftauchen, die alle mit Luft (Atem, Äußerung, natürliche Phänomene) und Hitze (Energie, Handlung, Gefahr) zu tun haben.

Beim Bearbeiten des Klangmaterials wurden auch andere Vorstellungen von Luft wichtig: Ihre Bewegung durch den Raum; ihre Flüchtigkeit; und Luft als das hauptsächliche Medium für die Übertragung von Klang an sich. Die Art und Weise, wie diese Übertragung geschieht, wurde zum Modell für die Strukturdes Stückes selbst. Langsam deckten dann die Aspekte des Stücks ein besorgniserregendes Bild eines aufgeblasenen Luftballons auf, als Metapher für die Zerbrechlichkeit der Erde selbst.

Aber Vorsicht! Gefahr!

Ich riskiere schon, daß ich durch die Wichtigkeit meines Themas zu eingebildet, zu „aufgeblasen" werde. Wenn jemand etwas sagt, das nur „heiße Luft" ist, dann fehlt es an Substanz, es ist Unsinn, bedeutungslos, bluff, Viel-Reden-und-Nichts-tun, es sind leere Worte ... „Hot Air" ist ein Auftragswerk für die Groupe de Recherches Musicales, das Klangmaterial wurde mit dem Syter und den Tools-Systemen von GRM bearbeitet; spätere Phasen im Kompositionsprozeß wurden im Privatstudio des Komponisten und in den Electroacoustic Music Studios der University of Birmingham ausgeführt.

Jonty Harrison
"Hot Air", 1995, 22:10 min

MATT HECKERT

COMPUTER MUSIC HONORARY MENTION

Matt Heckert (USA), BA vom San Francisco Art Institute; 1980–1988 Regisseur/Künstler bei Survival Research Laboratories, wo er Performance-Inszenierungen, Roboter, Requisiten und Bühnenbilder entwarf und baute und Soundtracks für Performances arrangierte. Seit 1989 arbeitet Heckert mit dem Mechanical Sound Orchestra zusammen, mit dem er auch Solo-shows bei Festivals und Museen in Europa absolvierte.

Matt Heckert (USA), BA of San Francisco Art Institute, 1980–1988 worked as director/artist with Survival Research Laboratories conceiving performance scenarios, designing and building robots, props, sets and generating entire performance soundtracks; since July 1989 independent work on Mechanical Sound Orchestra: therefore several solo shows at festivals and museums in Europe.

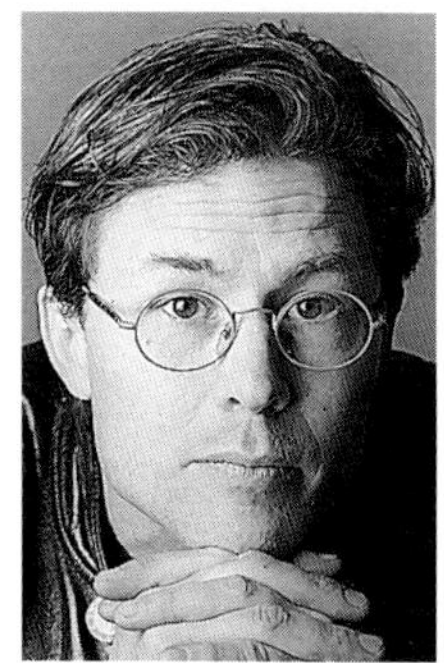

Ich entwerfe und baue Maschinen, die Klang produzieren. Für Klang-Performances werden sie oft dort, wo früher einmal Maschinen standen (in alten Fabriken, Kraftwerken usw.), installiert. Durch ein eingebautes digitales Steuerungssystem kann ich die Maschinen oder „Instrumente" von einem Computer-Interface aus steuern. Meine Methode der Komposition besteht darin, daß ich einzelne Maschinen laufen lasse, bis das gewünschte rhythmische Muster oder die gewünschte Klangqualität erreicht sind. Die Zahlen, die am Bildschirm ausgegeben werden, werden aufgezeichnet, benannt und einer Spur zugeordnet. Die Spuren werden dann mit einem Interlace-Verfahren miteinander verknüpft und als ein Musikstück gespeichert.
Das Werk „Salt Train" wurde entworfen und geschrieben, während ich an meiner Installation im Salzmagazin in Hall in Tirol arbeitete.

I design and build machines that produce sound. They are often installed for sound performance in former machine locations (old factories, power stations, etc.). A digital control system is set up, which allows me to run the machines or "instruments" from a computer interface. My method of composition is to run individual machines until a desired rhythm pattern or tonal quality is achieved. The displayed numbers on the computer screen are recorded, named and assigned a track. Tracks are then laced together and saved as a piece.
The piece "Salt Train" was conceived and written during the time I was working on my installation at the Salzmagazin in Hall in Tirol.

Matt Heckert
"Salt Train", 1994, 55:00 min

GORDON MONAHAN

Gordon Monahan (CDN), born 1956, Kingston, Ontario. Gordon Monahan's works for piano, loudspeakers, video, and kinetic sculpture span various genres from avant-garde concert music to multi-media installation and sound art. He is also artistic director of the KBZ 200, a group specializing in 14-hour "Vexations" performances of music from the 1950's Exotica movement.

Gordon Monahan (CDN), geb. 1956 ; seine Werke für Klavier, Lautsprecher, Video und kinetische Skulptur spannen einen Bogen von Avantgarde-Konzertmusik bis zur Multimediainstallation und Klangkunst. Er ist künstlerischer Leiter von KBZ 200, einer Gruppe, die sich auf 14stündige Performances der Musik aus der Exotica-Bewegung der 50er Jahre spezialisiert hat.

All sounds are produced acoustically (without loudspeakers), but are controlled by computer. The sounds are created by mounting variable speed (24 V DC) motors onto steel sheets of various sizes; the motors have off-centre weights attached to the shafts so that when the motors turn, a physical modulation is transferred to the metal sheeds. The motor speeds are varied so that an extreme spatial effect takes place, where the sound travels around the room as each of the six motors changes speed (causing timbral and dynamic changes) in relation to each other.

The piece is controlled using MAX music software to precisely control the speeds of the motors. Each motor is assigned to a MIDI note name, and velocity numbers from 0 to 127 correspond to voltage values from 0 to 24 volts DC. The velocity numbers can be preprogrammed or run in real time using mouse control. In the case of this recording, the velocity numbers were pre-programmed and read from a value table.

There are two large stainless steel sheets (3 meters x 1.2 meters x 1 mm.) that are hung vertically, the motors being mounted on the top of the sheet. There are 4 smaller sheets ranging from approximately 60 cm x 80 cm. to one square meter. Each of these four sheets has a motor mounted in the centre, and the sheets are hung horizontal to the ground.

Bei „Music for Mechanical Metal" werden sämtliche Klänge akustisch (ohne Lautsprecher) erzeugt, jedoch über Computer gesteuert. Die Klänge werden dadurch erzeugt, daß man Motoren mit verstellbarer Geschwindigkeit (24 V DC) auf verschieden große Stahlbleche montiert; bei jedem Motor ist am Schaft ein Exzentergewicht befestigt, wodurch eine physische Modulation auf das Blech übertragen wird, sobald die Motoren sich drehen. Die Geschwindigkeit der Motoren wird so variiert, daß eine extreme räumliche Wirkung entsteht, wobei sich der Klang im Raum umher bewegt, wenn die sechs Motoren ihre Geschwindigkeit verändern (dadurch entstehen Veränderungen in der Klangfarbe und der Dynamik).

Das Stück wird mittels MAX Musiksoftware gesteuert, um die unterschiedlichen Geschwindigkeiten der Motoren genau kontrollieren zu können. Jeder Motor wird einem MIDI-Notennamen zugeordnet, und die Geschwindigkeitszahlen 0 bis 127 entsprechen den Spannungswerten von 0 bis 24 Volt DC. Die Geschwindigkeitszahlen kann man entweder vorprogrammieren oder mittels Mauskontrolle in Echtzeit laufen lassen.

Für die Aufnahme wurden die Geschwindigkeitszahlen vorprogrammiert und von einer Wertetabelle abgelesen.

Zwei große Bleche aus Edelstahl (3 m x 1,2 m x 1 mm) werden senkrecht mit dem Motor am oberen Ende aufgehängt. Vier kleinere Bleche von 60 cm x 80 cm bis zu einem Quadratmeter werden waagrecht zum Boden aufgehängt, bei ihnen ist in der Mitte ein Motor montiert.

Gordon Monahan
"Music for Mechanical Metal", 1995, 13:23 min

GORDON MONRO

COMPUTER MUSIC HONORARY MENTION

Gordon Monro (AUS) begann 1989 zu komponieren; er unterrichtet an der School of Mathematics and Statistics an der University of Sydney; seine Forschungstätigkeit gilt u. a. mathematischen Aspekten des computergenerierten Klangs. Er unterrichtet auch einen Kurs in Computermusik-Komposition am Musik-Department der University of Sydney.

Gordon Monro (AUS) started composing in 1989; member of the faculty of the School of Mathematics and Statistics, University of Sydney; his research interests include mathematical aspects of computer sound generation. He also teaches a course in computer music composition in the Music Department, University of Sydney.

Angeregt wurde „Dry Rivers" durch eine Reise, die der Komponist durch den westlichen Teil von New South Wales, Australien, unternahm. Die Landschaft dort, von niedrigem Gebüsch überzogen, ist eher Steppe als Wüste. Das Land ist sehr flach, und über Hunderte von Kilometern sind Veränderungen kaum wahrnehmbar. Mit einer Ausnahme war jeder Fluß, an dem wir vorbeikamen, ausgetrocknet.

Das Werk verwendet eine digitale Synthese: genaugenommen fraktale Wellenformen. Es gibt neun parallele Klanglinien mit je einer anderen sub-hörbaren Frequenz (die langsamste wiederholt sich nur alle sechs Sekunden). Die Wellenformen sind jedoch ausreichend komplex, so daß jeder Zyklus getrennt gehört wird. Die Klangfarbe der Wellenformen ändert sich langsam im Laufe des Stückes.

Die neun Linien bestehen aus „Phrasen", die auf einfache, fraktalähnliche Weise angeordnet sind. Durch die zweifache Verwendung von Fraktalen – auf der Ebene der Wellenformen und auf der Ebene der Phrasen – entsteht der Eindruck, daß das Stück immer gleich bleibt, sich aber gleichzeitig kontinuierlich verändert.

„Dry Rivers" wurde an einer Workstation der School of Mathematics and Statistics an der University of Sydney verwirklicht.

"Dry Rivers" was inspired by a trip the composer took through the Western part of New South Wales, Australia. The country is semi-arid rather than desert, being covered by low scrub. It is very flat, and changes imperceptibly over hundreds of kilometres. Every river we came to, except one, was dry.

The piece uses digital synthesis; specifically, fractal waveforms. There are nine parallel lines of sound, each with a different sub-audio frequency (the slowest repeating every 6 seconds). However the waveforms are sufficiently complex to allow each cycle to be heard as a distinct sound. The timbres of the waveforms change slowly throughout the piece.

The nine lines consist of "phrases" arranged in a simple fractal-like manner. The dual use of fractals at the waveform level and at the phrasal level helps to give the impression of something that is always the same, yet always changing.

"Dry Rivers" was realised on a workstation belonging to the School of Mathematics and Statistics, University of Sydney.

Gordon Monro
"Dry Rivers", 1995, 12:00 min

 *212*

STEPHEN MONTAGUE

Stephen Montague (GB), born 1943 in Syracuse, New York, studied piano, conducting and composition at Florida State University, received a doctorate from Ohio State University. During 1992 and 1995 Guest Professor at the University of Texas at Austin and since 1993 has been Visiting Guest Professor at the Royal College of Music, London.

Stephen Montague (GB), geb. 1943 in Syracuse, New York, studierte Klavier, Dirigieren und Komposition an der Florida State University. 1972 erwarb er ein Doktorat an der Ohio State University. 1992 und 1995 war er Gastprofessor an der University of Texas, Austin, seit 1993 ist er Gastprofessor an der Royal College of Music, London.

"From the peaceful opening sounds of wind and breathing, String Quartet no. 1: in memoriam Barry Anderson & Tomasz Sikorski (1989–1993) expands into an incredible sound universe violent and nerve-tingling, then almost painful shrieking when the string quartet and electronics, in spite of their differences, work tightly together as one. It finishes as if the musicians are going away. Rising to their feet, their backs to the audience, they play a few faint, muted sounds. This is electronic music of the highest calibre, and one of the works from Musiana 93 that left the deepest impression." (Dansk Musik Tidsskrift)

„Von den anfänglich ruhigen Wind- und Atemklängen wächst „String Quartet No. 1: in memoriam Barry Andersen & Tomasz Sikorski" (1989-1993) zu einem unglaublichen Klanguniversum an, das gewaltig und aufreibend ist. Es wird zu einem fast schmerzhaften Schrei, wenn das Streichquartett und die Elektronik trotz ihrer Unterschiede so eng zusammenarbeiten, daß sie fast zu einer Einheit verschmelzen. Gegen Ende sieht es fast so aus, als ob die Musiker sich schon verabschieden würden. Sie stehen auf und spielen, mit dem Rücken zum Publikum, ein paar leise, gedämpfte Töne. Dies ist elektronische Musik der höchsten Qualität und eines der beeindruckendsten Werke bei der Musiana 93." (Dansk Musik Tidsskrift)

COMPUTER MUSIC HONORARY MENTION

Stephen Montague
"String Quartet no.1" 1989-1993

MICHEL REDOLFI

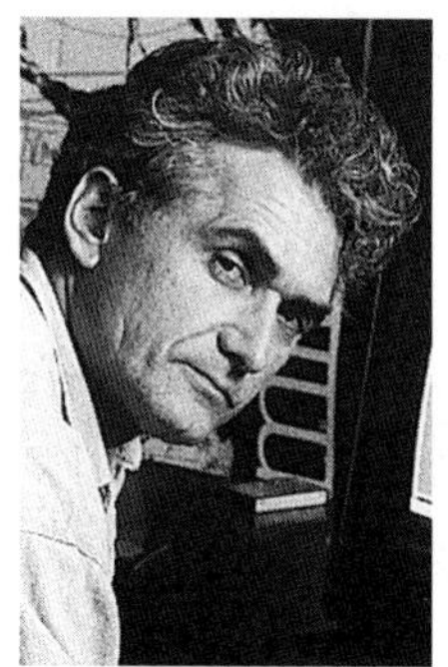

Michel Redolfi (F), geb. 1951 in Marseille, seit 1986 Direktor des Centre International de Recherche Musicale (CIRM) in Nizza, 1968 Mitbegründer der Groupe de Musique Expérimentale de Marseille (GMEM).

Michel Redolfi (F), born 1951 in Marseille, Director of the Centre International de Recherche Musicale (CIRM) in Nice since 1986, co-founder of the Groupe de Musique Expérimentale de Marseille (GMEM) in 1968.

80 Radierungen, die lange Zeit Rabelais zugeschrieben wurden, wurden in der ersten posthumen Neuauflage von „Pantagruel" aus dem Jahr 1565 veröffentlicht. Surrealismus und Symbolismus bilden den Hintergrund für das Ausschlüpfen einer Bevölkerung unmöglich schrulliger Wesen mit wunderlichen Körpern.

Unmenschlichkeit, Animalität sind in diesem düsteren Universum, einer der weniger bekannten Seiten des rabelais'schen Planeten, ebenfalls gegenwärtig. Die Vorstellung, diese in der Stille des Papiers gefangenen Monster durch die Computermusik wieder zum Leben zu erwecken, hat mich fasziniert.

Die computerklangliche Auferweckung der mittelalterlichen fiktiven Wesen verwendet Stimm- und Körpergeräusche, die vom Corpus Art Ballet, einer französischen Tanzgruppe, erzeugt werden.

Mikroskopische klangliche Details ihrer Aktionen wurden gesamplet (Roland 770), leicht bearbeitet (Syter) und als Mix digital neu zusammengestellt; alles wurde an einer Dyaxis Workstation (Mac Mix-Software) produziert.

Weitere in der Partitur vorhandene Geräusche und Strukturen sind Samples von vibrierendem Metall, quietschendem Holz, blubbernder Flüssigkeit sowie von diversen Substanzen, die ein Soundscape des Mittelalters evozieren.

Long attributed to Rabelais, the 80 etchings of Rabelais "Songes Drolatiques" appeared in the first posthumous reedition of Pantagruel in 1565. Surrealism and symbolism underlie the eclosion of a whimsical nation of impossible, quaint-bodied creatures. Inhumanity, animality are also present in this sombre universe, one of the lesser known sides of the Rabelaisian planet. I found the idea of using computer music to resurrect these creatures trapped in the silence of the page very appealing.

The computer-sound resurrection of the medieval fictional characters makes use of the voice and body sounds produced by the Corpus Art Ballet, a French group of dancers. Microscopic sonic details of their actions were sampled (Roland 770), slightly processed (Syter) and digitally reassembled in a mix, all produced on a Studer Dyaxis work station (Mac Mix software).

Additional sounds and textures found in the score include samples of palpitating metal, creaking wood, gurgling liquids and any substance evoking the soundscape of medieval times.

Michel Redolfi
"Songes Drolatiques", 1994, 15:45 min

JACOB TER VELDHUIS

Jacob Ter Veldhuis (NL), born 1951, studied composition with Willem Frederik Bon and electronic music with Luctor Ponse at the Groningen Conservatory in the Netherlands. His musical roots are found in the sixties and seventies. With a background in rock bands, he entered the Groningen conservatory, where he soon became involved with electronic music.

Jacob Ter Veldhuis (NL), geb. 1951, studierte Komposition bei Willem Frederik Bon und elektronische Musik bei Luctor Ponse am Konservatorium Groningen/Niederlande. Seine musikalischen Wurzeln reichen in die 60er und 70er zurück. Aus der Rock-Szene kommend, studierte er am Konservatorium in Groningen und begann bald, sich mit elektronischer Musik auseinanderzusetzen.

"De Zuchten van Rameau" ("The Sighs of Rameau") opus 71, a multi-media work for harpsichord, tape and slide projection, commissioned in 1995 by the Amsterdams Fonds voor de Kunst, was dedicated to Annelie de Man. The composition was inspired by "Les Soupirs" from the Suite no. 2, Pièces de Clavecin, 1724 by Jean Philippe Rameau. The French word "le soupir" means: sigh, but also: a quarternote rest.

The harpischord itself is subject of the composition. In 1987, Annelie de Man had her instrument re-designed by Sies Bleeker, who removed all original baroque characteristics. In "De Zuchten van Rameau" it's the other way around: in search of the nature of the harpsichord, Kerstens and Ter Veldhuis re-discovered baroque elements like symmetry, ornamentation, fugato structures, arpeggio's, a basso continuo and a passacaglia. "De Zuchten van Rameau" is a composition about, on, in, around, under, above and before the harpsichord, that was sampled in every possible way, by microphone and camera. The historical distance of nearly 3 centuries evokes a lot of drama: the music is rather centrifugal, and transforms the small sound of the harpsichord into a giant machine that threatens to explode, whereas the images are much more centripetal, still and intimate, focalizing.

„De Zuchten van Rameau („Das Seufzen von Rameau"), opus 71", ein Multimediawerk für Cembalo, Tonband und Diaprojektion, wurde 1995 von Amsterdams Fonds voor de Kunst beauftragt und ist Annelie de Man gewidmet. Inspiriert wurde die Komposition von „Les Soupirs" aus Suite Nr. 2, Pièces de Clavecin, von Jean Philippe Rameau (1724). Das französische Wort „soupir" bedeutet „Seufzer", bezeichnet aber auch die Pause auf der Viertelnote.

Gegenstand der Komposition ist das Cembalo an sich. 1987 ließ Annelie de Man ihr Instrument von Sies Bleeker neu gestalten, wobei alle Barockmerkmale des Originals entfernt wurden. In „De Zuchten van Rameau" kehrt sich dieser Vorgang um: Auf der Suche nach dem Wesen des Cembalos entdeckten Ter Veldhuis und Kristien Kerstens, die die auf die Deckel des Instruments projizierten Bilder entwarf, Barockelemente wie Symmetrie, Ornamentierung, Fugatostrukturen, Arpeggios, Basso Continuo und Passacaglia neu. „De Zuchten van Rameau" ist eine Komposition über, auf, um, unter, oberhalb und vor dem Cembalo und wurde auf jede erdenkliche Weise mit Mikrophon und Kamera gesamplet. Durch die historische Entfernung von beinahe drei Jahrhunderten entsteht eine starke Dramatik: Die Musik ist eher zentrifugal und verwandelt den kleinen Klang des Cembalos in eine riesige Maschine, die zu explodieren droht, während die Bilder eher zentripetal, still und intim, konzentrierend sind.

Jacob Ter Veldhuis
"De Zuchten van Rameau", 1995, 13:52 min

ALEJANDRO VIÑAO

Alejandro Viñao (RA), geb. 1951 in Buenos Aires, studierte Komposition, Gitarre und Dirigieren in Buenos Aires; setzte 1975 seine Studien am Royal College of Music und an der City University, London, fort. Derzeit arbeitet er im Auftrag für dasZentrum für Kunst und Medientechnologie (ZKM) in Karlsruhe an einer Kammeroper und an einem Werk für Orchester.

Alejandro Viñao (RA), born 1951 in Buenos Aires, studied composition, guitar and conducting in Buenos Aires, continued studies at Royal College of Music and the City University in London in 1975. At present Viñao is working on a chamber opera commissioned by the Zentrum für Kunst und Medientechnologie in Karlsruhe and on an orchestral piece.

Die ersten drei Sätzen des Quartetts „Phrase & Fiction" basieren auf der Öffnungsphrase des Stückes. Jeder Satz untersucht diese Phrase aus einer anderen Perspektive. Im ersten Satz wird die melismatische Natur der Phrase untersucht. Die Melodie entwickelt sich aus dem Rhythmus anstatt auf harmonische Weise. Der Computerpart entfaltet sich aus den Melodien, woraus sich eine Verwandlung ergibt, die man als Klang-"Morphing" beschreiben könnte. Der zweite Satz ist eher statischer Natur und konzentriert sich auf die harmonisch/klangfarblichen Implikationen der ursprünglichen Phrase. Mich interessiert vor allem die „Grauzone", in der man Klangfarbe und Harmonie nicht mehr unterscheiden kann. Im dritten Satz werden die ursprüngliche Phrase und die davon abgeleiteten Sekundärphrasen gleichzeitig mit unterschiedlichen Tempi behandelt. Das Konzept für diesen Satz bezieht sich auf Ideen, die in der Musik von Conlon Nancarrow gefunden werden. Trotzdem wollte ich den Eindruck vermeiden, daß sich die Komposition, sobald die einzelnen Instrumente in ihrem eigenen Tempo eingesetzt haben, in fast vorhersehbarer Weise entwickelt. Mit einem solchen „Determinismus" werden keine starken musikalischen Beziehungen zwischen den sich verschiebenden

The three movements of the quartet "Phrase & Fiction" are based on the opening phrase of the piece. Each movement looks at this phrase from a different perspective.
In the 1st movement the melismatic nature of the phrase is explored. Melody develops through rhythm rather than by harmonic means. The computer part grows out of the melodies, often resulting in transformation that could be described as sound "morphing". The 2nd movement is more static in nature focusing on the harmonic/timbral implications of the original phrase. I was interested in that "grey" area where timbre and harmony may no longer be told apart. In the 3rd movement different tempi are applied simultaneously to the original phrase and to secondary phrases derived from it. The concept in this movement is based on ideas found in Conlon Nancarrow's music. Yet, I tried to avoid the feeling that once every instrument sets out at its own speed the composition progresses in an almost predictable fashion. Such 'determinism' does not establish strong musical relationships

between the drifting tempi. I have tried to solve this problem by making the different tempi move in and out of synch with respect to one other, before their predetermined cycle is completed. I created the illusion that the cycles of the tempi coincide at points where they do not. In the creation of such "fiction" the computer played a major role, since it can perform irrational rhythmic values with complete accuaracy.

Alejandro Viñao
"Phrase & Fiction", 1995, 20:00 min

JURY

Hannes Leopoldseder

Geboren 1940 in St. Leonhard, Dr. phil., seit 1967 als Journalist beim Österreichischen Rundfunk tätig, seit 1974 Landesintendant des ORF, Landesstudio Oberösterreich. 1979 Mitbegründer der Ars Electronica und der Linzer Klangwolke. 1987 Initiator des Prix Ars Electronica, 1991 Projektidee zum Ars Electronica Center als Museum der Zukunft in Linz (Eröffnung anläßlich Ars Electronica 1996).

Hannes Leopoldseder

born in 1940 in St. Leonhard; Ph.D., journalist for the Austrian Broadcasting Corporation from 1967, Managing Director of the Upper Austrian Region since 1974. Co-founder of the Ars Electronica Festival and the Linzer Klangwolke in 1979, initiator of the Prix Ars Electronica competition in 1987, originator of the 1991 Ars Electronica Center idea for a museum of the future in Linz. 1991 set the idea in motion of the Ars Electronica Center as a museum of the future in Linz (Opening Ars Electronica 1996).

WORLD WIDE WEB JURY

David Blair

David Blair (USA) ist Mastermind der Webpage „Waxweb" und einer der profundesten Kenner des weltweiten Netz(verkehrs) in all seinen Inhalten und Ausdrucksformen.

David Blair (USA) is the mastermind of the Webpage "Waxweb" and has an expert knowledge of the ins and outs of worldwide networks (traffic) with all its contents and forms of expression.

Oliver Frommel

Oliver Frommel (D), geb. 1969. 1990 Studium in München. 1994 Medienlabor, München. 1996 Ars Electronica Center, Linz. Mitglied von FirstFloor electronix (http://www.firstfloor.org).

Oliver Frommel (D), born 1969; studied in Munich in 1990. In 1994, Medienlabor in Munich, 1996 Ars Electronica Center, Linz. Member of FirstFloor electronix (http://www.firstfloor.org).

Joichi Ito

Joichi Ito (J/USA), Entwickler und Produzent in den Bereichen Virtual Reality und Multimedia. Japan-Korrespondent für Mondo 2000, Wired u. a. Ausgedehnte Publikationstätigkeit, vor allem im Bezug auf Netzwerke.

Joichi Ito (J/USA), developer and producer in the areas of virtual reality and multi-media. Japan correspondent for Mondo 2000, Wired and other. Numerous publications, particularly on networks.

Karin Spaink (NL), born 1951, was trained as a teacher and a programmer. Works as a writer and has published seven books on various subjects, that somehow tend to be linked to that unstable object which we refer to us as "the body": on sex, health, quack therapies, cyborgs etc. Spends as much as eight hours per day on the Net and is currently being sued by a cult, Scientology, because of her Homepage.

Karin Spaink (NL), geb. 1951, Ausbildung als Lehrerin und Programmiererin. Arbeitet als Schriftstellerin und hat sieben Bücher veröffentlicht, deren Themen alle irgendwie mit jenem unbeständigen Objekt, das wir „Körper" nennen, zu tun haben: Sexualität, Gesundheit, fragwürdige Therapien, Cyborgs usw. Sie verbringt bis zu acht Stunden täglich im Netz und wird zur Zeit wegen ihrer Homepage von der religiösen Vereinigung „Scientology" gerichtlich belangt.

Karin Spaink

David Traub (USA) defines himself as an "Educational Warrior", earned a masters in education with a focus on human potential and the instructional use of virtual environments and multimedia from Harvard University while conducting classwork in interactive cinema and artificial intelligence-based narrative at the MIT Media Lab, undergraduate degrees in rhetoric and film with honors form University of California. Has produced, written, consulted upon or co-developed several multimedia projekts, e.g. "The Lawnmower Man" or "Real World" (Peter Gabriel), produced three virtual reality festivals (1993 – 1995) at Brazil's Centro Cultural de Candido Mendes.

David Traub (USA) definiert sich als „Bildungskrieger". Magisterdiplom in Pädagogik mit dem Schwerpunkt „Human Potential" und didaktischer Einsatz von virtuellen Environments und Multimedia, Harvard University; Unterricht in interaktivem Kino und Narrativem auf Basis der künstlichen Intelligenz am MIT Media Lab. Abgeschlossene Studien der Rhetorik und des Films, University of California, Berkeley. Produzent, Autor, Berater bzw. Mitinitiator bei diversen Mulitimedienprojekten, z. B. „The Lawnmower Man" und „Real World" (Peter Gabriel); Produzent für drei Virtual Realitiy Festivals (1993–1995) in Brasilien am Centro Cultural de Candido Mendes (Rio Janeiro).

David Traub

INTERACTIVE ART JURY

Alex Adriaansens

Alex Adriaansens (NL) studierte an der Königlichen Akademie der Künste in s-Hertogenbosch und arbeitet seit 1976 als Künstler. Gemeinsam mit Joke Brouwer gründete er die V_2-Organisation als ein Zentrum für Kunst und (Medien-)Technologie in Rotterdam (Institute for the Unstable Media), wo er derzeit Direktor ist. 1987 initiierten Alex Adriaansens und Joke Brouwer das „Manifesto for the Unstable Media". Adriaansens ist Mitglied einiger nationaler Beratungsgremien (Bildung, Kunst), die sich mit (Medien-)Technologie im weiteren Sinn befassen.

Alex Adriaansens (NL) studied at the Royal Academy of Arts in 's-Hertogenbosch and has worked as an artist since 1976. Together with Joke Brouwer, he initiated the V_2 Organisation as a centre for art and (media) technology in Rotterdam (Institute for the Unstable Media), of which he is now the director. In 1987, Alex Adriaansens and Joke Brouwer launched the „Manifesto for the Unstable Media". He is a member of several national advisory boards (education, art) that deal with (media) technology in a broad sense.

Harvie Branscomb

Harvie Branscomb (USA) bereichert seit 1975 die Welt der interaktiven Kunst mit Anregungen, Beiträgen und Unterstützung. Zunächst als Wissenschaftler ausgebildet, erfindet/entwickelt er nun sowohl Hardware wie auch Software für Produkte und Kunstwerke und lebt als Künstler. 1994 war er Wettbewerbsleiter des Interactive Media Festival, wo ein einzigartiger Prozeß unmittelbarer Erfahrung angewandt wurde, um 27 internationale Werke für die Ausstellung in Los Angeles auszuwählen. Derzeitige Projekte sind u. a. eine Web-interaktive Brunnenskulptur in Aspen, die Ausarbeitung eines historischen Rückblicks in Verbindung mit einigen Leuten, die in der Zeit Teenager waren, als Elvis Presley populär war.

Harvie Branscomb (USA) has been a catalyst for, contributor to and supporter of the interactive art world since 1975, primarily trained as a scientist, works as an inventor/developer of both hardware and software for products and artworks, and lives as an artist. Harvie was the Director of the Competition of the 1994 Interactive Media Festival which used a unique process of direct experience to select 27 interactive works from around the world to be shown in Los Angeles. His current projects include a web interactive sculptural fountain in Aspen, and a historical perspective on a few people who shared their teenage years with Elvis Presley.

Coco Conn (USA) has provided vision and leadership in the computer graphics field for more than twenty years. As President of Digital Circus, her efforts have focused on introducing technology to young people, designing and developing interactive media, and producing live events showcasing cutting-edge technologies. Her work today is a synthesis of her interdisciplinary experience as a producer, designer, computer and Internet techie, business entrepreneur, and teacher.

Coco Conn (USA) ist seit über zwanzig Jahren eine Vorreiterin im Bereich der Computergraphik. Als Präsidentin von Digital Circus konzentriert sich ihre Arbeit auf die Gestaltung und Entwicklung interaktiver Medien und die Produktion von Live-Veranstaltungen zur Präsentation zukunftsorientierter Technologien. In ihrer Arbeit verbindet sie ihre grenzüberschreitenden Erfahrungen als Produzentin, Designerin, Computer- und Internetspezialistin, Managerin und Lehrerin.

Perry Hoberman is an installation and performance artist. His installation "Bar Code Hotel" was awarded the top prize at the 1995 Interactive Media Festival in Los Angeles, and has also been shown at Ars Electronica. Other ongoing projects include a variety of stereo 3D installations and performances, and "The Empty Orchestra Cafe", a radical Neo-Karaoke Bar. Hoberman currently teaches in the graduate Computer Art Department at the School of Visual Arts in New York. He is the Art Director at Telepresence Research, a company specializing in virtual reality and telepresence installations for arts and industry.

Perry Hoberman ist Installations- und Performance-Künstler. Für „Bar Code Hotel" bekam er den ersten Preis des 1995 Interactive Media Festival in Los Angeles; diese Installation wurde auch beim Ars Electronica Festival gezeigt. Weitere aktuelle Projekte sind u. a. verschiedene Stereo-3D-Installationen und Performances und „The Empty Orchestra Cafe, A Radical Neo-Karaoke Bar". Hoberman unterrichtet an der Graduate Computer Art Department der School of Visual Arts in New York. Er ist künstlerischer Direktor bei Telepresence Research, einer Firma, die sich auf Virtual Reality und Telepräsenz-Installation für Kunst und Industrie spezialisiert hat.

Gerfried Stocker (A), born 1964. In 1991, he founded x-space, a group of artists-technicians who are involved in interdisciplinary projects. Up to 1995, numerous x-space projects have been carried out, including EXPO-Sevilla '92, Venice Biennial '93, FISEA '93/94/-Minneapolis/Helsinki, SIGGRAPH '94/95-Orlando/Los Angeles, ISEA '95 Montreal. In 1992/93 Stocker was the artistic director of the „Steirischen Kulturinitiative" and was also involved in setting up the artists network ZEROnet. Since 1995, Gerfried Stocker has been the artistic director of the Ars Electronica Festival and the managing director of the Ars Electronica Center.

Gerfried Stocker (A), geb. 1964, gründete 1991 x-space, eine Künstler-Technikergruppe zur Realisierung interdisziplinärer Projekte. Bis 1995 wurden zahlreiche x-space-Projekte realisiert, u. a. EXPO-Sevilla '92, Biennale Venedig '93, FISEA-'93/Minneapoli/Helsinki, SIGGRAPH '94/95-Orlando/Los Angeles, ISEA '95 Montreal. In den Jahren 1992/93 war Stocker künstlerischer Leiter der „Steirischen Kulturinitiative" und widmete sich u. a. dem Aufbau des Künstler-Netzwerkes ZEROnet. Seit 1995 ist Gerfried Stocker künstlerischer Leiter des Ars Electronica Festivals und Geschäftsführer des Ars Electronica Center.

COMPUTER ANIMATION JURY

Valie
Export

*Valie Export (A), geb. 1940. Ihre Arbeit um-
faßt Filme, Video- und Computerarbeiten,
Fotografie, Installationen, Performances
usw. Zahlreiche Publikationen zur zeit-
genössischen Kunstgeschichte. Teilnahme
an internationalen Ausstellungen und
Film/Videofestivals, u. a.: Centre Georges
Pompidou, documenta Kassel, Museum of
Modern Art New York, Cannes, Internationale Berliner Filmfestspiele, Filmfestspiele
Hongkong. 1980 offizielle österreichische
Vertreterin bei der Biennale von Venedig.
Zahlreiche Preise, u. a. 1995 Skulpturen-
preis der EA Generali Foundation. Lehrtätig-
keiten im In- und Ausland, u. a. 1989–1991
Full Professor für Film und Video an der
University of Wisconsin, 1991–1995 Professorin an der Hochschule der Künste Berlin,
1994–1995 Vizepräsidentin der Hochschule
der Künste, seit 1995 Professorin für Multi-
media/Performance an der Kunsthochschule
für Medien Köln.*

Valie Export (A), born 1940. Her work
includes films, video and computer works,
photography, installations, performances, etc.
She has published numerous articles on contemporary art history and has participated in
international exhibitions and film/video festivals, including: Centre Georges Pompidou,
documenta Kassel, Museum of Modern Art
New York, Cannes, International Film Festival
of Berlin, Hongkong Film Festival. In 1980, she
officially represented Austria at the Biennale in
Venice. She has received numerous awards,
including the 1995 Sculpture Award from the
EA Generali Foundation, and has held teaching
positions at home and abroad, including:
1989–1991 Full Professor for Film and Video
at the University of Wisconsin, 1991–1995
Professor at the Hochschule der Künste Berlin,
1994–1995 Vice-President of the Hochschule
der Künste; Professor for Multimedia/
Performance at the Kunsthochschule für
Medien in Cologne since 1995.

Lisa Fisher (USA) is a visual effects producer at Mass. Illusion, a feature film visual effects company in Lenox, Massachusetts, USA. From 1982 to 1988, she was a producer of feature film advertising and visual effects commercials at R/Greenberg Associates in New York. She then became vice president/executive producer for visual effects at Editel New York and in 1994 was promoted to vice president/general manager at Editel. A graduate of Princeton University, she attended the Yale School of Drama in the MFA program in Theatre Management.

Lisa Fisher (USA) ist Produzentin für visuelle Effekte bei Mass. Illusion, einer Firma in Lenox, Massachusetts, die sich auf visuelle Effekte für Spielfilme spezialisiert hat. Von 1982 bis 1988 war sie Produzentin für Spielfilmwerbung und Werbespots mit visuellen Effekten bei R/Greenberg Associates in New York. Danach wurde sie Vizepräsidentin/leitende Produzentin für visuelle Effekte bei Editel New York und wurde 1994 zur Vizepräsidentin/Geschäftsführerin bei Editel befördert. Sie ist Absolventin der Princeton University und besuchte auch die Yale School of Drama im MFA-Programm für Theatermanagement.

Lisa Fisher

Rolf Herken (D), born 1954, studied Theoretical Physics and Mathematics at the Freie Universität Berlin. In 1986 he founded the company „mental images" in Berlin, which specializes in the development of high image quality visualization software. His interests are in computer graphics with special emphasis on image synthesis, and in artifical intelligence, specifically mental imagery and vision.

Rolf Herken (D), geb. 1954, studierte Theoretische Physik und Mathematik an der Freien Universität Berlin. 1986 gründete er in Berlin die Firma „mental images", die auf die Entwicklung von Hochleistungs-Visualisierungssoftware spezialisiert ist. Sein Hauptinteresse gilt der Computergraphik, vor allem der Bildsynthese, und der künstlichen Intelligenz, vor allem der Rolle von Vorstellungsbildern.

Rolf Herken

A. J. Mitchell (GB), born 1947; Camera Man at BBC-TV; 1976 Video Effects Supervisor; 1980 freelance als Lighting Cameraman mainly on effects and pop promotions; 1981 The Moving Picture Company as a Comerical Director, Cameraman and Effects Supervisor; 1987 Director of Special Effects; 1990 Director of Printed Picture Company.

A. J. Mitchell (GB), geb. 1947; Kameramann bei BBC-TV; 1976 Leiter Video-Effects; 1980 freischaffender Beleuchtungskameramann hauptsächlich für Special-Effects und Pop-Werbung; 1981 Geschäftsführer, Kameramann und Special-Effects-Leiter der Moving Picture Company; 1987 Direktor für Special Effects; 1990 Direktor der Printed Picture Company.

A. J. Mitchell

Michael Wahrman (USA) lives and works in New York; he works with and creates his own computer animations and visual effects.

Michael Wahrman (USA) lebt und arbeitet in New York. Er arbeitet selbst an und mit Computeranimationen und Visual Effects.

Michael Wahrman

COMPUTER MUSIC JURY

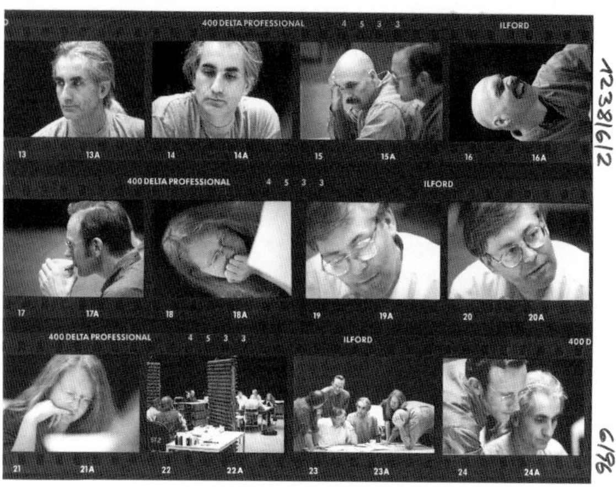

<table>
<tr>
<td>

Stephen Arnold

Stephen Arnold (GB) studierte bei Peter Maxwell Davies, Jonathan Harvey und Alexander Goehr sowie an den Universitäten von Southampton und Nottingham. Für sein Doktorat schrieb er eine Studie über den amerikanischen Komponisten Milton Babbitt. Er ist Direktor der Computer Music Studios an der University of Glasgow, wo er ein Team leitet, das sich der Komposition, Lehre und Forschung im Bereich der Musiktechnologie widmet. Sein derzeitiges Forschungsgebiet ist die Entwicklung von Musik- und Audioanwendungen zur Nützung der Hochleistungen der ATM-Netzwerken. 1990 leitete er die International Computer Music Conference in Glasgow. Er ist Vizepräsident für Konferenzen der International Computer Music Association.

</td>
<td>

Stephen Arnold (GB) studied with Peter Maxwell Davies, Jonathan Harvey and Alexander Goehr, and at the Universities of Southampton and Nottingham, gaining a Ph.D for a study of Milton Babbitt. He is Director of the Computer Music Studios at the University of Glasgow, where he heads a team engaged in composition and research relating to Music Technology. His present research relates to the development of audio applications designed to exploit the high performance of ATM networks. In 1990, he directed the International Computer Music Conference in Glasgow. He is Vice-President for Conferences for the International Computer Music Association.

</td>
</tr>
<tr>
<td>

Ludger Brümmer

Ludger Brümmer (D), geb. 1958. 1978–1983 Studium der Psychologie/Soziologie an der Universität Dortmund. 1983–1989 Kompositionsstudium an der Folkwanghochschule in Essen bei Nicolaus A. Huber und Dirk Reith. 1992 Arbeit mit den Nederlands Dansteater und Susanne Linke. 1991–1993 Stipendium am Center for Computer Research in Music and Acoustics (CCRMA) an der Stanford University California. 1995/96 am elektronischen Studio der TU Berlin, Zusammenarbeit mit Archimedia Linz, Aufträge und Forschung am Studio der Akademie der Künste Berlin und am Zentrum für Kunst und Medientechnologie (ZKM) Karlsruhe. Seit 1993 Lehrauftrag am elektronischen Studio der Folkwanghochschule Essen (ICEM).

</td>
<td>

Ludger Brümmer (D), born 1958; studied psychology/sociology at the University of Dortmund from 1978–1983; studied Composition at the Folkwanghochschule in Essen with Nicolaus A. Huber and Dirk Reith 1983–1989. He worked with the Nederlands Dansteater and Susanne Linke in 1992; awarded a scholarship to the Center for Computer Research in Music and Acoustics (CCRMA) at Stanford University from 1991–1993. 1995/96 Technische Universität Berlin; Archimedia Linz, Akademie der Künste Berlin, Zentrum für Kunst und Medientechnologie (ZKM) Karlsruhe. Lecturer at the Electronic Studio of the Folkwanghochschule Essen (ICEM) since 1993.

</td>
</tr>
</table>

Werner Jauk (A), born 1953; assistant professor and lecturer in systematic musicology at the University of Graz. Founder and director of the "Grelle Musik" studio for experimental acoustic and visual art forms. Author of scientific works in the area of technology of music, psychology of music, sociology of music, computer music and avantgarde rock, with an emphasis on the carrying over of principles inherent in technology into the aesthetics of music.

Werner Jauk (A), geb. 1953, Assistenzprofessor und Lehrbeauftragter für Systematische Musikwissenschaft an der Universität Graz. Gründer und Leiter des Studios „Grelle Musik" für experimentelle Formen der akustischen und visuellen Künste. Verfaßt wissenschaftliche Publikationen in den Bereichen Musiktechnologie, Musikpsychologie, Musiksoziologie, Computermusik und Rock-Avantgarde, wobei ihn die Übertragung technologieimmanenter Prinzipien auf die Ästhetik von Musik interessiert.

Bob Ostertag (USA) is a San Francisco-based freelance composer. He performs widely as a soloist, with his own ensembles, and with ad hoc groups. He has recorded 12 CD's of his compositions. His collaborators range from the Kronos Quartet to rock star Mike Patton, from avantgarders such as John Zorn and Fred Frith, to drag queens and dyke punk rocker Lynn Breedlove. He has received prizes and commissions from US National Endowment for the Arts, the Lincoln Center, and many others.

Bob Ostertag (USA) ist freischaffender Komponist in San Francisco; zahlreiche Auftritte im In- und Ausland als Solist, mit seinen eigenen Ensembles und ad hoc-Formationen. Er hat zwölf CDs mit eigenen Kompositionen aufgenommen und arbeitet mit ganz unterschiedlichen Künstlern zusammen, vom Kronos Quartet bis hin zum Rockstar Mike Patton, von Avantgardekünstlern wie John Zorn und Fred Frith bis zu Drag Queens und Dyke-Punk-Rocker Lynn Breelove. Preise und Aufträge von US National Endowment for the Arts, Lincoln Center und anderen.

Andrea Sodomka (A), born 1961 in Vienna; studied at the Hochschule für angewandte Kunst in Vienna 1982–1989, studied electro-acoustic music at the Hochschule für Musik und Darstellende Kunst, Vienna 1984-1987. President of the Austrian Gesellschaft für Elektroakustische Musik 1991–1994; lecturer as composer in residence at the Musikhochschule Graz; member of the advisory council for media art at the Offenes Kulturhaus, Linz, since 1995. She has worked in the areas of intermedia performance, artistic photography, video, computer music, telecommunications and radio art and has designed and realized numerous intermedia projects since 1986.

Andrea Sodomka (A), geb. 1961 in Wien. 1982–1989 Studium an der Hochschule für Angewandte Kunst in Wien, 1984–1987 Studium der Elektroakustischen Musik an der Hochschule für Musik und Darstellende Kunst. 1991–1995 Präsidentin der Gesellschaft für Elektroakustische Musik Österreich, 1994 Lehrauftrag als „composer in residence" an der Musikhochschule Graz. Seit 1995 Medienkunstbeirat am Offenen Kulturhaus Linz. Andrea Sodomka arbeitet in den Bereichen Intermedia-Performance, künstlerische Fotografie, Video, Computermusik, Telekommunikation und Radiokunst. Seit 1986 Konzeption und Realisation zahlreicher intermedialer Projekte.

Adt Reinhold
Blumenstr. 5
78601 Mahlstetten, D
Site: Kleine
KünstlerKonkordanz
URL: http://www.
uni-wuppertal.de7FB5-
Hofaue/Brock/

Anstey Josephine
628 W. Surf 1B
Chicago, IL 60657, USA
josephin@evl.eecs.uic.edu
Site: Les Girls
URL:
http://evlweb.eecs.uic.
edu/josephin

Asmus Stefan /
Roetel Sabine
Roonstr.10
42115 Wuppertal, D
asmus@urz.uni-
wuppertal.de
Site: Lehrstuhl für Ästhetik
URL: http://www.uni-
wuppertal.de/FP5-
Hofaue/Brock

Auer Martin
Rotenmühlg. 44/30
1120 Wien, A
100571.2073@
compuserve
Site: STORYWEB
URL:
http://ourworld.compuserv
e.com/homepages/Poetry_
Machine/storyhom.htm

Bader Markus
Hermannstr. 22
63069 Offenbach a. M., D
ammon/mbader/hoepfel/c
weber@stud.uni-frankfurt.de
Site: Plateau Mind Mycel
URL: http://www.igd.fhg.
de/plateau

Badiner Allan Hunt
Deer Point-Lime Creek
Big Sur, CA 93920, USA
ahbadiner@igc.org
Site: Sustainability
Consciousness
URL: http://www.well.com/
www/suscon/esalen

Baker Colin
107 Alton Ave
Toronto M4L 2M3, CDN
cwcjb@interlog.com
URL: http://www.interlog.com/
~cwcjb/home.html

Bazelmans Det
Oeienbos 8
5511LE Knegsel, NL
det@IAEhv.nl
Site: TRACKS, a hikingtour
in Cyberspace
URL: http://www.IAEhv.nl/
users/det/hiking.html

Beaman Darin
Art Center College of Design
1700 Lida St.
Pasadena, CA 91103, USA
gudrun@artcenter.edu
Site: Art Center Web Site
URL:
http://www3.artcenter.edu

Becker Scott
P.O. Box 578956
Chicago, IL 60657-8956
USA
artscb@interaccess.com
Site: Scott Becker
URL: http://homepage.
interaccess.com/~artscb/s
cb.html

Beloff Zoe
153 Norfolk Street #5H
NewYork, NY 10002, USA
zoe@interport.net
Site: Beyond
URL: http://www.users.
interport.net/users/~zoe

Benech Jean-Michel
9, bd Ledru Rollin
34000 Montpellier, F
jmbenech@mnet.fr
Site: Dianying
URL: http://www.mnet.
fr/dian.ying

Berg Il / Jerry L.
3129 La Selva Cir. #2
San Mateo, CA 94403, USA
jberg@golfmedia.com
Site: „Virtual Portfolio"
URL: http://www.ksu.
edu/~jberg/

Bergk Benjamin
Overbeckstr.76
50823 Köln, D
100072.162@compuserve.com
Site: Virtual Brain
URL:
http://www.virtualbrain.com

Bernardi Daniele
Via Don Minzoni 7
20025 Legnano, I
danieber@galactica.it
Site: Solidarity &
International Adoption Web
URL: http://www.citinv.
it/associazioni/AMI

Bernhard L. /
Udatny D. /
Zai M. Etoy
Lorenz-Mandl-G. 33/1
1160 Wien, A
mailme@etoy.com
Site: The Digital Hijack
URL: http://www.hijack.org

Bertrand Ennio
Via Giulia di Barolo, 48
10124 Torino (TO), I
ennio.bertrand@torino.
alpcom.it
Site: Smell-Link
URL: http//www.alpcomit/
bertrand/foto.html

Bielicky Michael
Borivojova 92
13000 Prague, CZ
bielicky@mbox.cesnet.cz
Site: Exodus
URL: http://exodus.bgu.ac.il/
exodus/

Blase Christoph
Wiener Weg 3b
50858 Köln, D
100444.3467@
compuserve
Site: Blitz Review
URL: http://www.thing.or.at/
thing/blitzreview/

Boersma Jay
416 West 34th, #201
Steger,IL 60475, USA
gamma@bgu.edu
Site: Boersma, Jay Page,
Web
URL : http://www.ECNeT.
Net/users/gas52ro/Jay/
home.html

Bonaventura Paul
116a Walton Street
Oxford OX2 6AJ, GB
paul.bonaventura@
ruskin-school.ox.ac.uk
Site: The Laboratory at
the Ruskin School of
Drawing and Fine Art
URL: http://ruskin-sch.
ox.ac.uk/lab

Bongiovanni Pierre
BP 5
25310 Herimoncourt, F
ole@cicv.fr
Site: OLE-THE WEB OF
THE CICV
URL: http://www.cicv.fr

Bourrel Jean-François
C.N.B.D.I.
121, rue de Bordeaux
16000 Angoûlème, F
rj@altern.com
Site: The Merlin Unk
URL: http://www.cnbdi.fr

Brace Brad
2434 SE Belmont St.
Portland,
OR 97214-2621, USA
bbrace@netcom.com
Site: Reverse Solidus
URL: http://www.teleport.
com/~bbrace/bbrace.html

Brooks Kevin Sawad /
Szelo Gong
18 Tufts St. #3
Cambridge, MA 02139, USA
swad@media.mit.edu
Site: Aporia: Doubt in
Forms (1995)
URL:
http://www.media.mit.
edu/~sawad/proj/aporia/

Burgos Maria de Fatima
ShinQI13-Conjo8-Casa11-
Lago no
71535-080 Brasilia, BR
fburgos@guarany.unb.br
Site: A virtual Museum to
Computer Art
URL: http://www.unb.br/
vis/museu/museu.htm

Burkhart Benno
K 2, 33
68159 Mannheim, D
burkhart@rummelplatz.
uni-mannheim.de
Site: Bruchweiler-
Bärenbach – Das Dorf im
Netz
URL: http://rummelplatz.
uni-mannheim.de/~
burkhart/index.html

Burt Butz Marcy
Keltenstraße 23
8044 Zürich, CH
burtz@burtz.ch
Site: Burtz Virtual Atelier
URL: http://www.burtz.ch

Cassani Tina / Beusch
Bruno
51, rue Piat
75020 Paris, F
cassani@cnam.fr
Site: sos RADIO TNC
URL: htpp://www.cnam.fr/
museum/radio/

Cavender Lisa N. /
Safan Jessica
17 Greenwich Ave. #11
New York, NY 10014, USA
cavender@echonyc.com
Site: Review
URL: http://www.itp.tsoa.
nyu.edu/~review

Christensen Murry C.
34 Coryell Street
Lambertville, NJ 08530, USA
murry-christensen@ktic.com
Site: The MC2 Web
(Got Webs In My Eyes !)
URL:
http://www.ktic.com/~mc2

Clarage Jim
4403 Verone St.
Bellaire, TX 77401, USA
clarage@rice.edu
Site: ClickMe
URL:
http://www.bioc.rice.edu/
~clarage/clickme/prix/

Coenen Arno
Ipemaheerd 21
9718 BG Groningen, NL
rene@scan.media-gn.nl
URL: http://www.media-
gn.nl/people/arno+rene/

Colonna Jean-François
14, rue de la Vieille Poste
78350 Jouy en Josas, F
colonna@poly.
polytechnique.fr
Site: The Space Time
Travel Machine
URL: http://blanche.
polytechnique/
lactamme/Mosaic/
descripteurs/demo_14.html

Cubacub Arturo
3744 N. Hoyne
Chicago, IL 60618, USA
arturo@i-cubed-fx.com
Site: Arturo's Room
URL: http://i-cubed-
fx.com/people/arturo/

Cunningham Stephanie
1616 E. Lasalle Ave.
South Band, In 46617, USA
cunningham.24@nd.edu
Site: Voice
URL: http://www.nd.edu/~art/
face/lead.html

Danelli Diana
Via Magenta, 34
20075 Lodi, I
dianadnl@ipo.tesi.dsi.unimi.it
Site: @rs&
URL: http//www.dsi.unimi.it/~@rs

Day Gary
5621 Erskine Street
Omaha,NE 68104, USA
gday@unomaha.edu
Site: Hypergarden
URL: http://www.unomaha.
edu/~gday/

De Bardonneche-Berglund
Dominique
49, rue Louis de Savole, 49
1110 Morges, CH
debab@ping.ch
Site: Manufactures du
Virtuel
URL: http://www.synaptic.ch

De Nijs Petra
2e Jan Steenstraat 62-1
1074 CR Amsterdam, NL
pdenijs@xsyAll.nl
Site: The Virtual Temple
URL: http://www.desk.nl/
~pdenijs

Debrini Marusa I.
321 East 21st street, #2E
New York, NY 10010, USA
marusa@sva.edu
Site: Rudy's Diary
URL: http://www2.sva.
edu/thesis/marusa/
Rudy/Rudy.html

Demmers Jim / Prince Chea /
Cheatham Robert
1299 Oakdale Rd.
Atlanta, GA 30307, USA
jdemmers@pd.org
Site: Topos
URL: http://noel.pd.org./
Public_Domain.html

Diemer Bernd
Saarstraße 2
66111 Saarbrücken, D
bernd@hbks.uni-sb.de
Site: SUBconciousNET
URL: http://www.wjp.cs.
uni-sb.de/art/bernd/p3/
subnet.html

Dieter Michel/Klaus
Wittekindstr. 16
33615 Bielefeld, D
michel@kcp.teüto.de
Site: ART WAR PEACE
SCULPTURE PLAN
URL: http://www.zerberus.de/
kcoopawp

Ditsch Matthias
Gedonstraße 2
80802 München, D
into@infinite.de
Site: Digital Mirror-Das
Magazine für Onliner-
URL: http://www.infinite.de

Domingues Diana
Marechal Floriano 531
95020-370 Caxias Do Sul, BR
diana@visao.com.br
Site: Netlung
URL: http://www.unb.br/vis/
netlung.htm

Donath Judith S.
144 Marlborough St. #2
Boston, MA 02116, USA
judith@media.mit.edu
Site: The Electric Postcard
URL: http://postcards.
www.media.mit.edu/
Postcards/

Eike
Falk Miksa u. 8
1055 Budapest, H
eike@samon.aszi.sztaki.hu
Site: The Naked Eye-
Experiment
URL: http://www.sztaki.
hu/sztaki/gallery.html

Ennio Bertrand
Via Giulia Di Barolo, 48
10124 Torino, I
ennio.bertrand@torino.
alpcom.it
Site: Smell-link
URL: http://www.
alpcom.it/netville/

etoy
Ruetschistraße 29
8000 Zürich, CH
mailme@etoy.com
Site: etoy.TANKSYSTEM -
www.etoy.com
URL: http://www.etoy.com

Evans Matt
1631 Park Avenue Apt#7
Baltimore, MD 21217, USA
atlas@charm.net
Site: Matt Evans: Personal
website & Potfolio
URL: http://www.charm.
net/~atlas/

Fasola Marco
6994 Aranno, CH
mfasola@dial.eunet.ch
Site: The Table
URL: http://www.TINET.
CH/table

Favela Collaborative
530 Molino St. #204
Los Angeles, CA 90013, USA
glenn@bait.themarket.com
Site: FAVELA!
URL: http://www.favela.org

Feigl Franz /
Hobijin Eric /
Solomon Debra / Verduel
Dick
Postbus 3970
1001 AT Amsterdam, NL
netband@xs4all.nl
Site: The Egg of the Internet
URL: http://www.xs4all.
nl/~netband/

Fenster Diane
287 Reichling Ave.
Pacifica, CA 94044, USA
fensterR@sfsu.edu
Site: The Attic Window
URL: http://www.srt.net/

Ferzi Konuk
Hilschbacherstraße 31
Berlin, D
Site: The 2nd Temple/Just
slipped my mind
URL: http://www.wjp.cs.
uni-sb.de/art/ferzi/p2

Flint Joost
Prins Benedikkade 193a
1011 TD Amsterdam, NL
joost@dds.nl
Site: De Digitale Stad 3.0
URL: http://www.dds.nl

Forest Fred
Territoire du M2
60540 Anserville, F
terr@monaco.mc.
Site: Le Territoire des
Réseaux
(=Cyberterritories)
URL: http://www.monaco.
mc/exhib/territories

Fraga Tania
SQN 107, BLH, Apt. 106
70743-080 Brasilia, BR
tfraga@guarany.unb.br
Site: Interactive
Stereoscopic Simulations
URL: http://www.lsi.usp.br/
~tania/tania.html

Franken Bernhard
Institut für Neue Medien
Daimlerstr. 32
60314 Frankfurt, D
offrece@inm.de
Site: Skylink Frankfurt
URL: http://www.inm.de/
projects/people/
bernhard/skylink.html

Frenkel Vera
692 St.Clarens Ave.#1
M6H 3X1 Toronto, CDN
vfrenkel@yorku.ca
Site: The Body Missing
URL: http://www.yorku.
ca/BodyMissing

Fujihata Masaki
326-23 Nagae
240-01 Hayama-Cho,
Miura-gun,Kanagawa, J
masaki@sfc.keio.ac.jp
Site: Global Clock Project
URL: http://www.flab.
mag.keio.ac.jp/GClock

Fundberg Björn
Flogstav. 37c
75273 Uppsala, S
Fundberg@bahnhof.se
Site: Bjorns Artworks
URL: http://www.mps.mde.se
/~frv95beg

Gesellschaft für
Untertagebau
Prüfeninger Str. 19
93049 Regensburg, D
peter.nowotny@t-online.de
Site: Memopolis
URL: http://rsls8.sprachlit.uni-
regensburg.de/memopolis

Goldbaum Howard
813 N. Maplewood Ave.
Peoria, IL 61606, USA
howard@bradley.bradley.edu
Site: The Digital
Photography Exhibit
URL: http://www.bradley.
edu/exhibit/

Goldberg Ken /
Santarromana Joe
1079 Tennessee Street
San Francisco, CA 94107
USA
goldberg@ieor.berkeley.ed
Site: The TeleGarden
URL: http://www.usc.edu/
dept/garden

Gondolat-jel
Ö Utca 5
1066 Budapest, H
dash@caesar.elte.hu
Site: dASH
URL: http://caesar.elte.hu/
gondolat-jel/

Grassi Pietro
Via della Dataria 94
00187 Rome, I
grassi@ansa.it
Site: Ansa news agency
on Internet
URL: http://www.ansa.it

Grohs Fritz
Mechelgasse 6/9
1030 Wien, A
fgrohs@to.or.at
Site: und ... und ... und ...
URL: http://www.
DerStandard.co.at/
DerStandard/.

Gržinić Marina /
Smid Aina
Cesnikova 12
1000 Ljubljana, SLO
margrz@zrc-sazu.si
Site: Axis of Live
URL: http://lois.kud-fp.
si/quantum.east

Gurley Jason W.
8501 San Marcos Dr.
Knoxville, XX 37938, USA
ovation@utkux.utk.edu
Site: Jason's Web!
URL: http://funnelweb.utcc.
utk.edu/~ovation

Guzak Karen
7075, Snognalmine
Studio 5A
Seattle, WA 98108, USA
guzak-blake@msn.com
Site: Karen Guzak: Art
Works
URL: http://www.artswire.org/
Artswire/guzak/kgfront.html

Haberfellner Sabine
Ortliebgasse 31/16-18
1170 Wien, A
sabin.aell@silverserver.co.at
Site:Fuckhead /
Bodymusic
URL: http://www.
silverserver.co.at/
rawpower/fhead.htm

Hack Hermann Josef
Hangweg 11
53757 Sankt Augustin, D
hack@oz.gekko.
technopark.gmd.de
Site: Virtuelles Dach über
dem Ruhrgebiet
URL: http://www.
hack-roof.gmd.de

Hartill Robert
562 Central Ave. Apt. #1
Los Alamos, NM 87544, USA
robh@imbd.com
Site: Internet Movie
Database WWW Interface
URL:
http://www.us.imdb.com

Haveman Josepha
47 Del Mar Ave.
Berkeley,CA 94708, USA
JosephaH@aol.com
Site: Art of Two Worlds
URL: http//www.
illuminated.com/
JH_ArtArchive

Haznal Nemeth
Kolzsvar u.34
1181 Budapest, H
Site: Ten Commandments
URL: http://frcij.inf.bme.hu/
internet.galaxis/kepzom/

Hennrich Kurt
Thaliastr.164 (Altbau)
1160 Wien, A
KHennrich@fishnet.co.at
Site: Art-up-Austria
URL: http://www.art-up-
austria.co.at

Hershman-Leeson Lynn /
Sartain Jarrod /
Nguyen Kim
Hotwire Productions
327 Ritch
San Francisco, CA 94108,
USA
lynn2@well.com
Site: Byte my Button...
URL: http://arakis.
ucdavis.edu/hershman/

Heyrman Hugo
Belgielei 202
2018 Antwerp, B
hugohey@innet.be
Site: Interactive Dreams
URL: http://www.innet.
be/isdm/isdm_2.0/
i_dreams/start.html

Hovagimyan G.H.
11 Harrison Street
New York, NY 10013, USA
gh@Thing.net
Site: Terrorist Advertising
URL: http://www.thing.
net/~gh/artdirect

Huppert Leslie
Adalbertstraße 22
10997 Berlin, D
leslie@hbks.uni-sb.de
Site: The Robe (Das
Gewand)
URL: http://www-wjp.
cs.uni-sb.de/art/leslie/p1

Hutton Lisa
4606 Castelar St.
San Diego,
CA 92107-1412, USA
lhutton@ucsd.edu
Site: Variety is ...
URL: http://art-slab.ucsd.
edu/ARTSLAB/
LisaHutton/LLHpage.html

Hypermedia Research
Centre
School of Design & Media
University of Westminster
Waterford Rd.
Harrow HA1 37P, GB
hrc@hrc.wmin.ac.uk
Site: Hypermedia
Research Centre
URL:
http://www.hrc.wmin.ac.uk

Kac Eduardo
207 Fine Arts Bldg.
Lexington,
KY 40506-0022, USA
ekac1@pop.uky.edu
Site: Kac Web
URL: http://www.uky.edu/
FineArts/Art/kac/kachome.html

Katzav Sigal
Nachalat.Binyamin St.
65163 Tel-Aviv, IL
impulsiva@reshet.co.il
Site: Why do we rave
URL: http://www.math.
tau.ac.il/~iddos/sigal

Kedem Benjamin
90 Aluf David
52241 Ramat-Gan, IL
kbenny@inter.net.il
Site: Benny Kedem's Web-
Site
URL: http://www.teletel.co.il/
benny

Kerne Andruid
S 19 W 26th St.,
Ste. 5000
New York, NY 10001, USA
info@creatingmedia.com
Site: Coded Messages:
CHAINS
URL: http://found.cs.nyu.
edu/andruid/chains.html

Khan Omar
66 Cumberland St.
San Francisco, CA 94110
USA
omar@harappa.com
Site: Harappa
URL: http://www.
harappa.com

Koch Olaf
Weissdornweg 3
50767 Köln, D
olafKoch@well.com
Site: KochWeb
URL: Http://www.well.com/
user/olafkoch/index.html

Kolnicker Michele
Kudlichgasse 38/13
1100 Wien, A
mkies@magnet.at
Site: 1002 Situations
URL: http://fgidec1.
tuwien.ac.at/

Konuk Ferzi
Hilschbacherstr. 31
Berlin, D
ferzi@hbks.uni-sb.de
Site: The 2nd Temple
URL: http://~www-wjp.cs.
uni-sb.de/art/ferzi/pz

Krahberger Franz
Schönburgstr.44/9
1040 Wien, A
crow@thing.or.at
Site: Electronic Journal
Literatur Primär
URL: http://ejournal.
thing.at/ejournal/

Kriesche Richard
Trauttmansdorffg.1
8010 Graz, A
kriesche@iis.joanneum.ac.
Site: Telematic Sculpture 4
(TS4)
URL:
http://iis.joanneum.ac.at/
Kriesche/biennale95.html

Kulakovich Bret
4. North Orchard St.
New Bedford,
MA 02740-3662, USA
BKulakovich@umassd.edu
Site: Five Billion Dreams
Interactive Metaspace.
URL: http://dreams.mth.
umassd.edu:1111/

Lapajne Andrej
Koprska 20A
1000 Ljubljana, SLO
Andrej.Lapajne@snet.fri.un
i-lj.si
Site: Slovenian Virtual
Gallery
URL: http://razor.fer.
uni-lj.si:8080/gal

Le Grand Yvonne
Oosterweg 85 B2
9724 CG Groningen, NL
ylg@scan.media-gn.nl
Site: LaZoyd's Metaverse
URL: http://www.media-
gn.nl/
people/n-zoyd/html/

Lee Iara
1120 5th Ave. #15A
New York, NY 10128, USA
iaralee@panix.com
Site: Synthetics Pleasures
URL: http://www.
caipirinha.com

Lewis Matthew
ACCAD, Ohio State Univ.
1224 Kinnear Rd.
Columbus, OH 43212-1154,
USA
mlewis@cgrg.ohio-
state.edu
Site: Abulafia Gallery
URL: http://www.cgrg.
ohio-state.edu/~mlewis/
Gallery/gallery.html

Liao Sabrina
719 Broadway, 12th floor
New York, NY 10003, USA
liaos@is.nyu.edu
Site: Sabrina's World -
When East Meets West
URL: http://c4dm.nyu.edu/
liaos/

Lintermann Bernd
Essenweinstr. 37
76131 Karlsruhe, D
linter@ira.uka.de
Site: Evolutionary Web
Sculpture
URL: http://i31www.ira.
uka.de/~linter

Löffler Sandra
Plastic Reality
Am Treptower Park 50
12435 Berlin, D
plastic@bbtt.com
Site: Love Version
URL: http://www.
technohouse.de

Loudon Annette
448, Bryand St.
San Francisco, CA 94107
USA
Site: Stratus:VRML artspace
URL: http://www.construct.net/
perhelion/gallery/

Lyster Gavyn
11/57 Darlinghurst Rd.
Kings Cross, NSW 2011, AUS
exile@matra.com.au
Site: Exile
URL: http://www.matra.
com.au/~exile/

Määttä Arto
Kevätkatu 18 as 4
15240 Lahti, SF
amaatta@ameba.ipt.fi
Site: The Artless
Homepage v1.0
URL: http://web.lpt.fi/
~amaatta

Malloy Judy
2140 Shattuck, Suite 2340
Berkeley, CA 94704, USA
jmalloy@well.com
Site: Marketplace of the
Mind
URL: http://www.well.com/
user/jmalloy/cyberagora.html

Marroquin Raul
Da Costakade T10 91A
1053 XK Amsterdam, NL
hksteen@desk.nl
Site: De Hoeksteen Net
URL: http://www.desk.
NL/~hksteen

Martin Juliet
450 6th Avenue #2F
New York, NY 10011, USA
juliet@sva.edu
Site: Answers
URL: http://www2.sva.
edu/threads/juliet/

Maturana Mariano /
Scharreberg Joost
Linnaeusdwstr. 15 B
1048 AW Amsterdam, NL
webmaster@mundolatino.
org
URL: http://www.
mundolatino.org/lacosa/

McClurg Scott Alan
5 Natalie Lane
Newark, DE 19713, USA
scotalan@udel.edu
Site: A Search for Balance
URL: http://128.175.
43.100/Galleries/
Grad.Gallery/SMcCl

McRae Matthew
5814 Flambeau Road
Palos Verdes, PA 19103, USA
mcrae@eniac.seas.
upenn.edu
Site: Apple Flavored Java
URL: http://www.seas.
upenn.edu/~mcrae/
projects/macjava/

Meads Arthur /
Mansell Alice
1341 Birmingham St.
Halifax,
Nova Scotia B3J 2J3, CDN
ameads@isisnet.com
Site: bioGraphics:
enGendered Positions
URL: http://tuweb.ucis.
dal.ca/~cohn

Mirage Merel
c/o KHM/
Peter Welter Platz 2
50676 Köln, D
merel@khm.uni-koeln.de
Site: Poem* Navigator
URL: http://www2.khm.
uni-koeln.de/~merel

Mitchell Bonnie
102 Shaffer Art Bldg.
Syracuse Univ.
Syracuse, NY 13244, USA
bonniem@syr.edu
Site: ChainReaction
URL: http://chain.syr.edu

Mnich Georg Th.
Kamminerstr. 5
10589 Berlin, D
mnich@blacksun.de
Site: „Pointworld"
URL: http://www.pointcom.
com/vrml/home.wrl

Moberly Jonathan
55 Charlotte Rd.
London EC2A 3QT, GB
...@ellipsis.co.uk
Site: ellipsis
URL: http://www.gold.
net/ellipsis

Mokka group
Kisrókus 1, Illem 8
10240Budapest, H
100324.1201@
compuserve.com
Site: Present Time
URL: http://www.met.hu/
mokkahp.htm

Morice Anne-Marie /
Larsen Lulu
Associate Synthésie
171 rue André Karman
93300 Aubervilliers, F
synesthe@worldnet.fr
Site: Synesthesie
URL: http://www.cicv.fr/
SYNESTHESIE/
homepage.html

Müller Jens
Barerstr. 32
80333 München, D
kl511ab@sunmail.lrz-
muenchen.de
Site: Space Collector
URL: http://www.
lrz-muenchen.de/Adbk/
collect.htm

Murphy Robbin
73 East Second Street Apt#9
New York, NY 10013, USA
murph@artnetweb.com
Site: artnetweb
URL: http://artnetweb.com

Nakano Yuzo
1060 Heinz St.
Berkeley, CA 94710, USA
kakano@kala.org
Site: Kala Art Institute
URL: http://www.kala.org

Nideffer Robert F.
UC Santa Barbara
Dept. of Art Studio
Santa Barbara, CA 93106,
USA
nideffer@arts.ucsb.edu
Site: „ASCII Alphabet"
URL: http://www.arts.ucsb.
edu/~nideffer/
ascii_alphabet/intro.html

Nikolic Svetislav
7 Jula 12
22320 Indjja, YU
Site: Swing

Nohe Timothy
P.O. Box 13712
La Jolla, CA 92039, USA
tnohe@ucsd.edu
Site: Limbiferous
URL: http://jupiter.ucsd.
edu/~ntim/
limb_welcome.html

Novak Lorie /
Castiglia Willig /
Kershaw Betsy / O'Neill
Kerry
60 Pineapple Street #4G
Brooklyn, NY 11201, USA
cvisions@play.nyu.edu
Site: Collected Visions
URL:
http://cvisions.nyu.edu

O'Donovan William
134 Cathedral St.
Woolloomooloo,
NSW, 2011, AUS
Site: Johnny Ice: Digital
Detective
URL: http://www.mm.com/
amn/johnnyice

O´Neill Maria de Mater
Calle trigo 557 Bajos
00907 Miramar, PUE
mmoneill@caribe.net
Site: El cuarto del
Quenepon
URL: http://www.ponce.
inter.edu/cuarto/
quenepon.html

Obereder O. /
Jahrmann M.
Lorenz-Mandl-Gasse 33/1
1160 Wien, A
oskar@silverSERVER.co.at
Site: Digitall-
Silverservernet
URL: http://www.
digit-ALL.or.at/digit-ALL

Oberleitner Gerwald
Flurschützstr. 36/12/5
1120 Wien, A
oberleit@ccc.or.at
Site: CCC – Computer
Communications Club
URL: http://www.ccc.or.at

Paesmans Dirk /
Heemskerk Joan
Aelbrechtskade 49A
3022 HN Rotterdam, NL
mail@jodi.org
Site: Jodi
URL: http://www.jodi.org

Pantic Drazen
Makedonska 22
11 000 Belgrad, YU
www@www.opennet.org
Site: opennet.org home
page
URL: http://www.
opennet.org

Pasko Alexander /
Savchenko Vladimir /
Sourin Alexei
University of Aizu
Aizu-Wakamatsu
Fukushima Pref. 965-80, J
pasko@u-aizu.ac.jp
Site: Shape Modeling and
Computer Graphics with
Real Functions
URL: http://www.
u-aizu.ac.jp/public/www/
labs/sw-sm/FrepWWW/
F-rep.html

Peppermint Cary
746 Euclid Ave
Syracuse,NY13210, USA
capepper@mailbox.syr.edu
Site: This is the Place
URL: http://chain.syr.
edu/~cgrgrad/cary/
origin.html

Pickover Clifford
37 Yorkshire Lane
Yorktown Hts, NY 10598
USA
cliff@watson.ibm.com
Site: Cliff Pickover's
Computer Art + Virtual
Caverns
URL: http://sprott.
physics.wisc.edu/
pickover/home.htm

Pighi Isabella
Luigi Pagani 11
29010 Pontenure (PC), I
isa@lim.dsi.unimi.it
Site: Welcome to Lim
URL: http://lim.dsi.unimi.it

Plewe Daniela Alina
ZKM
Gartenstr. 71
76135 Karlsruhe, D
dap@zkm.de
Site: Muser's Service
URL: http://www.icf.de/
musers-service

Pope Nina /
Guthrie Karen
3 Shaws Terrace
Edinburgh EH7 4PJ, GB
n.pope@ucl.ac.uk
Site: A Hypertext Journal
URL: http://www.unity.
co.uk/hypertext/journal

Porett Thomas
673 Aubrey Avenue
Ardmore, PA 19003, USA
tporett@netaxs.com
Site: The Beautiful
URL: http://www.op.net/
~tporett/ambeau/ambeau.ht
ml

Von Rahden Mark
Goetheplatz 4
28203 Bremen, D
farm@is-bremen.de
Site: Saludo! Tango
URL: http://www.is-
bremen.de/~tocco/Tango

Rapoport Sonya
6 Hillcrest Court
Berkeley, CA 94705, USA
rapop@qarnet.berkeley.edu
Site: Smell your Destiny
URL: http://www.lanminds.
com/local/sr/srapoport.html

Reardon Michael
742 SW Vista #21
Portland, OR 97205-1219,
USA
reardon@teleport.com
Site: House of Reardon
URL: http://www.teleport.
com/~reardon

Reijnders Mark
Witte van
Haemstedestraat 12d
3021 SW Rotterdam, NL
mare@luna.nl
Site: mare@luna.nl
Website
URL: http://www.luna.nl/
~mare/

Reinisch Wolfgang
Idlhofgasse 52
8020 Graz, A
reinisch@sbox.tu-graz.ac.at
Site: Banale III
URL: http://hyperg.tu-graz.
ac.at/banale

Ribuoli Andre
333 W. 52nd Street
New York, NY 10019, USA
dreko@aol.com
Site: The Digital Atelier
URL: http://home.dti.net/
irisprnt

Ritsch Winfried
Leitnergasse 7a
8010 Graz, A
ritsch@iem.mhsg.ac.at
Site: The House of
Sounds
URL: http://iem.mhsg.ac.
at/slives

Ritter Don
130 McGill St., #3
Montréal, QC H2Y 2E5, CDN
ritter@alcor.concordia.ca
Site: Percept Plus
Presents Interactive Video
Artist Don Ritter
URL: http://www.
odyssee.net/~percept/

Rosen Avi
Hashoshanim 22,
P.O. Box 12075
20300 Nesher, IL
avi@rotem.technion.ac.il
Site: Avi Rosen, Media
Artist (Homepage)
URL: http://www.
technion.ac.il/~ravi

Rosen Peter
2263 Sacto St. #2
San Francisco, CA 94115
USA
peter@creativity.net
Site: Creativity Cafe
URL: http://www.
creativity.net/ccafe

Rosenberg Stuart
Vogelsangerstr. 53
50823 Köln, D
stuart@khm.uni-koeln.de
Site: West Bank Industries
URL: http://www.
westbank.org

Rosenstein Mark
44 Hill St.,
Apartment 5K
Morristown, NJ 07960, USA
mbr@bellcore.com
Site: Mark Rosenstein's
Sailing Page
URL: http://community.
bellcore.com/mbr/
sailing-page.html

Ross Aaron
643 Divisadero St. #202
San Francisco, CA 94117
USA
dryo@best.com
Site: Aaron Ross:
Electronic Artist
URL: http://www.best.
com/~dryo/

Roth Rob
268 East Broadway
NYC, NY 10002, USA
glamnerd@interport.net
Site: Interjackie
URL: http://www.echonyc.
com/~interjackie

Sag Dave
187 Rundle St.
Adelaide 5000, AUS
va@va.com.au
Site: Adelaide Cyberfringe
URL: http://www.va.com.
au/afringe

De Sales Aymon
456 W. 20th Street
New York, NY 10011, USA
Aymon@moobird.com
Site: The Brown Moobird
URL: http://moobird.com

Salgado Neto /
Luiz Antonio
João Luis Alves,
82 ap.301
22291-090 Rio de Janeiro, BR
lasalgado@fund.cepel.br
Site: Uma Incursáo Na
Arte Por Computador
URL: http://www.rionet.
com.br/~lasalgado/
index.html

Santeix Elizabeth
321 East Houston Street
New York, NY 10002, USA
karen@tiedrich.com
Site: Crude Rom
URL: http://www.
tiedrich.com/crude_rom

Sappington Rodney /
Gomez Pat /
Lazrus Julia
1620 1/2 Westerly Terrace
Los Angeles, CA 90026, USA
artqueen@aol.com
Site: Territory of Blows
URL: http://itchy.calarts.
edu:80/~julia/territory

Scaletti Carla
P.O. Box 2530
Champaign, IL 61825-
2530, USA
symsound@symbolic
Sound.co
Site: Public Organ
URL: http://www.
prairienet.org/~scaletti/
PublicOrgan.html

Schäffer Jörg
Linzer Straße 352/3/6
1140 Wien, A
office@kraftwerk.co.at
Site: kraftWerk Homepage
URL: http://www.
kraftwerk.co.at/kraftwerk

Schedel Gerhard
Elisabethstraße 39
80796 München, D
100633.2627@
compuserve.cm
Site: Analogue
Synthesizer Connection
URL: http://ourworld.
compuserve.com

Schilcher M. /
Palmetzhofer G. /
Offenhuber D.
Sonnensteinstr. 8
4040 Linz, A
relais@relais.khs.linz.ac.at
Site: VVV A journey as an
Exile
URL: http://193.170.97.45/vvv/

Schoppen Erik
Ypemaheerd 21
9736 ME Groningen, NL
kilko@scan.media-gn.nl
Site: Welcome to the
World of Imaginary
Thoughts
URL: http://www.
media-gn.nl/post-grad/
kick/kick.html

Schulthess Markus
Hirschengraben 13
6003 Luzern, CH
mas@centralnet.ch
Site: Container City
URL: http://www.
centralnet.ch/userpages/
masworld/container_
city/menu.html

Schultz Pit
Kleine Hamburger Str.15
10117 Berlin, D
pit@contrib.de
Site: Fechner
URL: http://www.ilf.de/
fechner/

Sechtlova Marie
Dukelskych bojovniku
1944
390 03 Tabor, CZ
hubicka@paru.cas.cz
Site: M. M. Sechtlova -
homepage
URL: http://www.paru.
cas.cz/~hubicka/Sechtl/Ma
rie/English

Scott Brent
2100 Mary St.
Pittsburgh, PA 15203, USA
Bscott@andrew.cmu.edu
Site: manIFESTation
URL: http//www.
BrentScott.com

Secuya Dong
750 Phase II St,Jude
Acres,Par
6000 Cebu City, RP
dsecuya@durian.usc.edu.ph
Site: CAI Art Gallery
URL: http://www.usc.
edu.ph/cai/

See H. / Lenman S. /
Century M. / Swain D.
17575 Chomedy Blvd.
Laval, H7V 2X2, CDN
henry@pd.org
Site: Merz Project
URL: http://merzban.citi-
doc.ca/merz/merz.html

Selichar Günther
Seidengasse 26/2
1070 Wien, A
Site: Who's Afraid of Blue,
Red and Green?
URL: http://www.lot.or.
at/LOT/EXTENS/selichar/

Shulgin Alexei / Detkina
Tania /
Nikolaev Alexander
Polotskaya 29-1-39
Moscow 121355, R
easylife@glas.apc.org
Site: Moscow WWWArt
Centre
URL: http://sunsite.cs.
msu.su/wwwart

Smolan Rick
110 Caledonian Street, Suite
1
Sausalito, CA 94965, USA
rick519@aol.com
Site: 24 Hours in
Cyberspace
URL: http://www.
cyber24.com

Srečo Dragan
Hrenova 13
1000 Ljubljana, SLO
TRIBE@ARXEL.si
Site: ROTAS WWW
URL: http://lois.kud-fp.
si/video/sreco/rotas

Stastny Ed
PO Box 241113
Omaha, NE 68124-5113,
USA
ed@synergy.net
Site: Hygrid
URL: http://www.sito.
org/synergy/hygrid

Stasuk Rose
1210 Ryan
Clermont, FL 34711, USA
roric@gate.net
Site: The Body Internet
URL: http://www.ucet.ufl.
edu/~rstasuk/intro.html
oder /figure.html (image
sp)

Stösser Achim
Haupstr. 83
76448 Durmersheim, D
stoesser@ira.uka.de
Site: HyperLiteratur
URL: http://i31www.ira.
uka.de/~stoesser/Lit/
index.html

Stuermer Wolfgang
230 EL 5th Street #5C
New York, NY 10010, USA
webmaster@arcananet.org
Site: ARCANA-Artist
Research,Composers'Aid
& Network Access
URL: http://www.
arcananet.org/

Swartzbeck Michael
214 5th Street N.E.
Washington, DC 20002
USA
sinkers@his.com
Site: A Human Life
URL: http://myhouse.com/
mikesite/garcia

Szegedy-Maszak Zoltan
Németvölgyi út 67
1124 Budapest, H
szmz@inf.bme.hu
Site: Crytogram
URL: http://www.inf.bme.
hu/~zoli/cryptogram

Szyhalski Piotr
2444 Stevens Ave South
Minneapolis, MN 55404
USA

piotr_szyhalski@mn.mcad.
edu
Site: The Spleen
URL: http://www.mcad.
edu/home/faculty/
szyhalski/Piotr

Timcke Henning
Stadtturmst.5
5400 Baden, CH
timcke@aart.ch
Site: Zapperlot!!
URL: http://www.kunst.ch/
zapperlot/home.html

Torinus Sigi
816 Bancroft Way
Berkeley, CA 94710, USA
sigi@sirius.com
Site: browsing beauty
URL:
http://www.sfai.edu/~sigi/bb

Touma Michael / Wolf
Christian
Kochstr. 34
04275 Leipzig, D
michael@hgb-leipzig.de
Site: Ort ohne Raum
URL: http://www.hgb-
leipzig.de/projekt/wwwgal/
wwwgal.htm

Trippi Laura
100 Sullivan Street #5C
New York, NY 10012, USA
latrippi@interport.net
Site: Drawing On
Air(dn/a):an evolving
system for distributed art
URL: http://adaweb.com/
~dn/a

Troeger Andreas
Zero Tolerance
160 1st Ave. #2D
New York, NY 10009, USA
at@escape.com
Site: Zero Tolerance
URL: http://zero.
tolerance.org//

Tuomola Mika /
Vainionpää / Aki Kivela
Coronel Interactive Oy Ltd.
Mannerheiminhe 66 A 9, SF
k22051@kyyppari.hkkk.fi
Site: Daisy's Amazing
Discoveries
URL: http://www.
kolumbus.fi/daisy/en1

Umstätter Antya /
Heschkal Steffen
Tucholskystr. 35
10117 Berlin, D
antya@artcom.de
Site: Ping
URL http://www.artcom.
de/ping/mapper

Up Mathilde
Tuinstraat 11
1015 NX Amsterdam, NL
mupe@desk.n1
Site: A-Maze
URL: http://www.desk.nl/
~mupe/test/amaze/
index.html

Van der Cruijsen Walter
2E Van Swindenstraat 39 C
1093 VH Amsterdam, NL
wvdc@desk.nl
Site: Thing Desk
URL: http://thing.desk.nl

Vassilev Vesselin
K-s „Krasno selo"
gl.17,vHA
1680 Sofia, BG
Site: „The Gate of the
Magic Mirror"

Venturelli Suzete
Colina, Bl.j-Apto 107-
Campus un
70910-900 Brasilia, BR
suzetev@guarany.unb.br
Site: LIS-Image and
Sound Laboratory
URL: http://www.unb.br/
vis/liso.htm

Vesna Victoria
Dept. of Art Studio
Santa Barbara, CA 93105,
USA
vesna@humanitas.ucsb.edu
Site: Bodies INCorporated
URL: http://www.arts.ucsb.
edu/concrete

Wagenaar Akke
Krefelderstraße 48
50670 Köln, D
akke@khm.uni-koeln.de
Site: Quite A Portait
URL: http://www.khm.
uni-koeln.de/people/
akke/Portrait

Warnke Robert
Küstriner Str. 39
13055 Berlin, D
rowa@is.in-berlin.de
Site: Weltmusik e.V.
URL: http://www.is.
n-berlin.de/Culture/
weltmusik

Waser Bruno
Sonnenbergstr. 20
6005 Luzern, CH
brw@mital-u.ch
Site: mital U
URL: http://www.mital-u.ch/

Weintraub Anette
2 Bond Street
New York City, NY 10012
USA
anwcc@cunyvm.cuny.edu
Site: Realms
URL: http://artnetweb.
com/artnetweb/projects/
realms/notes.html

Whiteland Dave
Beholder Graphics
Hailsham BN27 4ZR, GB
dave@beholder.co.uk
Site: The Concuspidor &
the Grand Wizard of Many
Things
URL:
http://www.beholder.co.uk

Wohlgemuth Eva
Kriehubergasse 5/18
1050 Wien, A
evasys@ping.at
Site: Siberian Deal
URL: http://www.to.or.
at/~siberian/vrteil.htm

Wortzel Adrianne
19 East 7th ST #5
New York,NY 10003, USA
sphinx@fly.net
Site: The Electronic
Chronicles
URL: http://artnetweb.

Addison Rita / Thiébaux
Marcus / Zeltzer David
MIT, Room 36-763,50
Vassar Street
Cambridge, MA 02139, USA
dz@vetrec.mit.edu

Ahuva Mu'alem
63/53 Stern
96750 Jerusalem, IL
ahumu@cs.huji.ac.il

Alexander Amy
California Institute of Arts
24700 McBean Pkwy.
Valencia, CA 91355, USA
amy@emsh.calarts.edu

Anderson Elliot W. /
Campbell Jim
108 Dolores Street
San Francisco, CA 94103
USA
elliota@ix.netcom.com

Ando Yasuhiko/ Kosugi
Mihoko
53, Shimokanegura,
Enmyoji
618 Kyoto-fu, J
ksgand@mbox.kyoto-
inet.or.jp

AntiRom
20 Earlham Street
London WC2H NLW, GB
antirom@movie.demon.
co.uk

Art Group Archimediala
Ruzveltova 34
91000 Skopje, MK
mpandil@soros.org.mk
Art-Réseaux
10 rue Véronèse
75013 Paris, F

Auer Martin
Rotenmühlg. 44/30
1120 Wien, A
100571.2073@
compuserve.com

Bachschneider Wolf
Harunk
C-ART Design Studios
Unertlstr. 11
80803 München, D

Bauer Christian
Bauer & Bauer
Medienbüro GmbH
Friedrichstr. 49
90408 Nürnberg, D
headwork@axis.de

Becker Scott
P.O. Box 578956
Chicago, IL 60657-8956
USA
artscb@interaccess.com

Beerman Burton
Vitual Media Foundation
713 Champagne Ave
Bowling Green,
OH 43402, USA

Benda Lubor
tr. Miru 71
530 02 Pardubice, CZ
lbenda@ffa.vutbr.cz

Beöthy Balázs
Falk Miksa u.8
1055 Budapest, H

Bertrand Ennio
Via Giulia di Barolo, 40
10124 Torino (To), I
ennio.bertrand@torino.
alpcom.it

Beuter Stefan
Seestraße 36
72764 Reutlingen, D

Binkley Timothy
School of Visual Arts
209 E. 23rd St.
New York, NY 10010, USA
binkley@sva.edu

Bookchin Natalie
University of California
9500 Gilman Drive
La Jolla, CA 92093-0327
USA

Britton Benjamin Jay
3404 Middleton #10
Cincinnati, OH 45220, USA
benjamin.britton@uc.edu

Bure-soh Gwek
83 rue du Commerce
75015 Paris, F

Burns Kristine
Dartmouth College
Dept. of Music,
6187 Hopkins Ctr.
Hanover, NH 03755, USA
kristine.burns@
dartmouth.edu

Cajaraville Maite
c/Sorgo 53
28029 Madrid, E
maite@neptuno.ciberteca.es

Campbell Jim
1161 De Haro Street
San Francisco, CA 94107
USA
73677.2706@
compuserve.com

Cevro Vukovic Renzo
Via Machiavelli 12
30026 Portogruaro, I

Choi Seungjun
111 River Road #H-9
Edge-Water, NJ 07020, USA
alien.big@aol.com

Christian Dani /
Veli Kleeb
Pilatusst. 1
6300 Zug, CH

Cirincione Janine/ Ferraro
Michael
299 Pearl Street
New York, NY 10038, USA
janine@panix.com

Cmielewski Leon /
Starrs Josephine
5/19 Blair Str., Bondi
Sydney 2026, AUS
leon@sysx.apana.org.au

Courchesne Luc
3484 Laval Street
Montreal,
Quebec H2X 3C8, CDN
courchel@ere.umontreal.ca

Davies Char
SOFTIMAGE Inc.
3510 Boulevard St.
Laurent/400
Montreal Quebec
H2X 2V2, CDN
charlotte.davies@
softimag

Delannoy Jean Christophe /
Jaspart Celine /
Flores Jacko
Animacao
14, rue Saint Bertrand
31 500 Toulouse, F
101571.2600@
compuserve.com

Dement
15/21 St. Neot Ave./Potts
Point
Sydney, NSW 2011, AUS
Linda@real.com.au

Demers Louis-Philippe /
Vorn Bill
6585 Jeanne-Mance, Unit 301
Montreal H2V 4L1, CDN
d356644@er.uqam.ca

Dimon Roz
Dimon Arts, Inc.
New York,
NY 10014-4916, USA
rozdimon@interport.net

Dodge Chris
148 Fifth Street, Apt. #1
Cambridge, MA 02141, USA
cdodge@media.mit.edu

Doespirito-Santo Eiko /
Doespirito-Santo Rivaldo
P.O. Box 12694
Berkely, CA 94712, USA
eiko@dnai.com

Draves Scott
CMU Box 154, 4902
Forbes Ave.
Pittsburgh, PA 15213, USA
spot@cs.cmu.edu

Drees Holger /
Hoffs Max
Camphausenstr. 16
40479 Düsseldorf, D

Driessens Erwin /
Verstappen Maria
Eikenweg 9
1092 BW Amsterdam, NL
notnot@xs4all.nl

Dusman Linda
Clark University
950 Main St.
Worcester, MA 01610, USA
ldusman@vax.clarku.edu

Endlicher Ursula
116 S. 2nd Str., Apt #3
Brooklyn, NY 11211, USA
ursz@fly.net

Engineering Animation, Inc.
2625 North Loop Dr.
Ames, IA 50010, USA
lattie@eai.com

Ennio Bertrand
Via Giulia Di Barolo, 48
10124 Torino, I
ennio.bertrand@torino.
alpcom.it

Fadon Vicente Carlos
Rua Livreiro Saraiva 236
01237-020 São Paulo, BR

Feingold Ken
140 5th Ave.
New York, NY 10011, USA
kenf@panix.com

Fischnaller Franz /
Singh Yesenia Maharaj
F.A.B.R.I.CATORS
Via Fratelli Bronzetti 6
20129 Milano, I
fabricat@galactica.it

Fisher Shana
I/O 360
133 W. 19th Street Floor 3
New York, NY 10011, USA
shana@io360.com

Fleischer Joachim
Schlosserstr. 5
70180 Stuttgart, D

Fleischmann Monika /
Strauss Wolfgang /
Bohn Christian
GMD
Schloß Birlinghoven
53754 Sankt Augustin, D
fleischmann@gmd.de

Fogar Alessandro
Via Venezia 26
34073 Grado (GO), I
sfogar@xnet.it

Forgacs Peter
Mese köz 10
1121 Budapest, H
pforgacs@mail.datanet.hu

Förster Friedrich /
Cajthaml David
Hechinger Straße 203
72072 Tübingen, D
f.foerster@proaudio.de

Freedlander Paul
43 Narcissus Road
London NW6 1TL, GB
praskovi@uk.pi.net

Freitag Rosa
21 Brook Walk, Strawberry
Vale
London N2 9RB, GB
rosa@freitag.demon.co.uk

Fujihata Masaki
Keio University
5322 Endo
252 Fujisawa, Kanagawa, J
masaki@sfc.keio.ac.jp

Funk Gerhard
Weesestr. 3
4060 Leonding, A
funk@khsa.khs-linz.ac.at

Gardiner Jeremy
CyberArts
300 NE 2nd Avenue
Miami, FL 33132, USA

Geelhaar Jens
Werrg. 7
69120 Heidelberg, D
jens@hbks.uni-sb.de

Geith Stefan/ Akimo /
Kremling Bernd
New Frame Projekt
Steuiheilstr. 34
97080 Würzburg, D
geithman@mail.iMNet.de

George Phillip / Wayment
Ralph
Zographics
11 Miller St. Bondi
Sydney, NSW 2026, AUS
p.george@uws.edu.au

Gerber Karl
Deisenhofenerstr.102
81539 Münchnen, D

Gilardi Piero
Corso Casale, 121
10132 Torino, I

Gillerman JoAnn
Viper Vertex
950 61st St.
Oakland, CA 94608, USA
viper@metron.com

Gillman Clive
94 Magazine Lane
Merseyside L45 1LX, GB
clive@mg.u-net.com

Goldring Elisabeth
Center for Advanced Visual
Stu
Same as above, USA
goldring@mit.edu

Grancher Valéry
15, rue des Beaux Arts
75006 Paris, F
mhll@clavacom.fr

Gruppe „Sincretica"
Via Molise 6
20090 Limito (MI), I
gcospito@micronet.it

Grüneis Gerd / Mayer Pavel
/ Sauter
Joachim / Schmidt Axel
ART + COM
Budapesterstraße 44
10787 Berlin, D
js@artcom.de

Guyaux Françoise
4255 St-André
Montreal, QC H2J 2Z3, CDN
guyaux@sim.qc.ca

Györfi Gábor
Káldy Gyula u. 1
1061 Budapest, H
janna@osiris.elte.hu

Hachiya Kazuhiko
Atelier-K; 5-31-6 Nishi
Gotanda
141 Tokio, J
hachiya@shrine.cyber.ad.jp

Hales Christopher
Royal College of Art, Film &
TV
Kensington Gore
London SW7 2EU, GB
c.hales@rca.ac.uk

Hanlin Heath
1820 G. Street
Iowa City, IA 52240, USA
hhanlin@inav.net

Harwood Graham
ARTEC
257–258 Upper Street
London N1 1RW, GB
harwood@artec.org.uk

Haug Annette
Franklinstr. 77
70435 Stuttgart, D
100734.3457@
compuserve.com

Haveman Josepha
A/PIX
P.O. Box 9063
Berkeley, CA 94709, USA
JosephaH@aol.com

Heindl Josef
Münchnerstr. 35
82069 Hohenschäftlarn, D

Herbst Claudia
University of Maryland
Baltimore County Campus,
ECS
Baltimore,
MD 21228-5398, USA
claudia@irc.umbc.edu

Hershman-Leeson Lynn
Hotwire Productions
B 27 Ritch St.
San Francisco, CA 94123
USA
lynn2@well.com

Hinreiner Christian
Orleansstraße 55
81667 München, D
binreiner@zeilbeck.spacee

Hirschmann Heribert
Weidweg 50
8051 Graz, A

Hoffs Maximilian
Parkstr. 1
40477 Düsseldorf, D

Hooykaas Madelon /
Stansfield Elsa
Grote Bickerssstraat 44
1013 KS Amsterdam, NL
elsa@euronet.nl

Huang Liju
2 Almond Ct.
Lawrenceville, NJ 08648
USA
li-ju@sva.edu

Ikam Catherine /
Féri Louis
IRCAM / Territoires Virtuels
8, rue des Haies Fleuries
93100 Montreuil, F

Ishii Haruo
Trident School of Design
1-15-3 Noritake Nakamura-ku
Nagoya-shi 453, J
MXC00275@niftyserve.or.jp

Itapura Fabio / Domschke
Gisela
12, rue Notre Dame des
Champs
75006 Paris, F
fitapura@pratique.fr

Iwata Hiroo
Institute of Engineering
Mecha
1-1-1 Tennoudai
305 Tsukuba, J
iwata@kz.tsukuba.ac.jp

Jake
230 rue Saint Charles
75015 Paris, F

Janney Christopher
PhenomenArts, Inc.
75 Kendall Rd.
Lexington, MA 02173, USA
phenom@tiac.net

Jennings Pamela
Mind Field Productions
471 Bergen Street #3
Brooklyn, NY 11217, USA
pamela@panix.com

Johannsen Kirsten
Yorckstr.3
10965 Berlin, D
101557.706@compu
serve.com

Kamarotos Dimitri
36, Michalakopoulou Str.
11528 Athen, GR
dimik@forum.ars.net.gr

Kärkkäinen Aarre /
Okkonen Hilkka
Aallonhuippu 5 B 33
02320 Espoo, SF
aarre@karkka.pp.fi

Kinosita Seiko
Senriyama-nisi 5-43-1
Osaka Suita 565, J
ksp@yo.rim.or.jp

Kit
9 Nab Close, Bollington
Macclesfield SK10 5RB, GB

Kleingarn Dieter
Albertstr. 34
01097 Dresden, D

Knowbotic Research
Schillingstr. 32
50670 Köln, D
kr+cf@khm.uni-koeln.de

Köpnick Andreas
Helios Str.4
50825 Köln, D

Kosugi Mihoko /
Ando Yasuhiko
53, Shimukanegura,
Enmoji,
Oyamazaki-cho
Kyoto-fu 618, J
Ksgand@mbox,kyoto-
inet.or.jp

Kriel Charles
Chelsea College of Art
Manresa Road
London SW3 6LS, GB
ckriel@noel.pd.org

Kupisz Zbigniew
Open Studio / WOR
P.O. Box 1385
54-137 Wroclaw, PL
wro@info.wcss.wroc.pl

Kutscher Vollrad /
Marker Peter /
Viragh Laszlo /
Sterna Thomas
Bruchstr.7H
60594 Frankfurt/M. 70, D

Lahr Christian
Ackerstr. 18
10115 Berlin, D

Lakicevic Yohana
IBA-Israel Television
Romena
91071 Jerusalem, IL

Lara Felipe /
Phillipuk Mary
340 Broadway, 4th Floor
New York, NY 10013, USA
flaragar@pratt.edu

Lavaud Sophie
Art 3000
Chateau de L'Eglantine
78350 Jouy en Josas, F
art3000calvanet.
calvacom.fr

Lazarus Julia
24401 Jennifer Place
Newhall, CA 91321, USA
jlazarus@muse.calarts.edu

Lee Cheong-hyun
159 E. 30 St. #6A
NewYork, NY 10016, USA
cheong@sua.edu

Lee Youn H.
School of Visual Arts
141 W. 21st Str. 19th Floor
New York, NY 10010, USA
youn@sva.edu

Löffler Sandra / Yastas
Andreas / Zielke Bettina
Plastic Reality
Am Treptower Park 50
12435 Berlin, D
plastic@bbtt.com

Lois Viktor
Bükkös Part 72
2000 Szentendre, H

Longavesne Jean-Paul
GRIP
64 avenue Jean Moulin
75014 Paris, F
grip@cnam.fr

Löschner-Gornau Andreas
Am Kirchtor 14
06108 Halle/Saale, D
03452003916@t-online.de

Lutz Michael
Domagkstr. 33
Haus 38
80807 München, D

Machover Tod
MIT Media Lab
E15-494, 20 Ames St.
Cambridge, MA 02139, USA
tod@media.mit.edu

Maebayashi Akitsugu
Mitaka Simorenjaku
4-14-22-201
Tokyo 181, J
KGH01323@niftyserve.or.jp

Mamber Stephen
UCLA Dept. of Film/TV
Los Angeles, CA 90024, USA
smamber@ucla.edu

Martinez Luc
CIRM
33 ave. Jean Medecin
06000 Nice, F
100665.175@
compuserve.com

Martino Jacquelyn
Philips Research Labs
345 Scarborough Rd.
Briarcliff, NY 10510, USA
jam67@columbia.edu

Maun Patrick
255 E. Kellog Blvd., Studio
509
St. Paul, MN 55101, USA
butoh@well.com

McTavish Kevin
Zentrum für Kunst &
Medientechno
Kaiserstr. 64
76133 Karlsruhe, D
Kevin@zkm.de

Mehrain Thessy
140 East 28th Penthouse B
New York, NY 10016, USA
thessy@gramercy.ios.com

Meltzer Julia /
Ramos Amanda
236 4th St
Troy, NY 12180, USA
meltzj@rpi.edu

Merewether Janet
241 Denison St, Newtown
Sydney, NSW 2042, AUS

Mintz Ronen / Duggan
Brian / Ditmars Jason
Bridge Interfaces
345 So. Wetherly Drive
Berverly Hills, CA 90211
USA
bduggan@sdsc.edu

Mork Knut / Pendry Kate /
Stenslie Stahl / Watz Marius
Trondheimsvn. 170 D
0570 Oslo, N
senseless@hok.no

Mork Loren
Cool Software
355 NW 200th
Seattle, WA 98177, USA
lmork@coolsoft.com

Möslinger Sigi
43 West 16th St. #10D
New York, NY 10011, USA
sgm8943@is2.nyu.edu

Négyessy András
Tihanyi Arpad Ut. 69
9023 Györ, H
andrasn@eps.hu

Novakovic Gordana
ReVision
Dragorska 4
11000 Belgrade, YU

Orazem Vito /
Steingen Hans
Max-Reger-Str. 17–19
45128 Essen, D
101727.1366@
compuserve.com

Oschatz Sebastian / Bott
Martin /
Kliem Karl
Am Braunen Berg 4
64342 Seeheim, D
oschatz@gmd.de

Pannucci Cynthia
Art & Science
Collaborations
P.O. Box 358
Staten Island,
NY 10301-3225, USA
asci@fly.net

Paraschiv Christian
152 rue Rateau Atelier no. 8
93120 La Courneuve, F

Paterson Nancy
475 The West Mall #1513
Étobicoke,
Ontario M9C 4Z3, CDN
nancy@utcc.utoronto.ca

Perfahl Ernst
Goethestr. 16
4020 Linz, A
100444.3502@
compuserve.com

Petit Marianne
mutant productions
104 Suffolk Street, Apt.3
New York, NY 10002, USA
petit@echonyc.com

Plewe Daniela Alina
ZKM
Gartenstr. 71
76135 Karlsruhe, D
plewe@is.in-berlin.de

Proy Gabriela
Lacknergasse 100/24
1180 Wien, A
r.orlando@magnet.at

Radova Elen
Svidnická 5
18100 Prague, CZ

Raunig Gerald
PolyTroboi / Ibe
Währinger Str. 59
1090 Wien, A
lucas.filz@serv.univie.ac.at

Redl Erwin
65 South 11th Street 2nd
Floor
Brooklyn, NY 11211, USA
parallel@thing.net

Redolfi Michel
CIRM
33 ave Jean Medecin
06000 Nice, F
100673.1127@
compuserve.cm

Reichelt Nicolas
Institut für Neue Medien
Daimlerstr. 32
60314 Frankfurt, D
nico@inm.de

Rice Dixon Tennessee /
Gasperini Jim
270 Riverside Drive 12A
New York, NY 10025, USA
jimg@well.com

Richards Catherine
41, Delaware Ave.
Ottawa, Ont. K2P OZ2
CDN
crichard@ccs.carleton.ca

Roberts Sara
13709 Yellowstone Drive
Pine Mountain,
CA 93225, USA
sroberts@shoko.
calarts.edu

Robertshaw Simon
38 Oxford Drive, Waterloo
L22 7RZ Liverpool, GB

Rodemer Michael
School of the Art Institute
of Chicago
112 S. Michigan Ave.
Chicago, IL 60603, USA
rodemer@artic.edu

Rodriguez Nino
506 N. Flores Street #7
West Hollywood,
CA 90048, USA
nino@pobox.com

Rosen Peter
V.A.R.I.O.U.S.
2263 Sacramento St. #2
San Francisco, CA 94115
USA
peter@creativity.net

Roth Rob
Jackie Factory
648 Broadway #906
New York, NY 10012, USA
glamnerd@interport.net

Rudolf Klaus
Christburgerstr. 36
10405 Berlin, D

Rudolph Mark
107 Tunnel Mountain Road
Banff, Alberta ToL oCo
CDN
mfr@banffcentre.ab.ca

Kim Sanghun
School of Visual Arts
209 E. 23rd Str.
New York, NY 10010, USA
sanghun@aol.com

Schiphorst
Digital eARTh
1128 Rose Street
V5L 4K8 Vancouver BC
CDN
thecla@cs.sfu.ca

Schloss Arleen
A's WAVE
330 Broome St.
New York, NY 10002, USA
atel@panix.com

Schmidt Arthur
Gerichtstr. 23, a. 5. H.
13347 Berlin, D
7133.3650@compuserve.com

Schnell Ruth
Große Neugasse 12/7
1040 Wien, A

Schönwandt Barbara
Kastanienstr. 10
65719 Hofheim/T., D

Scott Jill
ZKM
Gartenstr. 71
76135 Karlsruhe, D
jscott@zkm.de

Seaman Bill
117 N. Beaumont Ave.
Catonsville, MD 21228, AUS
seaman@umbc.edu

Soros Center For
contemporary Art
Ryzveltova 34
91000 Skopje, MK
scca@soros.org.mk

Sekiguchi Atsuhito
Academy Media Arts and
Science
3-95 Ryoke-cho
Gifu Pref. 503, J
guchi@iamas.ac.jp

Serra Marius / Pares
Narcis / Pares Roc.
Galeria Virtual
Rambla 31
08002 Barcelona, E
gvirtual@harrison.upf.es

Choi Seungjun
1111 River road #H-9
Edge Water, NJ 07020, USA
Alien big@aol.com

Shaked Osnat
221 W. 16th Str. Apt. 3B
New York, NY 10011, USA
osnat@sva.edu

Shortess George
3505 Hecktown Road
Bethlehem, PA 18017, USA
gkso@lehigh.edu

Silver
U Akademie 4
17000 Prague, CZ
silver@avu.cz

Smetana Pavel
10, rue Hechner
67000 Strasbourg, F
p_smetana@la_cigogne.te
chlink.fr

Smith Graham
317 Adelaide St. W. #302
Toronto,
Ontario M5V 1P9, CDN
grahamt@intacc.web.net

Smolan Rick
Against All Odds
Productions
110 Caledonia Street,
Suite #1
Sausalito, CA 94965, USA
rick519@aol.com

Snibbe Scott Sona
Adobe Systems Inc.
411 1st Ave. S.
Seattle, WA 98104, USA
ssnibbe@adobe.com

Sparacino Flavia /
Chao Chloe / Wren
Christopher / Kotani Akira
/ Pentland Al
MIT Media Laboratory
20 Ames Street
Cambridge, MA 02139 USA
flavia@media.mit.edu

Spiegel Stacey
21 Glenholme Ave
Toronto M6H3A8, CDN
Spiegel@infovamp.net

Stampfl Gottfried
Florianistr. 25
8523 Frauental, A

Steggell Amanda Jane
Ulfstensgt. 1A
0355 Oslo, N
maggies@pobox.com

Stelkens Jörg
Akademikerstr. 2
80799 München, D
kl51101@sonmail.lvz-
muenchen.de

Stevenson Carl
127 East Dulwich Grove
London SE228 8PU, GB
carl@tier.demon.co.uk

Stytz Martin R.
Air Force Institute Of
Technology
2950 P Street,
Bldg 640, Room48
WPAFB, OH 45433, USA
mstytz@afit.af.mil

Sugár János
Varoshaz u. 4
1052 Budapest, H
sj@dial.isys.hu

Suzuki Nobuya
Academy of Media Arts
3-95 Ryokechon
Oogaki-city 503, J
zuckey@iamas.ac.jp

Svobodova Lucie
Factory Art,a.s.,
Ovenecká 15
17000 Prague, CZ
lucie@factory.cz

Szegedy-Maszák Zoltán
Németvölgyi út 67
1124 Budapest, H
szmz@inf.bme.hu

Tamblyn Christine
Florida International
University
Visual Arts Dept.
University Park Campus
DM 382
Miami, FL 33199, USA
tamblyn@ipof.fla.net

Thomson Jon / Graighead
Alison
149b Upper Tooting Rd.
London SW17 7TJ , GB
j.thomson@ucl.ac.uk

Tosa Naoko /
Ryohei Nakatsu
ATR Media Integration
& Communications
Research
Seika-cho Soraku-gun
Kyoto 619-02, J
tosa@mic.atr.co.jp

Truckenbrod Joan
School of the Art Institute
of Chicago
112 S. Michigan
Chicago, IL 60603, USA
truckenbrod@physics.niu.u

Tubak Bortnyik Eva /
Tubak Csaba
Bossigasse 16/5
1130 Wien, A

Underkoffler John
MIT Media Laboratory
20 Ames Street
Cambridge, MA 02139, USA
jh@media.mit.edu

Up(=µp) Mathilde
Tuinstraat 11
1015 NX Amsterdam, NL
mupe@desk.n1

Vanouse Paul
412 Hastings Street
Pittsburgh, PA 15206, USA
pv28@andrew.cmu.edu

Veldhoen Martijn
Madelievenstr. 14
1015 NV Amsterdam, NL

Verostko Roman
5535 Clinton Ave 5
Minneapolis, MN 55419, USA
roman@mcad.edu

Vila Doris / Rowe Robert /
Singer Eric
445 Grand St.
Brooklyn, NY 11211, USA
vila@dorsai.org

Watson Margaret
EVL / University of Illinois
851 S. Morgan Street,
R. 2032
Chicago, IL 60607, USA
watson@evl.eecs.vic.edu

Weidenaar Reynold
William Patreson College
Dept. of Communication
Wayne, NJ 07470-2152, USA
weidenaa@email.njin.net

Weiss Doris
M. Hock – Photosynthese
Lenzhalde 28
73732 Esslingen, D
100407.454@
compuserve.com

Werner Marc
Sabotage GBR
Solmische Weiherstr. 1
63303 Dreieich, D

Williams Nik
104 2nd Avenue Apt.#10
New York, NY 10003, USA
nik@panix.com

Wipfler C. Wilma
Hochschule f. Film &
Fernsehen
Karl-Marx-Str. 33–34
14482 Potsdam, D

Woolford Kirk
Rheing.14
50676 Köln, D
kwolf@khm.de

Abel Adam
Open Studio
P.O. Box 1385
54-137 Wroclaw 16, PL
wro@info.wcss.wroc.pl

Aberle Douglas
ABERLE FILMS
12800 NE 191st. Circle
Battle Ground,
WA 98604, USA
daberle@teleport.com

Adamczyk John
728 N. Wilson Ave.
Pasadena, CA 91104, USA
jwalt@sre.sony.com

Akiyama Yuko
23 Wharf Road,
Flat C,21/F,Bl.2
Hong Kong, HK

Alexander Amy
California Institute of Arts
24700 McBean Pkwy.
Valencia, CA 91355, USA
amy@emsh.calarts.edu

Apikian David
32, rue George Sand
75016 Paris, F

Arcadias Laurence
1231 #A Oxford St.
Berkeley, CA 94709, USA
arcadias@slip.net

Bailly-Basin Hervé
Electrons Libres
24 bis rue de la Paix
74000 Annecy, F

Basso Alain
Electrons Libres
24 bis rue de la Paix
74000 Annecy, F

Batten Trevor
Kanaalstraat 15
1054 WX Amsterdam, NL

Bauer Dominik
Friedrich-List-Schule
Kriegstr. 116
76133 Karlsruhe, D

Bell Alyson
PO Box 367 Terrey Hills
NSW 2084 Sydney, AUS

Beriou
AGAVE SA.
Cap. 108-67
Rue Robespierre
93558 Montreuil
cedex, F

Billion Philippe
Toshiba / ExMachina
22 Rue Hegesippe Moreau
75018 Paris, F

Borgmann Tim
Ravensburger Str. 20
42117 Wuppertal, D

Boustani Christian
Video Lune
36, rue Marceau
94200 Ivry/Seine, F

Britto Vera
University of Michigan
2108 School of Education
Ann Arbor,
MI 48109-1259, USA
fiatlux@umich.edu

Buffin Pierre /
Gondry Pierre
Buf compagnie
9 avenue de Villiers
75017 Paris, F

Büttner Manfred
Hernalser Haupt-
str. 24-26/19
1170 Wien, A

Calcagno Paolo
Alphaville Studio
Via Statuto 8
20121 Milano, I
alphavil@mbox.vol.it

Chen Raymond
4422 Via Marina #P 79
Marina Del Ray,
CA 90292, USA
chen@rhythm.com

Cheung Tim
541 Del Medio Ave. #133
Mt. View, CA 94040,USA
tcheung@pdi.com

Choi Song-won
ECAL-USINE
46, rue de l'Industrie
1030 Bussigny, CH
ggarcia@ulys.unil.ch

Clement Pierre
Z. A Production
64 rue de la Folie
Mericourt
75011 Paris, F
zap@club.internat.fr

Clyne John
National Center for
Atmospheric Research
1850 Table Mesa Dr.
Boulder, CO 80303, USA
clyne@ncar.ucar.edu

Coenen Arno/ Bosma René
Produced at Scan
Hoendiepshade 23/2
9718 BG Groningen, NL
rene@scan.media-gn.nl

Coggins Sigrid
21 Blvd. Taine
74000 Annecy, F

Coleman Connie
Coleman and Powell
Video
9215 Old Easton Rd., PO
Box 130
Ferndale, PA 18921, USA
ccoleman@netaxs.com

Colonna Jean-François /
Polieri Jacques
Lactamme
Ecole Polytechnique
91128 Palaiseau Cédex, F
colonna@poly.
polytechniqu

Coppel Christine
ECAL-USINE
46, rue de l'Industrie
1030 Bussigny, CH
ggarcia@ulys.unil.ch

Cotillas J. E. /
Jiménez M. /
Briz F. I. / Agulló J. /
Sancho E. /
Jiménez A.
TVE, SA Spanish Public
Televio
Alcade Sainz de Baranda,
92-7a
28007 Madrid, E

Cotte Olivier
Pascavision
4 place du 18 Juin 1940
75006 Paris, F
100767.2053@
compuserve.com

Coulter Allen
Coulter Studios
209 N.Niagara St.
Burbank, CA 91505, USA
adcoulter@aol.com

Cryer Chris
223 Calwell Ave
Los Gatos,CA 95032, USA

Curtis Cassidy /
Conner Judy
Pacific Data Images
3101 Park Boulevard
Palo Alto,CA 94306, USA
jconner@pdi.com

Dajez Julien
Mikros Image
7 rue Biscornet
75012 Paris. F

De Lorenzo Peter
P.O. Box 138
Robertson, NSW 2577, AUS
pdls@ozemail.com.au

Degen Markus
Piaristengasse 56-58/16
1080 Wien, A

Derlich Karin
U1, 24
68161 Mannheim, D
karin@wild.de

Detev Jordan Petrov
Computer Music
Laboratory
P.O. Box 15
1712 Sofia, BG
july@bgearn.acad.bg

Detkina Tanya / Nikolaev
Alexander
CORONADO Films
18 rue Faventines
26000 Valence, F
easylife@glas.apc.org

Dimke H-P. Karl
Scrollheim Kunstforschung
Fichtestr. 22
10967 Berlin, D

Dodge Chris
148 Fifth Street, Apt. #1
Cambridge, MA 02141, USA
cdodge@media.mit.edu

Drott Hajo
Platanenstraße 3
82024 Taufkirchen bei
München, D

Du Boulay Zoe /
Merrie Tessa
School of Television &
Imaging
13 Perth Road
Dundee DD1 4HT, GB
cryoung@dux.dundee.ac.uk

Duesing James
University of Cincinnati
ML# 0016 Clifton Ave.
Cincinnati,OH 45221-0016,
USA
jduesing@headchesse.
daa.uc.edu

Emami Nousha
School of the Art Institute
112 S. Michigan
Chicago, IL 60603, USA
nemami@dune.artic,edu

Engineering Animation,
Inc.
2625 North Loop Dr.
Ames, IA 50010, USA
lattie@eai.com

Esneault David
Texas A&M University
College of Architecture
College Station, TX
77843, USA
esneault@viz.tamu.edu

Facklam Heike /
Kolenda Michael
SZM Sendezentrum
München
Bahnhofstraße 28
85774 Unterföhring, D

Farrell Anne
VideoGraficArts
131 Huddleson Street
Santa Fe, NM 87501, USA
afarrell@santa-fe.cc.nm.s

Fong Weiming
Savannah College of Art &
Des.
548E. Broughton St., Norris
Hall
Sayannah, GA 31401, USA
buncheung@delphi.com

Foss Gregory
Pittsburg Supercomputing
Cente
4400 Fifth Avenue
Pittsburg, PA 15213, USA
foss@psc.edu

Furio Jean Marc
ENSAD
31 rue d'Ulm
75005 Paris, F
pierre@enoad.fr

Gasaway Mike
12790 Primrose Lane #313
Eden Prairie, MN 55344, USA
mikeg@ivi.com

Geith Stefan / Akimo /
Kremling Bernd
New Frame Projekt, D
geithman@mail.iMNet.de

Gibson James
3126 Bell Drive
Boulder, CO 80301, USA

Gill Jason
School of Television &
Imaging
13 Perth Road
Dundee DD1 4HT, GB
cryoung@dux.dundee.ac.uk

Goodwin Victoria /
Quintanilla Grace
School of Television &
Imaging
13 Perth Road
Dundee DD1 4HT, GB
cryoung@dux.dundee.ac.uk

Grillo Glenn
Nighttribe
228 Main St.#A
Venice, CA 90291, USA

Gsteu Peter
Rohrbach 40
6850 Dornbirn, A
bad.factory@
computerhaus.at

Guida Rosanna
SINCRETICA
Via Molise 6
20090 Limito (MI), I
gcospito@micronet.it

Guilminot Virginie
DEUS
100 rue du Faubourg
St. Antoine
75012 Paris, F

Dan Hanna /
De Graf Brad
Protozoa
2800 Third Street
San Francisco, CA 94107
USA

Heil Matthias
SFB288, Mathematik, TU-
Berlin
Str. des 17 Juni 136
10623 Berlin, D
matt@sfb288.math.
tu-berlin.de

Heyduck Nikolaus / Krüger
Roland
Leipzigerstraße 71
60487 Frankfurt, D

Nakazawa Hideo
NHK HDTV Division
2-2-1 Jinnan, shibuya-ku
Tokio 150-01 Tokio, J
nakazawa@hi-vision.
nhk.or.jp

Hodgins Jessica
College of Computing
801 Atlantic Dr
Atlanta, GA 30332, USA
jkh@cc.gatech.edu

Hoffman Charles R.
R/Greenberg Ass.
350 W. 39th St.
New York, NY 10018, USA
crh3@rga.com

Huitric Hervé/ Nahas
Monique
Université Paris 7
2, Place Jussieu
75251 Paris-Cedex 05, F
nahas@ccr.jussieu.fr

Hulse Matt/ Simpson
Joanne
School of Television &
Imaging
13 Perth Road
Dundee DD1 4HT, GB
cryoung@dux.dundee.ac.uk

Husain Oliver
Wendelsweg 4
60059 Frankfurt /M., D

ILM
P.O. Box 2459
San Rafael, CA 94912, USA
debra@kerner.com

Inakage Masa
The Media Studio, Inc.
2-24-7 Shichirigahama-
Higashi
Kamakura 248 , J
inakage@media-studio.co.j

Jäger Gottfried /
Holzhäuser Martin
Fachhochschule Bielefeld
Lampingerstr.3
33615 Bielefeld, D

Jeanneret Xavier
ECAL-USINE
46, rue de l'Industrie
1030 Bussigny, CH
ggarcia@ulys.unil.ch

Jouannet Mathilde
ENSAD
31 rue d'Ulm
75005 Paris, F
pierre@enoad.fr

Juhasz Attila
ENSAD
31 rue d'Ulm
75005 Paris, F
pierre@enoad.fr

Justel Elsa
Studio Phonos
La Rambla 31
08002 Barcelona, E

Karasova Monika
Academy of Fine Arts -
Prague
U Akademie 4
17000 Prague 7, CZ
monika@avu.cz

Kelomees Renee
Estonian Television
Faemlmanni 12
EE0100 Tallin, EV

Kinney Don /
Priore Dreux
Space Monkey Prod.
5001 Baum Boulevard-
Suite 676
Pittsburgh,PA 15213, USA
DonKinney@aol.com

Kitahara Satoshi
SEGA Enterprises, Ltd.
1-2-12 Haneda, ohta-ku
Tokio 144, J

Kular Jerzy
ExMachina
22 Rue Hegesippe Moreau
75018 Paris, F

Kuntzsch Betina
Schwalbacher Str. 2a
12161 Berlin, D

Lachapelle Pierre
TFX Animation Inc.
305 de la Commune
Ouest, Suite
Montreal H2Y 2E1, CDN
pierre@taarna.qc.ca

Lamarlette Arnauld /
Groce Pasquale
Buf Compagnie
9 Ave. de Villiers
75017 Paris, F

Lamine Bendjama
Mohamed
ENASD
31 rue d'Ulm
75005 Paris, F
pierre@enoad.fr

Landreth Christopher
ALIAS/Wavefront Inc.
110 Richmond Str. East
Toronto M5C 1P1 , CDN
landreth@aw.sgi.com

Larson Stephan
P.O .Box 288, Univ.
Station
Syracuse, NY 13210, USA
shlarson@mailbox.syr.edu

Lasseter John
Pixar Animation Studios
1001 West Cutting Blvd.
Richmond, CA 94804, USA
nancy@pixar

Le g.r.éggco
c/o Cooper Görres Straße 30
80798 München, D

Lee Kelvin
SONY Pictures
Imageworks
10202 W. Washington Blvd.
Culver City,
CA 90232-3195, USA
kelvin@spimageworks.com

Lefdup Jerome
Mikros Image
7 rue Biscornet
75012 Paris, F

Lelong Denis
24700 McBean Parkway,
BOX MJ-31
Valencia, CA 91355, USA
denis@emsh.calarts.edu

Levy Stuart /
Gunn Charly /
Munzner Tamara u.a.
Univ. of Minnesota,
Geometry Center
1300 S. 2nd Street, Suite
500
Minneapolis, MN 55454
USA
slevy@geom.umn.edu

Lin Serena
University of Maryland
5401 Wilkens Avenue
Baltimore, MD 21228, USA
slin1@gl.umbc.edu

Magnenat-Thalmann
Nadia
MIRALab-CUI, Université
de Genève
1211 Genève 4, CH
thalmann@cui.unige.ch

Maltman Gregor
School of Television &
Imaging
13 Perth Road
Dundee DD1 4HT, GB
cryoung@dux.dundee.ac.uk

Marguin Moira
ENSAD
31 rue d'Ulm
75005 Paris, F
pierre@enoad.fr

Marini Claudia /
Zava Sergio /
Ghisolphi Giorgio
Chinatown
Via Aleardo Aleardi 12
20154 Milano, I

Masin Tomas
Dawson Prod.
Starostrasnicka 16/25
10000 Prague 10, CZ

Mayr Andrea
Tivolig. 18/14
1120 Wien, A
mayr@etoy.com

McSherry Stewart
1777 Yosemite Ave. #3-b
San Fancisco, CA 94124
USA
mcsherry@sgi.com

Medical Broadcasting
Company
555 North
Coushohocken, PA 19428,
USA
lattie@eai.com

Merewether Janet
241 Denison St, Newtown
Sydney, NSW 2042, AUS

Merrie Tessa
School of Television &
Imaging
13 Perth Road
Dundee DD1 4HT, GB
cryoung@dux.dundee.ac.uk

Moilanen Milla
Kroma Productions Ltd.
Magnusborg
06100 Porvoo, SF

Monnet Penelope
ENSAD
31 rue d'Ulm
75005 Paris, F
pierre@enoad.fr

Moragues Jordi
Institut Universitari de
l'Audiovisual
La Rambla 31
08002 Barcelona, E

Murgatroyd Steve
School of Television &
Imaging
13 Perth Road
Dundee DD1 4HT, GB
cryoung@dux.dundee.ac.uk

Nikolić Milan Peca
ReVision Consulting
Group
Dragorska 4
11000 Belgrad, YU

Nir Karen
Florida Center for
Electronic Communication
220 SE Secound Ave.
Fort Lauderdale,FL 33301
USA
nir@Laureate.cec.fau.edu

Noji Suma
Nippon Electronics
College
1-25-4, Hyakunincho,
Shinjuku-ku
Tokyo 169, J

Oda Hideyuki
A202 Maison Higashi-
Ogaki,
5-21 Imajuku
Ogaki-City, Gifu 503, J
odada@iamas.ac.jp

Oertl Stefan / Lung
Michael
Neustiftgasse 84/6
1070 Wien, A
stefan@stellaris.cg.
tuwien.ac.at

Oh K. Hee
24700 McBean Parkway
Valencia, CA 91355, USA
hee@itchy.calarts.edu

Oschatz Sebastian
Am Braunen Berg 4
64342 Seeheim, D
oschatz@gmd.de

Pagoni Girini
Plaguata 50
114 73 Athen, GR

Perrier Cedric
ENSAD
31 rue d'Ulm
75005 Paris, F
pierre@enoad.fr

Pickles Martin
Rectory End,
Church Lane
York 406 4JQ, GB

Pignon Dinka
Saterbacken 14 BV
142 32 Stockholm, S
71662.321@
compuserve.com

Pinel Marc
ENSAD
31 rue d'Ulm
75005 Paris, F
pierre@enoad.fr

Polthier Konrad /
Arnez Andreas /
Steffens Martin
TU Berlin, MA8-3
Straße des 17. Juni 136
10623 Berlin, D
polthier@math.tu-berlin.de

Prisse Edouard
ENSAD
31 rue d'Ulm
75005 Paris, F
pierre@enoad.fr

Pushpathadam Thomas
Visual Lab, Texas A&M
Univ.
216A Langford Center
College Station,
TX 77843-3137, USA
qmot@viz.tamu.edu

Rigaud Olivier
ENSAD
31 rue d'Ulm
75005 Paris, F
pierre@enoad.fr

Robert Thierry
Bandgasse 11/13
1070 Wien, A

Robin-Prevalle Matthieu
ENSAD
31 rue d'Ulm
75005 Paris, F
pierre@enoad.fr

Robinson Matthew
School of Television &
Imaging
13 Perth Road
Dundee DD1 4HT, GB
cryoung@dux.dundee.ac.uk

Robinson Robert
240 Collins Street
San Francisco, CA 94118
USA

Rosendahl Carl
Pacific Data Images
3101 Park Boulevard
Palo Alto, CA 94306, USA
jconner@pdi.com.

Rudolph Mark
107 Tunnel Mountain Rd.
Banff, Alberta ToL oCo
CDN
mfr@banffcentre.ab.ca

Salles Valérie
ENSAD
31 rue d'Ulm
75005 Pais, F
pierre@enoad.fr

Satoshi Koreki
7275 Franklin Ave. #504
Los Angeles, CA 90046
USA
koreki@primenet.com

Schulz Thomas
Bismarkstr. 7
24768 Rendsburg, D

Schuster Klaus
Luthergasse 4
8570 Voitsberg, A

Seblatnig Heidemarie
Krallgasse 6
1220 Wien, A
ferschin@osriris.iemar.te

Sirgado de Sousa
Evangelina
Bournemouth University
Talbot Campus,
Fernbarrow
Poole, Dorset BH12 5BB, GB
angel@bournemouth.ac.uk

Simon Loic
ENSAD
31 rue d'Ulm
75005 Paris, F
pierre@enoad.fr

Simpson Joanne
School of Television &
Imaging
13 Perth Road
Dundee DD1 4HT, GB
cryoung@dux.dundee.ac.uk

Sreco Dragan
TV Slovenia - Arxel Tribe
1000 Ljubljana, SLO
TRIBE@ARXEL.si

Staeger Jörg / Wimmer
Stefan
digital media münchen
Gneisenaustr. 15
80992 München, D

Stephan Alexander
Virchowstr. 23
14482 Potsdam, D
pixel@pixel.of.EUnet.de

Stöckl-Prochazka Eduard
TND – The New
Dimension
Obkirchergasse 33/8
1190 Wien, A

Struwe Gerd
Heinrichstr. 45
50676 Köln, D
101727.3330@
compuserve.co

Sturm Matthias
Tandervision
Wörenstieg 33c
22415 Hamburg, D

Stytz Martin R.
Air Force Institute Of
Technology
2950 P Street, Bldg 640,
Room48
WPAFB, OH 45433, USA
mstytz@afit.af.mil

Svobodova Lucie
Factory Art,
Ovenecka 15
17000 Prague, CZ
lucie@factory.cz

Sylvestre Pierre
SCRATCH Prod.
5302 Fabre
Montreal H2J 3W5, CDN
debeat@vir.com

Szczesny Ches
Weidenallee 10A
20357 Hamburg, D

Szleszynski Jacek
Ul. Zielinskiego 28/44
53-534 Wroclaw, PL

Takenaka Takahiro
Links Corporation
2-14-1 Higashi-gotanda
Tokyo 141, J
takenaka@links.imagica.c
o.jp

Theill Signe
Laubacherstr. 32/2
14197 Berlin, D

Thomason Kevin
Texas A&M Univ.
216 A Langford Center
College Station, TX
77843-3137, USA

Tibursky Jan /
Kolenda Michael
SZM Sendezentrum
München
Bahnhofstraße 28
85774 Unterföhring, D

Tremblay Marjolaine
Industrial Light & Magic
P.O. Box 2459
San Rafael, CA 94912
USA
marjo@kerner.com

Ursyn Anna
Univ. of Northern
Colorado
Department of Visual Arts
Greeley, CO 80639, USA

Vaskov Goce
Arxel Tribe & Zagreb Film
Samova 5
1000 LJUBLJANA, SLO
gozze@arxel.si

Wagner Anna
1915 18th Street
San Francisco, CA 94107
USA
anna@xaos.com

Waliczky Tamás
ZKM
Gartenstr. 71
76135 Karlsruhe, D
tw@ZKM.de

Watson Margaret
EVL/University of Illinois
851 S.Morgan Street,
R.2032
Chicago, IL 60607, USA
watson@evl.eecs.vic.edu

Wedge Chris
Blue Sky Prod., Inc.
100 Executive Blvd.
Ossining, NY 10562, USA
chrissie@blueskyprod.com
Weston Stephen
Whitehorse Films
24 Belsize Grove
London NW3 4TR , GB

Wipfler C. Wilma
Hochschule f. Film &
Fernsehen
Karl-Marx-Str. 33-34
14482 Potsdam, D

Wright Dominic
London Guildhall
University
Commercial Road
London NW6 3A4, GB

Wright Maurice
Boyer College of Music
Rock Hall 113
Philadelphia, PA 19122, USA
wright@astro.ocis.temple.
edu

Wright Richard /
White Jason
Soft Future Prod.
90 Netherlands Road
New Barnet,
Herts. EN5 1BU, GB
SFP@DIG-
LGU.DEMON.CO.UK

Zajec Edward
Syracuse University
102 Shaffer Art Bldg.
Syracuse, NY 13244, USA
ezajec@mailbox.syr.edu

Zervos Kominos
Konstantin
477 Milton Rd,
Auchenflower
4066 Brisbane, AUS
S271502@Student.ug.
edu.au

Zorin Denis
Caltech
139-74 Caltech
Pasadena, CA 91125, USA
dzorin@gg.caltech.edu

Abrams Frederick
c/La Fransa, 31, 2-2
08004 Barcelona, E
100743.1717@
compuserve.com

Acquaviva Frédéric
9, rue de l'Arc de
Triomphe
75017 Paris, F

Adám Kálmán
Marvany u. 46
1126 Budapest, H

Adkins Mathew
University of East Anglia
Music Department
Norwich NR4 7TJ, GB
m.adkins@uea.ac.uk

Ainger Marc
334 E. Beechwold Blvd.
Columbus, OH 43214, USA
ainger.l@osu.edu

Amin Dzamal
Herndlgasse 22/27
1100 Wien, A

Amin Irina
Herndlgasse 22/27
1100 Wien, A

Apollyon Nicolay
Grinivn. 34
0756 Oslo, N
nicolay@notam.uio.no

Argersinger Charles
Washington State
University
School of Music and Theatre
Pullman,WA 99164-5300
USA

Ascione Patrick
Les Augerats
18510 Menetou-Salon, F

Ashley Robert
Performing Artservices, Inc.
260 West Broadway
New York, NY 10013, USA
76221.330@
compuserve.com

Austin Larry
2109 Woodbrook
Denton, Texas 76205, USA
austin@cube.cemi.unt.edu

Averill Ron
University of Washington
School of Music, DN 10
Seattle, WA 98195, USA
raverill@u.washington.edu

Bandt Ros
14 Collings St., Brunswick
West
Melbourne, Victoria 3055
AUS
rossart@vaxc.cc.
monash.edu.au

Barrett Natasha
City University
Northampton Square
London ECIV OHB, GB
db553@city.ac.uk

Basso Alain
Association Electrons Libres
24 bis rue de la Paix
74000 Annecy, F

Batchelor Peter
University of Wales,
Bangor
College Road, Bangor
Gwynedd LL57 2DG, GB
muu005@bangor.ac.uk

Bebris Egils
223 Wright Ave.
Toronto, Ontt. M6R 1L4
CDN

Beerman Burton
Vitual Media Foundation
713 Champagne Ave
Bowling Green,
OH 43402, USA

Bennett Justin / Grosveld
Geurt /
Vanderwalle Daan
BMB con.
BICE
Laag Veen 14
2544 RZ Den Haag, NL
justin@koncon.nl

Berenguer José Manuel
Cóchlea
Sardenya 516-6-2
08024 Barcelona, E
jmberenguer@l
onestar.es

Berry Michael
5947 Laird Ave.
Oakland, CA 94605, USA
mikeb@mills.edu

Bianchini Laura
Centro Ricerche Musicale -
CRM
Via Lamarmora 18
00185 Rome, I

Bischoff John
Center for Contemporary
Music
5000 MacArthur Blvd.
Oakland, CA 94613, USA
bischoff@ella.mills.edu

Bless Karl Heinz
Hermanngasse 25/8
1070 Wien, A

Bless Markus
Lederergasse 9
4861 Schörfling, A
bless@khsa.khs-linz.ac.at

Blyth Andrew Robert
13 Standard Ave.
Box Hill, Victoria 3128, AUS
ablyth@ozemail.com.au

Bodin Lars-Gunnar
Helgalunden 17
11858 Stockholm, S

Bolewski Christin
Thumbstr. 72
51103 Köln, D
christin@khm.uni-koeln.de

Bomben Massimo
Via dei Roveri 45
33080 Fiume
Veneto (PN), I

Bonardi Alain
5 Impasse du
Debarcadère
78000 Versailles, F

Bönn Georg
Franz-Liszt-Str. 7
28209 Bremen, D
0421343796-1@t-online.de

Boschetto Francesco
c/o EMS Södermälerstrand
61
11825 Stockholm, S
boschetto@composer.
ems.srk.se

Bradley Stephen
University of Maryland
5401 Wilkens Avenue
Baltimore, MD 21228, USA
sbradley@umbc.edu

Breitenfeld Roland
Moosgrund 8
79110 Freiburg, D

Brizzi Aldo
GRAME
6 Quai Jean-Moulin
B.P. 1185
69202 Cedex 01 Lyon, F
grame@applelink.apple.com

Brncic-Isaza Gabriel
Phonos, Foundation
La Rambla 31
08002 Barcelona, E
gabriel@phonos.upf.es

Brown Chris
Mills College Center for
Music
5000 MacArthur Blvd.
Oakland, CA 94613, USA
cbmus@mills.edu

Bürck Rainer
Am Samuelstein 9
72574 Bad Urach, D
101515.35149.
compuserve.com

Burgoyne Diana
2735 St.Catherines St
Vancouver V5T 3Y6, BC
CDN
d_burgoyne@mindlink.
bc.ca

Burt Warren
c/o ACAT
GPO Box 804
Canberra, ACT 2601, AUS
waburt@melbourne.dialix.u

Burtner C. Matthew
820 Park Avenue #4
Baltimore, MD 21201, USA
mburtner@peabody.jhu.edu

Camilleri Lelio
Conservatorio di Musica
G. B. Martini
Piazza Rossini 2
40126 Bologna, I
lelioc@mailserver.idg.fi.cnr.it

Cardano Claudio
Via Adamello, 13
37011 Bardolino (VR), I

Ceccarelli Luigi
Edison Studio
Viale Mazzini, 6
00186 Rome, I
l.ceccarelli@agora.stm.it

Chagas Paulo
Marsilstein 9-13
50676 Köln, D

Chandra Arun
702 S. McCullough
Urbana, IL 61801, USA
arunc@ux1.cso.uiuc.edu

Cizek Martina / Musil
Wolfgang
Rotenlöwengasse 9/22
1090 Wien, A

Cooper Robert
University of Missouri
4949 Cherry
Kansas City, MO 64110, USA
rlcooper@cctr.umkc.edu

Copeland Darren
1588 Spring Rd.
Mississauga,
Ontario L5J 1N3, CDN
darcope@interlog.com

Corona Edgardo
Lope de Vega 5499
1605 Carapachay, RA

Cospito Giovanni
Sincretica
Via Molise 6
20090 Limito (MI), I
gcospito@micronet.it

Crowley Timothy
Texas A & M University
College Station, TX 77843
USA
timc@jing.tamu.edu.edu

Dall'Osto Diego
Corso Palladio 114
36100 Vicenza, I
d.dallosto@vi.nettuno.it

Dapelo Riccardo
Via Valente 40
16015 Casella (GE), I

Dashow James
Loc. Le Contra
02030 Poggio S. Lorenzo
(RI), I
j.dashow@agora.stm.it

Davidson Christopher
67 Glen Avenue #107
Oakland, CA 94611, USA
antimatter@earthlink.net

De Chenerilles Bruno
Audiorama
BP 161
67004 Strasbourg Cedex, F

De Man Roderik
1e Tuindwarsstraat 3
1015 RT Amsterdam, NL

DeLaurenti Christopher
P.O.Box 45655
Seattle, WA 98145-0655
USA
composer@scn.org

Devers Patrick
44, rue de la Crete
74960 Cram-Gevrier, F

Dhomont Francis
3355, Chemin Queen Mary,
App. 317
Montreal (Qc) H3V 1A5, CDN

Di Scipio Agostino
Via Salaria
Antica Est 33/A
67100 L'Aquila, I
lms@aquila.infn.it

Doati Roberto
Via Giorgione 66
35020 Albignasego (PD), I
doati@csc.unipd.it

Dodd Rose
The Flat, The old Barn
Norwich NR86EE, GB
R.Dodd@uea.ac.uk

Dong Kui
2005 California St. #6
Mountain View,
CA 94040, USA
kui@ccrma.stanford.edu

Doyle Roger
Rynville Mews,
Killarney Road
Bray, Co. Wicklow, EI
INFO@CMC.IE

Drever John Levack
5 Park Road, Eskbank
Midlothian EH223DF, GB
J.Drever@uea.ac.uk

Duesenberry John
514 Harvard St. #3B
Brookline, MA 02146, USA
johndu@world.std.com

Eagle David
University of Calgary
2500 Univesity Dr. NW
Calgary, AB T2N 1N4, CDN
eagle@acs.ucalgary.ca

Eberhard Alexander
Salesianergasse 10/28
1030 Wien, A

Eckert Gerald
Viehauser Berg 9
45239 Essen, D
eckert@folkwang.
uniessen.de

Edwards Michael /
Trevisani Marco
Stanford University,
CCRMA
Lomita Street Knoll 203
Stanford,
CA 94305-8180, USA
michael@ccrma.
stanford.ed

Enström Rolf
Helgestavägen 127
12541 Älvsjö, S
enstroem@kacor.kth.se

Essl Karlheinz
Am Ölberg 26-30
3400 Klosterneuburg, A
essl@ping.at

Favotti Gino Didier
8, rue Joseph Serlin
69001 Lyon, F

Feuerstein Thomas
Amraserstr.103
6020 Innsbruck, A
bik@ast5.nibk.ac.at

Field Ambrose
South House, Ullenwood
Cheltenham,
Glos. GL53 9QX, GB
Ambrose.Field@
City.ac.uk

Fischer Nirto Karsten
Forced Media
Karl-Marx-Str. 156
12043 Berlin, D
100407.3635@
compuserve.com

Forró Daniel
Lucni 40
616 00 Brno, CZ
2:421/13.20@fidonet.org

Frers Karlheinz
Th. Körnerstr. 17
28203 Bremen, D

Fumarola Martin A.
Universidad Nacional de
Cordoba
Estafeta 56
5001 Cordoba, RA
maralefu@famaf.uncor.edu

Furukawa Kiyoshi
Sillemstr. 61
20257 Hamburg, D
kf@zkm.de

Gaigne Pascal
LIMCA
Route de Toulouse
32000 Auch, F

Gena Peter
School of the Art Institute
of Chicago
112 S. Michigan Ave.
Chicago, IL 60603, USA
pgena@artic.edu

Gerwin Thomas
ZKM
Kaiserstr. 127
76133 Karlsruhe, D
TG@ZKM.DE

Gibbons Mark Edward
116 E 73rd Street
Apt. 10
New York, NY 10021, USA
megibbons@aol.com

Giomi Francesco
Via Silvani 180
50125 Firenze, I
art@mailserver.idg.fi.cnr.it

Giraudon François
Groupe de Musique
Experimentale
1 Place André Malraux
18001 Bourges, F
agmebio@calvacom.fr

Gluck Robert J.
43 Elm Court,
P.O. Box 276
Sheffield, MA 01257, USA
rjgluck@aol.com

Gobeil Gilles
5043 A Bordeaux
Montreal (Qc) H2H 2A5
CDN

Gololobov Andrey
Bela Coona 17-1-66
192241 Sankt Petersburg, R

Gottifredi Antonello
2, Place Neuve
1204 Genève, CH

Grana Edgar / Weiss Art
Edgar Grana Music
315 West 53rd Street
New York, NY 10019, USA
Green Peter / Dred Mike
60 Norvic Drive
Norwich NR4 7NW, GB

Grippe Ragnar
Öraker
196 93 Kungsängen, S
grippe@composer.ems.
srk.e

Gründler Seppo / Klammer
Josef
Grasbergerstr. 47
8010 Graz, A
sego@iem.mhsg.ac.at

Halac José
544 Court St. #3
Brooklyn, NY 11231, USA
jose@interport.net

Harrison Jonty
University of Birmingham
(UK)
Music Department
Edgbaston, Birmingham,
B15 2TT, GB
d.j.t.harrison@bham.ac.uk

Harvey Scott
Kent Inst. of Art & Design
Oakwood Park
ME16 8AG Kent, GB

Hatzis Christos
35 Eaton Avenue
Toronto, Ontario M4J 2Z4,
CDN
chatzis@epas.utoronto.ca

Heckert Matt
2245 Quesada Ave.
San Francisco, CA 94124
USA
monk@slip.net

Hedas Kim
Högbergsgatan 24 III
116 20 Stockholm, S

Hinkle-Turner Anna
Elizabeth
University of Illinois
Undergraduate Library
Urbana, IL 61801, USA
hinkletu@uxl.cso.uiuc.edu

Hoffman Elizabeth
11235 Evanston Avenue N.
Seattle, WA 98133-8220
USA
ehoffman@u.
washington.edu

Hoffman Paul
Unit 6/50 Ormond Road
Elwood 3184, AUS

Hoffmann Norbert
Föhrenwald 464
6100 Seefeld, A

Hoffs Maximilian
Parkstr. 1
40477 Düsseldorf, D

Hortobagyi Laszlo
Tarnok u. 26
1014 Budapest, H

Howard Earl
39-39 45th Street
Sunnyside, NY 11104-2103,
USA

Humpert Hans
Hochschule f. Musik
Dagobertstr.38
50668 Köln, D

Hyde Joseph
University of Birmingham
Barber Institute of Fine Arts
Edgbaston,
Birmingham B16 0NU, GB
hydej@bham.ac.uk

Iges José
Meson de Paredes, 46
28012 Madrid, E

Jaffrennou Pierre Alain
GRAME
6 Quai Jean Moulin B.P.
1185
69202 Lyon Cedex 01, F
jaf@rd.grame.fr

Jelinek Robert
Sabotage Communications
eV.
Seegasse 12/14
1090 Wien, A

Jones Stuart
610 W.113th St #3A
New York, NY 10025, USA
sj33@columbia.edu

Jünger Patricia
ANIGMA Acoustic Arts &
Edition
Muttenzerstr. 11
4142 Münchenstein /
Basel, CH
anigma-
juen.wag@datacomm.ch

Justel Elsa / Lopez
Armand
Studio Phonos
La Rambla 31
08002 Barcelona, E

Kagel Mauricio
Wolfgang-Müller-Str. 18
50968 Köln, D

Kahn Frédéric
36, Grande Rue de Vaise
69009 Lyon, F

Kan-no Shigeru
Filmakademie Baden-
Württemberg
Mathildenstr. 20
71567 Ludwigsburg, D

Kanding Ejnar
Oestergade 38
4000 Roskilde, DK

Karlsson Erik Mikael
Junkergatan 16/II
126 53 Hägersten, S
emk@composer.ems.srk.se

Kayn Roland
Zuidereind 124
1243 KL 's-Graveland, NL

Kellow Markus
1 Butler St., Northcote
Melbourne,
Victoria 3070, AUS

Kempf Davorin
Universität Zagreb
Gunduliceva 6
10000 Zagreb, HR

Kestellikian Cyril
11 ave. des Coccinelles
13012 Marseille, F

Kirschner Kenneth
211 East 11th Street, App. #3
New York, NY 10003, USA
jhs6@columbia.edu

Kiwus Wolfgang
Alexanderstraße 78
70182 Stuttgart, D

Klammer Josef
Neuholdaugasse 51
8010 Graz, A

Koenders Michel G. M.
p/a. Dieter Bothstraat 18
3531 GZ Utrecht, NL

Koller Gerald
Froschaugasse 7/59
8010 Graz, A

Kopecky Pavel
Na Maninách 25
170 00 Prague, CZ

Korte Karl
University of Texas
School of Music
Austin, TX 78712-1208, USA

Kosk Patrick /
Enckell Agneta
Ulrikagatan 1A/8
00140 Helsingfors, SF

Kratochwil Martin
Jagdschloßgasse 24A/5
1130 Wien, A

Kreger Tim
ACAT
Baldessin Cres.
Canberra, 2601, AUS
tim.kreger@anu.edu.au

Kruppa Birgitta
Vision Music LAB
Peter-Strasser-Weg 17
12101 Berlin, D

Kuljuntausta Petri
Tunnelitie 9 G 53
00320 Helsinki, SF
tiina.kevajarvi@helsinki.fi

Kupper Leo
Studio de Recherches
23, Avenue Albert-Elisabeth
1200 Bruxelles, B

Kuriyama Yuusuke
8-1-201 Shiratori-cho
040 Hakodate-City 040, J

Lane Cathy
78, Sandringham Road
London E8 2LL, GB
c.m.lane@city.ac.uk

Lanza Alcides
McGill University
555 Sherbrooke West
Montreal (Qc) H3A 1E3
CDN
alcides@music.mcgill.ca

Larmor Luc
Le Goulumer
56 760 Penestin, F

Laronde Claire
185 rue du Chevaleret
75013 Paris, F

Le Prado Cecile
116 rue des Pyrenées
75020 Paris, F
leprado@ircam.fr

Lech Jury
Insolit Prod.
Espolsasacs 4-4-1a
08002 Barcelona, E
insolit@hen.servicom.es

Leduc Daniel
15 Rue Waterman
App. 606
Saint-Lambert (Qc)
J4P 1R7, CDN
leduc@ere.umontreal.ca

Le Nobel Bob
Timbre Productions
Vogelsanglaan 5
3571ZM Utrecht, NL

Leonardson Eric
1550 N.Milwaukee Ave.
Chicago, IL 60622-2008
USA
eleon@tezcat.com

Lesso Drew
201 S. Santa Fe Ave. #300
Los Angeles, CA 90012, USA
drewlesso@aol.com

Lewis Andrew
1 Victoria Park
Bangor,
Gwynedd LL57 2EW, GB
a.p.lewis@bangor.ac.uk

Lillios Elainie
Route 1, Box 121
Ponder, TX 76259, USA
elillio@cube.cemi.unt.edu

Lippe Cort
University at Buffalo
222 Baird Hall
Buffalo, NY 14260, USA
lippe@acsu.buffalo.edu

Little David Clark
Sweelink Conservatory
V. Baerlestr. 27
1070 LP Amsterdam, NL
19521952@xs4all.nl

Lo Yee On
Independent
Laurel Ave.
Merlo Park, CA 94025, USA
acoustic@netcom.com

Loizillon Guillaume
24, rue Simart
75018 Paris, F

Lopez Manuel / Espinoza
Eugenio
Pasaje San Lorenzo 53M
La Reina
Santiago, RCH
gold@lactiva.cl

Lopez-Lezcano Fernando
CCRMA/Music Department
Stanford University
Stanford, CA 94305, USA
nando@ccrma.stanford.edu

Lupone Michelangelo
Centro Ricerche Musicali
CRM
Via Lamarmora 18
00185 Rome, I

Lyon Eric
M.I.T. W102, 46-1
Gakudencho
Ogari City, Gifu 503, J
eric@cmlab.sfc.keio.ac.jp

MacDonald Alistair
43 High Street West
Anstruther KY10 3DJ, GB
a.n.macdonald@bham.ac.uk

Mahin Bruce P.
Radford University
Box 6968
Radford, VA 24142, USA
bmahin@runet.edu

Maldonado Gabriel
Il Fantalogico
Via Donna Olimpia 166
00152 Roma, I
g.maldonado@agora.stm.it

Marsanyi Robert
6510 South Deer Lake
Road
Clinton, WA 98236, USA
Robert.Marsanyi@3do.com

Martínez Patricia E.
Tacuarí 453 P.B. „A"
1071 Buenos Aires, RA

Marcelo Mary Mario
23, rue Benard 6 - 67
75014 Paris, F
mmary@ircam.fr

Mazza Tommaso
C/da Gorgofreddo 144/C
70043 Monopoli (BA), I

Mendelssohn Vladimir
Obrechtstraat 81A
2517 VN Den Haag, NL

Michael Doug
2889 Seville Circle
Antioch, CA 94509, USA
dmic27@ccnet.com

Milicevic Mladen
University of South
Carolina
Columbia, SC 29208, USA
mmladen@sc.edu

Minsburg Raul
Bravard 1172
1414 Buenos Aires, RA
minsburg@pinos.com

Mion Philippe
Rue Montmartre 49
79002 Paris, F

Miranda Eduardo Reck
University of Glasgow
Dept. of Music
14, University Gardens
Glasgow G12 8QH , GB
miranda@music.gla.ac.uk

Mittendorf Hans
35A Bisson Road
London E15 2RD, GB

Moenne-Loccoz Phillippe
Collectif et Compagnie
11 ave. des Vieux Moulins
74000 Annecy, F

Monahan Gordon
R.R. #4
Markdale N0C 1H0, CDN

Monro Gordon
School of Mathematics &
Stat.
University of Sydney
Sydney, NSW 2006, AUS
monro_g@maths.su.oz.au

Montague Stephen
2 Ryland Road
London NW5 3EA, GB
100767.767@compuserve.
com

Moore Adrian J.
7, Mossfield Road,
Kings Heath
Birmingham, B14 7JE, GB
a.j.moore@bham.ac.uk

Morgenroth Inge
Naunynstr. 36
10999 Berlin, D

Morikawa Hiroto
YA Heights Koenji 807
1-4-2 Koenji Minami
Tokyo 166, J

Moschos Konstantin
Forschungsinstitut für
Musik
Adrianou 105
10558 Athen, GR
kmos@culture.gr

Mowinckel Johan
Salstagatan 11 C
642 36 Flen, S

Nagashima Yoichi
Art & Science Laboratory
10-12-301, Sumiyoshi-5
Hamamatsu, Shizuoka
430, J
nagasm@kobe-
yamate.ac.jp

Nagy Sabine
Das Andere Gitarrenstudio
Hauzenbergerstr. 20
80687 München, D

Nakamura Shigenobu
Kyoto College of Art
2-116 Uryuyama
Kitashirakawa,
Sakyo-ku
Kyoto 606, J
GGB00251@niftyserve.or.jp

Nakatani Akira
Nikken Sekkei Ltd.
1-4-27 Koraku,
Bunkyo-ku
Tokyo 112, J

Nelson Gary Lee
Timara Department
Conservatory of Music
77 W. College
Oberlin, OH 44074, USA
fnelson@oberlin.edu

Nelson Jon Christopher
Florida Internat. University
U. Park Campus DM342A
Miami, FL 33199, USA
nelsonj@servax.fiu.edu

Nillni Ricardo
2 Allée de la Motte
93400 Saint-Ouen, F

Norman Katharine
University of Sheffield
38 Taptonville Rd.
Sheffield, S10 5BR, GB
k.a.norman@sheffield.ac.uk

Normandeau Robert
2023, rue Marie-Anne est
Montréal H2H 1M5, CDN
normandr@ere.
umontreal.ca

Novotny Josef
Schiffamtsgasse 8/8
1020 Wien, A

Núñez Adolfo
LIEM-CDMC
Santa Isabel 52
28012 Madrid, E
adolfo.nunez@cdmc.es

Oberlinninger Bernd
Tendlergasse 15/5
1090 Wien, A

Ollertz Ralf R.
32, Avenue Louis
Bertrand
1030 Bruxelles, B

Oppenheim Daniel
20 Mt. Green Road
Croton, NY 10520, USA
music@watson.ibm.com

Pampin Juan Carlos
CCRMA / Music
Department
Stanford, CA 94305, USA
juan@ccrma.stanford.edu

Pantaleão Aquiles
City University
Northampton Sq.
London EC1V 0HB, GB
a.pantaleao@city.ac.uk

Parmerud Ake
Backeskärsgatan 27
42159 Västra Frölunda, S
ake.parmerud@musik.gu.se

Patella Gianatonio
Via Verdi, 3
35012 Camposampiero
(PD), I
toni@nexttis.unipd.it

Payri Blas
Limsi B.P. 133
91403 Orsay, F
blas@limsi.fr

Pennycook Bruce
McGill University
555 Sherbrooke St. West
Montreal, QC H3A 1E3, CDN
brp@music.mcgill.ca